✦ *The Sorrows of the Quaker Jesus*

The Sorrows of the Quaker Jesus

James Nayler and the Puritan Crackdown on the Free Spirit

Leo Damrosch

Harvard University Press
Cambridge, Massachusetts
London, England
1996

Library of Congress Cataloging-in-Publication Data

Damrosch, Leopold.
    The sorrows of the Quaker Jesus: James Nayler and the Puritan
crackdown on the free spirit / Leo Damrosch.
    p. cm.
    Includes bibliographical references and index.
    ISBN 0–674–82143–2 (alk. paper)
    1. Naylor, James, 1617?–1660   2. Quakers—England—Biography.
3. Naylor, James, 1617?–1660—Trials, litigation, etc.   4. Trials
(Blasphemy)—England—Lancaster.   5. Puritans—England—Discipline—
History—17th century.   6. England—Church history—17th century.
I. Title.
BX7795.N3D35   1996
289.6'092—dc20   96–12530
[B]

To Joyce Van Dyke

whose keen editorial eye has improved every page of this book, in large matters as in small, and who has often had occasion to remind its author, "Let your words be few."

✤ Contents

❖ *Illustrations*

✤ *Acknowledgments*

I am grateful for valuable advice given by Hugh Barbour, David Damrosch, Scott Gordon, Barbara Lewalski, Joyce Van Dyke, and the two readers for the Press, John Morrill and David Underdown. Eloise Pasachoff acted as a very able research assistant.

✤ *The Sorrows of the Quaker Jesus*

✤ *A Note on Quotations*

I have regularized spelling throughout in order to avoid an unnecessary impression of archaism and illogical differences among texts. (Some of Nayler's works would be quoted with the peculiarities of the 1650s and others with those of a 1716 collection, while many of his contemporaries, Bunyan and Hobbes for instance, must be cited in modern editions that have widely differing standards as to modernization.) I have adjusted punctuation slightly when the meaning would otherwise be obscure and have substituted quotation marks for the italics that Nayler and his contemporaries used for direct quotations, since italics strike a modern eye with misleading emphasis. Certain words—Seed, Light, Spirit, Word—are regularly capitalized to indicate their importance as key terms in Quaker discourse and their status as indicators of divine power.

Introduction: Receding Echoes of a Cause Célèbre

In late October of 1656 a strange party approached Bristol, the largest city in the west of England. Apparently indifferent to a deluge of rain, a small group of men and women, some on horseback and others on foot, sang hosannas before a mounted figure who was unmistakably imitating Christ's entrance into Jerusalem on Palm Sunday seated upon an ass. This was James Nayler, formerly a soldier and now a well-known preacher in the nascent Quaker movement. The incident immediately became notorious. It looked like deliberate and outrageous blasphemy to the established ministers of Bristol and to many other people as well, and since the confrontational tactics of the Quakers had aroused great resentment throughout England, it ignited official outrage and furnished a convenient test case for anti-Quaker action. Several detailed accounts of what happened were promptly published,[1] and the case was soon a cause célèbre at the national level. What actually happened at Bristol was never in doubt, but its significance proved to be endlessly disputable. Many intelligent people—not least of whom was Nayler himself—struggled repeatedly to explain what it meant, and the records of the controversy illuminate an exceptionally turbulent moment in British history.

The known facts of Nayler's life are few and, as is true of many of his contemporaries, what facts do survive tell us little about his personal relationships or his private feelings and thoughts. Such biographical information as is available will be presented at appropriate places during the course of this study, in historical and intellectual contexts that can help to illuminate it. In brief, Nayler (sometimes spelled Naylor) was a Yorkshire farmer and small landowner who joined the Parliamentary army in 1643 at the age of twenty-five. He remained in the army for eight years, rising to the highly responsible rank of quartermaster, and like many soldiers became a lay preacher. Ill health forced him to return to civilian life in 1651. Almost immediately he underwent a dramatic conversion experience, hearing a call from God while plowing in the fields, and for the rest of his life he was an itinerant preacher with no fixed address. Around the time of his conversion he met George Fox, with whom he was thenceforward associated as one of the founders of the Quaker movement. Nayler proselytized extensively throughout the north of England, and together with his colleagues he was interrogated and imprisoned by local authorities. When the movement spread southward he went to London and by 1655 was regarded as the leading figure among the Quakers there.

Nayler's career came to a catastrophic end in 1656 when, after a painful falling-out with several colleagues, he enacted the symbolic performance at Bristol. He was immediately arrested and interrogated, and was then sent to London to be the subject of a ten-day debate by the entire Parliament. Convicted of "horrid blasphemy," he was brutally punished: the skin was flayed from his back by more than three hundred lashes, his forehead was branded with the letter B (for "blasphemy"), and his tongue was bored through with a red-hot iron. Consigned afterwards to solitary confinement in Bridewell, Nayler spent three years there before a general amnesty released him in 1659. He died a year later, after being robbed (and possibly beaten) on the highway while attempting to travel home to Yorkshire.

Strange and curious though his story is, the present book is not intended to be a biography of James Nayler, but rather an exploration of the meaning of the Nayler affair as his contemporaries perceived it and as he himself seems to have understood it. The "sign" (to use the Quaker term) that Nayler and his companions exhibited at Bristol condensed into a single symbolic act an immense complex of overlapping and competing values and beliefs. To investigate its contexts is to go to the imaginative heart of the early Quaker movement, in which radical antinomianism made a last-ditch bid for expression before Puritan conservatism drove it underground, and to clarify many of the conceptual issues through which the political, religious, and intellectual conflicts of the Interregnum were fought out.

Some notion of Nayler's persistent symbolic interest may be gathered from the account given a century later by David Hume in his *History of England*. The urbane ironies Hume deploys cannot altogether dispel the harrowing power of the story he elliptically relates. Hume has been deploring the fanaticism of the seventeenth-century Puritans and pauses to give a narrative example:

> James Naylor was a Quaker, noted for blasphemy, or rather madness, in the time of the protectorship [of Oliver Cromwell]. He fancied that he himself was transformed into Christ, and was become the real saviour of the world; and in consequence of this frenzy he endeavoured to imitate many actions of the Messiah related in the evangelists. As he bore a resemblance to the common pictures of Christ, he allowed his beard to grow in a like form; he raised a person from the dead; he was ministered unto by women; he entered Bristol, mounted on a horse: I suppose, from the difficulty in that place of finding an ass; his disciples spread their garments before him, and cried, "Hosanna to the highest; holy, holy is the Lord God of Sabbaoth." When carried before the magistrate, he would give no other answer to all questions than "thou hast said it." What is remarkable, the parliament thought that the matter deserved their attention. Near ten days they spent in enquiries and debates about him. They condemned him to be pilloried, whipped, burned in the face, and to have his tongue bored through with a red hot iron. All these severities he bore with the usual patience. So far his delusion supported him. But the sequel spoiled all. He was sent to Bridewell, confined to hard labour, fed on bread and water, and debarred from all his disciples, male and female. His illusion dissipated; and after some time, he was contented to come out an ordinary man, and return to his usual occupations.[2]

Hume's account begins with easy deadpan mockery: anyone might choose to wear his beard like Christ's and be ministered unto by women, and these accomplishments are presented as identical in kind with raising a person from the dead. The entry into Bristol is made ridiculous by the substitution of an English horse for the Biblical ass.

Even the expression "Thou hast said it" has a faintly ludicrous effect, as if Nayler solemnly and literally parroted Christ's answers to Pilate. But in fact the original transcripts contain no such language. At various points Nayler did deflect a question by objecting that it was couched in his questioners' terminology rather than his own, but he never once echoed Christ's "Thou hast said it." Hume probably never saw the obscure original sources; he got the idea, I believe, from Hobbes's *Behemoth:* "This year also it was that James Nayler appeared at Bristol, and would be taken for Jesus Christ. He wore his beard forked, and his hair composed to the likeness of that in the *Volto Santo;* and being questioned, would sometimes answer, Thou sayest it."[3] Only a decade later, Nayler was a mythic figure, and one who was constructed for the most part by those who had least reason to understand or approve of him.

Yet that is not the whole of what Hume does with Nayler, short though his narrative is. "Thou hast said it" actually signals a change in viewpoint, since from the moment that Nayler's interrogators are identified with Pilate, it is the self-righteous judges who attract the ironies of the Enlightenment *philosophe.* Nayler endures his torture in a way that even Hume might concede to be Christlike, and the real pathology is exhibited by the members of Parliament, whose sadistic judicial torments suggest that it was the entire leadership of the nation that was mentally ill. If anyone comes off well in Hume's account it is poor Nayler, who eventually returns to his senses.

In recent times the Calvinistic Puritans have been intensively studied by historical and literary scholars. Psychologically, their program of relentless self-scrutiny and their deterministic theology created whole new modes of behavior, contributing greatly to modern modes of self-understanding and of fictional narration.[4] Sociologically, they provided a driving energy and a system of organization that have fascinated theorists from Max Weber to Michael Walzer, and paradoxically were at once sponsors of radical change and architects of what eventually became the conservative orthodoxy of British commercial and family life. Modern scholarship has thus been able to repair the damage caused by the Restoration rewriting of the story of the 1640s and '50s; as Macaulay said long ago, "The friends of liberty labored under the disadvantage of which the lion in the fable complained so bitterly. Though they were the conquerors, their enemies were the painters."[5] But people who were still more radical than the mainstream Puritans have fared less well, for they were losers not only during the Restoration but in the 1650s too, marginalized and to a large extent suppressed by the Presbyterians and Independents who won the day and who eventually mutated, once monarchy had been restored, into hardworking and dependable "Nonconformist" pillars of society.

Among the many groups that competed for influence during the 1650s, the Quakers are particularly interesting because their movement in those formative years was extraordinarily different from what it later became. By the eighteenth century—as depicted in Fielding's *Tom Jones*, for instance—Quakers struck their neighbors as deliberately drab and taciturn, cautious among strangers and notable mainly for shrewdness in business. But in the 1650s they seemed very different, both to themselves and to a culture that felt threatened by them. As for James Nayler, at the time of his much-publicized catastrophe he was considered crazy even by many of his fellow Quakers. I shall argue, however, that what was diagnosed as madness was at a deep level an imaginative understanding of principles that all antinomians, and many orthodox believers too, claimed to accept. I use the term "antinomian" in the sense in which Nayler himself understood it, as the replacement of an external moral law by an internal, spiritual one. In its extreme form, which the Quakers firmly repudiated, this might be taken to mean that the Ten Commandments had become irrelevant and that a saved person was liberated from moral obligations of any kind.[6] The Quaker position was that the law was still binding, but that participation in Christ made it possible to live up to its demands instead of endlessly failing to do so. In the opinion of the Quakers, the Calvinists, refusing to understand this consequence of the Incarnation, remained trapped in the punitive legalism of the Old Covenant and had yet to understand the real message of Christ. "My covenant is the new one, and the law in the heart," Nayler declared in *A True Discoverie of Faith, and A Brief Manifestation of the Ground upon which we stand, to those who desire to know it*, "and here Christ is the rule of life to me for ever, and my law is spiritual and not moral."[7]

This theology lies at the heart of early Quaker thinking, but in making literal what was normally figurative Nayler put it to the test: he articulated the implications of antinomian thought with great clarity and consistency, and his eventual recantation, comforting though it was for later Quaker historians, was really a reluctant and very limited backing-down in the face of total ostracism. His ideas may not have been conventionally "rational" but, like the antirationality of William Blake with which they have much in common, they embodied a coherent and powerful critique of the usual ways of holding, and living, beliefs. In addition, they implied a critique of mainstream Calvinism in its institutional aspects and in its rigorous program for internalized self-discipline, and advanced a doctrine of the free spirit so threatening to the established authorities that it had to be energetically suppressed.

In the twentieth century Nayler has been studied mainly by Quaker biographers and historians, who have naturally been interested in his relationship to their movement and in the reasons for his "fall," as it is usually called, which has been regarded as an unlucky aberration. As one such writer remarked, he quickly became "the skeleton in the Quaker cupboard"[8] and in the decades following the Restoration was virtually erased from official memory. William Crouch's memoir, *Posthuma Christiana*, published in 1712, gave a detailed account of the early days of the movement in London without a single reference to Nayler.[9] He had become an unperson. It was therefore an act of unusual generosity, and perhaps of courage too, when in 1716 Nayler's former colleague George Whitehead published a selection of his writings as *A Collection of Sundry Books, Epistles and Papers, Written by James Nayler, Some of which were never before Printed, With an Impartial Relation of the Most Remarkable Transactions Relating to His Life*. This publication seems to have been the culmination of a project of collecting Nayler's writings that had been begun much earlier by Quaker archivists but was long postponed, no doubt due to uneasiness about his reputation.[10] Whitehead knew Nayler well in the 1650s and had actually lodged with him during the last year of his life;[11] by the early eighteenth century he had become the de facto leader of the movement and was in a position to rehabilitate those parts of Nayler's work that still seemed edifying. But none of Nayler's writings was reprinted again after Whitehead's collection, and many were never reprinted after 1660.

So long as the early Quaker movement was studied mainly by inheritors of its religious assumptions, Nayler's "fall" could only be regarded as a lamentable setback, forgiven no doubt but deeply deplored. Thus the distinguished religious historian Geoffrey Nuttall (a non-Quaker) could conclude that "his behaviour may be seen as the natural outcome of a certain mistaken line of thought and feeling, in which a widespread but regrettable tendency came suddenly to a head."[12] Interpreters who might have been sympathetic to Nayler were thus motivated to marginalize him as aberrant, except insofar as he could be shown to have repudiated his own actions. It was from this perspective that William Braithwaite introduced Nayler in his magisterial *Beginnings of Quakerism* (1912, but still standard): "James Nayler's career, both in its lights and shadows, is of the utmost significance to any one who desires a true understanding of early Quakerism, and until his fall he was the ablest speaker and one of the most trusted leaders of the movement. His final repentance and recovery rank among the great personal experiences in Church-history."[13] An explanation of the hinted-at "shadows" is reserved for a much later place in the history, and emphasis falls on "repentance and recovery." What happened to Nayler after his disaster may indeed have constituted a "great personal experience," but as we will see, his own explanations of it were highly elliptical and by no means cancelled out the significance of what happened when he "fell."

For political and social historians of the period, as opposed to those directly concerned with Quaker history, Nayler is necessarily a minor figure since he did not achieve political power, or become the undisputed leader of a sect, or write books with lasting literary prestige. Misleading or mistaken accounts of him have therefore been common. One justly admired historian, for example, after describing the antipredestinarian belief that all individuals could be saved by responding to the inner Light, comments that "this had its dangers, as when Nayler, the Quaker, believed that he was the Messiah."[14] Nayler never believed that, as his statements under interrogation plainly show, and as his own writings, after the Bristol debacle as well as before it, confirm by placing his actions in a coherent context of antinomian symbolism. There had indeed been a number of self-styled Messiahs over the years, some manifestly deranged, some putting on an act. Nayler turns up during the course of Keith Thomas's judicious survey of such cases: "This failure to distinguish between the inner spirit and its earthly vessel underlay the messianic delusions of the Quaker James Nayler."[15] But Nayler was not deluded, as Thomas's other examples may have been, and it is far from clear that even the most "enthusiastic" of his followers thought that he was literally and personally the Messiah.

The same inherited assumptions regularly appear whenever Nayler is mentioned in general accounts of the period, where he serves to provide a passing exemplum in the story of Cromwell's struggles with his parliaments. Thus we read in a well-respected survey:

> In October 1656, then aged 36, [Nayler] re-enacted at Bristol Christ's entry into Jerusalem, seated on an ass, accompanied by hysterical women singing and casting their garments in the muddy ruts before him. (Such was the state of the main road from Glastonbury to London!) The extraordinary, somewhat comical, strangely pathetic incident might have been just a local sensation had not an M.P., confessing himself shattered to the soul, directed the attention of the House to this "blasphemy."[16]

The facts are accurate but the presentation is tendentious. The women were not necessarily "hysterical," the incident was surely far from comical, and there is no reason to imply that the local M.P. was ridiculous (or, more probably, hypocritical) when he claimed to be "shattered to the soul."

Historians who have looked more closely into the Nayler case exhibit a subtler sense of its complexity, but they too tend to assume that he and his followers were merely demented.

> In October of 1656, James Naylor, a Quaker who had slipped into a private world of religious ecstasy, rode a mule into Bristol in a pathetic parody of Christ's entry into Jerusalem. Obviously suffering severe mental disturbance, Naylor gazed fixedly ahead as companions, singing hosannas and spreading garments before him, led his mount into the city . . . Examination of Naylor demonstrated his unbalanced mental condition, but his examiners, shocked by the wild statements of his followers, saw him only as a horrid blasphemer and not as the sick man he was.[17]

Nayler was undoubtedly deeply distressed at the time of the Bristol episode, both because of a wounding quarrel with his colleague and rival George Fox and because of anxiety about the appropriateness of the "sign" that he was helping to enact. But there is no evidence whatever that he had retreated, let alone "slipped," into a "private world of religious ecstasy," and his replies upon interrogation, far from demonstrating an "unbalanced mental condition," were impressively lucid and intelligent.

The fullest of modern interpretations of Nayler deserves more extended discussion, since it has been widely influential and is, in its own terms, deeply sympathetic. In a number of books and essays Christopher Hill has discussed Nayler, and an important chapter is devoted to him in the most powerful of these works, *The World Turned Upside Down*. In this account Nayler is treated as a political spokesman, and Hill averts his eyes completely from the messianic entry into Bristol, the details of which, he surprisingly declares, "are well known." Hill's conclusion is that conservatives in Parliament made a public example of Nayler because, unlike various "holy imbeciles" who similarly claimed to be Christ, he was a well-known leader in a movement that posed a serious threat to social control. Reasoning from premises diametrically opposed to Hume's, who wanted to depict the parliamentary judges as crazy fanatics rather than as self-protective conservatives, Hill laments the political consequences for the radical movement in general: "Nayler's case was a tragedy for the Quaker movement . . . [It] strengthened the arguments for more discipline, more law and order . . . James Nayler became a black shadow lying across memory."[18]

In the story that Hill has repeatedly told, the Nayler episode is part of a tragedy of failed aspirations, an attempt to turn England upside down that would have wrought much good if it had been allowed to succeed. Hill's more recent version of the story, *The Experience of Defeat*, is a bleak review of individual disappointments and sellouts, with several Quakers among them.[19] But from a different point of view it is much easier for later generations, with their desire to identify and honor brave precursors, to romanticize revolution than it was for the revolutionaries themselves. A useful analogy is suggested by the case of William Blake: he was vehemently radical in the atmosphere of 1789, and in the remaining four decades of his life he never relented in his bitter attacks on privilege, oppression, and institutional politics and religion. Nevertheless, Blake has always been an awkward figure for modern celebrators of revolution, because even in the early 1790s his political critique was embedded in a set of religious and metaphysical assumptions that have much more in common with thinkers of the first century than with socialist theorists of the twentieth century. And by the middle of the 1790s, when the catastrophic failure of revolution was all too apparent, Blake turned to a quietism that located the essential issues in an interior rather than a political theater of conflict. Blake was certainly not apolitical if by that term one implies indifference to institutional oppression, but like the seventeenth-century Quakers, he was no longer radical as that term is commonly understood today.[20] At various points in this book I refer to Blake, whose highly intellectual version of antinomianism can help to make sense of Nayler's beliefs and actions.

Hill's romantic vision of what he calls the seventeenth-century "counter-culture" centers on the short-lived flowering of the Ranters—whose very existence is now a subject of some dispute among historians—and reveals the Quakers to be rather a disappointment. "Rejecting private property for communism, religion for a rationalistic and materialistic pantheism, the mechanical philosophy for dialectical science, asceticism for unashamed enjoyment of the good things of the flesh, [the counter-culture] might have achieved unity through a federation of communities, each based on fullest respect for the individual."[21] The Quakers of the 1650s did argue very strongly indeed for respect for the individual, but they never objected to private property, and abhorrence of "the good things of the flesh" formed a principal basis of their quarrel with the Ranters. But if they did not anticipate the Marxism of the 1930s in which Hill's attitudes were formed, much less the counterculture of the late 1960s from which his rhetoric in this passage is derived, neither were they covert allies of the mainline Puritans. They were much stranger than that, and their rebellion against established modes of life, though not framed in terms that would make them congenial to Hill's thesis, was nonetheless deep and implacable.

Without question the civil wars of the 1640s produced a program for change that constituted a revolution and not just a rebellion, but it does not follow that all who participated in it were programmatically "radical" or "conservative." Conrad Russell, in his trenchant analysis of causes, asks, "Does the attempt to impose a common label of 'revolution' on many disparate events result in a typology which makes us misunderstand those events by treating them as more generic, and less individual, than they really were?" In particular, the religious attitudes of individual people, and the political alliances those attitudes helped to undergird, often failed to correlate with class or institutional affiliations. As Russell says, "The Civil War did not produce a division between the members of an established order and its opponents, but divided people on almost entirely non-institutional lines."[22]

The Nayler case brings just such divisions into the open: in defiance of Cromwell's commitment to religious toleration, some of his strongest political supporters took a conservative religious line in interpreting Nayler's offense and determining how to punish it, and theological considerations interacted with political ones in complicated ways. The members of Parliament who condemned Nayler wanted to send a decisive political message to insubordinate sectarians, but they also intended to honor (in some cases, perhaps, to propitiate) the Almighty by punishing a horrible blasphemy. Their extended debate about blasphemy was not merely a coded way of making a political point; it was what they said it was. For them religious language and political language ran in tandem. They did not always run comfortably, and the points of friction and blockage are of particular interest, but that should not lead us to conclude that one language was the real one and the other a mere mask, or at best a historically dated misunderstanding that can be dispelled by translating it into other terms.

My own beliefs, I should state explicitly, are entirely secular; yet I am suspicious of historical scholarship that translates religious concepts into what they "really" meant, and I shall try to do justice to their original contexts. To give a quite obvious example, it is remarkable how seldom scholars look up Biblical references even when they are explicitly invoked. But to read Puritan and Quaker tracts without pondering the Biblical texts they refer to (often only allusively) is to hear only half of a dialogue and, very often, to miss its point.

To be sure, it is not always easy to detect and explain such references, since the writings of Nayler and most of his colleagues have never been edited in even a cursory way. A few historians have wondered whether the 1716 texts accurately reproduce the originals, but no one seems ever to have actually compared them, and I believe I am the first to have done so. In fact the 1716 volume makes many alterations, usually for stylistic reasons but sometimes for significant doctrinal ones, as I shall point out when they suggest interesting points of interpretation. But more important, these are writings of great imaginative and intellectual power, and they deserve a fuller and more engaged reading than they have yet received.

Nayler's three twentieth-century biographers have winnowed the manuscript collections of Quaker letters with great thoroughness, but the contemporary trove of printed material has been much less thoroughly explored. The early Quakers quickly developed a comprehensive and efficient system for the dissemination of tracts, which were sold in bookshops and on the streets, distributed by local Quaker Meetings and by travelers on horseback, and sent to influential politicians and merchants.[23] Most of these were cheaply and hastily printed, with uneven type and frequent misprints (usually acknowledged in scrupulous lists of errata at the end). The orthodox regarded them as an exasperating plague—"hellish printed pamphlets sent hither into these parts before any of the cursed [Quaker] generation arrived in this jurisdiction," as a New England court complained.[24] Nayler was the most prolific of the Quaker writers, producing nearly fifty publications between 1652 and 1656.

The great majority of the quotations from Nayler in the present book, and more than a few of those from his contemporaries, have not appeared in print since their original publication. Modern scholars mainly quote from Whitehead's *Collection of Sundry Books* (commonly misdescribed as *Works*), which stressed homiletic writings that would be of interest to Quakers two generations later and therefore omitted many of the controversial pamphlets Nayler published during his life. Even in Whitehead's volume, which is over seven hundred pages in length, there is much of interest that has never really been studied, and Nayler's other publications have seldom been examined at all. The writings of Fox, by contrast, have been edited and interpreted with exhaustive care, but Nayler is in many ways a subtler and more perspicuous writer and thinker than Fox. The contrast is still more striking with Nayler's contemporary John Bunyan. Thanks to the deserved prestige of *The Pilgrim's Progress*, lavish editorial care has been given to Bunyan's early tracts, such as *Some Gospel-Truths Opened* and *Some Sighs from Hell*, which are highly derivative, exasperatingly repetitive, and far less interesting than Nayler's writings of the same period.

I ought to add that I have been trained as a literary scholar rather than as a historian, and my approach remains literary in that I look closely at particular passages in order to understand how they make sense or evade it; I try to listen attentively to notes of uneasiness and ambiguity rather than interpreting all texts as declarative statements. But I address this book to historians as well; its methods may not entirely be those of their discipline, but its deepest assumptions are. I attempt to work at the intersection of literary and historical studies in order to understand a set of confused and ambiguous particulars that once seemed pregnant with social, political, and spiritual meaning. My subject is the many layers, overlapping but also conflicting, in the construction of James Nayler. There are his own attempts, and the often unfriendly attempts of his Quaker colleagues, to explain his mission and its apparent failure. There are the interpretations of his avowed enemies and judges, who had no trouble establishing what he had done but needed to ascertain why he had done it and what it meant. And finally, there are the accounts of later interpreters, working from documents that recede into the past and with assumptions that have been very different from those of the original participants. My aim is to recover the significance of a scandal that once preoccupied a nation, and of ideas for which people, in a time of bewildering change, were willing to overturn their lives and even, if necessary, lose them.

In recent years stories like Nayler's have attracted the attention of literary scholars known as New Historicists, who have studied the imaginative assumptions that underlie cultural phenomena of many kinds. But the New Historicists tend to rely upon a Foucauldian model of power and subversion that works better for authoritarian monarchies (whether French or British) than it does for the Puritan regime of the Interregnum, and they have consequently devoted more attention to the Elizabethan and Jacobean courts than to the up-welling of demotic expression between 1640 and 1660. The great paradox that I examine in this book is the crisis of authority that developed when the Puritans, who had always defined themselves as individualist and oppositional, found that they had no choice but to assert control in much the same ways as their predecessors had done. The ambiguous figure of Oliver Cromwell is particularly interesting in this regard: in accordance with his general program of toleration he was anxious to limit the scope of Nayler's punishment, but in the end he felt obliged to let it go forward in all its exemplary brutality. Still more paradoxically, the Quaker movement too, despite its ideology of absolute individualism, was forced in its turn to impose discipline. These interrelated developments throw much light on the fatal logic by which every antinomianism contains the seeds of its own collapse. Rather than representing an exhilarating challenge to order posed by freedom (or "transgression"), whether in the New Historicist model or in the older Marxism of Christopher Hill, this process represents the systematic transformation of freedom into order as each radical movement in turn becomes conservative in order to survive. At bottom it was an anti-antinomianism that asserted itself within the Puritan and the Quaker movements, and the Nayler case is indispensable in exposing how it did so.

G. M. Trevelyan observed long ago that "the past was once as real as the present and as uncertain as the future."[25] In 1656 nobody knew what was coming next; we cannot help knowing, and for us the unerasable date is 1660. The members of Parliament who debated Nayler's fate thought they were consolidating the revolution and making it secure; we know that their drift toward conservatism participated in a larger reaction that would soon end it. The Nayler drama was filled with paradoxes and ironies that were apparent to people at the time but was shadowed as well by historical ironies that were then dormant and invisible. Hindsight also permits us to grasp more clearly than was possible at the time the symbolic foundations of the opposition between Calvinistic Puritans and Quakers. Identity is always positional: you identify what you are, to yourself as well as to others, by contrast with what you are not. The early Quaker movement, before it consolidated and conventionalized itself, involuntarily played the role of scapegoat for the ascendant Puritans. In effect, the Puritans ascribed to Quakers versions of beliefs and practices for which they themselves were criticized but wished to repudiate, and they confirmed their sense of righteousness by throwing Quakers in jail. This process was much assisted, in turn, by the willingness of many Quakers to persist in forms of behavior that were virtually guaranteed to elicit punishment.

As for James Nayler, his fate was to be a double scapegoat. His beliefs and his notorious "sign" at Bristol were perfectly consistent with familiar antinomian attitudes. In fact, as more than one member of Parliament admitted at his trial, his beliefs came disturbingly close to what all Protestants claimed to believe. But the Quakers, defending themselves against oppression and suppression, needed a scapegoat of their own. Nayler was available to play that role. He may even, in some deep sense, have wanted to play it.

1

The Quaker Menace

Puritans, Seekers, and Quakers

James Nayler was born in 1618 at West Ardsley in Yorkshire, the son of a farmer who seems to have been relatively well-to-do. In an interrogation in 1652 he gave his occupation as "husbandman,"[1] and we know that he was a landowner rather than a farm laborer. At the age of twenty-one he married Anne, of whom virtually nothing is recorded, and they moved to the nearby town of Wakefield, where their three daughters were baptized in 1640, 1641, and 1643. There was apparently a brother named William who was also to join the Quaker movement, but nothing is known of him but the name.[2] Mere worldly relationships were in effect irrelevant. In Nayler's own understanding, as in that of his contemporaries, his life was significant only in the context of the Quaker movement, which means that his story has to be grounded in the phenomenology of religious and political experience in the 1650s: what it felt like to those who lived it, what it looked like to those who hated it, and the ideas and arguments both sides developed to explain it.

In the later 1640s a series of unprecedented events seemed to announce the advent of genuine revolution. The Archbishop of Canterbury was executed in 1645, episcopacy abolished in 1646, and the House of Lords likewise abolished in 1649. In the same year, most momentous of all, King Charles I met his death on the scaffold, com-

15

pleting the equation proposed by James I forty-five years before: "No bishop, no king." At that moment it must have seemed that the erstwhile country gentleman Oliver Cromwell was ready to "cast the kingdom old / Into another mold."[3] But before long it became apparent that radical hopes had already reached their high-water mark and had begun to recede. So far as religious reform was concerned, as early as 1646 Milton was reproaching the Long Parliament for ejecting bishops only to "seize the widowed whore plurality / From them whose sin ye envied, not abhorred." Milton's sonnet ends, "New Presbyter is but old Priest writ large," exploiting the etymological fact that the word *priest* is a contracted form of the Latin *presbyter.*[4] By the end of the 1640s the lines were clearly drawn: the Puritan leadership was determined to establish a state church with the same privileges, if not the same doctrines, as the old Church of England, while a radical minority insisted on their right to independence from any such church, financially and in every other way.

As for politics, the army had become the controlling power in the state, but its leaders had no intention of permitting sweeping democratic reforms; when disaffected soldiers began to lobby for these they were efficiently suppressed. In the summer of 1649 a Leveller mutiny supplied a convenient occasion for repression. A number of soldiers refused to obey their officers and began to march across England, apparently hoping to pick up support as they went; a brigade dispatched by Cromwell caught up with them at Burford in Oxfordshire, where they had camped for the night, arrested them, and executed the ringleaders. The threat of radical insurrection was easily put down, in fact with very little bloodshed.[5] Civilian Leveller propagandists such as John Lilburne and William Walwyn were imprisoned in the Tower. In a recent publication Lilburne had pointedly commented on Cromwell's ability to proclaim godly renovation while siding with the conservatives: "Ye shall scarce speak to Cromwell about any thing, but he will lay his hands on his breast, elevate his eyes, and call God to record; he will weep, howl and repent, even while he doth smite you under the first rib."[6] Particularly futile was the occupation of "common" lands by small groups that called themselves True Levellers, or Diggers: action by local authorities was sufficient to dispel these minor threats (though modern historians have appreciated the suggestiveness of their leaders' ideas).

The turning point in Nayler's life, as in the lives of many of his contemporaries, was joining the Parliamentary army, which he did in

1643. It happens that records survive for the troop in which he first served, and they show it to have been a body of men from a single region, many of them neighbors. Two-thirds of the sixty-four soldiers lived in the West Riding of Yorkshire, and there were four other Naylers who, like James, came from the Wakefield area.[7] Nayler discharged successfully the challenging duties of quartermaster in a regiment of horse under John Lambert, who would later become one of the famous major generals and for a time heir apparent to Cromwell. In the 1640s, a period of great scarcity and hardship, a quartermaster had to obtain provisions from the rural population without arousing their resentment, and was also expected to keep records of every soldier, lodging, and meal.[8] Years later, when Nayler was on trial for his life, Lambert testified that he had been "a very useful person" and "a man of a very unblameable life and conversation, a member of a very sweet society of an independent church."[9]

The New Model Army was unprecedented in British history as a professional standing army with politically committed leaders, and from 1645 onward it was the ultimate guarantor of Cromwell's authority. Its soldiers were expected to be volunteers who freely chose to fight for their cause, and all over England they formed idiosyncratic "gathered churches" led by chaplains who often lacked formal theological training and were much more radical in their views than the civilian religious establishment. But if the army was the one institution in which radical ideas were joined to political power, it was by no means uniformly radical, and only a few of the officers sympathized with the protocommunist ideals of the Diggers or with the apocalyptic program of the extreme millenarians.[10] The rank and file were thus far more revolutionary than their leaders, and they used religious symbolism as their preferred vehicle of interpretation; in 1650 one army group affirmed that it had been "called forth by the Lord to be instrumental to bring about that which was our continual prayer to God, viz., the destruction of Antichrist," and declared further that King Charles I, "that man of blood," was "one of the ten horns of the Beast spoken of, Rev. 17: 12–15."[11]

Like many other soldiers, Nayler began to preach, and it would be hard to exaggerate the importance of the military origins of his religious vocation. Whereas the professional Puritan ministers had been trained in theology at the universities, army preachers formed their views in an atmosphere of ideologically committed militancy while acquiring habits of discipline and organized action. When the revolution turned irrevocably conservative, numerous ex-soldiers spilled out into English life as evangelists who knew how to plan a campaign, organize support, and keep opponents off balance. Moreover, Nayler was not just an eloquent speaker; he was also a deeply intelligent and interesting thinker. The "mechanic preachers" of the 1650s were autodidacts, as orthodox divines never tired of complaining, but their ideas were by no means half-baked or inconsistent with formal theology. On the contrary, these were often people of great linguistic gifts, passionate readers and interpreters of the Bible, whose thinking had been strongly influenced by learned clergymen whom the pressures of the 1640s had pushed into radical intellectual positions.[12]

In 1651 Nayler, suffering from poor health (probably consumption), left the army and returned to farming. Up until then he had been an Independent, or what would later be called a Congregationalist, as is indicated in his address "To them of the Independent Society: some grounds why I deny you to be a church in Christ, though in the times of ignorance I walked with you in these things, worshipping I knew not what."[13] Also in 1651 he met George Fox (who had not served in the army) and, according to Fox's *Journal*, was at once "convinced," the Quaker term for being converted.[14] But in fact it is likely that Nayler reached independently a position very similar to Fox's, at a time when there was a previously unheard-of freedom of the press and antinomian ideas were widely discussed. It seems also more than coincidental that the same radical minister once occupied the Leicestershire parish where Fox grew up and afterwards, when ejected from it for his insubordinate views, moved to West Ardsley.[15]

By Nayler's own account his conversion came as a specific and unrefusable instant of revelation. Early in 1652, during an interrogation for alleged blasphemy at Appleby in Westmoreland, he was asked "What was the cause of thy coming into these parts?" To this he returned an answer that may have been more comprehensive than his questioners expected:

> I was at the plow, meditating on the things of God, and suddenly I heard a voice saying unto me, "Get thee out from thy kindred, and from thy father's house;" and I had a promise given in with it . . . When I came at home I gave up my estate, cast out my money, but not being obedient in going forth, the wrath of God

was on me, so that I was made a wonder to all, and none thought
I would have lived: but (after I was made willing) I began to make
some preparation, as apparel, and other necessaries, not knowing
whither I should go. But shortly afterward going a-gateward with
a friend from my own house, having on an old suit without any
money, having neither taken leave of wife or children, nor thinking then of any journey, I was commanded to go into the West,
not knowing whither I should go, nor what I was to do there; but
when I had been there a little while, I had given me what I was to
declare; and ever since I have remained, not knowing today what
I was to do tomorrow.[16]

The promise, Nayler explained, was "that God would be with me:
which promise I find made good every day."

This account is full of interest. Having returned home after nearly a
decade in the army, Nayler is once again at the plow, but with his
mind abstracted in religious musings, when he hears a voice commanding him to leave both work and family and promising that God
will take their place. He immediately gives away most of his posses-
sions but is at first unprepared to leave home, whereupon he falls so
seriously ill that his life is despaired of. Recovering, he begins to pack
a few items for a trip, but still does not think of himself as ready to
leave; but as he approaches the gate that opens out to the world beyond, the command comes upon him once more and he takes to the
road without even saying goodbye. From then on he lives a life of tire-
less preaching, which is also, in point of motivation, extraordinarily
passive: he speaks as he is told to speak and never has any idea what
will happen next.

It is worth noting that Anne Nayler has been sentimentalized by
later writers because on two occasions when he was in trouble, once
with rival Quakers and once in prison, she visited her husband and offered support; but apart from those two interventions there is nothing
to support the touching picture of their marriage presented by biographers.[17] Between 1643, when Nayler joined the army, and 1660, when
he died on a belated and perhaps reluctant homeward journey, he
seems to have lived with his wife only during 1651 and almost immediately thereafter felt called to an itinerant ministry. As Christopher Hill
observes, "We may have here a case of *de facto* divorce by removal."[18]
The implications of such behavior were not lost on early critics of the

Quakers such as Thomas Weld, who noted "their forsaking the world (though to a sinful neglect of their callings and families)."[19]

At the Appleby interrogation one Colonel Briggs commented, "I never heard such a call as this is, in our time" and Nayler agreed: "I believe thee."[20] The authenticity of the inner voice was of course not obvious to people who distrusted Quakers. In *A Brief Relation of the Irreligion of the Northern Quakers* Francis Higginson recorded an exchange during the interrogation that he said was omitted from Nayler's printed version:

> Col. Briggs interrupted him with this question: "Friend," said he, "didst thou hear that voice thou sayest spoke unto thee?"
>
> Nayler answered, "Yea, I did hear it."
>
> Col. Briggs questioned him again thus, "Were there not some others besides thy self at plow with thee?"
>
> "Yea," saith Nayler, "there were two more besides my self."
>
> "And did not they," said the Colonel, "hear that voice as well as thy self?"
>
> "No friend," saith Nayler; "it was not a carnal voice, audible to the outward ear."
>
> "O then," said Col. Briggs, "I know what voice it was."[21]

Higginson, an intelligent and articulate critic whom I will often have occasion to quote, appears in the *Dictionary of National Biography* only as second son of the more famous Francis Higginson the elder, a leading Puritan in Leicestershire who emigrated to Massachusetts in 1629 and died there a year later. After leaving New England the younger Higginson received a thorough grounding in Calvinism during studies at Leiden before taking his parish at Kirkby Stephen in Westmoreland.

In Nayler's understanding the implied model was the apostolic one:

> And Jesus, walking by the sea of Galilee, saw two brethren, Simon called Peter, and Andrew his brother, casting a net into the sea: for they were fishers. And he saith unto them, Follow me, and I will make you fishers of men. And they straightway left their nets, and followed him.[22]

But from a secular point of view one might well guess that Nayler was unhappy at the plow, more than willing to leave his family, and deeply relieved by the removal of any obligation to take thought for the morrow. It was divorce from the Independents as well. His home congregation and its minister, Christopher Marshall, a distinguished Puritan who had been trained in New England, concluded that he had rejected them and expelled him from communion, though Nayler seems not to have been aware of it until much later.[23] His enemies made much of this expulsion, but far from being unusual, it was entirely characteristic of sects that were struggling to preserve a sense of identity in a time of confusion. "To judge by the surviving church books," Hill says, "excommunication was one of the principal activities of the early sects."[24]

Why were these Quakers so offensive to the Puritan establishment? By the time Cromwell had won decisive victories at Dunbar (1650) and Worcester (1651) it was clear that England was controlled by an oligarchy that, however "Puritan" in theory, was politically elitist and eager to get rich by pillaging the crown, the Church of England, and the expelled royalist magnates. It was against this newly stabilized establishment, so disappointingly similar to its predecessor, that the Quakers rose up in protest. Lilburne himself became a Quaker in 1655, converted at least in part by reading a book by Nayler, whom he described as "that strong, or tall man in Christ."[25] Not surprisingly, Nayler repeatedly had to repel false charges that he had been one of the mutineers at Burford:

Col. Briggs. Wast thou not at Burford among the Levellers?

James. I was never there.

Col. Briggs. I charge thee by the Lord that thou tell me whether thou wast or not?

James. I was then in the North, and was never taxed for any mutiny, or any other thing while I served the Parliament.[26]

In important ways the Quakers were indeed heirs of the Levellers,[27] but Leveller ideas could only survive if they underwent drastic transformation, in effect undergoing a process of depoliticizing. Among the sects, as John Morrill observes, "it was those with specifically religious visions that thrived (Baptists and Quakers especially), while those whose religious ends led them to seek to control the state (e.g. the Levellers) dissolve before our eyes."[28] But the Quakers did keep up a campaign of oppositional behavior, aggressively exposing what they saw as the hypocrisy of a newly ascendant orthodoxy that had itself been accustomed to think and act in oppositional terms.

Students of the New England Puritans have long recognized the scapegoat status conferred on a series of repudiated "others"—Indians, antinomians, witches; the Quakers played a similar role in England during the Puritan ascendancy of the 1650s. In the very year in which his parliamentary trial would take place, Nayler analyzed the situation in explicit terms: "Therein hath the Serpent beguiled the creature, by getting into somewhat of the form once used with the saints (whilst God dwelt therein) and to that adds inventions of his own, called decency and order, and the like, and with this hath deceived the creatures so as to serve his ends, to shed the blood of their brethren, under a pretence of error and blasphemy, and denying ordinances and worships, and as being leaders of dangerous sects and heresies, denying government, turning the world upside down, and the like."[29] The Jews of Thessalonica who rejected Paul and Silas cried, "Those that have turned the world upside down are come hither" (Acts 17: 6). In Nayler's usage the phrase becomes ironic, turned against the no longer radical Puritans who had themselves once gloried in turning the world upside down.

Recent research has revealed just how conservative religious practice in general remained throughout the Interregnum. In 1643 Parliament decreed a massive reorganization of the national church along Presbyterian lines, but this was widely ignored and never really went into effect. In 1649 at least two-thirds of the parishes in England (possibly as many as three-quarters) still had the same ministers who had been in place in 1642, and many of them went on using the supposedly illegal Prayer Book. Even if local and national committees wanted to eject "scandalous" ministers, they could only have accomplished this by direct military action, which the regime was unwilling to attempt. Cromwell in fact approved of permitting local parishes to choose their own ministers, so that if total reform had ever come to pass it would necessarily have had to be a very gradual affair. But in fact the reverse was the case. When it became clear in the 1650s that no consensus for a new national church was likely to be reached, parishes thereafter freely followed their own preferences as to the Prayer Book, holy communion, and so on. A wide variety of ministers occupied the established parishes, where tithes were still paid and lay patrons still had the right to choose incumbents. Many ministers were Independents, but rather surprisingly a majority of pre-Revolution Anglicans remained in place. This happened for the most part faute de mieux: the government would have preferred to replace them but had no appropriate substitutes available.[30] The majority of all of these ministers, whatever their sect or profession, undoubtedly hoped for moderation rather than drastic change. The Presbyterian (later Independent) John Owen spoke for many when he wrote of his attempt to locate "the habitable earth between the valley (I had almost said the pit) of democratical confusion and the precipitous rock of hierarchical tyranny."[31] And it seems certain that the high visibility of the radical sects, the eloquence of many of their writers, and their assumed affinities with later political attitudes have all conspired to make them seem stronger than they were. Membership figures are extremely hard to establish, but between 1643 and 1654 probably no more than five percent of the population attended religious assemblies other than those associated with their parish churches (many of which were now headed by "Puritan" ministers).[32]

Who, then, were the Puritans? Throughout this book I use the terms "Puritan" and "Quaker" rather than "Puritanism" and "Quakerism," agreeing with Michael Finlayson that the modern habit of thinking in reified "isms" is inappropriate for social and intellectual currents that were as shifting and ambiguous as these. It is interesting that use of the term "Puritanism" seems to have originated in the nineteenth century with Carlyle, who glorified it as "the last of all our Heroisms."[33] Admittedly the term "Puritan" is notoriously slippery, implying all too easily a coherent program or solidarity among individuals and groups who were constantly aware of their very real differences. This difficulty about usage bedevils everyone who works in the period, since the term "Puritan" is sometimes used to refer to orthodox Calvinist theology; sometimes to temporary political alliances that embraced such disparate groups as Presbyterians, Independents, and Baptists; and sometimes to the intellectual cast of mind of an individual such as Milton who began as a Calvinist and ended up an Arminian, representing, as Samuel Johnson long afterward remarked, a church of one.

In this book I use the term "Puritan" mainly to indicate the Calvinist orthodoxy that was accepted by all Presbyterians and many Independents, who represented the main centers of power in the "Puritan Revolution," and also by some groups that in certain respects were more radical, such as the Particular Baptists, to which Bunyan belonged. Originally this Calvinist orthodoxy was accepted as well by the "Puritan" wing of the established Church of England, which produced those formerly Anglican ministers who remained in their parishes during the Interregnum.[34] Before the 1630s Calvinist doctrine had been deeply entrenched in the Church of England, and the deep division within that establishment reflected an unresolved struggle to determine whose theology and other practices should prevail. As Conrad Russell says, "The division was not between the orthodox and the unorthodox: it was between rival claimants to the title of orthodox, and therefore between rival criteria of orthodoxy."[35] But under the pressure of the traumatic events of the 1640s the Anglican position became separated with increasing decisiveness from Puritan attitudes if not from an abstraction called "Puritanism."[36]

Calvinist orthodoxy affirmed the principles of the Synod of Dort of 1619, stressing predestination of the elect and an absolute reliance on the text of the Bible, and it demanded fidelity to professionally trained ministers who emphasized both.[37] In social and political terms the belief system had two essential elements: it affirmed the predestined triumph of the elect, which encouraged otherwise cautious temperaments to persist in rebellion against their king; and it internalized a conviction of sin and guilt, which promoted a rigorous self-control that both mirrored and reinforced the larger requirements of social control. This belief system was immensely empowering for those who believed themselves to be the elect, riding an irreversible tide of predestined events; and Providence was regularly invoked by countless people from Cromwell on down, all asserting God's irresistible plan and trying to convince themselves that contemporary events reflected it. Blair Worden, surveying a rich collection of examples, is inclined to reject claims by anti-Calvinists that appeals to Providence were self-serving rather than sincere (more accurately, they were self-serving *but also* sincere).[38] Many people nevertheless found this to be a chilling and anxiety-producing faith, and like Milton they gradually moved away from the tenets of strict Calvinism and to that extent ceased to be "Puritans." As William Haller summarizes the peculiar dilemma of this faith, "Orthodox Calvinism leveled all men under the law, made all equal in their title to grace, and then denied to most all prospect of realizing their hopes. It made the individual experience of God in the soul all-important, enormously stimulating individual spiritual experience, and then denied any freedom to the individual will."[39]

The antinomian response, in which the Quakers participated, asserted that all people could be saved and that their wills, having been released from selfish egotism, were radically free. These fundamental points of disagreement derived their capacity to infuriate Puritans from the fact that they appealed to a shared framework of assumptions in what were essentially family disputes. As J. C. Davis reminds us, debates within a culture of common assumptions and beliefs are often more furious than those between totally antithetical beliefs.[40] The conflict was greatly exacerbated by its participants' insistence that their beliefs really were antithetical: if you were not completely within the church of Christ as each group defined it, then you were necessarily an agent of Antichrist. From a sociological point of view the struggle reflected what Derek Hirst has called the "fissiparous history of the gathered churches,"[41] all claiming authority from the same Bible and overlapping in countless ways doctrinally as well as institutionally. So they were forever struggling to seal off their highly permeable boundaries, an effort that was made still more difficult by their rapid rate of mutation. The long lists of heretical sects compiled by the so-called heresiographers, particularly Thomas Edwards in *Gangraena*, have sometimes been cited as if they were reliable guides to real phenomena; it makes more sense to conclude, as Davis does, that there was something frantic about this effort to pin down precise categories in "what appeared as a seethingly promiscuous heterodoxy."[42]

Hobbes, hostile but characteristically perceptive, saw clearly the filial relationship between the radical groups and orthodox Calvinism (which was indeed an "ism"). As preachers got subtler and more competitive, he wrote in 1668, they evolved "many strange and many pernicious doctrines . . . and distracted their auditors into a great number of sects, as Brownists, Anabaptists, Independents, Fifth-monarchy-men, Quakers, and divers others, all commonly called by the name of fanatics: insomuch as there was not so dangerous an enemy to the Presbyterians as this brood of their own hatching."[43] They altered or rejected essential Puritan beliefs, but they continued to think within the categories that had produced those beliefs in ways that were absolutely maddening to their opponents, who possessed the political

power to do something about it. If the challenge had been merely oppositional the Puritan authorities would not have felt it to be so disturbing and dangerous: it was because the radicals seemed to parody
and subvert the most important truths that they had to be ruthlessly
suppressed. "These people called Quakers," one critic declared, "are
to me the saddest and most deplorable spectacles of revolted professors [those who profess true belief] that ever I have heard or read of."[44]

In 1655, reproaching "the Separatists and Anabaptists in England,"
the eminent preacher Richard Baxter proposed a malign genealogy for
the Quakers:

> The hand of God is apparently [i.e., evidently] gone out against
> your ways of Separation and Anabaptism; it is your duty to ob-
> serve it. You may see you do but prepare too many for a further
> progress; Seekers, Ranters, Familists, and now Quakers, and too
> many professed infidels do spring up from among you, as if this
> were your journey's end and the perfection of your revolt . . . I
> have heard yet from the several parts of the land but of very few
> that have drunk in this venom of the Ranters or Quakers, but
> such as have been first of your opinions and gone out at that
> door.[45]

Familists and Ranters, both tiny and elusive groups, will be considered
in the next chapter. Anabaptists were more easily described as dangerous, having had a bad name ever since their takeover of the German
city of Münster in the sixteenth century; conservative polemicists in
the 1640s constantly asserted that the heresies of their leader, John of
Leiden, were being spawned again in England.[46] Any apparent resemblance to Anabaptist practice was accordingly seized upon, for instance by Higginson with reference to the Quaker custom of meeting
at night: "Their holies, they think, are best dispensed while others are
asleep; these unseasonable dark assemblies of theirs, much like the
night-meetings of the Anabaptists in Munster, which afterward proved
fatal to that city . . . have been in some places a just cause of affright-
ment to the neighbouring inhabitants that are not of their way, who
have professed they could scarcely sleep in their beds without fear."[47]

Baxter's "Seeker" identification had more to recommend it. Insofar
as Seekers existed at all they were not a sect but an anti-sect: what they
had in common was a conviction that all existing churches were "part

of the apostasy" and that the Holy Spirit had yet to reveal the true dispensation.[48] Long afterwards Baxter defined them in essentially negative terms: "These taught that our Scripture was uncertain; that present miracles are necessary to faith; that our ministry is null and without authority, and our worship and ordinances [sacraments and customary practices] unnecessary or vain; the true church, ministry, Scripture, and ordinances being lost, for which they are now seeking."[49] And it is true that their position was a disillusioned and passive one: having worked their way through all of the available sects, they felt themselves to be waiting for some as-yet-unheard message or signal. In the opinion of people like Baxter, who were committed to a professional ministry and to well-defined parishes of the traditional kind, the Seekers were just another version of the restless misfits who had plagued England for a decade. In 1644 Richard Vines preached a sermon before the Lord Mayor and aldermen entitled *The Impostures of Seducing Teachers Discovered*, in which he denounced the "nomad" or "walker," who "wanders away the Sabbath by peeping in at Church-doors, and taking essay of a sentence or two, and then if there be no *scratch* for his *itch, lambit et fugit*, he is gone."[50] The frequent Quaker assertion that they had recruited large numbers of Seekers was, however, an interpretation through hindsight. They did indeed attract many distressed and alienated people, but these were not necessarily "Seekers" except in the metaphorical sense.[51]

In any case when a person was "convinced," by Fox or anyone else, it was not a question of learning something he or she didn't already know. Every one of the distinctive Quaker beliefs or attitudes was already current.[52] After 1660, when Fox was securely acknowledged as leader of the movement, its earlier history was reinterpreted—and some inconvenient documents probably suppressed—in order to antedate that role to 1650 or even earlier, but in fact he had been honored as a co-worker rather than as a leader or prophet with special authority that others did not possess.[53] What was new for Nayler and people like him was the realization that an actively charismatic movement might replace their former passivity and isolation, and that a mood of rooted pessimism could be transformed into its opposite.

In a much-quoted letter Cromwell remarked that "to be a seeker is to be of the best sect next to a finder; and such an one shall every faithful humble seeker be at the end. Happy seeker, happy finder!" But the sentence that follows this statement is less often quoted: "Who ever tasted that the Lord is gracious, without some sense of self, vanity, and badness?"[54] It was that initial conviction of "badness" that the early Quakers had acquired during their years as Puritans. In William Dewsbury's account, "I was conceived in sin and brought forth in iniquity, and in that state lived and delighted in pride and pleasures, lightness and vanity, as all do in that nature, until I was about eight years of age." Richard Vann comments, "We may wonder into what depths of worldliness a boy might sink by the age of eight."[55] But the crux of Dewsbury's statement is "as *all* do in that nature." In Calvinism it was human nature itself that was being rejected.

So also Bunyan remembered that he "did so offend the Lord, that even in my childhood he did scare and affright me with fearful dreams, and did terrify me with dreadful visions. For often, after I had spent this and the other day in sin, I have in my bed been greatly afflicted while asleep with the apprehensions of Devils and wicked spirits, who still, as I then thought, laboured to draw me away with them; of which I could never be rid."[56] Those dreams, which modern psychological theories might interpret as projections of guilt, were for Bunyan objective proof of his sinful condition, and *Grace Abounding to the Chief of Sinners* gives a harrowing account of a lifelong struggle to find peace. Bunyan's solution was to acknowledge himself, as Paul did, to be the "chief of sinners" (1 Timothy 1: 15). But as will be seen in the next chapter, the Quaker reply was that this emphasis made sin essential and institutionalized it, whereas the point was to accept Christ's promise that sin could be abolished.

For many people the preaching of Fox and his colleagues, with its emphasis on the transforming presence of Christ in each believer, was exactly what they had been waiting for without knowing it. The apocalypse was no longer an event to be enacted at some future date, but a total renovation here and now; Christ's return *had already happened* for those who could understand it.[57] Conversely, from a Quaker point of view, to remain a Seeker was to choose to remain in darkness. Quakers had come so that Seekers might cease to be. In a discourse on the victims of the fallen world Nayler referred to those who were "weary with seeking where nothing can be found, and are fallen asleep in the world of ease and carelessness," and he added sympathetically, "Many of you have had great travail, and gone through many sorrows to find rest, but have found none: many prayers and tears, but no answer of peace: many days of seeking, but have not found him whom your souls thirst after: and all this, because you have been seeking the living among the dead."[58] In another work Nayler proclaimed "the day of the Lord dawning" to "all people everywhere who profess that you love God, and have a desire to walk in his ways, and are in this dark world, wandering to and fro, enquiring the way, how you may come out of this great city which is Sodom and Egypt, where filthiness and darkness rules and is heard, wherein the Lord is crucified, and all the righteous blood hath been shed, and your selves are kept in bondage to sin and unrighteousness, blindness and thick darkness, and know not where you are, nor the way out of this condition; though many of you have been enquiring after the way so many years."[59] But now there was no time to lose, as an embedded scriptural allusion in this passage makes ominously clear: "Their dead bodies shall lie in the street of the great city, which spiritually is called Sodom and Egypt, where also our Lord was crucified" (Revelation 11: 8).

The name "Quaker" was originally a term of abuse, "slandering and nicknaming" true Christians, as Nayler complained, "the Quakers as thou scornfully callest us."[60] Their status as outsiders, even as outcasts, was one of which they were proud. In an early tract Nayler described them as "a poor, despised, persecuted, reproached people, whom God hath called out of the world's ways, words, works, worship, riches and pleasures, and so are become strangers and wanderers to and fro."[61] On the title page of another book he referred to Quakers as "the despised contemptible people trampled on by the world, and scorned by the scorners."[62] In an allusion that lurks behind this formulation, the scorners will themselves be scorned by God: "Surely he scorneth the scorners: but he giveth grace unto the lowly" (Proverbs 3: 34).

Their own self-description was at first "Children of the Light" and afterward "Friends," with authorization in the words of Christ: "Henceforth I call you not servants; for the servant knoweth not what his lord doeth: but I have called you friends; for all things that I have heard of my Father I have made known unto you." Christ goes on to say, as they certainly remembered, "Ye have not chosen me, but I have chosen you, and ordained you, that ye should go and bring forth fruit" (John 15: 15–16). It seems that the name "Society of Friends" came much later,[63] but from the beginning a strong sense of mutual support counterbalanced the isolation of the prophet, overcoming anomie by renouncing the larger community and focusing on a tiny one. Phyllis Mack has put it well: "Society made individuals; salvation made bonding."[64] This bonding tended to be horizontal through the nation—Quakers were prolific correspondents as well as energetic travelers—rather than vertical within a locality. Numbers are hard to determine, but by 1660 there were somewhere between 40,000 and 60,000 Quakers. Even the higher number would amount to less than one percent of the total population, but many hundreds of parishes had at least one Quaker family, and their influence was widely felt.[65]

Modern scholars have given much attention to the social status of the first Quakers, who tended to be people not at the very bottom of society, where fatalistic conservatism was common, but in situations where the failure of reform was particularly resented. R. H. Tawney, asked whether the Civil War was a bourgeois revolution, replied, "Of course it was a bourgeois revolution. The trouble is the bourgeoisie were on both sides."[66] The big merchants and bankers had as strong a stake in the status quo as the big aristocrats did; it was among artisans and independent farmers like Nayler who owned their land that the Quakers found their earliest and most effective recruits. Their appeal was also regional, strongest where economic and demographic change seemed threatening, including market-dependent pastoral regions such as Nayler's Yorkshire, which had been fiercely independent during the civil wars, many men refusing to join either side or to pay tithes.[67] Regions of arable farmland, with their many small villages, tended to be much more deferential to traditional order.[68] Often Quaker converts were people whose work required travel and who thereby came into contact with new ideas. Clothiers, for instance, who traveled constantly to "put out" wool for spinning and later to collect it, furnished a notably large number of early Quakers. So did the army, particularly the lower-ranking officers, who had been accustomed to form "gathered churches" with their own chaplains rather than to join existing churches where they might happen to be stationed.[69]

At the time, what most struck contemporaries was the youth and rootlessness of the Quaker itinerants. Fox, a weaver's son who became a cobbler, began preaching in 1647 when he was twenty-three, and a majority of the early Quaker preachers were very young. John Audland was twenty-two when he joined the movement; Edward Burrough was nineteen. According to their modern historian, "They were for the most part young men in the prime of their ardour and strength, who would follow the movings of life rather than the counsels of prudence."[70] Less piously Hill remarks that "it would be inter-esting to consider Quakerism as a revolt of teenage boys against their parents (not apparently of girls)."[71] This is a plausible suggestion: per-sons who felt repressed by patriarchy, in its most immediate and do-mestic form, were struggling not to turn into patriarchs themselves. And there is no reason to except girls, since from the start the Quaker movement had an unusual number of influential women members, often "convinced" in their teens. Certainly the young preachers, who were constantly on the move and often averaged thirty miles a day on foot,[72] were much freer than older people would have been to embrace a formless way of life and to live, as they themselves often said, like the lilies of the field. They acted as fully as possible upon Christ's direc-tive to his seventy disciples: "Behold, I send you forth as lambs among wolves. Carry neither purse, nor scrip, nor shoes" (Luke 10: 3–4). The original itinerant "First Publishers of Truth" were commonly referred to as the "valiant sixty," but their number was sometimes put at sev-enty to align it with this biblical precedent.

As the Quaker preachers moved west into Lancashire they found a powerful patron in Margaret Fell of Swarthmoor Hall and her hus-band Judge Thomas Fell, and Margaret Fell played a crucial role as coordinator and advisor of the growing movement. As a "mother in Is-rael" rather than as an administrator of the conventional kind, her role was entirely informal and depended on deference rather than author-ity.[73] For all its striking success, this was not an organized sect and de-liberately tried not to become one; nor did it expect to gain converts on a wide scale. It therefore represented, as Braithwaite says, "a spiri-tual Israel within the nation rather than a separated sect."[74] As Nayler expressed it, "We who are one do witness the unity in these things, and hereby are of one soul, heart and mind, and all who are not in this unity we deny, and see them to be in the sects, opinions, and the many names; but we which are one, witness one God, and his Name one."[75]

From the point of view of the establishment, Quaker converts were either inconsiderable persons or insubordinate ones. Baxter's account of their origins is suggestive, so long as one makes due allowances for his hostility:

It's no great encouragement to us to turn Quakers, when we con-sider who are their followers and society that make all this ado in the world. Very few experienced, humble, sober Christians that ever I heard of turn to them; but it's the young raw professors, and women, and ignorant ungrounded people that were but novices and learners in the principles, and such as are notorious for self-conceitedness and pride, being wise in their own eyes. And most of all these that ever I heard of, were Anabaptists or the members of some such sect, that by their division and error were prepared before.[76]

People already interested in antinomian ideas, whether abnormally proud or not, were, as Baxter says, "prepared" for the Quaker message; men who became Quakers in the 1650s did tend to be young, and an unusually high proportion of the membership was female.[77] Richard T. Vann observes that it seems significant that Margaret Fell and all her daughters became Quakers while her magistrate husband and their only son did not.[78]

The sincerity with which the Quakers tried to live like the lilies of the field also deserves to be emphasized, directly opposed as it was to the worldly asceticism that Weber has described in the kind of Puritan for whom faith was a stimulus to acquisition. As Thomas Camm remembered his father John, one of Fox's earliest converts in Westmoreland and thereafter a notable preacher,

> He was made willing to take up the cross and become a fool for Christ's sake [1 Cor. 4: 10], forsaking the world, and all the glory, delights, pleasures, wisdoms and riches of it, of which he had enjoyed a share equal, if not above, many of his degree; for naturally he was a wise man in worldly matters, having at that time great concerns and dealings therein; and the world seemed to smile upon him, and the riches and glory of it had exceedingly increased, and was then likely to increase more; yet notwithstanding all this, the Lord so prevailed by his power and spirit in his heart, that he was made willing to part withal, and counted it a blessed exchange to be made an heir in Christ of that durable riches laid up in heaven that his soul had traveled [travailed] for, so that it was no hard thing for him to forsake all for Christ's sake, and become a despised follower of him through many tribulations.[79]

If the earliest Quakers were often men and women of some substance, they voluntarily gave up much or even all of it. Social egalitarianism was a constant theme of Quaker preachers, expressed as an overturning of the customary relationships that prevailed among classes. As Nayler described it, this destabilization should work in both directions: "He that is called of the Lord being a servant, is the Lord's freeman; likewise he that is called being free, is Christ's servant."[80] The Quakers were not, however, communists (even the Levellers seem to have countenanced some distinctions within society); their ideal was a nation of small producers, none of whom would be allowed to gain inordinate wealth.[81] And even when they did grow rich in after years, Weber could rightly include the Quakers among "those sects whose otherworldliness is as proverbial as their wealth."[82]

Quaking and Solemnity

However interesting social origins and contexts are to modern interpreters, the early Quakers did not define themselves in those terms. Rather, they proclaimed a radical individualism that repudiated all worldly connections and declared an unmediated relationship with the divine Spirit. Their notorious quaking, the involuntary trembling and groaning that led Higginson to refer to them contemptuously as an "epileptic society,"[83] also represented a differentiation from their contemporaries that struck many as flagrant irrationalism. The Puritan elect were supposed to scrutinize ambiguous clues to their spiritual status and fate; the Quaker saints knew who they were because their status was confirmed by an entirely involuntary response. And they had plenty of Biblical authority for it. "To this man will I look," the Lord says in Isaiah, "even to him that is poor and of a contrite spirit, and trembleth at my word" (66: 2). Moses himself was a quaker, as Paul confirmed: "So terrible was the sight, that Moses said, I exceedingly fear and quake" (Hebrews 12: 21).

Not surprisingly, episodes of quaking often came on at times of stress, particularly when a preacher had to confront hostile crowds or authority figures. When Thomas Aldam faced the formidable Major General Harrison, who was holding a great court in the castle at York, and warned him against accepting bribes, "I was taken with the power in a great trembling in my head and all of the one side all the while I was speaking to them, which was a great amazement to the people, and they was silent."[84] The Quakers themselves, of course, did not interpret this behavior in psychological terms; for them it was a decisive manifestation of the prophetic power described in the Bible. Charles Marshall was "convinced" at Bristol at the age of seventeen when he heard John Audland speak:

> He stood up, full of dread and shining brightness on his countenance, lifted up his voice as a trumpet and said, "I proclaim spiritual war with the inhabitants of the earth, who are in the Fall and separation from God, and prophesy to the four winds of heaven." And these words dropped amongst the Seed; and so went on in the mighty power of God Almighty, opening the way of Life. But, ah! the seizings of souls and prickings at heart which attended that season; some fell on the ground, others crying out under the sense of opening their states, which indeed gave experimental knowledge of what is recorded, Acts 2. 37.[85]

The text Marshall cites says that Peter's hearers "were pricked in their heart" on the occasion of Pentecost, when tongues of fire descended upon the apostles and as an earlier verse records "they were all filled with the Holy Ghost, and began to speak with other tongues, as the Spirit gave them utterance" (Acts 2: 4). The whole of the chapter in Acts must have seemed immediately prophetic in the mid-1650s, when apocalyptic claims were being heard on all sides: "It shall come to pass in the last days, saith God, I will pour out of my Spirit upon all flesh: and your sons and your daughters shall prophesy, and your young men shall see visions, and your old men shall dream dreams; and on my servants and on my handmaidens I will pour out in these days of my Spirit; and they shall prophesy" (17–18).

As with so much that the Quakers did and said, these claims were not necessarily easy for Puritans to dismiss, for as Nayler shrewdly pointed out they were very willing to invoke as metaphor what they distrusted as reality: "Thou sayest, 'Work out your salvation with fear and trembling,' but scornest *quaking*, and sayest, 'it is from the power of the Devil.' . . . Thou wilt own the Scripture in notion and letter, but scornest and persecutest the power and practice of it."[86] Puritan writers therefore had to say, and in many contexts did indeed say, that the world of the Bible was utterly different from their own and that modern saints could no longer do what their ancestors had done. The Quaker counterclaim was that the saints of the Bible had no special powers that were not equally available in the seventeenth century. In defense of quaking Nayler wrote a tract made up of biblical quotations that showed how "the holy men of God do witness *quaking* and *trembling,* and *roaring,* and *weeping,* and *fasting* and *tears;* but the world knows not the saints' conditions."[87]

As so often, a fundamental disagreement about the nature of religious experience was at stake. Higginson, who witnessed the earliest manifestations of the Quaker movement, made the interesting assumption that quaking among north-country rustics could not be learned or imitative behavior and must therefore be diabolical, an inspiration of the reverse kind to what the Quakers claimed:

> It is an utter impossibility for any man, especially women, that never knew what belonged to stage-playing, and young children, to feign such swoonings, tremblings, palsy motions, swelling, foaming, purging, such great and horrid screechings and roarings; yea common modesty would restrain any man or woman that are themselves from such uncleanly excretions as do often accompany these sordid trances. Surely it must needs be some black art that works so turbulently on men's spirits or bodies, and conjures them into such surprises.[88]

The glance at stage plays, that favorite target of Puritan indignation, is particularly notable. The northern Quakers were like actors who had never seen real actors perform, and must therefore be playing out roles dictated subliminally by the prince of darkness. The Quaker response to this critique would be that Puritan revulsion betrayed an excessive preoccupation with the body and its processes, whereas the inspired saints were literally *not* "themselves," escaping the prison of corrupt selfhood and leaving behind the groanings and excretions of the rejected body as the spirit soared free. From the Quaker point of view Higginson's appeal to "common modesty" would betray an almost ludicrous dependence on the conventions of the ordinary social world.

This was one aspect of Quaker behavior; but it was accompanied by a totally different mode of behavior that, interestingly enough, offended the Puritans in the opposite direction. When not immediately inspired by the Spirit, Quakers were given to a gravity of demeanor that struck many contemporaries as an affectation of moroseness. The habit of gloom is illuminated by a striking recollection by

Thomas Ellwood, who later became a Quaker and Milton's pupil and friend, of a visit to the family of Isaac Penington. Penington, son of a leading Puritan and Lord Mayor of London, had bought an estate at Chalfont St. Peter in Buckinghamshire in order to lodge traveling Quaker preachers and to hold meetings. Ellwood was particularly interested in an attractive Penington daughter, with whom he tried to strike up a conversation when he came upon her picking flowers in the garden, but he found himself abashed by "the gravity of her look and behavior" and withdrew "not without some disorder (as I thought at least) of mind." The ensuing scene with the entire family was no better:

> We stayed dinner, which was very handsome and lacked nothing to recommend it to me, but the want of mirth and pleasant discourse: which we could neither have with them, nor, by reason of them, with one another amongst ourselves: the weightiness that was upon their spirits and countenances keeping down the lightness that would have been up in us. We stayed notwithstanding till the rest of the company took leave of them and then we also, doing the same, returned, not greatly satisfied with our journey, nor knowing what in particular to find fault with.[89]

In its rueful bafflement this account gives a good sense of the uneasiness the Quaker style of deliberate melancholy must have aroused in many people. Its purpose was to testify to a separation from the depraved world of everyday behavior: the Quaker could not avoid being in that world, but must not be of it. For as Penington himself wrote, "Our work in the world is to hold forth the virtues of Him that hath called us; to forget our country, our kindred, our father's house, and to live like persons of another country, of another kindred, of another family: not to do anything of ourselves and which is pleasing to the old nature: but all our words, all our conversation, yea, every thought in us is to become new."[90] This formulation has great psychological interest. At the moment of "convincement" a person might well feel intoxicated by a sense of total renovation, but as time went by it could become a strict duty to be achieved with effort, if not reluctance. To make every thought continually "new" is a daunting task indeed.

Itinerants and Hireling Priests

If the Quakers had been content to live in private gloom, quaking occasionally, they might have excited sarcasm but not outrage. They got into trouble above all because they refused to leave the established ministers in peace, traveling from place to place to challenge them and to stir up their parishioners against them. As one of the speakers in Parliament complained when Nayler was being tried, "Whatever they pretend, they cannot be a people of God. Christ's spirit is a meek spirit, but they are full of bitterness in reviling the ministers and magistrates."[91] There was nothing new about anticlericalism as such, but in the 1640s, when the institutional lid came off, there was an unprecedented upwelling of it. In what seemed a bitter irony to many, the Puritan leaders attempted in the 1650s to put the lid back on.[92] At a time when travel was still unusual and outsiders were held in suspicion, the Quakers were quintessential outsiders, and even when they remained settled in one place they set themselves apart by distinctive language, manners, and dress. They were irritating not only to the elite who ran the country but to the mass of ordinary people as well, who readily believed wild accusations that Quakers were witches or Papists in disguise, and who frequently took part in mob actions against them.[93]

The arrival of aggressive itinerant preachers in remote northern parishes must certainly have been alarming to ministers who believed that they themselves had renounced worldly rewards in order to bring the Gospel to the people. The Independent minister of Cockermouth in Cumberland wrote later that "like a mighty torrent, they had like to have swept down all the churches in the nation."[94] Higginson complained in 1653 that "last summer there came, or rather crept unawares, into the county of Westmoreland, and some parts of Yorkshire and Lancashire adjacent to it, George Fox, James Nayler, one Spoden, and one Thornton, all of them Satan's seeds-men, and such as have prosperously sowed the tares of that enemy in the forementioned fields."[95] A Westmoreland ministers' petition in the same year charged that "James Nayler and George Fox, men whose country, habitation, profession, and condition is to us generally unknown, merely of their own accord, without any passport, license, or authority whatsoever that they can show or we ever heard of, have entered into the County." To this Nayler retorted that no human passport or authority could possibly be relevant, and he added proudly, "It is true, our habitation is with the Lord, and our country is not of this world, neither are our conditions known to the world."[96]

Clearly Nayler and his fellows were powerfully drawn to the idea of perpetual wandering. In 1652 he wrote to Fox that he had been urged to remain for a while in a place where he was preaching, "but I am made to go on in the work, and I am made free to wander any way the Lord shall move me so that I may do his will, for there is my peace."[97] This practice had an explicitly anti-institutional rationale: the point was to resist any temptation to exert authority over a particular group of people or to extract a regular income from them. Christ's first disciples, Nayler wrote, "did watch for the soul, and not for tithes, pigs, and eggs, and geese, and sheaves . . . They might eat freely what was set before them, where the spirit was free; but they did not seat themselves in a town, or say 'This is my parish,' and 'This is my hire,' so much a year; but wandering to and fro, having no certain dwelling place; nor was their bellies any part of the bargain, as to coming, preaching, staying or going, as to any place."[98]

The force of the Quaker challenge should not be underestimated: it was not merely a case of occasional disputes with local ministers, such as the ministers themselves regularly engaged in. For strangers to arrive in a town and settle down there, gradually building up congregations of their own, would not have seemed nearly so threatening; the various Puritan sects were entirely familiar with that sort of competition. The Quakers represented a very different kind of challenge because their movement directly challenged principles of collective order in which the Independents believed just as much as Anglicans did.

One of Nayler's angriest critics, Ralph Farmer, prefaced his account of the Bristol episode with an elaborate metaphorical plea for order that would continue to reflect subordination. The church should be a unity, Farmer wrote, mirroring that of the physical universe, and to this end the original Apostles "planted and settled (as stars in their particular orbs) pastors and teachers, as fixed constant and abiding lights among them." Just as the stars are located high above the earth, so also these pastoral light-givers enjoy an authority derived from their superior position. Between them and their congregations, "as parent and children, shepherd and sheep, rulers and ruled, there is a firm relation." But what, then, are itinerant preachers? The Copernican analogy is irresistible: "How shall we reckon of those arrant omnitinerant and extravagant undertakers, who (having no fixed station) go up and down like gipsies; but as wandering stars and meteors, or rather as blazing comets, who commonly portend some mischief, a generation of men of whom we find no constitution in the Scripture?"[99] For an orthodox Puritan like Farmer, the Bible is at once the legal constitution whose provisions must never be altered and the guarantor of the quasi-physiological constitution of the church, in which the varying humors are "tempered" into one whole. But the Quakers wander constantly and everywhere, "omnitinerant" in Farmer's expressive coinage, like irregular invaders of the solar system that portend mischief. They are "extravagant" in the root sense of wandering out of bounds in a morally transgressive way, as when Othello is described as "an extravagant and wheeling stranger / Of here and everywhere."[100] Likewise by an implicit pun they are at once "errant" (in the old sense of wandering) and "arrant" in their insubordinate pride. Wandering was indeed at the heart of the Quaker message, which implied a drastic rejection of the whole conception of moral and social order that Farmer's traditionalist metaphors were intended to shore up.

Like other sectarians the Quakers insisted on calling church buildings "steeple houses," reserving the term "church" for the invisible company of the saints. This was not an eccentric position: ever since the sixteenth century there had been a widespread Protestant reaction against the "superstitious" Catholic practice of consecrating churches and the holy ground surrounding them and, as Keith Thomas comments, "the plain and functional Quaker meeting-house was the ultimate achievement of this school of thought."[101] The practice of invading steeple houses to incite their congregations was explicitly intended as an imitation of the first apostles, who entered synagogues to bring their members from the Torah to Christ.[102] A custom in fact already existed of permitting members of the congregation to speak when the service was over and the preacher had, as Fox put it, "done his stuff" (he actually did use that expression).[103] But to interrupt during the service was totally unacceptable, and modern historians are not exaggerating when they call the Quaker itinerants "professionally skilled hecklers" who were waging "a guerrilla war against the clergy."[104]

Whereas the Quakers insisted that the church was people and not buildings, the religious establishment, in their view, used the buildings as fortifications of war. When Nayler was preaching at Kendal in

Westmoreland, "spies being out upon the steeple top and other places, notice was given what way James passed from thence." Alerted by the spies on the steeple, a crowd assembled and stoned him, "but such was the power of the Lord, that neither he nor any with him received any harm."[105] Unauthorized preaching was clearly illegal when it took place inside the steeple house, and Quakers were always on their guard against being set up for prosecution on this account, as is illustrated by the same episode:

> Another of them desired him to go into the church, as he called it, [and] tempted him, saying, "The people may all sit and hear better;" but James perceiving their deceit, said, "All places were alike to him: he would abide in the field." Wherein they pulled out an ordinance of Parliament, forbidding any to speak, but such as were authorized to speak either in church or chapel, or any public place; and bade him speak at his peril, as he would answer the contempt of it. To which he answered, saying, "This is not a public place." "No?" said one of the priests, "is not this a public place, the town field?" and charged the constable of the town to do his office. (p. 22)

The apparent equivocation is significant. In Nayler's interpretation the law refers to such public places as are specifically set aside for official purposes. The town field is not public in that sense; it represents noncontrolled space, at once liminal and democratic, very like the "common" lands that the Diggers had vainly attempted to treat as if they were actually held in common.

The Quaker invaders were offensive not only for their obstreperousness, but also because they lacked academic training and conveyed a challenge that carried an unmistakable element of class antagonism. Years later, in a retrospective view of the movement, Nayler recalled that after Puritan preachers had left the path of truth, God sent "men of enlightened consciences" to prophesy, "though otherwise they themselves were neither prophets nor sons of prophets, but may be a herdsman, or a gatherer of sycamore fruit, a plowman or a shepherd, or some such which England's pride would call 'mechanic fellows;' yet in these was a Seed preserved, else the land might have become as Sodom, and not one have known the Lord or his word."[106] A marginal gloss identifies the allusion to one of the favorite prophets of the early

Quakers: "Then answered Amos, and said to Amaziah, I was no prophet, neither was I a prophet's son; but I was a herdman, and a gatherer of sycamore fruit: and the Lord took me as I followed the flock, and the Lord said unto me, Go, prophesy unto my people Israel" (Amos 7: 14–15). Another gloss connects the Quakers with the "small remnant" by whom Israel was preserved from becoming "as Sodom" (Isaiah 1: 9). It was from this perspective that Nayler reproached university-trained preachers with their difference from the original apostles. "What rule walk you by, who must have them to such a pitch of learning, and so many years at Oxford or Cambridge, and there study so long in books and old authors? And all this to know what unlearned men, fishermen, ploughmen, and herdsmen did mean when they spoke forth the Scriptures, who were counted fools and madmen by the learned generation when they spake them forth."[107]

Whatever education Nayler may have received, contemporaries testified and his writings confirm that he was highly literate and an acute reasoner. Thomas Ellwood met Nayler in 1659—one month after his release from three years' solitary confinement—and noticed that his intellectual power was all the more striking by contrast with an unsophisticated appearance. After accepting an invitation to visit a Quaker meeting, Ellwood's father, who fancied himself an amateur theologian, defended the Calvinist doctrine of predestination. Nayler's colleague Edward Burrough, "a brisk young man, of a ready tongue," attempted to reply, without much effect. "But James Nayler interposing, handled the subject with so much perspicuity and clear demonstration that his reasoning seemed to me irresistible; and so I suppose my father found it, which made him willing to drop the discourse . . . What dropped from James Nayler had the greater force upon me because he looked but like a plain simple country-man, having the appearance of an husbandman or a shepherd."[108]

Nayler expressed the anti-institutional view with great clarity in an imaginary exchange between Paul, who proclaims the right of all believers to be prophets, and Antichrist, who prefers the institutional training of the orthodox Puritans and welcomes their punitive measures against anyone who attempts to prophesy.

Saith Paul, You may all prophesy one by one, that all may learn, and all may be comforted; and if any thing be revealed to one that sits by, let the first hold his peace, for God is not the author of confusion, but of peace; and the spirits of the prophets are subject to the prophets, as in all the churches of the saints. 1 Cor. 14. 30–33.

Saith Antichrist, That was the order in the primitive times, but that prophesying is now ceased, and none shall now prophesy but such as are men of learning, and have been at the university, and have tongues, and study to fit them for that purpose, and have received orders either from the bishop, or are approved by some appointed by authority: and these shall be masters, and bear rule in every parish, none shall reprove or contradict what they say in public, nor speak any thing till they have done (notwithstanding whatever be revealed to any that sit by) for we have a law, and by that law all that do shall be imprisoned, and proceeded against as disturbers of the peace.[109]

Antichrist's speech here faithfully reproduces the standard Puritan claims, and Nayler proposes to refute it not by argument but by the superior authority of the Spirit, which inspired Paul long ago and has continued to inspire God's prophets in his own day.

The fundamental issue in these controversies has not always been clearly appreciated. It was not just that the ministers were exposed to criticism; they were well accustomed to internecine quarrels of their own that were often highly acrimonious. The issue was that they took for granted their professional custodianship of such disputes and their right to insist on institutional discipline from their followers. The antinomian challenge was shocking because it inverted the priority of discipline over doctrine. Even worse, doctrines were of interest to Quakers mainly in the negative sense, as they inveighed against the beliefs that underpinned the Puritan establishment. And they struck at church governance at its very root by claiming not merely that Puritan "priests" (as they called all paid ministers) were governing in the wrong way, but that any governance at all was intolerable.

Baxter's indignant counterattack shows how outrageous the orthodox ministers found this kind of criticism: "When they have called me Dog and Devil, and abundance of such names, and I have asked them what was my fault? forsooth, it was that I was called Master, that I stood above the people in a pulpit, that I preached by an hourglass, that I preached by doctrine, and use, and such like. And doth the Christian religion consist in such ridiculous accusations as these?"[110] To the Quakers such accusations, far from being ridiculous, exposed the Puritan betrayal of Reformation spirituality, and these attacks represented the only hope of rescuing errant congregations from the abyss. At the end of a furious denunciation of a "blood sucker" opponent, Fox protested, "Neither count this hard language nor revile at it, it's the love of the Lord God to thee."[111]

Nayler gave an extended exposition of this specialized form of love in a work appropriately entitled *Love to the Lost:*

> This is pure love to the soul, that deals faithfully therewith in declaring its condition; and that was the great love Christ showed the Jews, when he told them they were "hypocrites," "blind guides," "liars," and said, "Woe unto ye, ye serpents, ye generation of vipers, how can ye escape the damnation of hell?" And many such plain words he spoke in love to them. And that was the love of God in Paul, which said to Elymas, "O full of all subtlety and all mischief, thou child of the Devil, thou enemy of all righteousness, wilt thou not cease to pervert the right ways of the Lord?" For all the love that can be showed to any creature is to deal faithfully and truly with them, as they are seen in the light; and he who doth not so, loves neither God nor them (as will be found out in the Day of Judgment).[112]

Blair Worden has observed of the Puritans, "A religion which seeks to cure the world can be relied on to become infected by it."[113] Sharing the Puritan belief in the world's corruption but denying the belief in predestination, the Quakers clearly felt they had more right than their opponents to be polemical: their goal was to make viciousness apparent so that sinners might be inspired to turn away from sin before it was too late.

Denunciation was thus understood to be a prophetic duty, and if it gave offence, so much the better. "And now try whether that Spirit act in you," Nayler wrote, "which led the apostles and saints into the temple and synagogues daily, there to dispute against all idolatrous worships . . . or [whether] that spirit that was in them who persecuted the saints for so doing, and commanded them to be silent, and charged them with breaking their law, and turning the world upside down, and counted them madmen."[114] Godly Puritan divines who had themselves labored to turn the world upside down did not, of course, appreciate this usurpation of their role, much less the vituperation that was lovingly heaped upon them. Thomas Weld and his co-authors complained, "Our selves, some of us, have had a large measure of this revilings thrown upon us. In one paper of theirs, which one of us hath, you have all these horrid railings against the ministers, calling them priests, conjurers, thieves, robbers, Antichrists, witches, devils, Sir-Simons, serpents, bloody Herodians, scarlet coloured beasts, Babylon's merchants, wolves, dogs, swine, Sodomites, &c." To this impressive catalogue Nayler replied calmly, "For words which have been spoken to some of you, which you call railing, you will find them one day to be no railings but the language of the Spirit upon the head of the man of sin in you."[115]

Weld's conclusion, like that of many anti-Quakers, was that their alleged prophetic mission was actually an outlet for inward "cursing and bitterness" (p. 50). They were certainly comprehensive in their abuse, as Higginson documented from their publications as well as from imprecations in the streets: "They impiously revile, with open mouth, even all the ministry of England without exception; calling them the priests of the world, conjurers, thieves, robbers, Antichrists, witches, devils, liars, and a viperous and a serpentine generation, blasphemers, scarlet coloured beasts, Babylon's merchants selling beastly ware, whited walls, ravening wolves, greedy dogs, Baal's priests, tithe-mongers, deceivers, hirelings, etc."[116] And beyond language, public demonstrations of disrespect were particularly intolerable: "A man that professeth godliness, especially a minister, that endeavours to be faithful to Jesus Christ in the discharge of the duties incumbent upon him, cannot pass by them without their scorns. Against such they grin, and point at them with their fingers" (p. 34). Even small children could join in the abuse. Eight-year-old Mary Fell, described as a "little sensitive girl" by her mother's modern biographer, recorded the following sentiments about the local minister on a scrap of paper that her family affectionately preserved: "Lampitt, the plagues of God shall fall upon thee and the seven vials shall be poured upon thee and the millstone shall fall upon thee and crush thee as dust under the Lord's feet how can thou escape the damnation of hell. This did the Lord give me as I lay in bed. Mary Fell."[117]

Nayler's account of a controversy in which he got embroiled in

Derbyshire shows how each side, fully convinced of its own good intentions, could provoke the other into furious anathemas.

> Being moved of the Lord to go to Chesterfield about the 20. day of the 10. month, and coming to the house of John Firth, as I was in the house I heard a confused noise in the town, whoting [hooting], yelling, and swearing about a bull-baiting; whereat being much troubled in spirit, I waited to know the will of God, what he would have me to do; whether I should go and declare against that their ungodly practice; but after I had waited a while I was moved to write to him that is called their teacher [i.e., the Puritan minister], and was showed that I must lay the thing upon him, being the cause why the people knew no better, but perish under him for want of knowledge.[118]

Nayler's objection to the bull-baiting, incidentally, has no affinity to Macaulay's famous explanation of Puritan condemnations of bear-baiting (not because it gave pain to the bear, but because it gave pleasure to the spectators). It was wrong, Nayler says, because it was "setting one of the creatures of God against another to torment."

Nayler's tactics are notable here, since he deliberately refrained from denouncing the "multitude" who were enjoying themselves so much. Instead he took at its word the Puritan establishment that laid great stress on the didactic role of the ministry: if the people were in error it was their minister who ought to have known better. Nayler therefore wrote to the minister of Chesterfield, John Billingsley, in highly confrontational language: "God is risen to cut you off, and to deliver his people out of your mouths upon whom you have made a prey; and woe unto you, it had been good for you that you had never been born; and in that day thou shalt witness that this is the word of God." The signature expressed solicitude for Billingsley's flock, if not for their teacher: "Written by one that seeks the good of souls, called James Nayler" (p. 2). Billingsley, not surprisingly, did not appreciate this account of his work and lodged a formal complaint with the magistrate, declaring that Nayler "deserved to be hanged for these words writing" (p. 2). The law declined to prosecute, however, and Billingsley had to settle for a public disputation and a written exchange of furious doctrinal "queries" and "answers," all of which were afterwards printed by Nayler.

One may well feel sympathy for Billingsley, who was himself a gifted evangelical preacher. After holding a fellowship at Corpus Christi, Oxford, he had responded in his late twenties to "a call into one of the remote and dark corners of the kingdom to preach the Gospel," as Edmund Calamy recalled, and thereafter resisted all temptations to seek more advantageous preferments: "He would not yield to a thought of leaving that people, who were dear to him as his own soul, and it was in his heart to live and die with them." At the Restoration, though a convinced royalist, Billingsley refused to conform to the Church of England and had to give up the Chesterfield living, but he nevertheless remained loyal to his former parishioners and for the remaining twenty-five years of his life visited them twice every month, preaching and attending the sick.[119] This was no timeserver whose hypocrisy might be exposed by the Quaker critique, but a dedicated pastoral minister who had given up much to serve his remote parish.

In his rejoinder Billingsley characterized Nayler and his colleagues as "persecutors of the faithful ministers of the Gospel of Christ," to which Nayler retorted, "Thou art not ashamed to call me persecutor, who hath often suffered by you [i.e., "you" in the plural, the Puritan ministry], but never persecuted any" (p. 3). But it certainly looked like persecution to Billingsley when a total stranger to his town—"James Nayler wandering Quaker" (p. 2)—launched an unprovoked attack that was deeply insulting if not actually defamatory. This is not to say that Billingsley, any more than Nayler, was shy about using polemical language. Nayler reports Billingsley's rejoinder to the complaint about the bull-baiting: "He said he wondered at the patience of God, that when I took the pen into my wretched hand he did not cause it to wither up; nay, my heart to tremble and my knees to smite one against another, and make me a spectacle of his avenged power before his saints and before the world; but if I repented not of that wickedness, the Lord would shortly come in flames of fire, with the angel of his power to take vengeance on me" (pp. 4–5).

Ultimately the dispute was not just about clerical authority, but at a fundamental level about the possibility of compromise with a sinful world. Billingsley explained that he had in fact tried to persuade his parishioners to give up bull-baiting, but felt that their continued misconduct could not justify abandoning them, "pleading that Christ ate with publicans and sinners, and that the Hebrews' church was such a mixed multitude as was accustomed to meet in the Jewish synagogue"

(p. 5). Nayler's contempt for this position makes one appreciate that the early Quakers were more exclusionist than even the most rigorous Puritans. All men and women were capable of being saved, but if they persisted in sin they put themselves utterly outside the pale. Billingsley claimed to be declaring "the Lord's advice" to Nayler, but in Nayler's opinion such a claim was contemptible: "That Lord I deny, and his advice who pleads for sin and sects, bull-baiting and bear-baiting, above the servants of God who reproves sin in the gate" (p. 5).

The Chesterfield controversy also illustrates the tactical games played by anti-Quakers who wanted to entrap them by legal means. When Nayler showed up for the public disputation he received warnings that the ministers wanted to launch into a formal church service and then have him charged with illegally interrupting it. Nayler therefore waited outside the church to intercept them before they could enter, hurrying around to a different door when they at first tried to avoid him. Billingsley, however, "would not stay, but as he went looked back, saying 'Thou hast been a soldier, but I am not so hardy, we will go in'" (p. 8). It looks as if Billingsley may actually have feared physical violence. At any rate, the service did start and Nayler accordingly withdrew, so that it seemed that the appointed confrontation would be aborted. In Nayler's account,

As I was going I met with the town's mayor and spoke some words to him, who was very moderate, and said he would keep peace, and would have had me in; but I told him they had begun their work [their church service] and in their time I should not go in. Further, I said, "Let it be manifest this day, to thee and all magistrates in the nation, that we have no mind to break the law unless the Lord move us, though that law is contrary to Scripture; therefore let them come forth in the yard, the weather is calm." So he went in, but they would not come forth, so he came again and wished me to come in, and some others wished the same, saying there was no plot; upon which I was moved to charge some there in the presence of God to speak what they knew as to the plot, and they said they did believe such a thing. Then said the mayor, "None can imprison here but I, and thou shalt not be imprisoned for it." I answered, "I believe thou intendst not to imprison me for it, but thou canst not secure me; here are priests out of all quarters, and if complaint be made twenty miles from this place that I broke the law, a justice in the country will say he must execute it upon me, and thou canst not keep me free." (pp. 8–9)

This passage suggests how complex and, in fact, inhibited the "persecution" of Quakers was. They could not simply be imprisoned without cause, not only because the magistrates might well throw such cases out, but also because their "persecutors" really needed to believe that the Quakers deserved what they got. It was necessary, therefore, to create situations in which Quakers would indeed break laws, thereby providing legal as well as moral justification for their punishment. But the Quakers of course knew what was going on, and they too could maneuver, obeying the call of God but trying to keep clear of situations that would compel them to become martyrs. At a deep level, perhaps, some of them did welcome martyrdom, but there is ample evidence that often they tried to avoid it. And not infrequently they found themselves dealing with fairminded officials, as Nayler did with the mayor of Chesterfield, who simply refused to take part in the persecutory game.

Quakers were frequently subjected to beatings and stonings by angry mobs. In Quaker historiography these attacks have generally been presented as inexplicable except as artificially fomented by frightened magistrates and jealous ministers. In fact, however, the majority of ordinary people seem to have perceived Quakers as disruptive deviants. Demands for drastic moral reform were opposed, in the words of a historian who has closely studied popular culture, by "a strong popular nostalgia for the imagined good old days of neighbourliness and fellowship," and this attitude eventually did much to ensure the widespread acceptance of the Restoration.[120] And although Fox and others regularly expressed amazement that they had not been killed, it seems clear that the beatings were intended as public humiliations, not as homicidal assaults.

Still they can only have been terrifying, especially since the victims were determined to offer no resistance. On one occasion in Lancashire Fox and Nayler were stoned and beaten with pitchforks and sticks, retaining the bruises for many days afterward,

and then G. F. got up, and they thrust him towards the sea with intent to have drowned him. And the boat which brought them over being near, James Lancaster put G. F. into it and then threw it off into the water, and they took up a fishing pole of the said James Lancaster about 6 or 7 yards long, and struck again at G. F. but missed him. And when they were got out of reach of the pole, they again threw stones at them; and the said James Lancaster stood up betwixt G. F. and them to defend him from the stones, and some of the stones lit on James Lancaster's cheek and made it bleed; and then they rowed off by the seaside to seek for James Nayler, who had walked off into the island whilst they were beating G. F. as aforesaid, being unknown to them. But they after perceiving he was a Quaker also, they hunted him out and fell upon him, and with clubs and staffs beat him sorely also.[121]

It seems strange that Nayler would have deserted his colleagues in this way; but the account was written long afterward, no doubt with recollections of Nayler's later disgrace, and it may have been intended to portray him as a faithless associate of Fox. (As for "the said James Lancaster," with his eponymous county name, he continued to travel and preach with Fox, wrote a number of tracts, did time in jail for his beliefs, and lived until 1699.)

It was not uncommon for physical opposition to be supplemented by doctrinal opposition in a way that may seem strange today. On one occasion in Westmoreland Nayler refused to emerge from a house to confront the "priests," since they had treated him harshly the previous day,

which answer they told the priests, whereupon they [the mob] rushed violently in, and took him by the throat, haled him out of the door into a field, where was a man whom they called a Justice, and with a pitchfork struck off his hat, and commanded him to answer to such questions as the priests would ask him. Whereupon the priest began to ask many questions, as concerning the resurrection, the humanity of Christ, the Scriptures, and divers other questions, as the sacrament, and such like, to which he answered, and proved by Scripture.[122]

Having just been grabbed by the throat and compelled with a pitchfork to remove his hat, Nayler had to stand in the field and parry a series of theological queries, complete with references to the Bible. It is well to remember, however, that some Quaker stories of persecution may have been exaggerated. Higginson, who found himself named as a notable tormentor, insisted that he could prove that he and his fellow ministers had been maligned: "What was done there was not done in a corner, but before many witnesses, by whom the truth may easily be made to appear."[123]

More formal debates sometimes occurred, but it is impossible now to know how coherent or persuasive the arguments on either side were. One of the few references to Nayler in Fox's *Journal* records a triumph: "So the Lord did, that all the people saw the priests were nothing and foiled, and cried, 'A Nayler, a Nayler hath confuted them all.'"[124] But this is being reported from the Quaker point of view. Public gatherings were doubtless welcomed as a form of spectacle by many people who cared little about what was being said, and who mainly enjoyed the entertainment value of a debate between local ministers and traveling challengers.[125] The crowd that cried "A Nayler hath confuted them all" was not necessarily a crowd of newly minted Quakers. Their opponents were of course just as sure they had won as the Quakers were. According to Higginson the Quakers were usually reduced in debate to be "totally silenced, and as mute as fishes; yet when these champions of errors have gone away, they have boasted of their conquests, and how gloriously they had foiled and stopped the mouths of their adversaries."[126]

It was on the issue of tithes that hostilities consistently focused. The Quaker position was that the tithes that supported the professional ministry translated spiritual sustenance into worldly cash, so that, as Nayler succinctly put it, "the parishioners pay excise for their souls."[127] Tithes were objectionable from many points of view, since they represented the most burdensome form of taxation that the majority of people (as opposed to big property holders) had to pay; they were incompatible with religious liberty, since they had to be paid to the established church even if one did not belong to it; and by securing the power of that church establishment, they constituted a major obstacle to religious as well as political reform. Moreover, ever since the Reformation a large part of the tithe had been transferred from the church to "lay impropriators," which meant that in many cases the money directly supported the gentry or aristocracy rather than the church.[128] This was a question therefore not just of local abuses but of an entrenched economic system on a national scale. In Nayler's words,

"That which is called the Gospel is become so chargeable in this nation, in respect of [the] great sums of money, etc. that yearly are paid to uphold it, lest it should fall."[129]

Cromwell himself, whose income in his youth had come largely from administering tithes, at various times pledged to abolish them, claimed that he was prevented from doing so by opposition in his own Council of State, and argued that they must remain in force until a better system of supporting the clergy could be developed.[130] Many parishioners resented the sight of their ministers dining with the squire, exerting authority in all sorts of ways, and feeding on a guaranteed income that was extorted from the people they were supposed to serve. Two centuries later George Eliot mentioned "the bitterness of tithe" in rural parishes.[131] If that was so under restored Anglicanism, it was far more the case when the Puritans had ejected the Anglicans but not their financial arrangements. As Nayler pungently observed, "Such ministers lay the foundation of their call upon a fat benefice; no means, no ministers with the parish masters; no cash, no call."[132]

The attack on tithes thus exposed a point at which the conservatism of the Commonwealth was particularly apparent. Radical critics focused their attacks on the two institutions (or intertwined branches of a single institution) of divinity and law—in the words of one Quaker writer, "the judges that judge for rewards, and the lawyers that plead for money, and the priests that teach for hire."[133] They wanted the professions to be open to all men of talent (a few even included women of talent) rather than remaining the monopoly of Oxford, Cambridge, and the Inns of Court. In addition the radicals complained that a salaried or "feed" ministry, the "blind mouths" of Milton's *Lycidas*, must necessarily be obedient to its source of income. As Hugh Peter crisply stated it in 1651, "The state pays them, and thus they have dependence upon the state."[134] Some Puritan apologists, Baxter for instance, were fully prepared to acknowledge the basis of tithing in state power: "If the supreme rulers of the Commonwealth may lay an excise or tax on the nation, and pay soldiers with one part of it, what forbids but that they may pay ministers of the Gospel with the other part?"[135] In another work Baxter's indignant defence betrays a sense of entitlement that goes far to justify the Quakers' criticism: "The tenths are the Church's, and not the people's: and God saith, 'Thou shalt not steal;' and yet the Quakers make a religion of teaching the people to steal or defraud others of the tenths."[136]

The Quakers did not want tithes to be shared more equitably, they wanted them abolished altogether, along with the professional clergy they supported. At bottom was not just resentment of economic inequity but also a deep moral revulsion against the slavery entailed by the very existence of money. In a plea addressed to Cromwell urging abolition of tithes, Nayler appealed to personal experience as a preacher: "If you say this will soon bring the ministers to be poor, I say you know not God, nor his care for his, who so argues; for never was the righteous, nor that Seed begging bread. Against that desponding mind do I bear witness, who was sent out without bag or scrip or money, into the most brutish parts of the nation, where none knew me, yet wanted I nothing."[137] In another pamphlet Nayler put into the mouth of "Antichrist" the standard exposition of what we would now call the Protestant ethic: "Thou must live by thy wits that God hath given thee, and this is not covetousness, but a provident care . . . Therefore first lay up for thy self and children, that you need not fear want, and then take thy rest, and thou mayest have time to serve God, and thy riches need not hinder thee, but further thee in his service." To this widely held view the irrefutable reply, in Nayler's opinion, was the commandment "Thou shalt not covet."[138] Collecting tithes was thus seen as symptomatic of a profound sellout in every sphere of life. The Quakers never wavered from the belief that Satan was the very real "god of this world" (2 Corinthians 4: 4) and that his seductiveness was a constant threat. "If you look to the God of this world, you may easily have his favour," Nayler said in an address to the Puritans, adding grimly, "but then you must take upon you his form."[139]

Forms, Hats, and Pronouns

In the campaign against Puritan orthodoxy, a resistance to external "forms" was the central principle that unified what might otherwise seem a miscellaneous set of sticking-points. The Quakers saw very clearly that any institutional church had a stake in enforcing social control, even when it asserted liberation from popish rituals and hierarchy. In Nayler's analysis the routines of public worship are skillfully defamiliarized by literal description:

> Men would impose upon our consciences *to come once a week to such a great house in their parish*, which they call a *parish church*, and

there we must observe what one man shall read, preach or pray, for two or three hours that day, by an usual form; and this man will have a clerk, and he shall say *Amen* at the end of such a sentence or part of his prayer or speech; and to this church, and to this worship so called, must we be bound while we dwell in that parish; and either the tithes of all we have, or so much a year set maintenance, must be paid to the man calling himself a minister of Christ; and so much a year to his clerk, for saying *Amen* after him, in money and other things; and if this we do constantly, we may live peaceably by them, and go under the name of good Christians, and a religious man; but if we fail in any of these, but especially in that of tithes or wages, then they call us heretics, and complain of us to the magistrate, or sue us at law, till they have cast our bodies into prison and taken the spoil of our goods.[140]

Religious ritual sustains authority, which in turn is sustained by compulsory financial contributions, and whenever this system is challenged the parallel system of legal sanctions is mobilized to secure it. To be identified as a "good Christian" and a "religious man" one must play the prescribed role within the system; to defy the system is to expose oneself as irreligious and to incur severe penalties. Moreover, by setting aside certain days and observances as specifically religious, the Puritans were compartmentalizing life in a way that proved them to be creatures of the fallen world: "You have a time to pray, and a time to play; a time to abstain from your lusts, and a time to fulfill your lusts; a day to abstain from the world, and days to conform to the world."[141]

To Puritans it must have been peculiarly insulting to be accused of "formalism," since they regarded themselves as spearheading the Protestant attack on ritual. And if ritualism, as defined for instance by the anthropologist Mary Douglas, is "a concern that efficacious symbols be correctly manipulated and that the right words be pronounced in the right order,"[142] then certainly the Puritans were not ritualists any more than the Quakers were. But they did hold on to "ordinances," if only baptism and (in some cases) commemorative invocations of the Last Supper, and they did sometimes use set texts in their worship, so it was still possible for the Quakers to charge them with not going far enough in their antiritualism. And, as always with the Quakers, to go less than all the way was to fail utterly. In an apologia for the Quaker movement Isaac Penington explicitly charged the Puritans with having sold out: "This is our lamentation, that forms and ways of worship abound: but the Puritan principle, the Puritan spirit is lost and drowned in them all."[143]

Conversely, it was not just Quaker disruptions in steeple houses that upset the Puritans, but the formlessness of their devotion as well. Francis Higginson, the Westmoreland minister who observed them closely, gave an unusually full description of their practices.[144] (My interpolations indicate what Higginson and other Puritans would have regarded as the correct alternatives.)

> They come together on the Lord's Day, or on other days of the week indifferently, at such times and places as their speakers or some other of them think fit. [God ordered mankind in the fourth commandment to "remember the Sabbath day, to keep it holy"; not only do the Quakers disobey, but they respond to the irregular promptings of various persons rather than heeding established ministers.]

> Their number is sometimes thirty, sometimes forty, or sixty, sometimes a hundred or two hundred in a swarm. [These are shapeless ad hoc assemblies, not settled congregations.]

> The places of their meetings are for the most part such private houses as are most solitary and remote from neighbours, situated in dales and by-places; sometimes the open fields, sometimes the top of an hill, or rocky hollow places on the sides of mountains, are the places of their rendezvous. [They ought to meet in proper churches rather than in the open air like pagans.]

> In these their assemblies for the most part they use no prayer: not in one meeting of ten; and when they do, their praying devotion is so quickly cooled that when they have begun, a man can scarce tell to twenty before they have done. [Puritans emphasized public prayer as an essential act of communal devotion, and expected it to be protracted in keeping with its importance.]

> They have no singing of psalms, hymns, or spiritual songs; that is an abomination. [Likewise, communal singing expressed the solidarity of the Puritan congregation; but the Quakers refused to sing or say anyone else's words.]

No reading or exposition of holy Scripture, this is also an abhorrency. No teaching, or preaching; that is in their opinion the only thing that is needless. [Claiming the absolute primacy of the Bible, the Puritans enforced doctrinal uniformity by means of ministerial teaching and preaching; this kind of uniformity was precisely what the Quakers rejected.]

The interrelation of politics and ideas is vividly exposed in this quarrel of opposed indignations. The Puritans had developed a tremendously powerful political movement because they internalized, with rigid self-discipline, a yearning for order in a time of change. Putting it the other way round, they projected outward their interior discipline, and for a time at least they managed to impose a revolutionary program on an entire society.[145] The Quakers, coming of age amid the confusions and disappointments of the fading Puritan revolution, took exactly the opposite tack. In their view Puritan self-discipline was really repression, Puritan "godly rule" was really oppression, and both were doomed to failure. The solution was to stop trying to impose order, either within or without, and to surrender freely to the Lamb, illuminated by the Light. In asserting the irrelevance of forms, the Quakers insisted on an utter nakedness of the soul that many people found altogether threatening. The threat was particularly disquieting since practically everyone during the 1650s claimed to be opposed to "formality" but could not agree as to what that was, on the one hand seeking to honor the freedom of the spirit, on the other hand insisting upon practices that might hold anarchy at bay.[146]

Challenged in these ways, the Puritan establishment freely invoked state power against the Quaker menace. "We have reason to solicit the Lord in our prayers," Higginson said, "that he would still continue to spread the skirt of the magistrate's protection and power over the churches," and he denied that such defensive maneuvers could be described as persecution:

For Nayler's sufferings, which the unfaithful relator [in *Saul's Errand to Damascus*] calls persecutions, he knows, or might as well as we, that little restraint only which he suffered as an evil doer was by the order of the justices; and we know that we did not so much as desire his sufferings in the least, and that we sought and desired nothing but the preservation of religion and peace among us, and that those authors and fomenters of the disturbances of this poor county might return to their habitations and callings, and there, according to the Apostle's rule, study to be quiet and do their own business.[147]

Preaching in Westmoreland was the "business" of the local ordained ministers; it could not be the business of the itinerant Quakers, and their infuriating disruptions were very properly restrained therefore by the hand of the law.

Throughout the decade of the 1650s Quakers regularly went to prison for certain specific offenses on which they were wholly unwilling to compromise. For the most part these related to interrupting church services and refusing to pay tithes.[148] Their treatment in court was not helped by their absolute refusal to swear oaths, insisting on obeying literally Christ's injunction "Swear not at all" (Matthew 5: 34), or even to remove their hats out of respect to the magistrates. This adamant rejection of customary forms demands to be understood in sociological terms: instead of participating in the routine face-saving behaviors of their culture, the Quakers made a point of behavior that was positively "face-threatening."[149] And they seem indeed to have fully appreciated the social implications of what they were doing, as when the keeper of the Launceton prison doffed his hat (no doubt with sarcastic intent) and said, "How do you, Mr. Fox? Your servant, Sir," and Fox replied, "Major Ceely, take heed of hypocrisy and a rotten heart, for when came I to be thy master and thee my servant? Do servants use to cast their masters into prison?" Fox is here recounting an episode that occurred during a legal interrogation regarding Ceely's claim that Fox had literally struck him. "And this was the great blow he meant that I gave him and struck him and that wounded him so that he complained to the judge of it in the face of the country and open court, and yet made the court to believe that I struck him outwardly with my hand."[150] From Ceely's point of view, of course, Fox had indeed struck him a wounding blow.

In general the Quakers explained or rationalized their antisocial style as simple obedience to Christ:

After these things the Lord appointed other seventy also, and sent them two and two before his face into every city and place, whither he himself would come. Therefore said he unto them,

The harvest truly is great, but the laborers are few: pray ye therefore the Lord of the harvest, that he would send forth laborers
into his harvest. Go your ways: behold, I send you forth as lambs
among wolves. Carry neither purse, nor scrip, nor shoes: and
salute no man by the way. (Luke 10: 1–4)

The early Quakers liked to think that the original band of itinerant
preachers (later honored as the "First Publishers of Truth") numbered
seventy; they traveled in pairs; they were partial to the metaphor of
harvesting; and they made a special point of saluting no one (that is,
giving "hat honor") by the way. On this last practice Thomas Weld
commented sarcastically:

You may see that by the same command the seventy Disciples
were forbid to wear shoes or carry a purse; and yet these Quakers,
who do so imperiously impose upon all men this not saluting,
make no conscience at all of these commands of not wearing
shoes and not carrying purses, as is evident to any that observes
them, especially if they be travelling a far journey. And this was
very fitly objected by one in Lancashire to James Nayler . . . as
being guilty of the breach of that command by wearing shoes. Is
not this to pick and choose in the Scriptures?[151]

The point was well taken: since Quakers claimed to be free of the letter of the Bible, responding instead to the spirit within, it was not obvious why they should insist upon—indeed, be prepared to go to jail
for—specific observances that might seem to be mandated somewhere
in Scripture.

Nayler, answering Weld in print, ignored the shoes and purse but
summoned a cascade of scriptural texts to buttress the real foundation
of the Quaker position, its aggressive rejection of "the world." "We
witness and practice whatever they did in the old time; and here we
leave you who are in the world, to your traditions of the world, and
[we] follow Christ and so witness against all the vanities out of which
we are called."[152] This was a stance so oppositional that it could well
lead to martyrdom, and that too was seen as fulfilling the mission.
"Behold," Christ had told the seventy, "I send you forth as lambs
among wolves," and Nayler remembered the text when he was being
interrogated at Bristol about his own very literal imitation of Christ:

Q. Art thou the unspotted Lamb of God, that taketh away the sins of the world?

A. Were I not a lamb, wolves would not seek to devour me.[153]

Even when refusal of "honor" did not incur immediate punishment, it could not fail to be perceived as antisocial and alienating. Ellwood, who grew up in a gentry household, understood it as a refusal to acknowledge any relationship that was conventional rather than personal:

> I had many evils to put away and to cease from, some of which were not, by the world, accounted evils; but by the light of Christ were made manifest to me to be evils, and as such condemned in me . . . Again, *the giving of flattering titles to men*, between whom and me there was not any relation to which such titles could be pretended to belong. This was an evil I had been much addicted to, and was accounted a ready artist in: therefore this evil also was I required to put away and cease from. So that thenceforward I durst not say, "Sir," "Master," "My Lord," "Madam" (or "My Dame") or say, "Your Servant," to any one to whom I did not stand in the real relation of a servant; which I had never done to any.[154]

Even if a personal relationship did exist it must not be misrepresented in conventional terms. When Ellwood met some former college friends he bewildered them by seeming to ignore their familiar social gestures, failing to doff his hat or say "Your humble servant, sir." One of them suddenly got the point:

> At length the surgeon (a brisk young man) who stood nearest to me, clapping his hand, in a familiar way, upon my shoulder, and smiling on me, said, "What! Tom, a Quaker!" To which I readily and cheerfully answered, "Yes: a Quaker." And as the words passed out of my mouth, I felt the joy spring in my heart; for I rejoiced that I had not been drawn out by them into compliance with them; and that I had strength and boldness given to me to confess myself to be one of that despised people. (p. 34)

To be a Quaker was to redefine former connections, even affectionate ones, and to give unmistakable proofs of membership in a "despised" group. From this firmness might spring joy, but it was a joy that would henceforth diminish or even exclude other kinds of relationships. "They stayed not long with me," Ellwood concludes, "nor said any more (that I remember) to me; but looking somewhat confusedly one upon another, after a while took their leave of me, going off in the same ceremonious manner as they came on" (pp. 34–35).

More alarming was the result when Ellwood failed to doff his hat to his father, whom he had always previously treated with respect. "He could not contain himself, but running upon me, with both his hands, first violently snatched off my hat and threw it away; then giving me some buffets on my head, he said, 'Sirrah, get you up to your chamber'" (p. 54). Ellwood claimed to regard this performance as wholly "unaccountable" (p. 55), as he likewise regarded his father's reaction to Quaker language: "He gave me a parting blow, and in a very angry tone said, 'Sirrah, if ever I hear you say *Thou* or *Thee* to me again, I'll strike your teeth down your throat'" (p. 57).

It is possible that in the beginning the Quakers did not regard the use of "thee" as remarkable, since it was normal usage in the north, but elsewhere it unquestionably sent unwelcome signals because it was commonly used by superiors to inferiors, in what Nayler succinctly described as the practice of "ye-ing the proud, and thou-ing the poor."[155] To address an equal or a superior as "thou" was at the very least to show bad manners; Higginson rather pedantically complained, "They account it unlawful to use the civility of our language in speaking to a single person in the plural number."[156] The Quakers insisted that the offending pronoun was no matter of personal choice, but a command from God that could not be refused. "When the Lord sent me forth into the world," Fox wrote, "he *forbade* me to put off my hat to any, high or low; and I was *required* to 'thee' and 'thou' all men and women, without any respect to rich or poor, great or small."[157] The authorities, however, saw this not as a case of solemn principle but as one example among many of plebeian contempt for the respect due to superiors.[158] That the Quakers insisted on it so self-righteously, and claimed to have scriptural authority for doing so, only made their behavior more infuriating.

Similarly, Quakers claimed the right to address all people by their first names, thereby flouting the deeply rooted English custom of withholding the use of one's personal name from any except the most intimate acquaintances. Their enemies saw this liberal use of names as presumptuous if not deliberately insubordinate. In its defense Nayler wrote,

> It hath been laid upon us by the Lord to call men and women by their own names, which their fathers have given to them, to be known by amongst men . . . In this we differ from some sorts of people, who can give flattering titles to some people instead of their names . . . For this we have suffered also by this generation as evil-doers and contemners of authority, though we know that to call a man by his name contemns not his authority, nor do we [do] it for that end, but in obedience to truth, and for conscience towards God.[159]

But this use of first names rather than titles appeared to critics like Higginson to be a blatant challenge: "They do not give any title or colour of respect to those that are their superiors, in office, honour, estate—such as Master, or Sir, etc., but call them by their naked name, Thomas, or William, or Gervase, or Dorothy, and ignorantly mistake it to be disagreeable to the word of Truth."[160]

As some of their critics were aware, Quaker usage was further complicated by a practice of adopting among themselves names that the profane were not to know, and in their correspondence they usually referred to each other by initials rather than full names.[161] Fox wrote (in a work coauthored with Nayler), "My name is covered from the world, and the world knows not me, nor my name; the earthly name the earthly man knows, and he is afraid of reproach, and cannot bear it upon the earthly name; he that overcometh hath the new name, and knoweth it."[162] Nayler himself, in answer to critics who suspected equivocation in his customary formula "one whom the world calls James Nayler," gave a very clear explanation: "For first, are not the words true? am not I one whom the world calls James Nayler? and they know no other name; and yet the Scripture speaks (Rev. 2. 17) of 'him that overcometh' having 'a new name, that no man knows but he that hath it.'"[163]

The Quaker insistence on keeping hats on, not only in social encounters but even in court, was similarly grounded in egalitarian ideas. Fox wrote, "If a lord or an earl come into your courts, you will hardly fine him for not putting off his hat; . . . it is the poor that suffer, and the rich bears with [i.e., makes allowances for] the rich."[164] During one of Nayler's earliest interrogations the examining magistrate urged that honor ought to be paid "respecting persons in judgment," and Nayler replied, "If I see one in goodly apparel and a gold ring, and see one in poor and vile raiment, and say to him in fine apparel, 'Sit thou in a higher place than the poor,' I am partial, and judged of evil thoughts."[165] No doubt the magistrate wore a gold ring. To pay him honor, then, would be to show a wicked partiality to his affluence and prestige, and would in itself be clear evidence of harboring evil thoughts.

As always, resistance was enabled by a conviction that it was a matter not of personal choice but of divine injunction, as the same interrogation confirmed:

> *Justice Pearson.* Now Authority commands thee to put off thy hat; what sayest thou to it?
>
> *James.* Where God commands one thing and man another, I am to obey God rather than man.
>
> *Col. Benson.* See whether the Law commands it, or your own wills. (p. 29)

The "Law" here is the law of God, not of England. Were the fractious Quakers really responding to imperative "leadings" of the Spirit, or were they indulging their rebellious wills and pulling the wool over their own eyes? Remarkably, Anthony Pearson, the justice who presided at this interrogation, was so impressed by Nayler and the Quakers that he made contact with Margaret Fell at Swarthmoor Hall and became a Quaker himself (though he eventually defected after the Restoration).

The outrage generated by refusing "hat honor" was so predictable that Fox seems to have regarded it as a litmus test to distinguish true believers from false.

> Oh, the rage and scorn, the heat and fury that arose! Oh, the blows, punchings, beatings, and imprisonments that we underwent for not putting off our hats to men! For that soon tried all men's patience and sobriety, what it was. Some had their hats violently plucked off and thrown away so that they quite lost them. The bad language and evil usage we received on this account are

hard to be expressed, besides the danger we were sometimes in of losing our lives for this matter, and that, by the great professors of Christianity, who thereby discovered that they were not true believers.[166]

In seventeenth-century usage, *discovered* meant *disclosed* or *revealed:* challenging the pious "professors" in this way served to expose the depth of their pride in demanding what Fox called "an honour invented by men in the Fall, and in the alienation from God." Quakers well knew that their refusal to observe certain forms laid them open to grave risks: imprisonment, of course, and in chancery cases financial ruin. That they persisted in such behavior was motivated, I believe, by a deep desire to be sure that they could not possibly be condemned as self-interested. To refuse to swear oaths or pay respect to magistrates was a means of proving to oneself, and not just to others, that one had utterly renounced the "creatures" of this world. Richard Hubberthorne was not speaking metaphorically when he wrote, "To us the truth is more precious than our estates, lives, or outward liberties."[167]

The Apolitical Apocalypse

By challenging their contemporaries in so many ways, the early Quakers were clearly willing to appear threatening. Whether or not their threat should be understood as a specifically political one depends upon how one defines politics. Like other sectaries they regularly used apocalyptic language that might well seem to anticipate imminent revolution, showing a fondness for alarming military metaphors which, however familiarized by the Bible, sounded very much like a call to violence and had certainly been so used by their Puritan predecessors during the civil wars. In 1654 Fox proclaimed, "A day of slaughter is coming to you who have made war against the Lamb and against the saints . . . The sword you cannot escape, and it shall be upon you ere long." "Spare none, neither young nor old," Francis Howgill wrote the next year; "kill, cut off, destroy, bathe your sword in the blood of Amalek and all the Egyptians and Philistines, and all the uncircumcised." John Audland similarly declared, "The sword of the Lord is in the hands of the saints, and this sword divides, hews and cuts down deceit."[168] Not every reader would be confident that these expressions were merely metaphorical. Again and again Quaker writers referred to "the Lamb's War," and as Nuttall comments, "much will turn on where the stress falls."[169]

In 1653 a petition was filed against Nayler and Fox by a group of Westmoreland ministers, declaring that their blasphemies and heresies "tend not only to the disturbance of the public peace and safety of the Commonwealth, but to the subversion of all government." Nayler's reply cannot have been reassuring: "That is false; it is not our intention to destroy the Commonwealth of Israel, for a Commonwealth is to bring up all into purity and justice . . . but he that doth pretend justice, and is partial, and hath an evil eye, and rules with his own will and tyranny, that we deny."[170] Insofar as the Commonwealth of England was unjust it had ceased to be the Commonwealth of Israel, and the Quakers might well seem to be plotting its overthrow.

Similar anxieties are apparent in a 1654 "humble petition of several gentlemen, justices of peace, ministers of the Gospel, and people, within the County of Lancaster," which survives because Fox and Nayler quoted it in order to refute it:

Sheweth, That George Fox and James Nayler are persons disaffected to religion and the wholesome laws of this nation; and that since their coming into this country have broached opinions tending to the destruction of the relation of subjects to their magistrates, wives to their husbands, children to their parents, servants to their masters, congregations to their ministers, and of a people to their God: and have drawn much people after them; many whereof (men, women, and little children) at their meetings are strangely wrought upon in their bodies, and brought to fall, foam at the mouth, roar, and swell in their bellies. And that some of them affirmed themselves to be equal to God, contrary to the late Act . . .[171]

The petitioners' allegation of blasphemy comes almost as an afterthought as a way of explaining Quaker anarchism and as justification for punishing them (since claims "to be equal to God" would violate the Blasphemy Act of 1650). The real issue, clearly, was the severing of ties of obedience, together with the irrational behavior that would thereby be liberated.

To this charge the Nayler-Fox reply was strangely oblique if not actually equivocal:

Opinions do tend to break the relations of subjects to their magistrates, wives to their husbands, children to their parents, servants to their masters, congregations to their ministers, and of a people to their God; but opinions we deny, for they are without God, and there you are. And justice and purity is but one, and that we set up and own; purity and walking in the Spirit doth make a separation from all uncleanness, and can have *no fellowship with* them who are *unfruitful workers of darkness;* but there is a separation from them . . . The one is separated to God, the other is separated from God. (p. 4)

Fox and Nayler first agree that opinions break traditional relationships and duties, and doubtless they think that many such relationships should indeed be broken. But then they turn the tables: it is their accusers who hold mere "opinions," for the views of the Quakers are not opinions at all but simple expressions of "justice and purity." Is it not then the godless behavior of the hypocritical magistrates and ministers that really threatens social order? The italics at the end signal an allusion to Ephesians 5: 11, "And have no fellowship with the unfruitful works of darkness, but rather reprove them." The established order has separated itself from God, and the only recourse is for a small band of saints to be separated *to* God.

The Spirit is inimical to forms of all kinds, and those must inevitably include the forms of traditional social order as well as of conventional religion. Nayler proclaimed, with an allusion to the apocalyptic Book of Daniel, "Now shall the stone cut out of the mountain without hands, break thee and thy image in pieces, and he that is without form shall by his power break all your forms and formal worships in pieces."[172] Nebuchadnezzar dreamed of the stone cut without hands that smashed the great image (Daniel 2: 34), which Daniel interpreted as a prophecy of the messianic kingdom. With this emphasis the Quakers could regard themselves as the true Puritans, the saving remnant of a movement that had fatally succumbed to "forms and formal worships." Nayler proclaimed in 1653 from Appleby jail, "Now the Lord is risen to disquiet the earth, and them that are at rest, yea, *Woe to them that are at ease in Sion* [Amos 6: 1]."[173] This certainly implies a call for ongoing revolution, but it must be remembered that it is fundamentally a spiritual revolution; Quakers wanted social injustice abolished, but they had no interest in the negotiations of Cromwell and the gentry if they did not make straight the way for the kingdom of God. As J. F. Maclear observes, even the politically astute Winstanley's proclamation of a New Age has to be understood in eschatalogical terms: "He stood as a most severe critic of all social and economic injustice, but in the tradition of Amos rather than that of Marx."[174]

Modern historians have understandably interpreted apocalyptic pronouncements as evidence of a determination to bring about practical change, but it makes at least as much sense to say that after the disappointments of the radical program of the 1640s they reflected a weary desperation. Worden surely catches the right note: "A rash of millenarian speculation in the pamphlet literature reflected the yearning for an apocalyptic solution, beyond the exhausted resources of human responsibility and choice."[175] Quaker writers doubtless looked forward to an apocalypse in historical time that would dismiss their persecutors to eternal judgment, but they believed that they themselves had already experienced the only apocalypse that mattered, the one that takes place within.

At bottom the early Quakers were opposed not only to politics in the usual sense but to history as well. In a typical formulation, Thomas Lawson wrote, "There is a pure and heavenly cry in me to dwell out of time, in that which was before all time, out of willing and running, and when I am kept stilly and quietly in it I find joy and peace."[176] To abolish the will and to live outside of time do not represent a program for participation in the political process. And however militant the Lamb's War appeared to those who feared they would be its victims, by the time of the Restoration it had evolved into the pacifism that has characterized Quaker thought ever since. To have served in the New Model Army, as a majority of the "First Publishers of Truth" had done,[177] did not encourage confidence in the efficacy of force. Warfare, Fox wrote in *A paper to Friends to keep out of wars and fightings*, amounted to "destroying men's lives like dogs and beasts and swine, goring, rending, and biting one another . . . All this is in Adam in the fall, for all that pretends to fight for Christ, they are deceived, for his kingdom is not of this world."[178] Someday the historical apocalypse would arrive, but in the meantime the role of the saints was to proclaim an atemporal spiritual apocalypse to as many of their fellows as were prepared to hear the message.

No wonder then that the Quakers could never be reconciled with their former comrades in revolution. Nayler wrote at the end of his life, after enduring severe punishment at the hands of Parliament, that reliance on parliaments was a hopelessly inadequate goal.

> *First* (say you) "we judge a Parliament the best expedient for the preservation of the nation."
>
> *Answ.* The best expedient for the preserving of the nation is for all people in the nation to turn to God, that by his light you may be led to repentance and newness of life.[179]

For Quakers half-measures were worse than none at all, and they remained true to their yearning for a total change of heart rather than merely of regime. At the very end of the Interregnum Grace Barwick addressed the officers of the army with solemn eloquence: "It is not the changings of government into new titles and names, but it is truth and perfect freedom that the best of men delights in, and it is that that will satisfy the hungering people."[180] This was not a hunger that was likely to be satisfied on earth.

In a profoundly politicized culture the specifically confrontational tactics of the Quakers were obviously political, as was their judicial punishment for nominal crimes such as refusing on scriptural grounds to swear oaths in court even though they promised to tell the truth. "Action against oppression," a recent historian says, "was vital for Quakers just as it was for Levellers and Diggers." But the same writer admits that "Quakerism is devoid of any coherent and identifiable political philosophy," and that what he calls "action" very often took the form of "symbolic protest."[181] To risk everything for one's principles, to be willing to languish in jail indefinitely and even to die there, is certainly a mode of action. But as the experience of the 1650s conclusively showed, this was not action that was likely to effect political reform; on the contrary, it excited alarm at every level of society and helped the custodians of the status quo to consolidate their position.

The Quakers knew that, of course, but since they had only contempt for compromise and the art of the possible, their conduct generally took the form of fiercely asserting principles rather than promoting a program.[182] Though they regularly wrote and spoke in favor of a simplified legal system and abolition of tithes, they did so as intransigent prophets, not as participants in a political process that could have much chance of success. In 1659 Isaac Penington analyzed the lessons of recent history:

> There hath been often a naked, honest, simple pure thing stirring in the army, which the great ones (seeing some present use of) fell in with and improved for their own ends, but destroyed the thing itself; so that it attained not to the bringing forth of that righteous liberty and common good which it seemed to aim at (and did indeed aim at in those in whom the striving did arise) but was made use of as an advantage to advance them in their particular interest against their enemies, and so set them up.[183]

In Penington's bleak retrospective the army radicals had indeed aimed at liberty in a naked and simple way ("pure" was a favorite Quaker word of approbation); the "great ones," however, only seemed to aim at it, and made cynical use of the radical movement in order to advance their "particular interest" rather than the "common good." There being as yet no popular party that could effectively oppose the great merchants and gentry, efforts to bring about political change were now revealed to be utterly futile. So the Quakers turned inward, which is where their emphasis had always lain in any case, having been born of the disillusionment of the late 1640s, and they concentrated on preserving the purity of their faith while avoiding any political entanglements that might compromise it. Of course they still pleaded for toleration, and failing to receive it went to jail for their beliefs; in one sense that was a profoundly political act, but in another sense it was the ultimate antipolitical act.

As I understand it, therefore, the Quaker position was the diametrical opposite of the militant socialism celebrated by Christopher Hill. Rather than holding that this world would be wonderful if only the political system could be transformed, they held that this world was radically corrupting for all but the tiny minority of elect who had learned to spurn it utterly. Unlike the Puritan elect, the Quaker elect did not have to wait for the afterlife to experience perfection, but the price of perfection was unconditional rejection—not transformation or amelioration—of the world they lived in. Their psychological existence was not just unworldly but antiworldly, like that of the Calvinist sect in which Edmund Gosse was raised two centuries later: "They lived in an intellectual cell, bounded at its sides by the walls of their own house, but open above to the very heart of the uttermost heavens."[184] More than most people, Quakers like Nayler lived in ideas, and to outsiders they might well look like madmen. To borrow Wallace Stevens's words,

> He would be the lunatic of one idea
> In a world of ideas, who would have all the people
> Live, work, suffer and die in that idea
> In a world of ideas.[185]

But from the Quaker point of view it was the Puritans, not themselves, who were really lunatics of one idea, obsessed with a doctrine of predestination that made them at once confident persecutors and guilty self-critics, and traducers of the religion of the spirit which they claimed to believe and live.

2

God in Man:
Theology and Life

Doctrine, Prophecy, Truth

Christianity in nearly all of its forms is an exceptionally propositional religion, in which much depends on being able to assent to a series of statements of belief, and in which sectarian identities depend upon deciding which statements are taken as acceptable. The controversies of the Reformation were peculiarly complicated because both sides read the same Bible and deployed the same language while claiming that their opponents had it all wrong. "The symbols and codes of English Christianity," Nigel Smith says, "were like a hall of opposed mutually reflecting mirrors."[1] The Seeker Isaac Penington, later a distinguished Quaker, wrote in 1650, "Babylon was built—and is daily built—in imitation of Sion, painted just like Sion. The intention of its building was to eat out Sion, to suppress Sion, to withdraw from the truth by a false image and to keep her inhabitants in peace and satisfaction under a belief and hope that it is the true Sion, and therefore it must needs be made like Sion."[2]

For most of the competing Protestant sects, debate over fine points of doctrine was an important way of establishing group identity and differentiating one's own group from all others. But in opposition to those who made doctrine a principal weapon against Babylon, the Quakers set themselves firmly against the theologizing of belief. In their view the Puritans had grossly perverted the ideal of *sola fides*, justification by faith, by identifying salvation with a set of propositions and then invoking the propositions to excuse or even to justify sinful living. "Whose image do you bear," Nayler challenged them, "who are like the world, except in opinion or notion? . . . Will you boast in the saints' lines to make you a cover, whilst that lies crucified in you which should lead to their lives?"[3]

The distinction between lines and lives, between textual words and the living Word, lay at the heart of the Quaker quarrel with the Puritans. And more than this, the Quakers claimed that direct inspiration, commonly described as irradiation by the inner Light, gave them unmediated knowledge of Truth. Their Puritan antagonists, profoundly distrustful of individual claims to prophetic insight, regularly alleged (as Francis Higginson put it) that the Quakers "worship the mental idols of their own imaginations."[4] The Quaker reply, as typified by Nayler's attack on a "false prophet" named Thomas Winterton, was that the Spirit is able not just to redirect imagination but to abolish it: "No other spirit hath power to judge the imaginations, but this infallible Spirit which is above nature, and it only [i.e., it and only it] searches and judges the natural imaginations; and thou that hast searched and judged without this art led in thy imaginations still; and so one imagination searcheth and judgeth another in thee: and thou and thy imaginations are judged and searched by that Spirit of Christ which searcheth all things, even the deep things of God [1 Corinthians 2: 10]."[5] The infallible Spirit can "search" natural imaginations because it is above imagination altogether: it embodies Truth, rather than producing second-order images or simulacra of it. The natural imagination of seventeenth-century psychology, by contrast, cannot manage without the images from which its name is derived, and is therefore condemned to an infinite regress in which each imagination has to be searched and judged by another imagination. Nayler repeatedly calls his antagonist Winterton an "atheist," and indeed Winterton's psychology closely resembles that of the alleged atheist Hobbes. Hobbes's philosophy, if it is religious at all, assumes a desacralized world where the wishes of the far-off *deus absconditus* can only be guessed at.[6] Nayler's thought assumes a world filled with spirit, a condition of universal pneuma in which Christ is ever-present and liberates the individual from all ambiguities of behavior and choice.

In accordance with this concept of the Spirit, Quaker testimony was regularly represented as impersonal prophecy. When a group of

Puritan ministers at Swarthmoor complained that Fox was giving merely private testimony, rather than transmitting academic learning as they did, Fox reported, "One of them burst out into a passion and said he could speak his experiences as well as I; but I told him experience was one thing, but to go with a message and a word from the Lord as the prophets and the apostles had and did, and as I had done to them, this was another thing."[7] Prophesying had played a role in Puritan practice, but had been confined at first to occasional discussions of Scripture by lay people after the regular service had ended. Increasingly, however, it came to mean oracular pronouncements like those of Jeremiah or John of Patmos,[8] and this is certainly how the Quakers understood it. Fox and Nayler could confidently argue that their form of worship was expressly enjoined by Paul: "Ye may all prophesy one by one, that all may learn, and all may be comforted" (1 Corinthians 14: 31). Puritan ministers, believing that the age of prophecy had passed, insisted on their professional duty to expound the Scriptures in methodical fashion. But antinomians were certain that the age of prophecy had not passed, and invoked Moses' exclamation when Joshua urged him to suppress prophesying: "Would to God that all the Lord's people were prophets, and that the Lord would put his spirit upon them!" (Numbers 11: 29). On the title page of an apocalyptic work "written from the movings of the Lord in JAMES NAYLER," the author is identified as "one of England's prophets."[9]

To be a prophet was not to be a reasoner, but quite the contrary. Fox wrote in a general epistle to Friends, "After thou seest thy thoughts, and the temptations, do not think, but submit; and then the Power comes. Stand still in that which shows and discovers; and there doth strength immediately come. And stand still in the Light, and submit to it, and the other [temptation] will be hushed and gone; and then content[ment] comes."[10] It was through thinking too much that the Puritans, like Milton's intellectual devils, tied themselves in insoluble knots:

> Others apart sat on a hill retired,
> In thoughts more elevate, and reasoned high
> Of providence, foreknowledge, will and fate,
> Fixed fate, free will, foreknowledge absolute,
> And found no end, in wandering mazes lost.[11]

Rejecting the Calvinism of his earlier years, Milton developed an Arminian theology and a narrative expansion of the Christian story that might secure a place for human freedom within the confines of God's providence. Rejecting the Calvinism of their earlier years, Milton's Quaker contemporaries asserted a direct intuition of the divine Spirit that gave priority to immediacy of timeless experience rather than to a narrative of fall and redemption, and liberated them from the maddening exegetical labyrinth in which truth had become entangled.

Donne catches the note of painful struggle common to much of seventeenth-century Protestantism:

> On a huge hill,
> Cragged, and steep, Truth stands, and he that will
> Reach her, about must, and about must go,
> And what the hill's suddenness resists, win so.[12]

To Quakers such anxieties were irrelevant, and the theological speculations that flowed from them represented the merest logic-chopping. "Instead of answering plainly," Nayler accused one of his Puritan antagonists, "thou goest about making thy distinctions and crooked ways, as concerning God's teaching, dividing into numbers, when God is but one, and his way and teaching one; but the world is in the many ways."[13] By its mere existence theological disputation was evidence of blindness to the unitary truth. "Thou art labouring in all this mud," Nayler told an opponent contemptuously, "against the pure light of Christ his Spirit and Word within."[14]

For the same reason the mediating types and symbols of Puritan exegesis were rendered unnecessary. The goal was no longer to gesture toward the remote God who in *Paradise Lost* hints ambiguously through "many a sign" and must be painfully deduced by searching for "his steps the track divine."[15] The Quaker God manifested himself in a radiant light that banished all shadows. In Nayler's words, "The light which Christ lighteth every man withal, which comes from Christ the unchangeable priest, this light lets you see the end of all shadows, visions, and the end of the first priesthood, and all types and figures and guides, out of all changeable things, to the unchangeable priest from whence light comes, to him by whom the world was made."[16] Puritans too, of course, asserted the indwelling presence of the Spirit, but their conservative position was that it remained utterly distinct from its temporary human receptacles. Richard Hollinworth explained: "When I speak of the Spirit's being or dwelling in a saint: I mean not an essential or personal in-being or in-dwelling of the Spirit, as he is God, or the third Person of the Holy Trinity . . . The Spirit by a metonymy may be said to dwell in us when we partake of his gifts and graces, though these be not the Spirit itself; as when we say the sun comes into a house, we mean not the *body* of the sun (for that abides in its own orb) but the *beams* of it."[17] For Quakers the indwelling was indeed "essential" and "personal," no metonym but a literal fact.

These opposed conceptions of truth can also be seen, in slightly different terms, as opposed conceptions of knowledge and wisdom. Here Quaker thought frequently recurred to the mysterious relationship between the tree of life and the tree of good and evil that so puzzled Milton's prelapsarian Adam and Eve:

> . . . not to taste that tree
> Of knowledge, planted by the tree of life,
> So near grows death to life, whate'er death is,
> Some dreadful thing no doubt; for well thou know'st
> God hath pronounced it death to taste that tree.[18]

The symbolism of the two trees, in a context of speculation about the scope and status of good knowledge as contrasted with evil knowledge, was widely noticed in radical writing,[19] and Quaker references to them imply a determination to rewrite the myth of the fall or at least to redefine its application in the present-day world. The following points were included in a list of pointed queries with which Nayler, in a characteristic controversial move, challenged a group of Puritan ministers:

What the tree of knowledge is, which is forbidden; where it is, and how it may be known with its fruits?

What that death is which hath passed over all men? And what it is that dieth the day the forbidden is eaten, seeing the old Adam may live many years after?

What the tree of life is, and what the flaming sword and cherubims is; and how man may come to the tree of life? What is to be cut down and burnt up in man before he come to the tree of life, and where that paradise is that man was driven out of, with its ground, and what ground he was drove into: and how the flaming sword parts these two grounds?[20]

According to Nayler his opponents neglected to return any answers to these queries, which were implicitly directed against the Puritan belief that all knowledge since the Fall has been hopelessly contaminated. As Milton memorably put it, "It was from out the rind of one apple tasted that the knowledge of good and evil as two twins cleaving together leapt forth into the world. And perhaps this is that doom which Adam fell into of knowing good and evil, that is to say of knowing good by evil."[21] Milton's own practice in *Paradise Lost* acts upon this belief: we know good only by subtraction, by a kind of thought-experiment in which we struggle to imagine what the world would be like if its ubiquitous evil could somehow be deleted. But the Quaker position was that it *has* been deleted: Christ's sacrifice totally reversed the fall, and good can once again be known without reference to evil. As Fox expressed it in recounting his conversion, "Now was I come up in spirit through the flaming sword into the paradise of God. All things were new, and all the creation gave another smell unto me than before, beyond what words can utter. I knew nothing but pureness and innocency and righteousness, being renewed up into the image of God by Christ Jesus, so that I say I was come up to the state of Adam which he was in before he fell."[22]

A reminiscence by Rebecca Travers, who was to become one of Nayler's most loyal defenders in his time of trouble, gives a valuable glimpse of his views on this point (and also of his conversational manner, which seems to have been solemn if not oracular):

A friend of hers [Rebecca Travers'] invited her to dinner with J. N. and others. One called a gentleman, who had run through all [religious] professions and had high notions, [posed] many curious questions to J. N. which he answered with great wisdom, but not so plainly as she would have had him, because she coveted to know hidden things; on which J. N. putting his hand over the table, and taking her by the hand, said, "Feed not on knowledge, it is as truly forbidden to thee as ever it was to Eve: it is good to look upon, but not to feed on: for who feeds on knowledge dies to the innocent life;" which he spoke in power, and was received by her as the word of Truth; and she found it so in the deepest trials;

her access to the throne of grace was, as in the innocency she could approach, and the more she came to be emptied of her self-knowledge, etc. the more she came to feel that innocent pure life that was before transgression was; and this, with the power and holy self-denial she beheld in J. N. in those days, made her value him, and attend on him in his greatest sufferings.[23]

For Rebecca Travers this was no abstract doctrine: it assisted her toward an emptying out of self that could transform the fatal tree of knowledge into the prelapsarian tree of life, and it underlay her support of Nayler during the bitter experience that is elliptically referred to here as "his greatest sufferings."

To replace knowledge with life in this way was to render formal theology irrelevant, and the usual opinion of orthodox divines was that the Quakers had no theology at all. Richard Baxter wrote contemptuously, "The things that they agree in, besides the furious opposition of others, are but a few broken scraps of doctrine, which they never yet set together, as making the substance of their faith"; and he added accurately enough, "I never met with man that heard of any sum or body of their divinity, faith, or religion, which they have published."[24] In a pamphlet intended to justify the institution of professional ministers, Baxter made a point of distinguishing between the teaching of doctrine and the prophetic "calling" that Quakers claimed to have. "The truth of our doctrine depends not on our calling. Were we no ministers, [yet] we can prove the Gospel true which we deliver . . . Therefore let Quakers, and Seekers, and Papists first disprove our doctrine if they can: and not cheat the people by persuading them that our calling must first be proved; as a prophet's must be."[25] For the Calvinist one's "calling" was a profession, approved by God but also by man, that need not necessarily be grounded on a literal apprehension of an inward "call." For the Quaker it was an irresistible voice like the one Nayler heard at the plow, the sine qua non for all religious authority whatsoever. And the idea that anyone at all was free to hear the voice and go forth to prophesy lay at the heart of the antihierarchical threat.

Quaker attacks focused therefore not on doctrine as such, which they regarded as instrumental at best, but on the ministers' claim to exert authority by means of doctrine. This emphasis was not overlooked by their Puritan opponents. However painfully the ministers may have felt assaulted in their economic security, their professional *amour propre* was equally injured. In a letter purportedly addressed to a young friend who had turned Quaker, Baxter expressed this resentment with an almost obsessive indignation:

> You confess to me that you have long thought that infant baptism was an error, and that now you think the Quakers are in the right; and yet you neither did once read any one of those books which we have written to prove infant baptism to be a duty, nor did once seriously and impartially lay open your doubts to your teacher, nor ask his advice, as if you were even then too good to inquire, and would venture your soul to save you a little labour; yet are you now confident that you are in the right, and he and all of his mind are in the wrong. You know you are a young man, and have had little opportunity to be acquainted with the Word of God, in comparison of what your teacher hath had; if you presume that you are so much more beloved of God than he, that God will reveal that to you without seeking and study, which upon the greatest diligence he will not reveal to him, what can this conceit proceed from but pride? God commandeth study and meditating day and night in his laws; your teacher hath spent twenty if not an hundred hours in such meditation where you have spent one; he hath spent twenty if not an hundred hours in prayer to God for his spirit of truth and grace, where you have spent one . . . His office is to teach, and therefore God is as it were more engaged to be his teacher, and to make known his truth to him than to you.[26]

Baxter's tone here helps one to appreciate why the Quakers found the professionalism of their antagonists so infuriating. Baxter thinks it incredible that a mere stripling who claims to know God by spiritual intuition could really be as close to God as a professional "teacher" who has studied and prayed for hundreds of hours. Above all, how can the stripling be so presumptuous as to neglect to read Baxter's books, when it is Baxter whom God has "engaged" to be the authorized conduit of his message? In a telling metaphor, Baxter says without irony that a young believer who has abandoned his teacher to follow the Quakers is "like a dog that hath left his master, and therefore will be ready to follow anybody that first whistleth to him" (sig. C2).

In reply the Quakers could urge not only that theological distinctions were trivial if not pointless, but also that they failed dismally to edify the congregations for whom they were intended. With admirable frankness the Worcester association of ministers, whose leader was the same Baxter, admitted in 1656, "We find by sad experience that the people understand not our public teaching, though we study to speak as plain as we can, and that after many years' preaching, even of these same fundamentals, too many can scarce tell anything that we have said."[27] Nor did this sorry situation reflect recent backsliding from a time of greater doctrinal competence. On the contrary, religious customs had always been more important than articles of belief, and priests as well as ministers had long deplored the ignorance of their flocks.[28]

And if indifference was deplorable, for orthodox Calvinists matters were only made worse when theology became a subject for general discussion. The turmoil of the civil wars, which from the radical point of view was a seedbed of lifegiving debate, looked to conservatives like an appalling explosion of error. Baxter, who had himself been an army chaplain, complained in his immensely popular book *The Saints' Everlasting Rest,*

> It is as natural for both wars and private contentions to produce errors, schisms, contempt of magistracy, ministry and ordinances, as it is for a dead carrion to breed worms and vermin. Believe it from one that hath too many years experience of both in armies and garrisons: it is as hard a thing to maintain, even in your people [i.e., your own congregation], a sound understanding, a tender conscience, a lively, gracious, heavenly frame of spirit, and an upright life in a way of war and contention, as to keep your candle lighted in the greatest storms, or under the waters.[29]

From a Quaker point of view, these lamentations totally missed the point, and all of this emphasis on errors and ordinances was indeed a glorification of dead carrion. The only truth was the truth of the Spirit, as Nayler declared when he addressed the doctrine of election and reprobation from an anti-Calvinist standpoint:

> This is that doctrine which is sealed from all the world, nor can any one know it or receive it truly who are in the reprobate state; though many be disputing about it in the dark, which none know but the children of light. So, as one who had obtained favour to

have this mystery revealed, I shall according to permission write a few words, as it is received in Jesus, yet can be received by no man's wisdom, nor any who only are born after the flesh; but who knows what it is to walk in the Spirit, shall witness me herein.[30]

The prophet is not a theologian, and not even a teacher. His role is to utter truth that has been given to him to deliver, and it is precisely because the expression is unwilled that it can be accepted as authoritative. "No prophecy of old came by the will of man," Nayler said in 1653, "but against the wills of all men in the world, both he that was sent, and they to whom he was sent."[31] Three years later he would act upon this belief at Bristol, and very nearly lose his life for doing so.

Words, Silence, and the Word

Given the Quakers' conception of truth, their relationship to language, including the language of the Bible itself, was necessarily ambivalent. The silence of the Quaker meeting and, in general, a posture of calm expectation were crucial to the movement's concept of spiritual life. This, even more perhaps than disagreement about social behavior, lay at the heart of their difference from the Ranters, with whom they were often confused (and to whom we will presently return). The Ranters literally ranted; they didn't know how to shut up. As Fox says of one such group, which he visited in 1651, "They had great [i.e., large] meetings, so I told them after that they had had such meetings they did not wait upon God to feel his power to gather their minds together to feel his presence and power and therein to sit to wait upon him, for they had spoken themselves dry and had spent their portions and not lived in that which they spake, and now they were dry." Fox adds contemptuously that they smoked tobacco and drank ale at their meetings "and so grew light and loose." Many of this particular group, according to him, "came to be convinced and received God's everlasting Truth," but their leaders "came to nothing."[32] What is especially interesting is the slow-moving circularity with which Fox invokes the power that will gather the minds that wait to feel the power and thereby know how to wait. "They did not wait upon God—to feel his power—to gather their minds together—to feel his presence and power—and therein to sit to wait upon him." This kind of experience is fundamentally different from the Puritan practice of attending closely to the "heads" and "divisions" with which a preacher would "open" a scriptural text, and of course different also from the fondness for rhetorical display that Butler satirized in his Presbyterian knight: "For rhetoric, he could not ope / His mouth but out there flew a trope."[33]

The much-quoted injunction "Let thy words be few" comes from a biblical text that emphasizes the gulf between the spiritual and carnal planes: "Be not rash with thy mouth, and let not thine heart be hasty to utter any thing before God: for God is in heaven, and thou upon earth: therefore let thy words be few" (Ecclesiastes 5: 2). In such a context, preaching can only be directed to the unconverted (the not yet "convinced"). Once irradiated by the Light a believer has no need of words. Fox stated this very clearly: "It is a mighty thing to be in the work of the ministry of the Lord and to go forth in that, for it is not as customary preaching, but to bring people to the end of all preaching; for [after] your once speaking to people, then people come into the thing ye speak of."[34] Conversely Puritan preachers, as Nayler put it, "feed the ear, but starve the soul."[35] As so often, the Quakers were invoking a principle that had been dear to Puritans but seemed now to be neglected or betrayed by them. For decades Puritans had denounced Anglican ritualism and had insisted on spontaneity in worship; yet their own sermons were elaborately rhetorical and regularly printed, and could seem to install a new text-based devotion in place of the old.

With the Quakers it was entirely different. We can only guess at what their preaching was like, since by definition it had to be spontaneous (drawing, of course, on familiar formulas) and could not be written down. Clearly it was emotional rather than analytical, though not necessarily histrionic. The accounts of it that survive are full of indistinct grandeur without much actual detail:

> In the latter end of the eighth month [of 1651], William Dewsbury was moved to come into these parts [in northeastern Yorkshire] and travelled much from town to town, sounding the trumpet of the Lord. His testimony was piercing and very powerful, so as the earth shook before him, the mountain did melt at the power of the Lord, which exceedingly, in a wonderful manner, broke forth in these days of our holy assemblies, to the renting of many hearts, and bringing divers to witness the same state, mea-

surably, as the prophet or servant of the Lord did in ancient times, whose lips quivered and belly shook, that he might rest in the day of trouble. Oh! It was a glorious day, in which the Lord wonderfully appeared for the bringing down the lofty and high-minded, and exalting that of low degree.[36]

Writers like this one were accustomed to translate their experience into the high terms of biblical poetry: the trumpet sounded, mountains melted, hearts were rent, and the belly of the prophet shook. Apart from the note of *ressentiment*, common in radical texts of the period, of "low degree" against the "lofty" of the world, the account here is scrupulously general. This is no accident: the goal was to extinguish individual selfhood and achieve union with a community of the elect that stretched back to the saints of the Bible and participated in, rather than merely borrowed, the language of the Bible to express its experience. That language tended to be filled with challenges to the ungodly: in Deborah's song of triumph over the Canaanites "the earth trembled" and "the mountains melted from before the Lord" (Judges 5: 4–5). Equally militant here is the allusion to the prophet Habakkuk, who saw and heard the Lord's wrath against Judah: "My belly trembled; my lips quivered at the voice: rottenness entered into my bones, and I trembled in myself, that I might rest in the day of trouble: when he cometh up unto the people, he will invade them with his troops" (Habakkuk 3: 16).

Quaker style has sometimes been criticized as "loose, lax . . . almost a stream of consciousness."[37] But as Jackson Cope showed in a brilliant article long ago,[38] a deliberate program underlay its incantatory repetitions, which were regularly employed even by well-educated Quakers who could write conventionally enough in other contexts. The aim, by contrast with Calvinist discursive persuasion, was to interweave scriptural terms and metaphors in order to overwhelm rational resistance by endless variations on a few key words. The inward Light could not be demonstrated or even described; it could only be witnessed. The Book of Revelation provided an obvious model, and so did the far less hermetic Epistles of John: "Beloved, let us love one another: for love is of God; and every one that loveth is born of God, and knoweth God. He that loveth not knoweth not God; for God is love" (1 John 4: 7–8). It is important to recognize also that Quaker incantatory rhythms reflected oral practice and, even if intended to persuade readers, did not originate in a written context. Richard Bauman persuasively describes the "collaborative expectancy" that would have been aroused in an audience by rhythmic energy and repetitive formal patterns, generating "a sense of immediate co-participation in the utterance that would make the listener feel that the minister's words were echoed within himself."[39] Such a technique could go far toward creating a sense that the preacher's words were only confirming what the listener already knew.

Whether this attitude was "mystical" or not depends on definitions. Antinomian expressions of belief, the Quakers' included, can easily seem vague or—in the pejorative term of a slightly later time—merely "enthusiastic."[40] And if mysticism is defined simply as "the type of religion which puts the emphasis on immediate awareness of relation with God, on direct and intimate consciousness of the Divine Presence,"[41] then the Quakers, like a great many others, could certainly be described as mystics. But to conclude that they were asserting an ineffable, unspeakable union with the infinite is in itself to grant priority to what can be described discursively, which for the Quakers was the very point at issue. To invoke the concept of "ineffability" implies a polemical, rationalist distrust of whatever is being dismissed as "mystical," whereas in actual practice an assertion that God is ineffable may mean something like "God cannot be positively characterized in literal terms" rather than that nothing whatever can be said about him.[42]

An unusually full account of the way Quakers spoke in their meetings was given by Higginson:

Their speaker for the most part uses the posture of standing, or sitting with his hat on; his countenance severe, his face downward, his eyes fixed mostly towards the earth, his hands and fingers expanded, continually striking gently on his breast. His beginning is without a [scriptural] text, abrupt and sudden to his hearers, his voice for the most part low, his sentences incoherent, hanging together like ropes of sand, very frequently full of impiety and horrid errors, and sometimes full of sudden pauses, his whole speech a mixed bundle of words and heap of nonsense. His continuance in speaking is sometimes exceeding short, sometimes very tedious, according to the paucity or plenty of his revelations. His admiring auditors that are of his way [i.e., his persuasion] stand the while like men astonished, listening to every word, as though every word was oraculous; and so they believe them to be the very words and dictates of Christ speaking in him.[43]

Higginson is clearly baffled by this unrhetorical or antirhetorical mode, which is "full" in paradoxically opposite ways: full of errors, but also of gaps ("full of sudden pauses"). The paradoxes continue: it is a rope of sand that has no coherence and yet somehow manages to look like a rope; it is a mixed bundle of words and heap of nonsense that can somehow persuade people that they hear Christ himself speaking. Hostile as he is, Higginson thus confirms the theory of language implicit in Quaker discourse, an emptiness that claims to evoke a plenitude. He concludes with exasperated tautology, "Such stuff as this all their speakings are for the most part stuffed with."

Unfortunately it is nearly impossible to know what Nayler's speaking style was like. Since Quaker prayers and sermons were supposed to be spontaneous, they were never written down in advance and very rarely afterward. Even oral speech was considered a *post facto* report on inner experience, offered not as adequate in itself but in the hope that it might stimulate similar experience in others. Bauman observes that whereas our logocentric culture regards silence as "merely an abstention from speaking or an empty interval between utterances," for Quakers silence was Truth itself and language could never be more than a second-order allusion to Truth.[44] Contemporary collections of Quaker correspondence mention Nayler's preaching, but in the flattest of terms. Thus, not long after he began his ministry in London an admirer wrote blandly, "James is very serviceable here, and his fame begins to spread in the city, seeing that he hath had public disputes with many." Nayler himself wrote to Margaret Fell at about the same time, "Great is the day of the Lord in this place, his name is become very lovely to some, very terrible to others, mightily doth it spread."[45] It is hard to be sure how the Lord's name was "terrible to others" and what got said during Nayler's "public disputes with many." There is no doubt, however, that he was very good at speaking. One of his angriest opponents, the aptly named John Deacon, conceded handsomely that he was "a man of an exceeding quick wit and sharp apprehension, enriched with that commendable gift of good oratory with a very delightable melody in his utterance."[46]

We do have one memorable testimony to the power of Nayler's preaching, if not to its content. Long afterward a former officer recalled encountering a crowd of people as he rode away from Cromwell's famous victory at Dunbar in 1650:

> When I came thither I found it was James Nayler preaching to the people, but with such power and reaching energy as I had not till then been witness of. I could not help staying a little, though I was afraid to stay, for I was made a Quaker, being forced to tremble at the sight of myself. I was struck with more terror before the preaching of James Nayler than I was before the Battle of Dunbar, when we had nothing else to expect but to fall a prey to the swords of our enemies.

The officer's words are strong and eloquent, but it should be noted that they come to us at third hand. The speech, though given as if verbatim and quoted as such in modern biographies of Nayler,[47] was reported by the Quaker James Gough in his *Memoirs* (Dublin, 1781) as having been told to him many years before by an aged minister named James Wilson, who in turn was recalling the words of an aged officer whom he had heard at a public house in his youth. It may well be the case that the old officer did say something like this about Nayler, but the speech as we have it is no likelier to be a verbatim account than the speeches in Thucydides; and in any case, it doesn't tell us what Nayler said.

Some sense of Nayler's speaking style may perhaps be gathered from occasional passages in his printed works when he rises from polemical subtleties to express prophetic rage or grief. Thus at the end of a rather gnarled and tedious tract he advances a vision of the city of Newcastle-upon-Tyne, where his antagonists live:

> The thing that was seen concerning Newcastle: all his pillars to be dry, and his trees to be bare, and much nakedness, that they have not scarcely the bark, but are as a wilderness where much wind and cold comes, where there must be much labour before the ground be brought into order; for it's a stony ground, and there is much briars and thorns about her, and many trees have grown wild long, and have scarce earth to cover their roots, but their roots are seen, and how they stand in the stones, and these trees bears no fruit, but bears moss, and much wind pierces through, and clatters them together, and makes the trees shake,

but still the roots are held amongst the stones, and are bald and naked. FINIS.[48]

The eloquence resembles Bunyan's, but with a relentless forward march that has an energy all its own. From one point of view this passage is biblical pastiche; from another, it is a compelling poem.

What was appropriate for dialogue among the convinced was in any case not appropriate for debate with the unconvinced, and this the early Quakers prosecuted with immense energy. As early as 1653 Higginson was complaining not only of "your printed libels," but also of "your manuscripts that fly as thick as moths up and down the country."[49] Whether in print or orally, Quaker disputation obeyed its own rules and refused to play by those of its antagonists. It proceeded not by opposing logic to logic in the Puritan fashion, but by posing questions that opponents would be revealed as unwilling or unable to answer. This style of nonargument was acknowledged by an exasperated Baxter in an elaborate attempt to supply answers to Quaker questions: "Because they abhor syllogisms and disputings, I was fain to deal further with them in their own questioning way."[50]

The Puritans were particularly vulnerable on one essential point: however deeply they believed their position to be grounded in logic, they had simultaneously to believe that it was grounded in the text of the Bible. But as soon as they began invoking the Bible, the Quakers could propose counterinterpretations while claiming to be merely stating the plain meaning of Scripture. Public disputations between Quakers and anti-Quakers therefore usually resolved into citation and countercitation of Scripture. Rebecca Travers was still a Baptist when she went in 1656 to hear a public disputation between three Baptists and Nayler:

She would have been glad to have heard the Baptists get the victory; but when the time came it proved quite contrary, for the country-man [Nayler] stood up on a form over against the Baptists, and they were so far from getting the victory that she could feel his words smote them; that one or two of them confessed they were sick and could hold it no longer; and the third beset him with such confidence, as if he would have carried all before him, but shamed himself in bringing Scriptures that turned against him: and she was confounded and ashamed that a Quaker should exceed the learned Baptists, which brought her low, and made her desire to hear him.[51]

Puritans, though they too testified to illumination by the Spirit, were obliged to assert that the Bible was the sole authoritative word of God, in relation to which they themselves were belated and very possibly fallible expositors. The Quakers, by contrast, claimed to be direct conduits of the same Spirit that had originally inspired the authors of the Bible, offering not interpretation but reenactment of the living Word. This message promised a welcome release from doctrinal logic-chopping and from the endless doubts and paradoxes that underlay it.

There was also a strong class element in this opposition of interpretive modes. "For seventeenth-century English radicals," Christopher Hill observes, "the religion of the heart was the answer to the pretensions of the academic divinity of ruling-class universities."[52] Hobbes, less sympathetically, made a similar point in 1668: "After the Bible was translated into English, every man, nay, every boy and wench that could read English thought they spoke with God Almighty and understood what he said, when by a certain number of chapters a day they had read the Scriptures once or twice over."[53] "The ministers of the world," Fox wrote, "receive their learning at Oxford and Cambridge, and are taught of men, and speak a divination of their own brain, which is conjuring; and bewitch the people with those things which are carnal." To receive formal training in theology, then, was to acquire professional skill in a verbal magic diametrically opposed to the free movement of the Holy Spirit. Nayler added, in a contribution to the same pamphlet, "The true ministry is the gift of Jesus Christ, and needs no addition of human help and learning; but as the work is spiritual, and of the Lord, so they are spiritually fitted only by the Lord, and therefore he chused herdsmen, fishermen, and plowmen, and such like; and he gave them an immediate call, without the leave of man."[54] On a later occasion he retorted to a Puritan critic, "For your scoffing at the plow, I am not ashamed of it, knowing it to be a lawful employment, much better than the *hireling* that works not at all, but lives on other men's labours, taking by violence what's other men's labours; but seeing the plow is a reproach with you, why should not the tithes be so also, which are a fruit of the plow?"[55]

Like Bunyan, who failed to understand how a knowledge of Hebrew or Greek could be relevant,[56] when Quakers quoted the Bible they assumed that the Spirit enabled the English version to be definitive and its meaning unambiguous. Thomas Weld reports an occasion when, if his account is at all accurate, the well-known Quaker John Audland made a complete botch of a text in Jeremiah, "A wonderful and horrible thing is committed in the land; the prophets prophesy falsely, and the priests bear rule by their means; and my people love to have it so." Weld wrote,

> Their [the Quakers'] common expression is to him that opens or shows them the interpretation of any Scripture, "Cursed is he that adds," or "The plagues are upon thee for adding to the Scripture" [Revelation 22: 18; cf. Deuteronomy 4: 2]. John Audland, a few days since, being for his railing and public disturbance called before the magistrates, and there pleading against the ministry, alleging that text, Jer. 5. 31, "The priests bear rule by their means;" one of us laboured to convince him of his ignorance in that gross misinterpretation, for by *means* he understood *by their maintenance;* [we] showing that that text doth most evidently hold this sense, that those priests bare rule by the means of the false prophets. The said J. A. presently cried out, "Thou addest, thou addest."[57]

Audland, influenced by the Quaker idée fixe about tithes, evidently thought that Jeremiah was talking about the financial support of priests. But when arguments to the contrary were presented he did not, as anti-Quaker polemics might lead one to expect, dismiss the Bible as irrelevant. On the contrary, he continued to assert its importance; but he also asserted an unshakable confidence in his own interpretation. When the orthodox ministers urged their counterinterpretation he saw it not as a case of hermeneutic disagreement, but simply of unacceptable "adding" to the text as it stood. According to Higginson this was the standard Quaker position. "They hold that no exposition ought to be given of the holy Scripture, and that all expounding of Scripture is an adding to it; and that God will add to such a one all the plagues written in that Book. Opening, and applying the Scripture, is one thing they mainly declaim against, wherever they come."[58]

This confrontation happened in 1653, when Audland was twenty-three. According to Braithwaite "his strong understanding and great memory made him early proficient in scripture,"[59] but from the point of view of the ministers he had no training at all to qualify him for biblical exegesis. Responding to this accusation of Weld's, Nayler simply reasserted the authority of the Spirit: "Whereas you talk of things hard to be understood in the Scriptures, which the unstable and unlearned wrest: it is true, and you are those unlearned, who were never taught of God, nor heard his voice . . . Your own practice shows what openers you are, for they are a book sealed to your wisdom and carnal learning."[60] Audland's own preaching style was highly effective in an entirely different mode, with a face "full of dread and shining brightness" and a voice like a trumpet.[61] As for Weld, he was notorious for his rigid opinions and appetite for controversy. A few years later his churchwardens (unsuccessfully) lodged a formal complaint against him for arbitrarily excommunicating more than a thousand parishioners and reducing his ministry to fewer than a dozen true believers.[62]

The role of the Quaker teacher was not to "open" the text of the Bible, but to communicate its spiritual energy in an exaltation that transcended language. Baxter characteristically took the opposite course, insisting that even in silent reflection a person should in effect be engaged in verbal discourse:

> In thy meditations upon all these incentives of love, preach them over earnestly to thy heart, and expostulate and plead with it by way of soliloquy, till thou feel the fire begin to burn. Do not only think on the arguments of love, but dispute it out with thy conscience, and by expostulating earnest reasonings with thy heart, endeavour to affect it. There is much more moving force in this *earnest talking to our selves*, than in bare cogitation that breaks not out into mental words.[63]

Breaking out into words was exactly what Quaker devotion was meant to forestall; and preaching, though necessarily verbal, was intended to bring its hearers to the point where they would no longer need it, "the end of all preaching" as Fox expressed it.[64] Silence was not just a preparation for spiritual experience, it was an expression of renunciation, and was intended not as a descent into the self but as an escape from subjectivity. As Weber has well said of the Quaker meeting, "The purpose of this silent waiting is to overcome everything impulsive and irrational, the passions and subjective interests of the natural man. He must be stilled in order to create that deep repose of the soul in which alone the word of God can be heard."[65]

Concentrating on the text of the Bible, Puritans pored over individual verses and often were painfully haunted by them. "That sentence fell in upon me," Bunyan says, quoting a biblical verse; or again, "That Scripture did seize upon my soul"; and again, "Then fell with power that word of God upon me." Particular texts seemed aimed at him personally, often with ominous import: "Sometimes again I should think, O if it were not for these three or four words, now how might I be comforted! and I could hardly forbear at some times, but to wish them out of the Book." No wonder Bunyan poignantly exclaims, "Woe be to him against whom the Scriptures bend themselves!"[66] But to treat individual verses of the Bible in this way was in the opinion of Quakers to be victimized by the "priests" who, as Fox said, "have got the Scriptures and are not in that spirit which gave them forth; who make a trade of their words and have put them into chapter and verse."[67] Numbering the verses of the Bible was indeed a relatively recent Protestant innovation, having originated with the Geneva Bible of 1560. Widespread access to the Bible was even more recent: in 1640 the monopoly collapsed that had kept it too expensive for the poor to buy, and from then on Bibles could be bought for two shillings or less.[68]

For Quakers the crux was that the Bible, though full of value, was not a collection of definitive oracular texts but instead was a now-dated expression of the same Spirit that continued to inspire living persons. In their opinion Puritan bibliolatry reified the literal text and made a mockery of its spiritual significance. "If the writings of the Apostles be the man Christ Jesus," Nayler observed, "then have we part of him visible here on earth, and part is lost"; and he added still more trenchantly, "The visible part of the Apostles' writings is paper and ink; but so is not the visible part of the man Christ Jesus."[69] One of Nayler's dreadful blasphemies, as defined by John Deacon, was that "the Scriptures are not the word of God, but only a declaration of that word."[70] At Carlisle in 1653, when Fox was arrested and interrogated by the magistrates, "they asked me whether the Scripture was the word of God. I said, God was the Word and the Scriptures were writings; and the Word was before writings were, which Word did fulfil them."[71] The Bible was a valuable set of texts through which the Word had spoken at one time, but it could not have unique authority since the Word continued to speak just as it had always done. In an interrogation Nayler was asked whether the Scriptures were the word of

God, and he replied in the same way: "They are a true declaration of the Word that was in them who spoke them forth."[72]

It was the Puritans, on this view, who made an illegitimate inference from the doctrine that Christ is the Word and mistakenly equated word with letter. "Is the letter the Son?" Nayler demanded; "in Revel. 2. 17, he doth not say 'hear what the letter saith,' but 'hear what the Spirit saith;' or in Ephes. 6. 17, is it there called the 'sword of the Letter,' or the 'sword of the Spirit?'"[73] In debate the Puritans themselves had to admit that the Word could only speak to those whom the Spirit enabled to understand it. In a passage that gives some sense of Nayler's style in disputation, he reminded one of his antagonists, "Thou said that the Scriptures are the absolute rule and medium of faith; and when I asked thee if God could give faith without them, thou saidst, Yea; then I said, They was not the absolute rule and medium; then John Wray said, I catched at words." The crux, as always, was the immediacy and completeness with which the Quakers claimed to receive the Spirit. "Thou said I was a false witness in saying that I had seen Christ, and said thou had never seen him as Paul did; to which I said, I believed thou had not."[74] If the Bible is read in and through the Spirit it remains the word of God; but that is because it is being mediated and, as it were, re-uttered by Christ, the living Word. As Nayler put it on another occasion, "There is not nor can be any knowledge of God but by revelation from Jesus Christ which is before the letter was, which the letter declares."[75]

As the Quakers saw very clearly, the fundamental issue was that the text of the Bible could not supply its own interpretation without an infinite regress of prior interpretations to guarantee each interpretation. In vain might a Puritan theorist like William Whitaker declare, "The Scripture is *autopistos*, that is, hath all its authority and credit from itself."[76] Subsequent history would show that there were really only two alternatives: either the Bible would have to submit to critical textual analysis like any other document, or else its inner spirit must be revived by continued infusion of the same inspiration that had prompted its original writers. The Quakers chose the second alternative and held to it resolutely. Puritan exegetes, Nayler complained, treated the Bible as an endlessly obscure "parable and mystery."[77] In opposition to the parabolic mode of interpretation Nayler endorsed that side of contemporary thinking that insisted on the declarative message of the Bible and rejected the allegorical license that more intellectual exegetes preferred, as in Donne's "metaphorical God" whose "figures flowed into figures, and poured themselves out into farther figures . . . How often, how much more often, doth thy Son call himself a way, and a light, and a gate, and a vine, and bread, than the Son of God, or of man? How much oftener doth he exhibit a metaphorical Christ than a real, a literal?"[78] Nayler would reject as misleading any distinction between a metaphorical and a literal Christ. For the believer who is inspired by the Holy Spirit, the way and the light and the bread are exactly what the Bible calls them, just as real as—actually, more real than—the phenomena of everyday experience. On the one hand, then, the letter of the Bible is dead unless informed by the Word; on the other hand, when it *is* informed by the Word it is literally true, and not just a vehicle for interpretive flights by what Nayler condemns as "imagination."

In accordance with this emphasis, the Quakers insisted on spontaneous personal expression rather than repetition of texts. Nayler denounced the Puritan metrical versions of the Psalms as "leading people to sing David's conditions in rhymes and meter, in the invention and not in the Spirit; and so you join with the world to make songs of his words, but his condition you know not, but are enemies to it where it is witnessed; and singing in words what you are not in life, you are found liars, and lead others to lie also; but the saints sung by their gifts, and not other men's words, as you do."[79] The metrical Psalms were artificially structured words usurping the presumed spontaneity of the original. As Nayler put it, they "turned David's quakings and trembling into meter," or more largely, "as David's tremblings, quakings, wastings, weepings, roarings till his sight grew dim, and watered his bed with his tears, and roared all the day long prophecies, praises, prayers; these you sing, having turned them into rhyme."[80]

The ultimate ground of interpretation was an apocalyptic closure in which the spiritual Word would reveal itself as the agent of retribution against the merely literal word. For as Nayler warned, "Though the fleshly mind profess the letter, and call it the Word, and call it the Light, the Light they shall find to be their condemnation, and the Word they shall find to be as a hammer, and as a sword among them and upon them, and as a fire to burn them up."[81] Seen in an apocalyptic context the entire Bible organizes itself under a phrase from Revelation 14: 6, "the everlasting gospel," which was frequently invoked by antinomians. The symbolism of the Everlasting Gospel had roots in a heretical doctrine that originated with the twelfth-century mystic

Joachim of Flora (or Fiore), who held that the Age of the Father and the Age of the Son were being superseded by the Age of the Holy Ghost. In this new dispensation a nondoctrinal religion of eternity would supplant the historically based gospel of the New Testament just as the New Testament had supplanted the old Law, revealed now not in texts but in the hearts of men.[82] But the historical sequence of the three stages did not especially interest the Quakers. For them the whole point was the atemporal completeness of revelation, which had preceded the written Gospel of the New Testament and which continued to inspire human beings just as fully as it inspired the evangelists. "You that say the four books are the Gospel," Nayler declares; "you never knew him who is the glad tidings, which Gospel was manifest before these books were written, and is *everlasting.*"[83]

By 1660 a Baptist critic condemned the Quaker position for drastic antihistoricism: "They boast that Christ is come to them, neither look they for any other coming; that the world is ended with them, neither look they for any other end; that the Judgment is past with them, neither look they for any other Judgment."[84] This formulation is an exaggeration, since Quakers did anticipate a genuine Second Coming sometime in the future, but it catches the authentic interiority and immediacy on which they always insisted. To orthodox Puritans the Quakers did not look in the least like adherents of an Everlasting Gospel; they looked like false prophets who were substituting a new gospel of their own. Higginson betrayed a real anxiety about the seductiveness of their message, while asserting once again the absolute authority of the textual Word:

> The more heresies spread themselves and eat like cankers, and the sweeter they are to the palates of deluded multitudes that are greedy after them, the more should we labor to decline the contagion, to ballast our vessels, and settle our selves in the truth, so that if an apostle from the dead, or an angel from heaven, or all the seducers on earth should preach unto us another Gospel, they may not be able to remove us from that which we have already received, and which is preached to us in the Word of God.[85]

It is a remarkable thought that if an angel should descend from heaven to pronounce a new gospel, it must be firmly resisted even coming from such a source.

Christ Within

The foundation of Quaker theology is the full presence of Christ in each of the saints. "The Father dwells in the Light and changes not," Nayler wrote, "and the Son is the light of the world in his own image, by whom he changes all things that are out of him, and overturns shadows and customs, and makes the world new."[86] On the whole Quaker writers preferred not to talk about the Trinity, which they considered an unbiblical concept. "God and the Spirit hath no Person," Edward Burrough wrote, "nor cannot truly be distinguished into Persons."[87] This was no mere technicality in theology: if the indwelling Spirit and the savior Christ were synonymous, and if there was no angry and remote Father-God to be somehow placated by the Son, then the immediacy of the divine was secured. "The Quakers scoffed," Cotton Mather reported, "at our imagined God beyond the stars."[88] The same concept is implicit in the reply by Fox and Nayler to the accusation that Quakers thought "Christ's coming in the flesh was but a figure." They answered, "Christ in his people is the substance of all figures, types and shadows, fulfilling them in them, and setting them free from them."[89]

Establishing typological correspondences was thus not an end in itself, as it virtually was for many Puritans who pored over the events of their own lives in order to detect hidden "types." On the contrary, since Christ had entered into his people they were set free from the tyranny of old symbols. If typology did continue to have hermeneutic value, it was in a totalizing form in which everything in the world was given intense clarity and meaning by the Spirit that animated it.[90] In Nayler's words, "The shadow is swallowed up in the substance, the end of all shadows, which is life indeed, but the figures are not the life."[91] As so often, each party to the dispute ascribed a symmetrically opposed position to the other party. The Quakers, according to Bunyan in an early tract, rejected the Christ of flesh and blood who was crucified and ascended into heaven, and settled instead for an empty "shadow or type." Contrariwise, the Quakers accused the Calvinists of worshipping a God far off rather than the living God of the spirit. As Bunyan indignantly reports, "I was told to my face that I preached up an idol, because I said that the son of Mary was in heaven, with the same body that was crucified on the cross."[92]

The reality and importance of the historical Jesus were not in fact doubted by the Quakers, whatever their Puritan critics believed. Looking back at the controversies of the 1650s Fox categorically rejected "the slander raised upon us that the Quakers should deny Christ that died and suffered at Jerusalem, which was all utterly false, and never the least thought of it in our hearts."[93] Moreover, the dire wickedness of sin was fully affirmed by the Quakers, together with the doctrine of Christ's sacrifice to save mankind from its consequences. Nayler had no qualms about using orthodox language to invoke Christ's "propitiation" in which his "freely imputed" righteousness was "put into the creature" as a "free gift from the Father."[94] What was really in dispute was not the nature of Christ's role, but rather the extent to which its effects had already been fully accomplished. Whatever Puritan polemicists may have supposed, what was at issue between the Quakers and themselves was not the reality of Christ's sacrifice but the extent to which a human being could be made "perfect" and "free" by participating in it.

On the nature and fullness of that perfection Quaker claims of union with Christ hinged, and these were the claims for which Nayler would be tried for his life in 1656. The beliefs that got him and his companions in such trouble had been common among the Familists, followers of the "Family of Love" first proclaimed a century earlier by the Dutch merchant and prophet Hendrik Niclaes (commonly anglicized as Henry Nicholas). After a trial in 1654 the Familist minister John Pordage was ejected from his church living for such beliefs as: "That the fiery deity of Christ mingles and mixes itself with our flesh," "that Christ is a type, and but a type," and "that it was a weakness to be troubled for sins."[95] In Niclaes's memorable formulation, God "manneth himself according to the inward man with us," and likewise man, illuminated by divine light, becomes "godded . . . to the upright righteousness with him."[96] "Godded" was an anglicization of the German *vergottet*, a much more striking expression than the Latinate "deified" by which it was more usually translated. The near-Ranter Richard Coppin, who until 1648 was a minister in the established church, similarly asserted that "God is all in one, and so is in everyone. The same all which is in me, is in thee; the same God which dwells in one dwells in another, even in all; and in the same fullness as he is in one, he is in every one."[97] The favorite Quaker phrase "that of God in thee" indicated not just the indwelling presence of God, which any Puritan would accept with the caveat that the person inhabited by God remained vile and alien to the divine inhabitant. To the Quakers it implied a resemblance between human being and God that reflected a difference of degree only, not of kind. "Thou wilt come to feel," Nayler declared, "how that of God in thee answers to the things of God, as face answers face."[98] Paul of course promised that we would come to see God "face to face" (1 Corinthians 13: 12); what was outrageous in the Quakers was their insistence that this immediacy of contact was possible in the present life.

If Christ fully informs all men and women, are they then identical with Christ? There might have been nothing shocking when a Puritan minister declared that there is "but one Christ" and Nayler retorted, "That one Christ is in all his saints."[99] But as contrasted with the Puritan Christ afar off, this one was literally and physically present. "This is he who cannot be limited," Nayler wrote, "nor his person restrained in one place, who filleth heaven and earth with his presence, and appeareth at his pleasure to his own (though the wise of the world know him not, and therefore limit him only above the stars), who dwelleth in the bodies of his saints."[100] As it often did, the 1716 *Collection of Sundry Books* was silently altered from the first edition, in this instance to tone down the suggestion of Christ's physical immediacy: "his person" was deleted, as were the "bodies" of the saints in whom he dwells. Like Nayler, Fox often had to face charges that he claimed to be divine, and his reply was essentially the same as Nayler's, that God was so fully present in the saints as to have superseded the personal self. When questioners in 1655, visiting Fox in Leicester prison, asked if he was the Son of God, "I said, I was no more; but the Father and the Son was all in me, and we are one."[101] Here too there was emendation in the direction of orthodoxy: in his original manuscript Fox regularly referred to himself as "the son of God," but a later hand altered "the" to "a," and the phrase duly appeared as "a son of God" in the published version.[102]

This conception of the union of believers with Christ goes well beyond the traditional metaphor of Christ the vine, with individual believers as the branches (John 15: 5), and implies a merger into unity. Those who "feed in a clean spirit," Nayler says, are able to keep clear of the false "knowledge" and "wisdom" of the world, and will come to "know the power of the Word of Life in your selves, which as it passeth breaks the rocks, and melts the hardness in every heart, and melts you all into one heart, as one man, all into one mind in Christ Jesus, that you may be knit in one body, and one spirit, and one head, the Lamb over all, glorified over all."[103] Christ is still the head and is still exalted "over all," but by union with him the community of true believers may be said to have a single heart and mind. They are thus liberated from the doubleness of ordinary human experience and become, as Blake would later express it, the "one man" in whom multitudes merge when seen in their totality: "As they are written in the Bible these various states I have seen in my imagination; when distant they appear as one man but as you approach they appear multitudes of nations."[104] "We are all coexistent with God," Blake told the diarist Crabb Robinson; when asked about the divinity of Jesus he replied, "He is the only God," and added, "And so am I and so are you."[105] Such claims were daring even for a poet-painter at the beginning of the nineteenth century; they were dangerously heretical for preachers in the seventeenth century.

The Quakers always insisted that they fully grasped the difference that continued to exist between individual human beings and the spirit of Christ in which they participated. Fox made the distinction clearly in recounting a confrontation with some Ranters whom he had visited in prison: "Then seeing they said they were God, I asked them if they knew whether it would rain tomorrow. They said they could not tell. I told them God could tell."[106] But when theologically astute antagonists pressed them on this point their answers were not always so satisfactory. In an extended controversy with Thomas Weld, Nayler could not be brought to deny that Fox had called himself equal with God, but insisted instead that when he said this he was no longer Fox. There was no way the wrangling on this point could reach a conclusion, since the two sides were arguing from totally different premises. Nayler wearily returned to it in a 1655 pamphlet, two years after the debate with Weld began, and his explanation deserves to be read at length:

> Now for a few words to your reply to my answer; and first, to your first position: as touching your accusing George Fox, that he said "that he was equal with God;" and you say your proof is not at all denied. I answer, that those words were spoken is not denied; but that they are the words of George Fox, is denied. And you use many words, and say I make a difference between George Fox and himself . . . The sum of mine answer was this, "that

George Fox was denied as dust; but the Spirit that spoke in him is equal with God;" according to the Scripture, and the words of Christ, who saith, "When you are called before rulers for my name's sake, take no thought what to speak: for it is not you that speak, but the Spirit of your Father that speaketh in you." Matth. 10: 20. Now George Fox being called before rulers for the name of Christ, he denies George Fox to speak, and the creature who is but dust, and witnesseth the Spirit of the Father speaking in him (though the words pass through George Fox) and the words of Christ [are] fulfilled. And are not the Father and the Son and the Spirit equal, wherever they are? and must they not be suffered to speak where they are? But you [i.e., the plural "you"] that are carnal know not the voice.[107]

To the Puritan ministers this must have looked like blatant logic-chopping. To the Quakers it was the simple consequence of a radical dualism in which the carnal Fox and Nayler were mere dust, animated within by the eternal Spirit that made use of their vocal cords to express itself. In the understanding of Nayler's antagonists he was asserting a preposterous "difference between George Fox and himself"; in Nayler's understanding, the inspired George Fox no longer *was* "himself." In Fox's own words, "I was no more."

Nayler's responses at his Appleby interrogation expose the same paradoxes:

Mr. Pearson then asked, whether Christ was in him as man, as he had before affirmed?

Nayler replied, "Christ God and Man is not divided; separate God and Man, and He is no more Christ; Christ God and Man is everywhere."[108]

Pearson was asking whether the human nature of Christ as well as the divine was in Nayler, and Nayler was answering that the two natures could not be separated. In principle this was a perfectly orthodox position, but clearly the emphasis given to it by the Quakers was disturbing to their critics. The capital letters admirably express the equation of the three terms: Man (printed with a small "m" in Pearson's question) is raised to a level of identity with Christ and God, in a new trinity in which the three become one and govern a singular verb: "Christ God and Man *is* everywhere."

Despite constant denials that they believed themselves to be identical with Christ, the Quakers could thus seem like slippery equivocators to their critics. Nayler's defense of one of his colleagues must have looked like no defense at all:

> Thou wouldst charge James Parnell with blasphemy who, speaking of corrupt reason, saith "Before that was, I am." I say: thou here showest what thou knowest of the inward man, or being in the life of Christ. Is not he that is born again of the immortal Seed born of that which before corrupt reason is? Art thou a teacher, and calls this blasphemy? Nay, it is the blasphemer in thee that cannot own the voice of Christ, for if any thing of Christ speak in man, it was before corrupt reason was; and every one in their measures of Christ, as they have received.[109]

For those who have received Christ, even in limited "measure," grammatical distinctions of tense and person blur and become unimportant. Participating in Christ in this way, the Quaker saint could freely use the first-person and present-tense language that so scandalized the Puritan: "Before that was, I am."

Sin and Perfection

For Puritans the most offensive of Quaker positions was their insistence on taking literally Christ's command in the Sermon on the Mount, "Be ye therefore perfect, even as your Father which is in heaven is perfect" (Matthew 5: 48). Since God, in his manifestation as the sinless Christ, is fully present in human beings, they too have been liberated from the tyranny of sin. In a sense they are restored to the prelapsarian condition, but in fact they have been promoted to a condition even better than that, for as Fox put it, "I was immediately taken up in spirit, to see into another or more steadfast state than Adam's in innocency, even into a state in Christ Jesus, that should never fall."[110] But this does not mean that sin becomes irrelevant. Quite the reverse: the Quakers were just as convinced as any Puritan could be that most human beings were hideously corrupt, and they differed from Calvinists not in their valuation of fallen human nature but in their understanding of the condition of the elect whom Christ had saved. The Calvinist view was that Christ's vicarious sacrifice had saved the tiny number of elect who had been chosen before the beginning of time but that they continued to be vile sinners even though certain of salvation. (In this life, of course, knowing themselves to be vile sinners, they might find it hard to be confident that they *were* among the elect, which was a notorious source of anxiety among pious Puritans.) Quakers too, although they held that all men and women might potentially be saved, believed that only a tiny minority were likely to be. "Scarce one of ten thousand," Nayler wrote, "knows any call from God to any service for him, or hath an ear to hear his voice."[111] The fundamental point of disagreement was that whereas orthodox Calvinists believed election to be an unmerited originary fact that the individual could do nothing to alter, Quakers believed a person could choose to be entered and saved by Christ. If this did take place, the person so blessed ceased altogether to be a vile sinner and participated in Christ's holiness and perfection.[112] In Nayler's words, "The elect way is opened to the blind, with encouragement to enter and walk therein . . . Thus the Spirit of life draws with the light, and saith 'Come' to all that mind its voice; and as many as obey, he changeth and feedeth with the new life, whereby they become new creatures, born of the freedom."[113]

The symbolism of the "Seed," which was in common use well before the Quakers took it up,[114] was central to their position. Nayler's usage in *A Salutation to the Seed of God* clearly shows that the term was understood in both a plural and a singular sense. As the title of the tract implies, it could be a synonym for godly people considered collectively. But in addition it referred to the spark of divinity within each individual, as when Nayler in the same work addresses "all honest hearts, in whom a seed of God hath place."[115] People are plural, and each contains *a* seed; but all of these seeds are manifestations of *the* Seed. Later on Nayler quotes Galatians 3: 16: "Now to Abraham and his seed were the promises made. He saith not, 'And to seeds,' as of many; but as of one, 'And to thy seed,' which is Christ." It follows that "that Seed is but one, one heart, one mind, one soul, one spirit" (pp. 240–241). But of course the two senses ultimately merge, since the germ of Christ grows in each individual person until it achieves full union with the collectivity whom he has redeemed. On the title page of another pamphlet Nayler identifies himself as "a lover of Israel's seed, called James Nayler."[116]

The symbolism of the Seed lent itself also to expanded metaphorical use. Preachers invoked it to suggest the planting of God's grace, its sprouting in suitable soil, and its maturation toward the ultimate harvest. As Fox later recalled the first years of his ministry, "I saw the harvest white, and the seed of God lying thick in the ground, as ever did wheat that was sown outwardly, and none to gather it; and for this I mourned with tears."[117] In addition, Quakers took a near-Manichaean view that the Seed of righteousness was in constant conflict with an opposing seed of evil.[118] "He that is really born of God," Nayler wrote in *A Door Opened to the Imprisoned Seed*, "knows two several seeds and natures, which spring and bring forth from several [i.e., different] roots, and after their several kinds."[119] In the minds of people who used this metaphor in the 1650s, the divine Seed was preparing to join battle with its diabolical antitype in the final conflict. In 1653 Nayler published a tract entitled *A Word to the Seed of the Serpent, or Ministers of Antichrist, or Man of Sin, wherever found*, which begins with an apocalyptic proclamation: "Know this, thou subtle one, who hast long upholden a kingdom of sin, unrighteousness, injustice and oppression, that now the day of thy torment is at hand; for now is that Seed arisen, which is appointed to discover [i.e., expose] thee and thy deceitful workings, and to bruise thy head, and to lay all thy pride and glory in the dust."[120] "I will put enmity between thee and the woman, and between thy seed and her seed," God had told the Serpent after the Fall; "it shall bruise thy head, and thou shalt bruise his heel" (Genesis 3: 15). The metaphor of "threshing meetings" had a similar basis. Like the apocalyptic treading out of grapes in the Book of Revelation, the metaphor anticipated a radical separation between the saved and the damned: when the threshing has been completed the worthless husks will be thrown away.

Those in whom the good Seed is growing, meanwhile, have entered into a self-authenticating condition of wholeness that most other sects rejected as impossible in mortal life. Fox wrote in 1659, "I am not one of them which calls themselves Papists, Common Prayer men [i.e., Episcopalians], nor Presbyterians, Independents, Anabaptists, Puritans, nor heathens, which be out of the life of God; but that which God has called me to, that I am, and the elect before the world began." Fox went on to describe the condition of the elect in strikingly circular terms: "This is to go everywhere all abroad amongst friends, who are of the royal priesthood which destroys that [which] made the separation from God, from which royal seed goes the royal command, which seed remains for ever from the royal seed to the royal seed, which are the royal priesthood, which hath the royal law and love to friends and enemies, which is beyond the love of the world and before it was, for that's the royal love where no enmity can come."[121] The royal seed circulates in the royal priesthood, which enjoys the royal love and obeys the royal law, endlessly propagating itself in the elect, who have embodied the royal seed since before time began and are therefore invulnerable to the snares of the fallen world.

Despite what their enemies claimed, Quakers did not necessarily believe that the elect were already perfect in this life. What made the symbolism of the Seed particularly attractive was its promise of continued organic development. "As man beholds the Seed growing," Nayler wrote, "so he comes to see the new creation . . . So comes man to be reconciled to his Maker in the eternal unity, beyond what is to be expressed."[122] And elsewhere he was entirely clear about perfection as a gradual process rather than an achieved condition: "It is a lying slander that we say every saint is perfect: for we witness the saints' growth, and the time of pressing after perfection."[123] Describing those who are "born of the freedom" Nayler declared that "it's hard for such to do evil, being against nature, Seed and sonship which is in God."[124] Hard, but not impossible.

The somewhat obscure concept of the "measure" was often invoked to suggest limitations in individuals in whom perfection was growing but who were not yet unequivocally perfect. George Whitehead remembered a meeting at which Nayler was expounding "a mysterious place in the Revelation" and suddenly "made a stop, seeming to give a check to himself, intimating that he would not stretch or go beyond his measure, according to that saying of the Apostle, 2 Cor. 10.13, 'But we will not boast of things without our measure, but according to the measure of the rule which God hath distributed to us.' Ver. 14. 'For we stretch not our selves beyond our measure, &c.'"[125] The term is used by Paul in several places to indicate differences in the pastoral or prophetic gifts of individual believers—"Unto every one of us is given grace according to the measure of the gift of Christ" (Ephesians 4: 7)—and this is generally what Nayler has in mind. "As you arise out of the earthly bondage, you shall witness the glorious liberty, and so come to know your own measures, every one in particular to improve it, and not to boast above it in another man's line."[126] To know one's own measure is to renounce competitiveness, to accept one's own "line" without reference to other people's.

Still, perfection is perfection, and if the Quakers were willing to hedge somewhat they never repudiated it. One might suppose that if different people received the light in different measures, they must therefore fall short of perfection in varying degrees. But Nayler made it clear that an individual, with whatever measure he or she might possess, does participate in the total perfection of Christ. "That's the righteousness of God, which by faith in Christ alone is freely received, and the least measure is perfect."[127] The attractiveness of the notion of "measure" was thus that it allowed Quaker writers to speak of *incompleteness* without having to acknowledge *imperfection*. In reply to a Puritan writer who said that "the saints have a glorious light in them, but imperfect," Nayler made this distinction explicitly: "It is true, the Light is but manifest in the creatures by degrees, but the least degree is perfect in its measure, and being obeyed, will lead to the perfect Day, and is perfect in its self, and leads up to perfection all that perfectly follow it."[128]

To assert perfection was repugnant enough to orthodox thinking. To put it the other way round and to claim sinlessness was still worse, and was met with frank incredulity by antagonists like Baxter, who wrote, "Is it possible that any man in this life, that is not mad with spiritual pride, can indeed believe that he hath no sin? What? that he transgresseth no law? that he doth love God in the highest degree that he is bound to do? that he never hath a thought or word that is sinful, nor sinfully loseth one moment of his time?"[129] The Quaker answer to each question was "yes," as Fox made clear during an all-day interrogation at Derby in 1650, which was conducted under the terms of the recently promulgated Blasphemy Act:

At last they asked me whether I was sanctified.

I said, "Sanctified? yes," for I was in the Paradise of God.

They said, had I no sin?

"Sin?" said I, "Christ my Saviour hath taken away my sin, and in him there is no sin."

They asked how we knew that Christ did abide in us.

I said, "By his Spirit that he has given us."

They temptingly asked if any of us were Christ.

I answered, "Nay, we are nothing, Christ is all."

They said, "If a man steal is it no sin?"

I answered, "All unrighteousness is sin."

A Ranter might well have believed that stealing was no sin. Fox denied that, and denied also that he considered himself personally to be Christ; but he did acknowledge that he was sanctified and sinless in Christ, which was all the authorities needed to hear: "And so they committed me as a blasphemer and as a man that had no sin." Fox adds sardonically that this event stimulated Puritan orthodoxy to reassert its stake in the existence of sin: "Many people came from far and near to see a man that had no sin; and then did the priests [i.e., paid ministers of any denomination] roar up for sin in their pulpits, and preach up sin, that people said never was the like heard. It was all their works to plead for it."[130] The irony is biting: the same Puritans who preached faith, not works, were devoted to the "works" of preaching the ubiquity of sin.

This was the Quaker view. Their opponents saw the claim of sinlessness very differently, as a self-righteous presumption of moral superiority. "To give one example," Higginson says, "Nayler at a private meeting in Sedburgh asked an honest Christian, Samuel Handley, whether he was without sin, or no? Handley replied, he was a sinner. Hereupon Nayler called him a thief, a murtherer, a Cain, and justified himself to be without sin."[131] Nayler often made the same point in print: "My sin being taken away by Christ, my repentance stands sure; but thou who says thou hast repented, and hast committed the sin again, art turned with the dog to the vomit, and hath overthrown thy repentance, and none who knows Christ will give the hand of fellowship to any such."[132]

As usual, the two sides used the same terminology but constantly talked past each other. For Calvinists the way out of despair was to recognize that even God's elect continue to wallow in sin, and can never deserve approval except as conferred by unmerited grace. A conscientious Calvinist was expected to schedule specific occasions for self-contempt, as Cotton Mather was still doing half a century later: "This day I set apart for the duties of a secret fast. Inexpressible self-abhorrence, for my abominable sinfulness before the Holy Lord, was the design and the very spirit of my devotions this day."[133] Obligatory guilt formed a central part of Puritan faith.

It is certainly true that the more sensitive a Puritan was, the more likely he was to experience the torments of unappeasable guilt, as Thomas Brooks testified:

> Ah! did not the Lord let in some beams of love upon the soul, when it is *Magor-missabib,* a terror to itself; when the heart is a hell of horror, the conscience an *Aceldama,* a field of black blood; when the soul is neither quiet at home nor abroad, neither at bed or board, neither in company nor out of company, neither in the use of ordinances nor in the neglect of ordinances; how would the soul faint, sink, and despair for ever!

In a footnote Brooks added, "An awakened conscience is like Prometheus's vulture, it lies for ever gnawing."[134] Magor-missabib is the "terror to thyself" imposed by an angry Jehovah (Jeremiah 20: 3–4); Aceldama is the "field of blood" bought with Judas's thirty pieces of silver (Acts 1: 19). Nayler well understood the comprehensive particularism of the Puritan attention to sin: "He that saith the letter is his rule must not miss it in any thing, for if they break it in one he is guilty of all."[135] Such a theology fed upon the notorious arbitrariness of Calvin's God. "That's the Devil's hope," Nayler commented, "which hopes not freedom from sin, as much as freedom from Hell. And with this hope would he make God a liar, and partial like himself, that he should find some in sin, and save them, and others in sin and condemn them."[136]

Implied in this controversy is a searching critique of the motives underlying Puritan teaching, which could be seen as promoting self-hatred as a mechanism of social control. In *A Word to the Seed of the Serpent, or Ministers of Antichrist, or Man of Sin, wherever found* (1653), Nayler addressed orthodox Calvinist ministers as agents of the Antichrist, preaching sin on behalf of the Man of Sin who is identified (as a marginal gloss indicates) in 2 Thessalonians.

> Now you are forced (lest the Man of Sin should fall) to tell the same people to whom you have been all this while talking against sin, impurity, and imperfection, that they must never look while

they are here to overcome sin, the world, and the Devil, nor ever come to purity and perfection; and thus you labour to keep a hold for the Man of Sin as long as people live; and so persuade them to leave the work of redemption and freedom till after death, or you know not when, and thus encourage people to spend their days in folly, and leave the world with torment and horror at their death.[137]

Nayler here puts his finger on a paradox of Puritan piety. In such an ethic psychic relief is endlessly deferred until "you know not when," because death itself, which ought at least to liberate the sufferer from this world of woe, threatens the possibility of irrevocable damnation and thus presents a prospect of "torment and horror." According to the Quaker critique, the Puritan needs sin to exist even while he denounces it, and recognition of the real and adequate presence of Christ in human beings would actually put an end to Puritan piety.

The Puritan could thus try to score points against the Quaker by claiming to be, in effect, viler than thou, while the Quaker could retort that anything less than complete holiness in Christ was really a hollow parody of holiness. The quarrel over the efficacy of works was similarly mirror-like. Since both sides agreed that works without faith were worthless, their positions were close to identical, and there was again an echo-chamber quality to the controversy, in which each side maintained that the other was corrupted by belief in works. Like other Protestants, Quakers regularly asserted the absolute priority of faith. In prison in 1659, noting elliptically that "the Enemy hath spread so many false reports of me, touching my faith in Christ Jesus," Nayler launched a tract entitled *What the Possession of the Living Faith Is* with the unequivocal assertion, "A right faith is the only ground of man's eternal happiness, and the only thing which gains the creature an entrance towards his Creator, and without which it is impossible to please God." But simply to believe in Christ, or even to preach him as the Puritans did, was no guarantee of anything, for as Nayler went on to say, "the devils believe the holiness that was in Christ, and can preach it, but cannot inherit it, because they love not to live the life of it."[138]

But what of the saint who failed to remain in the state of perfection? For Puritans that was the inevitable experience of daily life; for Quakers it was a terrifying catastrophe. Sins that had been committed in time of preconvincement "darkness" might be forgiven, but future sins must be immeasurably disastrous. In this context Nayler quoted the Epistle to the Hebrews: "If we sin willfully after that we have received the knowledge of the truth, there remaineth no more sacrifice for sins, but a certain fearful looking for of judgment and fiery indignation, which shall devour the adversaries."[139] These considerations help to explain why misconduct, especially sexual, was a common ground for expulsion from the Quaker community. A Calvinist might sin and, with suitable self-condemnation, vow to try to sin no more. But a Quaker was supposed to be perfect; repeated sins simply showed that he or she was an unregenerate sinner and therefore not a Quaker. The Quaker position thus resembles that of Augustine's great enemy Pelagius, whose doctrine of free will was far from being the relaxed and encouraging one implied by modern allusions to Pelagianism. As has been well said, Pelagius believed that "since perfection is possible for man, it is obligatory."[140]

Since perfection is obligatory, any who fail to achieve it must face the dark side of the God of love. "With the froward he appears in frowardness," Nayler wrote; "the kisses of his lips are life eternal, but who may abide his wrath?"[141] Far from liberating believers from the rigors of the law, the doctrine of perfection might seem to push those rigors to an extreme, even while it promised relief for true believers. Nayler's *Love to the Lost* holds out no comfort at all for those who remain lost:

> Whereas it was said in the letter, "Thou shalt not commit adultery," he saith, "Thou shalt not lust;" in the letter it was said, "Thou shalt not swear falsely," but in the Spirit he saith, "Swear not at all;" in the letter, "Thou shalt not kill," but in the Spirit, "Thou shalt not be angry;" and whosoever doth any of these things is guilty before God, and this is far from making it void, which declares it in its purity, so as they who might seem to be clear in the letter might be found guilty in the law of the Spirit; that by Christ Jesus, who is the end of that law, they may come to see their condemnation, and by faith in him come to be set free.[142]

A deep conceptual disagreement is implicit here. Puritans stressed the abolition of the old law of Moses, which no mortal could hope to satisfy, and its replacement by the new law of Christ. Quakers, very differently, took the antinomian position that through participation in Christ's perfection the law was satisfied, not abolished. In a passage of coded spiritual autobiography Nayler wrote,

> Then came I to see that I through the law must be redeemed from the law, and that my redemption from it must not be by making it void, but by fulfilling of it . . . and the words of Christ I found true, "I came not to destroy the law, but to fulfill it" [Matthew 5: 17] . . . And I find that Christ never believed that he could never be perfect, nor overcome the Devil or sin; it was never the faith of Christ to make void the law of his Father unfulfilled in him.

The 1716 edition made a crucial alteration in this passage, changing "Christ never believed that he could never be perfect" into "it is not *the faith of Christ* to believe that *men* could never be perfect."[143] In Nayler's original formulation it was the divine element in Jesus Christ the man that brought him to perfection, just as it has continued to do in all of the saints since that time. In the same work Nayler defined the "mystery of Godliness," which the worldly do not understand, as "God manifest in flesh, not God flesh, but manifest IN flesh" (p. 434). On this comprehensive identification with Christ hinged Puritan charges of blasphemy against Quakers, both for their published opinions and, as would happen disastrously to Nayler at Bristol, for the actions they sometimes based on those opinions.

In asserting freedom from sin, the Quakers constantly had to protect themselves from accusations that they were no better than the Ranters. Whether or not an actual Ranter movement ever existed,[144] Quakers as well as Puritans were always on the lookout for "ranterish" claims that people were free to do anything they liked. It was common for anti-Quaker writers to assert that Quaker principles somehow condoned immorality. Thus the Baptist Thomas Collier in 1657: "The Ranters would have no Christ but within; no Scripture to be a rule; no ordinances [sacraments], no law but their lusts, no Heaven or glory but here, no sin but what men fancied to be so, no condemnation for sin but in the consciences of ignorant ones, &c. And what the Quaker is more or less, let their own consciences be judge."[145] Quakers did insist that Christ was within, that the letter of Scripture was superseded (though not contradicted) by the Spirit, and that "ordinances" were unacceptable; but far from refusing to condemn sin, they condemned it vehemently, and far from acting out an amoral antinomian liberty, they insisted on absolute moral uprightness in the most traditional sense. Insofar as Quakers did resemble Ranters they would have to be seen as inverted Ranters, as Baxter rather sourly confirmed when he wrote, "The Quakers . . . were but the Ranters turned from horrid profaneness and blasphemy, to a life of extreme austerity on the other side." In the margin of his copy of Baxter's book Coleridge wrote, with unusual conciseness, "Observe the *but*."[146] Bunyan charged similarly in 1657, "The very opinions that are held at this day by the Quakers, are the same that long ago were held by the Ranters. Only the Ranters had made them threadbare at an alehouse, and the Quakers have set a new gloss upon them again, by an outward legal holiness, or righteousness."[147] From the Quaker point of view this was an unconscionable misrepresentation: to live a virtuous life was surely to be the diametrical opposite of a Ranter.

The widespread tendency to associate the Quakers with their opposites suggests that the real issue was not so much doctrinal as moral, the threat implicit in the Ranter claim that all things were lawful, as Bunyan ruefully recalled when describing his own brief flirtation with their beliefs: "O these temptations were suitable to my flesh, I being but a young man and my nature in its prime."[148] The most effective Quaker defense was therefore to stress not doctrine but behavior. "For those thou callest Ranters," Nayler demanded of an anti-Quaker writer, "is there any people in the nation that more differ in practice from us than they?"[149] In another place he complained, "The greatest profession now set up by many is to make the redemption of Christ a cover for all licentiousness and fleshly liberty, and say they are to that end redeemed."[150] The early Quakers, just as much as their Calvinist antagonists, utterly repudiated the Ranter appeal to nature as guarantor of the appropriateness of human behavior, since in their view nature was irremediably corrupt except for the intervention of Christ.

The Abolition of Self

A frequent accusation of their enemies was that in claiming perfection the Quakers were swollen with spiritual pride. As Baxter said, "Some may take them to be humble that judge by their clothes and crying down high titles. But alas it is a childish pride to be proud of fine clothes. This is too low a game for them to play. The greater the matter is that men are proud of, usually the greater is their pride: it is the supposed spirit of God, and extraordinary holiness and inspiration and abilities, that they are proud of."[151] Baxter's charge is understandable in the light of comments like this one by Nayler: "In humility we find a power above pride, higher than oppression, higher than men's wills, higher than the lusts of the eye; yea higher than all that in man would exalt against it."[152] It is easy to see why their assertive behavior struck their critics as not humble in the least, but this remained its fundamental justification: it would indeed have been assertive if there were any self left to assert, but since selfhood had been abolished, there could no longer be any possibility of pride. Nayler's sequence of terms is noteworthy here: a person who has successfully escaped that most fundamental of human impulses, "the lusts of the eye" (1 John 2: 16), no longer has anything to fear from oppression and from other men's wills. In sin-obsessed Calvinists, according to Nayler, "The will of the Devil and his power is present, and acts you at his pleasure."[153] This is a superb formulation of the Puritan intuition of desperate unfreedom, analogous to the Freudian view that the neurotic person is lived by repressed compulsions. The Quaker counterclaim was that union with Christ entailed full participation in the freedom of Christ, cutting the Gordian knot of the free-will problem by dismissing it as irrelevant.

Quakers commonly reported an overwhelming conversion experience that was directly assimilated to an apostolic model. When he heard William Dewsbury preach, George Canby recalled long afterward, "I fell down on the house floor as dead to all appearance as any clog or stone. When I came to sense again he had got me up in his arms (it was about the year 1652); so that I can truly say I was smitten down to the ground by the living power of the Lord, as surely as ever Saul was in his way to Damascus, and my beastial will at that time got a deadly wound that through the loving kindness of God was never healed to this day."[154] The conversion experience is decisive, but it is also only a stage: once the bestial self (with its fallen will) has been exposed and wounded it begins to fight, and there are many accounts of the anguished struggle that inevitably follows.

Richard Hubberthorne wrote to Fox, also in 1652, in terms that clearly imply a comprehensive interior apocalypse, with all of the suffering and drama that the imagery of the Book of Revelation would imply:

Dear heart, since I saw thee, the hand of the Lord hath been mightily exercised upon me, and his terrors hath been sharp within me. The consumption determined upon the whole earth hath [been] and is passing through me; which hath been terrible unto the brutish nature, which could not endure the devouring fire, it being so hot and unquenchable that I saw nothing that could live or pass through it, but that all as stubble must be destroyed . . . All things which is pure and holy is hid from man, for he is separate from God and knoweth not any of his ways; but when the Lord revealeth any of his ways within man, man must die and know his own ways no more, but must "be led in a way which he knoweth not," contrary to his will, contrary to his wisdom, contrary to his reason, and to his carnal mind. For none of these must enter, but must be cast out into the lake which burneth.[155]

The extinction of the carnal self—which most psychologies would identify simply as *the* self—is supposed to be absolute, and the outcome will then be emergence into peace on the other side of the devouring fire. Hubberthorne explicitly invokes the Lord's promise "I will bring the blind by a way that they knew not; I will lead them in paths that they have not known: I will make darkness light before them, and crooked things straight" (Isaiah 42: 16). But the promise cannot be fulfilled until ordinary reason is utterly rejected, and not just reason but wisdom too; and not just wisdom, but the very will itself. This model of salvation assumes a truly radical unmaking of the self, an abolition of fallen dualism after which the saint can repose in an unconflicted monism.

The necessary corollary of the obligation to be perfect was thus rejection of everything that was not perfect, in one's self as well as in the world. Accordingly a second birth was called for, which was also a kind of death. In Hubberthorne's account of "the consumption determined upon the whole earth" that was "passing through me," he first had to experience the interior apocalypse in all of its terrifying power. The essence of this experience is that it is horribly painful, a surrender and extinction of the old self that fights for its very life. Consequently it "hath been terrible unto the brutish nature, which could not endure the devouring fire." God's mercy, of course, raised Hubberthorne up from the fire, but in a way that could never be understood or accepted by the unregenerate self, all of whose wishes and initiatives must be abolished: "contrary to his will, contrary to his wisdom, contrary to his reason." The individual will is perceived as the source of rebellion and therefore of suffering; it is what Rousseau, like Hubberthorne brought up as a Calvinist, would later reject as *amour propre*, and Blake as Self-hood. The anguish of apocalypse, too, is a frequent theme in Blake: "But in the wine presses the human grapes sing not nor dance, / They howl and writhe in shoals of torment in fierce flames consuming."[156] Quaker conversions were commonly slow and painful experiences, and the converts' eventual assertions of calmness and peace were expressions of profound relief at having come out at last on the other side.

When the self was burned away, so must be the sinful flesh in which it had been incarcerated. To Puritan critics, as we have seen, "quaking" looked like a gross lapse in self-control, disgusting proof of surrender to the body. But from an anthropological perspective, as the work of Mary Douglas has emphasized, quite the opposite is actually true. In movements of millennial tendency "society appears as a system which does not work" and "the human body is the most readily available image of a system." A free and undifferentiated life of the spirit is therefore symbolically expressed by contrasting it with the structuring rigidities of the body. "The millennialist goes in for frenzies; he welcomes the letting-go experience, and incorporates it into his procedure for bringing in the millennium."[157] As Nayler says plainly, not only is "self dead" for those who are truly righteous, but for them "flesh and blood is an enemy."[158] The consequence of union with Christ is that his perfect body has taken the place of the sinful flesh. Dismissing controversies about the symbolic significance of the Lord's Supper, Nayler says that whenever people eat any food whatsoever they "discern Christ's body in their eating, who is the body of all creatures, and filleth all things in heaven and in earth." (No doubt this idea came to seem disturbingly heterodox even to Quakers: the 1716 edition silently respiritualized Nayler's thought by calling Christ "the life and upholder of all creatures," whereas Nayler had provocatively called him "the body of all creatures.")[159] No act of eating should ever be secular or indulge in the fleshly pleasures that, according to Nayler, attended the routine meals of the same theologians who argued so earnestly about the Lord's Supper.

Quaker solemnity was intended to bear witness to this antiworldly ideal. Although Puritans were notorious enemies of sports and games, in Nayler's opinion they fell woefully short of practicing what they preached, as he declared in a critique of his former colleagues among the Independents:

> Many other things I cannot own [i.e., approve] you in, as your hunting, coursing, keeping dogs for your pleasure, bowls, shuffleboard, or such sports used by the heathen; but never by any of the saints, for they were redeemed from these vanities, and prayed that their eyes might not behold vanities, and waited to redeem the time they had spent in the lusts of the flesh. Also your vain laughters, wanton jestings: but they who know Christ, know him a man of sorrows and acquainted with grief; but the wicked are as chaff, who shall not stand in judgment.[160]

A satirist might relish the image of saints playing shuffleboard, but a sense of humor is precisely what Nayler's position repudiates. Christ was a man of sorrows, and Christians should be wary of laughter.

Still the purged, solemn, and selfless self does have to go on living in the fallen world, where a constant awareness of its extreme vulnerability is unavoidable. The ambiguities of the self are strikingly brought out in a letter by Richard Farnsworth:

> I am now as a butt to be shot at . . . I am as Noah's dove turned out of all, and hath none to fly to but the Lord alone . . . I have no life nor comfort in anything whatsoever but in doing of his will . . . I am out of all friends and creatures whatsoever, and lives only by faith in the sense of the love and power of the Lord, and readeth in the Revelation much, and often that is the book that I preach out of. I am as a white paper book without any line or sentence, but as it is revealed and written by the Spirit, the revealer of secrets, so I administer.[161]

Any positive sense of self has been emptied out so that inspiration can be directly received, as it was by John of Patmos, of whose individual personality there is little if any hint in the Book of Revelation. Divine truth flows in upon the spiritualized mind just as literally and continuously as the data of phenomena flow in upon the empiricist mind, yet somehow the self in its negative sense is not altogether abolished after all: it is the butt at which the arrows of enemies are discharged, the

Friend who must live without friends, the creature that can have no contact with creatures, the dove that can find no firm ground but must believe by faith that the Lord's ark is waiting to receive it. This is very much an unselved self, liberated from the egotism of ordinary identity, yet threatened by the anomie of nonidentity. But the potential rewards are correspondingly great: not only the prestige of being a conduit of God's secrets, but also the mandate to carry out God's will: "so I administer."

Insofar as one does retain personal individuality, it must be in a new mode of existence irradiated by light and made "perfect" by total participation in Christ. All that survives of the old self is the eye, now open to divine illumination. According to Nayler, in Christ's covenant "we can truly say, here he is all and self is nothing, but abhorred because it is polluted, the eye being now open that's only taken with affection to that which is holy."[162] Wrong seeing is inexcusable, in the spirit of Christ's uncompromising demand in the Sermon on the Mount: "If thy right eye offend thee, pluck it out, and cast it from thee: for it is profitable for thee that one of thy members should perish, and not that thy whole body should be cast into hell" (Matthew 5: 29). So also Nayler on the eye of the flesh: "Were that eye plucked out, and you turned within, to see with that eye that is single, then the whole body would be full of light."[163] Conversely, to continue to see with a worldly eye is to be trapped in a fatal doubleness, as Fox declared: "These are they that have double eyes, whose bodies are full of darkness . . . Your eyes are double, your minds are double, your hearts are double."[164]

For the paradoxically selfless self, the everyday world is thus an occlusion, and Nayler pleads with his readers to struggle free from it so that "with the light of Christ in your own hearts you may see how the world's lusts have spoiled your souls of that heavenly image, and hath captivated your minds into its self and likeness, and how you lie dead in sin, covered with earth, and daubed over with the words of men."[165] In this formulation, fallen language both mirrors and creates the fallen state of bondage, as the earth with which the sufferer is "daubed over" is made up of "the words of men." But properly understood the world is irradiated by divine light and can take on a full reality of which the state of suffering is merely an illusory shadow. The language of John Everard's 1642 translation of a German mystical writer closely anticipates the attitude of the early Quakers:

The exterior world, and whatsoever outwardly is to be seen or is done, is only an accident and a certain signifying figure of the true and interior nature: and there is nothing true in all those things which are seen with the eye, that is substantial; for it behooveth that the frame of this world perish, because it is nothing else but an imaginary world, and a figure of the right true eternal, and by itself the constant world.[166]

As with Blake, who made similar assertions about a world transformed by vision, there is a strong temptation to Gnostic dualism, in which the ordinary phenomena of experience become merely "dirt upon my feet, no part of me."[167] A learned Independent divine, John Owen, who was vice-chancellor of Oxford University and close to Cromwell, published a Latin work in 1658 entitled *Pro Sacris Scripturis Adversus Hujus Temporis Fanaticos*, in which he expressly compared Quaker perfectionism with the heresies of the early Gnostics.[168]

All of these formulations are inevitably slippery, referring as they must to an interlocking structure of highly volatile beliefs. So far as Gnosticism goes, the Puritans have often been described as emphasizing Old Testament attitudes rather than Greek ones, but the remoteness and implacability of their God does not, in fact, make one think of the loving though offended parent of the Hebrew Bible. As Harold Fisch has cogently argued, "The stress upon the utterly transcendent nature of God; the purely spiritual character of our relation to him; his distance from the world, which becomes a place of evil under the dominion of Satan; the necessity for some Mediator to overcome this distance by standing between 'our pollution and the spotless purity of God'; these are in essence not Hebraic, but Greek and Gnostic modes of thinking."[169] The Quakers began as Puritans, and they did agree with the Puritans that Satan was lord of this world; but the Quakers' God was utterly immediate rather than mysterious and remote, and it was by participating fully in him that the saints were enabled to soar free from the pollution of the world. This position too, however, is a mode of Gnosticism, claiming to live in a world illuminated by the spirit while rejecting nearly all of the phenomena that are normally associated with the world. Fox describes how in his youth he "fasted much, and walked abroad in solitary places many days, and often took my Bible and went and sat in hollow trees and lonesome places till night came on; and frequently in the night walked mournfully about by myself." This isolation was deliberate. Belonging to no sect, he had given himself to the Lord, "and taken leave of father and mother and all other relations, and travelled up and down as a stranger in the earth." Indeed, a principal reason to keep forever on the move was a fear of what human contact might lead to: "For I durst not stay long in any place, being afraid both of professor and profane, lest, being a tender young man, I should be hurt by conversing much with either."[170]

Perfect because passive, selfless because assimilated into physical union with Christ, the early Quakers comprehensively denounced the Puritan psychology in which they had grown up, the theology by which it was undergirded, and the social order whose enabling ideology it had become. In all of this their posture of superiority and their prophetic wrath made them outstandingly offensive to the majority of their contemporaries. By the middle of the 1650s their critics, secular as well as clerical, were more than ready to deal them a blow if an opportunity should happen to occur. Riding into Bristol on horseback while his companions sang hosannas and strewed garments before him, James Nayler would give them that opportunity.

3

Nayler's Sign
and Its Meanings

Leadership and Charisma

James Nayler's quick intelligence was particularly needed when the Quaker movement reached London, where some of the north-country missionaries found themselves out of their depth. As Francis Howgill reported with evident alarm, "Here are the highest and the subtlest that we have to deal withal that ever was in any age. It is for none to come here but hath a sharp sword and well skilled to handle it."[1] Nayler was an accomplished spiritual swordsman, holding meetings that were attended by members of Cromwell's entourage, army officers, and prominent clergymen.[2] According to theory all Quakers were equal and there could be no such thing as leaders. In practice some people did become leaders, and Nayler was obviously one of them. It had certainly been under Fox's influence that the movement originally gained self-awareness in the north, where Higginson in 1653 called him "the ring leader of this crew."[3] By 1656, however, many outsiders believed that Nayler rather than Fox was the "head" or "chief" person in the movement; the Genoese ambassador referred to him as the *capo dei Tremolanti*.[4] It appears that Fox, despite his immense success as an itinerant preacher in the north and west, was relatively ineffective in London; certainly he rarely spent much time there.[5]

Nayler's preaching style seems to have been at once challenging and comforting, as an early convert indicated in a letter: "The words which you wrote to me were exceedingly serviceable to me; . . . they were like arrows in my heart and yet like ointment."[6] Outsiders got the impression that Nayler was more than just an admired preacher: his charisma had gained for him a potent degree of authority. When John Deacon complained to a London Quaker that Nayler thought perfection was possible in the present life, "the aforesaid A. A. called me liar and child of the Devil, till producing the book itself I read unto him Nayler's own words; which when he heard, he said, 'Doth James say so?' I answered, 'Yes.' 'Nay then,' said he, 'It is truth.' So far are they bewitched with his delusion, as to steer their faith by his unstable and vitiated brain."[7]

Visiting London in October 1656, less than a week before Nayler's disaster at Bristol, a northerner wrote anxiously to Margaret Fell, "It's like there is an evil thing begot amongst Friends in that city, the same as was amongst the church at Corinth, divisions and strife and contention, one saying 'I am of James,' another saying 'I am of Francis [Howgill] and Edward [Burrough]': so it's like that Truth will suffer by them."[8] The writer was alluding to Paul's plea for unity and his repudiation of any primacy in his own name: "It hath been declared unto me . . . that there are contentions among you. Now this I say, that every one of you saith, I am of Paul; and I of Apollos; and I of Cephas; and I of Christ. Is Christ divided? Was Paul crucified for you? Or were ye baptized in the name of Paul?" (1 Corinthians 1: 11–13). The allusion is complicated, since the whole point of Paul's comment in the epistle is to urge that Christians should not divide into parties. Nayler's supporters certainly knew this, and if they really did go around saying "I am of James," they must have intended a sarcastic allusion to the epistle, implying that Nayler represented the true Spirit and that his rivals were the sort of schismatics to whom Paul objected. Yet Paul did become the acknowledged leader after all; we speak of Pauline, not of Cephasine, Christianity.

The fullest account of what happened in London in 1656 was given half a century later by George Whitehead in a biographical introduction to his *Collection of Sundry Books* by Nayler. Whitehead clearly saw his main problem to be an explanation of Nayler's scandalous "fall." One epigraph on his title page is Daniel 11: 35, "And some of them of understanding shall fall, to try them, and to purge, and to make them white, &c." The remainder of the verse in Daniel, which Whitehead perhaps prudently omitted because of its millenarian theme, is "even to the time of the end: because it is yet for a time appointed." According to Whitehead the catastrophe that befell Nayler was, very simply, an assault by Satan, "that wicked one, the son of perdition, that spiritual Judas and betrayer, that Man of Sin" (p. v). Nayler's experience was thus explained as the result of a diabolically deluded imagination from which Christ eventually set him free.

Satan, it turns out, had accomplices in the clouding of Nayler's understanding: his "turbulent" and "imaginary" female admirers. Whitehead's account deserves to be read in full, in all the prolixity and indistinctness of its indignation:

> And some too much glorying in and admiring the said J. N. above his brethren, tended to his hurt and loss, as soon after followed; insomuch that he came to be ensnared through the subtle Adversary's getting advantage upon him by means of some persons who too much gloried in him, and endeavoured to exalt him above his brethren; and also to cause division between him and them. For so it came to pass, according as J. N. related to me some time after the Lord had restored him out of his bewildered and suffering state, that a few forward, conceited, imaginary women, especially one Martha Simmonds and some others, under pretence of some divine motions, grew somewhat turbulent, and interrupting the ministry and service of the said F. Howgill and E. Burrough in some public meetings, they reproving her and her party and manifesting their dislike thereto, seeing their forwardness, indiscretion and hurt they did in some meetings, interrupting the public service wherein those faithful and able ministers, F. H. and E. B. were engaged. Whereupon the said Martha and another woman went and made their complaint to James Nayler against the said F. H. and E. B. endeavouring to set him against them, and to draw a judgment from him against them; which not obtaining from him (for he was afraid to pass judgment upon his brethren as they desired) whereupon the said Martha fell into a passion in a kind of mourning or weeping, and bitterly crying out with a mournful shrill voice, saying, "I looked for judgment, but behold a cry!" And with that cried aloud in a passionate lamenting manner, which so entered and pierced poor James Nayler that it smote him down into so much sorrow and sadness that he was much dejected in spirit or disconsolate; fears and doubting then

entered him, that he came to be clouded in his understanding, bewildered, and at a loss in his judgment. Thus (poor man) he stood not in his dominion (as he should have done) over that dividing, false transforming spirit, which sought to sow discord among brethren; which for a time caused some estrangement and distance in him from his brethren and true friends. The substance of the foregoing relation, how J. N. came to be ensnared and to such a loss, he himself gave me the account, as we were walking together in the field at Great Strickland in Westmoreland, 1657, after we had both been at a meeting of Friends on Stricklandheath. (pp. vi–vii)

(The date, incidentally, cannot be right; in 1657 Nayler was in solitary confinement in Bridewell.)

In this account, the actual nature of Nayler's "fall" is utterly opaque. It looks as if the women's interruptions in Quaker meetings had some connection with their excessive adoration of Nayler, but that is far from explicit. All we are told is that they interrupted Howgill and Burrough, who were two of the most eminent Quaker preachers in London, and that when they were reproved they demanded that Nayler give a "judgment" against his colleagues. This he was unwilling to do; not only was he evidently reluctant to assert authority, but these were old friends. Howgill had been imprisoned with Nayler at Appleby at the very inception of the movement, and had written at that time, "James . . . is as a father to me."[9] But somehow Nayler's refusal to judge precipitated a psychological collapse. Once he had refused to give "a judgment" his own "judgment" was occluded: "bewildered and at a loss in his judgment." Whitehead's explanation is a demonizing one that identifies an agency external to all of the people involved: the women were merely instruments of "that dividing, false transforming spirit" who acts in continual subversion of the true Spirit and can transform everything into its opposite.

However Whitehead may have understood the story long afterward (and he had in any case tactical reasons for reducing it to a simple case of psychological disturbance), homage to charismatic figures was common in the early Quaker movement. Margaret Fell wrote to Fox (whom long afterward she married), "O thou fountain of eternal life, our souls thirsts after thee, for in thee alone is our life and peace, and without thee have we no peace: for our souls is much refreshed by seeing thee, and our lives is preserved by thee, O thou father of eternal felicity." This was hardly a private communication: it was cosigned by two of her daughters and by four other Friends. Quoting this letter, Braithwaite admits, "Such a document reveals the tendencies which in their acute form produced the disaster of James Nayler's fall. If the countryside had seen it, it would have confirmed the belief that Margaret Fell was bewitched and that Fox was a blasphemer."[10] Fox's other associates often addressed him in writing with epithets that suggested the Messiah: "who art one with the Father," "who is dead and alive, and forever lives," "thou god of life and power," and so on.[11] For many early Quakers, Fox clearly took the place of the father against whom they had rebelled. Francis Howgill, whose own status would later be threatened by Nayler's followers in London, wrote to Fox: "Glory for evermore, I am melted, I am melted with thy love it is not lawful to utter, pray for me thy dear son."[12] It is unclear what was "not lawful to utter," but Howgill's enthusiasm is unmistakable.

Since Quaker perfectionism depended on total abolition of selfhood, charismatic leadership could be acceptable only if it seemed impersonal, an irradiation by the divine Spirit rather than a consequence of personal abilities. Richard Farnsworth cautioned in an early letter to Nayler, "Mind that which keeps in humbleness and lowliness of mind. See the condition of the souls that went before; they exhort to lowliness of mind." Nayler himself was ready to reprove severely those who violated this ideal. "Richard Myers," he wrote in 1653, "thou gets above thy condition. Mind the babe in thee, and it will tell you so. And, Friend, thou that calls thyself a prophet art run up into the air. Lowly consider it."[13] The gift of prophecy was the very reverse of a mandate for self-promotion. It is notable that a year before the Bristol crisis Nayler himself received a prophetic warning from an elderly minister:

Take good heed while thou forbears to have outward reverence of men, as capping and kneeling and the like, that thou steal not men's hearts away from God to thyself and so lord it on their conscience that they have neither God, nor Scripture, nor any privilege of their own experience, but take thee as a demi-god and to make a mental idol, which is a worse kind of idolatry than all that thou reproves, for this hath more possibility to deceive, if it were possible, the very elect.[14]

Unlike the Calvinist elect, the Quaker elect were entirely capable of being deceived to their eternal damnation, and this warning suggests that Nayler's personal magnetism was attracting adverse comment well before his "fall."

Prophetic charisma, also, seemed to skeptics to have a dangerously coercive aspect. Contemporaries spoke of Fox's ability to stare at people as if he could see into their very souls—"Don't pierce me so with thy eyes! Keep thy eyes off me!"[15]—and parents often complained that their teenaged children had been seduced by the irrational when they became Quakers. The modern analogy would be the appeal of cults, whose assumptions are so deeply internalized that they can only be overcome by elaborate "deprogramming." What was at stake was not simple delusion, let alone "madness" (except in a few cases, which the Quakers themselves repudiated) but rather a deep commitment to an all-embracing belief system that was felt to supersede completely the person's prior life. Puritan preaching, with its constant emphasis on conversion and spiritual rebirth, made it natural to expect a total change of this kind, and unlike most sects at the time the Quaker movement claimed to provide unqualified inner happiness. From their own point of view the Quaker prophets were simply acting as passive conduits for divine authority; any power that was exerted was entirely that of the Spirit. But this made it all the more difficult for Nayler to know what to do when followers who admired him were demanding that he assert himself.

What did go on, then, in those months of disruption in London before Nayler reenacted Christ's entry into Jerusalem? An important key to understanding the situation is the role played by the "turbulent" women who proclaimed his primacy, urged him to reprove Burrough and Howgill, and somehow precipitated a breakdown when he refused.

Turbulent Women and the Erotics of Belief

Ever since the Middle Ages, radical movements and sects, with their promise of spiritual if not social equality, had attracted an unusually large proportion of female members. This was especially true of the Quakers. Of approximately three hundred women of all sects who wrote or prophesied during the 1650s, more than two-thirds were Quakers; there were many women among the itinerant preachers, and many who went to jail.[16]

In all of the radical sects there were women who "prophesied," but they were generally regarded as marginal and went virtually unmentioned in official histories of the Independents and Baptists. And although there were a good many women visionaries in the 1640s and 1650s, it makes no sense to lump them together as a single category. Some were mentally disturbed, and a few were obviously crazy; there are stories of trances that lasted for months at a time. At the other extreme, some were perfectly rational, and their "visions" were clearly allegorical. Most of these women, not surprisingly, were co-opted by men, who seized the chance to use their prophecies for polemical purposes, as the militant Fifth Monarchists did with Anna Trapnel. The author of one survey, who does not mention the Nayler case, has found no instances in which women were alleged to have "led" or deluded men.[17]

Only the Quakers, for whom any notion of an authorized ministry was anathema, permitted women to preach regularly as opposed to occasional utterance of prophetic mysteries. The reactions of non-Quakers ranged from condescension to outrage, indicating that women preachers were felt to be much more threatening than women visionaries. Unfortunately the women themselves left few writings—Quaker preaching by definition was spontaneous and oral—and we know them mainly through their antagonists, who have been accurately described as "invariably emotional, hostile, inexact, banal, and polemical."[18] Still, it is clear that Quaker women differed in a fundamental way from other visionaries of the time such as Anna Trapnel and Sarah Wight, who entered passive trance states and pronounced their message in traditional female imagery of motherhood and whoredom. The Quaker women preachers were more disturbing to their hearers because there was nothing passive or unconscious about their preaching. Moreover, instead of confirming traditional female roles they proclaimed a genderless state of self-transcendence that gave them the same authority as the male prophets of the Bible, identifying with Amos and Isaiah rather than with Deborah and Jael.[19]

The full implications of what was meant by the presence of Christ in each believer are suggested by an anecdote related by the baffled Higginson and repeated by later polemicists:

One Williamson's wife, a disciple of [James] Milner's, when she came to see him at Appleby, said in the hearing of divers there . . .

that she was the eternal Son of God; and when the men that
heard her told her that she was a woman, and therefore could not
be the Son of God, she said, "No, you are women, but I am a
man." These last words I insert, that the reader may see how
strongly the spirits of some of these people are transported, and
how ready they are to affirm any thing however impious or
absurd.[20]

Here again is an indication of the radicalism of the early Quakers:
gender distinctions that were fundamental to orthodox theology were
dismissed as both mistaken and irrelevant. If Christ can be present
only in men, then Mistress Williamson is a man; conversely, if those
who are incapable of receiving the indwelling presence of Christ are
women, then her accusers are women. The result, from the point of
view of non-Quakers, was a threatening oxymoron, "their mankind
women" as John Deacon called them.[21]

Genderlessness, however, is not affirmation of gender equality, and
may even seem to be the reverse. During the first decades of the seventeenth century, court records indicate an intense concern with
keeping "unruly women" in their place, and although the Quakers
professed spiritual equality and permitted women to preach, they too
continued to assert traditional standards of sexual hierarchy: they were
no more willing than the rest of their contemporaries to give up the
authority of men over women, fathers over children, masters over servants, or colonial planters over Indians and Negro slaves.[22] And in fact
nearly all of the Quaker women preachers combined their homiletic
and prophetic performances with domestic competence and depend-
ability of a traditionally feminine kind.[23]

The symbolism of the female likewise remained conflicted. To
some extent writers of both sexes used imagery of feminine passivity
and nurturing in deliberate contrast to masculine aggressiveness,
which they identified with the repudiated selfhood.[24] But more usually
female symbolism remained negative, as Nayler demonstrated in a
meditation on the marriage of the soul with Christ its spouse:

Now Christ and he is one, married to him, and Christ is his head
and husband; and now the head speaks, prayeth, and praiseth, and
prophesies, and is uncovered; and here is the church of the first-
born, the pillar and ground of truth, where the woman must be

covered and kept silent, and is not to speak in the church, is not to usurp authority, but is to be in subjection; and if she would know any thing, let her ask of her husband at home, and he is to her a covering of the eyes for ever.[25]

In a fascinating way the Quaker position on "hat honor" merges here with the Pauline symbolism of the female. "Every man praying or prophesying," Paul says, "having his head covered, dishonoreth his head" (1 Corinthians 11: 4). This was the basis of the Quaker willingness to remove the hat when praying, while refusing to remove it when addressing anyone lower than God himself. But in the next verse Paul adds, "Every woman that prayeth or prophesieth with her head uncovered, dishonoreth her head." And three chapters later he issues the directive that Nayler interprets allegorically in the passage just quoted: "Let your women keep silence in the churches: for it is not permitted unto them to speak; but they are commanded to be under obedience, as also saith the law. And if they will learn any thing, let them ask their husbands at home: for it is a shame for women to speak in the church" (14: 34–35). Precisely the same paradox appears in Blake, who urged spiritual (and also sexual) freedom for women, but retained the symbolism of the "female will" as a dark and destructive force. Nayler, like his Quaker colleagues, gave great encouragement to individual women, but continued to invoke the symbolism of the female as the part of the self that must be obedient and silent, "covered" by the male principle on the analogy of being covered by a hat during worship. No doubt the metaphor gained force from the common-law principle of *feme covert*, by which a married women was under the protection of her husband and lacked legal rights of her own.

Given this complicated view of gender, the early Quakers had a particularly ambiguous relationship to what may be called the erotics of faith. Conversion stories are frequently rich in erotic analogies, especially when they claim direct invasion of a human being by the divine Spirit, for which the metaphor of sexual union is irresistible and may well seem to be more than merely metaphorical. The language of the Song of Songs was regularly used by early Quakers of both sexes. "My dear and precious sister in whom my life is bound up," Ann Audland wrote to Margaret Fell, "after thee my life breatheth . . . My dear and near and eternal mother, by thee I am nourished . . . My heart is open into thy bosom." Margaret Fell received similar tributes from Ann

Audland's husband John: "Thou art bound up in me sealed closed and enjoyed for evermore: thy garments are sweet thy countenance is beautiful and glorious; breathe to me more and more and I shall feel thee I am open to thee my most dear sister."[26] "My heart, my life, my oneness," Farnsworth addressed Fox, "thou art ever with me. Thou lies within my bowels. Thou knowest where I am, I cannot be hid from thee, thou knowest my secrets."[27]

If anything, the strongest emotional relationships of the "First Publishers of Truth" were homosocial, though doubtless not overtly homoerotic. The itinerant preachers traveled in same-sex pairs to deflect any suspicion of illicit relationships, which of course made male bonding all the stronger. Thomas Camm described the marriage of John and Ann Audland in tepid terms as "a great comfort and blessing to each other, while they both lived together." But most of the time they did not live together, since Audland was traveling with Thomas Camm's father John: "Their hearts being firmly knit together, as David and Jonathan, by the bond of unspeakable love, their very lived being endearedly bound up in each other." This was not an exclusive relationship; something very similar also subsisted between young Thomas and his father's colleague: "I was from my childhood very intimately acquainted with him, and loved him with a brotherly love . . . Many comfortable days and times have I enjoyed with him, whom I loved and honoured in the Lord, and I am not unsensible of his love to me, our hearts being perfectly united and knit together, in that love that's everlasting, passing the love of women."[28] Francis Howgill used the same allusion to lament separation from Edward Burrough: "My beloved yokefellow and I now must part, who hath borne the yoke so long together, which was precious one to the other as our own lives . . . My very life I have with him whose bow, sword and spear never returned empty from the slain of the mighty, and often we have sung together at the dividing of the spoil."[29] Howgill was recalling David's lament for Jonathan: "From the blood of the slain, from the fat of the mighty, the bow of Jonathan turned not back, and the sword of Saul returned not empty" (2 Samuel 1: 22). A few verses later comes the famous text, "Thy love to me was wonderful, passing the love of women" (1: 26).

Along with these passionate declarations by both men and women went an extreme prudery regarding actual sex. As Mary Douglas observes, virginity is often a special ideal of minority groups that feel themselves to be threatened, symbolizing the body "as an imperfect container which will only be perfect if it can be made impermeable."[30] Officially, at least, celibacy was never a Quaker principle.[31] But a number of Quakers did make a point of practicing it, and the itinerant preachers were separated from their spouses for many months, sometimes even years, at a time, not to speak of their long periods of incarceration. And even if sexual relations were not actually discouraged, an excessive interest in them would certainly have been seen as symptomatic of attraction to the things of this world. Baxter accused the Quakers of "extolling monastical community and virginity."[32]

Whatever their theoretical position, Quakers had a practical motive to be more "puritanical" than the Puritans on the score of sexual temptation, since sin of any kind was catastrophic evidence of lack of grace, and sexual lapses were obvious to oneself if not to others. In his attack on Puritan attitudes, Hobbes observed:

> Whereas they did, both in their sermons and writings, maintain and inculcate that the very first motions of the mind, that is to say, the delight men and women took in the sight of one another's form, though they checked the proceeding thereof so that it never grew up to be a design, was nevertheless a sin, they [thus] brought young men into desperation and to think themselves damned, because they could not (which no man can, and is contrary to the constitution of nature) behold a delightful object without delight.[33]

That was certainly the Calvinist position: in man's fallen state "the very first motions of the mind" are irretrievably corrupt, and if they give pleasure, so much the worse. This heritage the Quakers never cast off. No wonder then that they denounced the "love of creatures" every bit as fiercely as the Puritans did. The fact that their hated doppelgangers, the Ranters, rejoiced in the pleasures of the flesh made it all the more essential to "check the proceeding" before it could get started.

Contemporary critics were particularly eager to find evidence that Nayler had sexual relations with his female admirers, and if possible to prove that he thought it harmless to do so, which would have identified him with the Ranter position. Such charges formed a central part of the "short history of Nayler's life" that was presented to Parliament during his trial, alleging that he was "a member of an Independent church, but cast out for blasphemy and suspicion of lewdness with one Mrs. Roper. After he had been up and down, he went to visit the Quakers in Cornwall, where he was committed as a wanderer; his principles being, that he may lie with any woman that is of his own judgment."[34] In response Nayler declared indignantly, "All that knew me, in the army and elsewhere, will say I was never guilty of lewdness, or so reputed. I abhor filthiness. See if any can accuse" (p. 46). But on the metaphorical level he had to acknowledge the erotic language his admirers had used: "As to those words of the woman, 'Arise my love, my dove, my fairest one, why stayest thou amongst the pots?' I own it no other way than as it was spoken in the Canticles, of Christ's church."[35]

Metaphorically, then, the Quakers rejoiced in the lush erotic imagery of the Song of Songs, but in a literal sense their ideal was asexual. As William Sewel concisely summarized Nayler's temperament, "He was a man of great self-denial." Sewel also reported that "as to what hath been divulged concerning his committing of fornication, I never could find, though very inquisitive in the case, that he was in the least guilty thereof."[36] Swift would have loved the hint of prurience in "though very inquisitive in the case," but Sewel was certainly anxious to clear Nayler's good name. As for the preachers' wives, they, like Anne Nayler, had to manage their farms, shops, or estates by themselves, as well as care for children. One wife complained that she would rather have married a drunkard than a Quaker preacher, because then she would at least have known that she could find him at the ale-house.[37] Nayler, it seems, was unusual in inspiring fervent devotion in female admirers, and this may well have influenced the way he was regarded by his fellow preachers as well as by later interpreters.

And what of Martha Simmonds, the presumed ringleader of the women's group? She has had an exceedingly bad press even from biographers of Nayler, let alone from partisans of Fox. Even the recent author of a defense of "the women around James Nayler" comes only to the weak conclusion that some of his male followers were just as outrageous as his female ones.[38] But Martha Simmonds was an intelligent and arresting person, and the significance of her role in the Nayler story can be deduced between the lines of the surviving evidence. In 1655 and 1656, in her early thirties, she published two pamphlets of apocalyptic tendency at the printing house of her brother, Giles

Calvert, who was Nayler's regular publisher; her husband, Thomas Simmonds, was the other leading publisher of Quaker books.[39] In her writings realities supplant types in a way that anticipates Nayler's enactment at Bristol: "All that have a desire to come this way must lay down your crowns at the feet of Jesus, for now a profession of words will no longer cover, for the Lord is come to look for fruit, all types and shadows is flying away; and he that will come in may inherit substance, and he that will not shall be left naked."[40] She was also interested in exhibiting "signs" of the kind that we will consider shortly; at Colchester during a period of proselytizing she "was moved to walk in sackcloth barefoot with her hair spread and ashes upon her head, in the town, in the frosty weather, to the astonishment of many."[41] In addition to the many Old Testament precedents, this was probably an apocalyptic gesture: "I will give power unto my two witnesses, and they shall prophesy a thousand two hundred and threescore days, clothed in sackcloth" (Revelation 11: 3).

Above all Martha Simmonds was a "seeker" who, by her own account, was perpetually unsatisfied by those who presented themselves as guides. A glimpse of her spiritual biography can be gathered from her 1655 pamphlet *A Lamentation for the Lost Sheep of the House of Israel.* Before referring to her own experience, Simmonds urges an entirely standard version of Quaker theology, imploring the reader to open the "inward eye" in order to discover "the royal diadem hid in thy unclean heart" (p. 1). One passage may conceivably allude to Nayler: "I counsel thee to prize thy time, and be still and staid and seek diligently for that messenger who is one of a thousand, who brings the glad tidings, who is the true teacher that cannot be removed into a corner" (3). But in any case this must refer to a John the Baptist figure—an analogy we will meet again in connection with Nayler—rather than to a reincarnation of Christ. For Christ is already fully present within each person, waiting for the soul to recognize him there: "Mind the light, the measure of Christ in you, that with it you may see where you are, that you may see his eternal love, how he calls and invites you into the kingdom, that he may take off your filthy garments, that he may clothe you with the garment of righteousness and marry you unto himself" (5).

After this plea Simmonds closes the pamphlet with a personal account of earnest seeking, which was apparently interrupted by a period of complacency, if not license, over a period of two decades (divided into biblically conventional seven-year segments). The account is solemn and totally unfanatical, testifying to an interior pilgrimage rather than to public controversy, and it deserves to be read at length:

> And now in the tenderness of my heart longing for your soul's good am I made open to you, having had a habitation in this city of London some time; for seven years together I wandered up and down the streets enquiring of those that had the image of honesty in their countenance, where I might find an honest minister, for I saw my soul in death, and that I was in the first nature, and wandering from one idol's temple to another, and from one private meeting to another; I heard a sound of words amongst them but no substance could I find, and the more I sought after them the more trouble came on me, and finding none sensible of my condition, I kept it in, and kept all close within me; and about the end of seven years hunting and finding no rest, the Lord opened a little glimmerings of light to me and quieted my spirit; and then for about seven years more he kept me still from running after men, and all this time I durst not meddle with any thing of God, nor scarce take his name in my mouth, because I knew him not, it living wild and wanton not knowing a cross to my will I spent this time; it something I found breathing in me groaning for deliverance, crying out, "Oh when shall I see the day of thy appearance;" about the end of the last seven years the Lord opened my eyes to see a measure of himself in me, which when I saw I waited diligently in it, and being faithful to it I found this light more and more increase, which brought me into a day of trouble, and through it, and through a warfare and to the end of it, and now hath given me a resting place with him; "and this is my beloved, and this is my friend O daughters of Jerusalem" [Song of Songs 5: 16] (5–6)

One thing is clear: Martha Simmonds had always been anxious to "find an honest minister," and her way of asserting interior peace made her a constant irritant to the many ministers whose claims she found wanting. Her crying out for the day of the Lord's appearance was perceived by the Quaker leadership as a direct challenge to themselves, especially since she freely interrupted them in their meetings. Richard Hubberthorne poured out a heartfelt complaint on this score in a letter to Margaret Fell, who constantly monitored Quaker activity from her stronghold in the north:

> When we had waited in silence a while, she stood up and spoke, judging all Friends that they were not come to the cross . . . And then she fell on singing, with an unclean spirit. And the substance of that which she said in her singing was, Innocency, innocency, many times over, for the space of one hour or more, but in the power of the Lord I was moved to speak soon after she begun . . . Then the word of life in others rose against her, and when she saw the power of God arising against her, and reign over her in those that were ready to be stumbled by her before then, she was tormented against me, and cried of deep subtlety, for a long time together, turning it into a song, And that we were all the beast, and I [was] the head of the beast, but the day was a day to the Lord, that the life of God in many was raised from under a thick cloud which was come over, and it was a day of washing of the garments of many that were spotted and stained through offence, but the Lord God is arising to his eternal glory, and is bringing his image and brightness from under a cloud, and chaining the dragon.[42]

This was to turn the Quakers' weapons against them with a vengeance: just as they resented having their own meetings disrupted in the way that they disrupted others, so they were furious at being identified with the servants of Antichrist, whom they regularly identified with orthodox Puritan "priests."

Since Nayler had been a particularly eloquent critic of "antichristian" ministers who presumed to exert authority, it is easy to see why Martha Simmonds would be drawn to him as her champion. The Quaker movement was supposed to permit total freedom and equality for all of its members, but Hubberthorne and his allies Burrough and Howgill (who had recently returned to London after a missionary journey) were now boldly asserting authority. They were, in fact, turning themselves into professional ministers, which by definition might seem to make them servants of the Beast. The ultimate confrontation was bound to be with Fox, who was seldom in London but had clearly assumed headship of the movement everywhere in England. By 1655 Fox was routinely telling itinerant preachers where they should go, even if it meant countermanding "drawings" or "leadings" that they felt they had received to travel in some particular direction.[43]

A letter Burrough wrote to Martha Simmonds herself tells the same story of uncontrolled prophesying and resistance to authority.

> This is the truth from the Lord God concerning thee Martha Simmonds, thou and [those] who follows thy spirit: you are out of the truth, out of the way, out of the power, out of the wisdom, and out of the life of God; for you are turned from the light of Christ Jesus . . . and doth disobey it, and follow a lying spirit . . . It is not the spirit of God, but the voice of the stranger [John 10: 5] which you follow; and are become goats, rough and hairy. Though some of you have prophesied in the name of Christ, yet now are you workers of iniquity.[44]

Nayler's refusal of Simmonds's request to give a "judgment" against his colleagues was consistent with his belief that it would be presumptuous to take sides in the workings of the Spirit, and he evidently felt that now she was herself asserting an authority no person should claim. According to Hubberthorne, Nayler "told her that she sought to have the dominion and charged her to go home and follow her calling," presumably as a housewife.[45] When she and her companions met his refusal with passionate lamentation, however, he abruptly fell into fears and doubts.

Whitehead's account contains an important clue in Martha's bitter exclamation, "I looked for judgment, but behold a cry!" This comes from Isaiah; in the passage just preceding it Isaiah foretells that after the Lord has passed judgment on the proud daughters of Zion, "seven women shall take hold of one man, saying, We will eat our own bread, and wear our own apparel; only let us be called by thy name, to take away our reproach" (Isaiah 4: 1). No doubt this was applied to their own case by the Naylerite women. In Isaiah the coming of the Messiah is then foretold, followed by the song of the vineyard from which Martha Simmonds was quoting: the rejected vineyard will be trodden down and laid waste, since it has brought forth nothing but wild grapes, "for the vineyard of the Lord of hosts is the house of Israel, and the men of Judah his pleasant plant: and he looked for judgment, but behold oppression; for righteousness, but behold a cry" (5: 7). Evidently the symbolic implication was that Nayler had abdicated his role as prophet, and that by refusing to give a judgment he abetted oppression, from which a helpless cry but no righteousness then ensued.

To the Quaker leaders it appeared that Nayler had simply lost his reason, and he does seem to have experienced some kind of collapse. Hubberthorne, writing at the time, was vague about what the women said but clear about its result:

> Something to that effect did she [Hannah Stranger] and Martha speak to him, which word he received to be the word of the Lord, and coming under the power of their words, judgment came upon him, and trembling night and day, while he was in London, for some nights lying upon a table. And then their reigns and deceits got up especially in Martha to glory and boast over all, and now an exceeding filthy spirit is got up in her, more filthy than any that yet departed out of the truth, and with it labours to break and destroy the meetings if it were possible.[46]

The harmony of the meetings was obviously imperiled, and Nayler, overcome by Martha Simmonds's prophetic rebuke, lay trembling on a table. Nayler's group may possibly have interpreted this reaction as a salutary trance state during which he was opening himself to divine guidance.[47] But the great majority of the Quakers were clearly alarmed and regarded it as evidence of serious mental disturbance. To them it seemed that Martha must have subjected Nayler to some species of witchcraft, and Dewsbury told her so: "The righteous seed is burthened with thee, who hath in thy deceitful practice opened the mouth of the enemies of God to blaspheme his name, and through thy sorcery hath abused the simplicity."[48] Burrough likewise accused her of bewitching Nayler and in a letter to her claimed that she had a "lying spirit of divination."[49] This became the standard Quaker position, excusing or at least explaining Nayler's errors by displacing them onto his female associates. But of course charges of supernatural influence could just as well run the other way, as they did in the government-controlled newspaper *Mercurius Politicus:* "Thus you see how this wretched impostor hath prevailed upon his followers, to bewitch them to the committing of strange absurdities and the uttering of many horrible blasphemies, the like for all circumstances never heard of in any age before."[50] How could so many people have been persuaded to adore Nayler unless Nayler himself had somehow seduced them?

Martha Simmonds herself, responding to the charge that she had
bewitched Nayler, defended her behavior with eloquent clarity:

> Being among the people called Quakers in London, I was moved
> to declare to the world, and often they would judge me exceed-
> ingly, that I was too forward to run before I was sent, and never-
> theless I loved them well, as being men of pure life, but I was
> moved by the Power, I could not stay though they sometimes de-
> nied me, yet I was forced to go, and my word did prosper; . . . and
> then I was moved of the Lord to go to James Nayler, and tell him
> I wanted justice, and he being harsh to me, at length the words
> came to me to speak to him, which I did, and struck him down:
> 'How are the mighty men fallen, I came to Jerusalem and behold
> a cry, and behold an oppression,' which pierced and struck him
> down with tears from that day; and he lay from that day in ex-
> ceeding sorrow for about three days, and all that while the Power
> arose in me, which I did not expect . . . Then they all concluded
> that I had bewitched him, when alas I was as innocent as a child,
> and they (because he could not go amongst them) all set upon me,
> that I had bewitched him.[51]

As always in this complicated story, there was no disagreement about
what had happened; it was the meaning of it all that was so hard to
establish.

The Howgill-Burrough version, not surprisingly, became the
Quaker authorized one. According to William Sewel in the next century, narrating these events as Whitehead did from a distance of more
than sixty years, "Some forward and inconsiderate women, of whom
Martha Simmons was the chief, assumed the boldness to dispute with
F. Howgill and E. Burrough openly in their preaching, and thus to
disturb the meetings: whereupon they, who were truly excellent
preachers, did not fail, according to their duty, to reprove this indis-
cretion." Sewel's magisterial periods could not altogether obscure his
uneasiness about rebuking women for doing what men were freely
permitted to do, so he added a somewhat casuistical footnote to distinguish mere speaking from prophesying:

> These women's practice we may suppose to be somewhat like that
> which gave occasion to the apostle Paul to say, "Let your women

keep silence in the churches, for it is not permitted unto them to speak." 1 Cor. xiv. 34. This prohibition of speaking must be voluntary discourse by way of reasoning or disputing, and not when they had an immediate impulse or concern to prophesy; for the apostle in the same Epistle has defined prophecy to be speaking unto "men to edification, exhortation, and comfort," chap. xiv. 3. And has also, chap. xi, made express mention of women's praying and prophesying together with the men.[52]

Martha Simmonds, of course, would have retorted that the immediate impulse to prophesy was precisely what had inspired her, but it seems clear that prophecy was acceptable only when it was directed outside the group. If a woman was presumptuous enough to criticize the male leaders of the movement, she automatically opened herself to accusations of self-promotion and of a disputatiousness that proved she had lost "the power." When Simmonds was accused of having bewitched Nayler the implication was obvious that she was no longer a prophet but a witch.[53]

From Martha Simmonds' point of view, however, it was the leadership that was at fault and Nayler, with his often-expressed insistence on the emptying out of selfhood, who stood for true openness to the Spirit. Another autobiographical account, filled with anguish about the sinful self, helps to explain her later attraction to Nayler:

> O pure, eternal, perfect Lord God! . . . How I have been tossed to and fro in this dark world! Surely thou hadst a purpose to make use of me in thy will and time; for the devil hath set very sore against me; for before ever I saw the light of the sun, or received a natural birth in this visible world, I was rejected of men, for my parents denied me a birth; and as concerning self, it had been good I had not been born; for I have not had pleasure in this world, but have stood as one alone; and since I knew the way to thee, I have exceedingly hasted out of it.[54]

The normal Puritan cure for this condition was homeopathic: by dwelling ever more intensely on one's utter sinfulness, one gained conviction of God's grace and patience to wait for the consolations of the afterlife. The Quaker cure was diametrically opposed, seeking to escape immediately from a world in which the devil had the power to torment human beings with feelings of unworthiness. Simmonds's sense of radical isolation is particularly striking. Her parents seem to have somehow "denied" her a second, spiritual birth, condemning her to the world of sin; the solidarity of the Quaker group (including marriage to a sympathetic believer) became a refuge from the fallen world in which each person stands "as one alone." For such a temperament Nayler's appeal rested in the depth and conviction with which he seemed able to renounce self, to serve as a conduit or mouthpiece for the holy Spirit. But since this was a charisma based on radical passivity, it would have been grossly violated if Nayler had presumed to admonish, much less discipline, his followers. No wonder then that he suffered anxiety and doubt when Martha Simmonds and her allies demanded that he rebuke Burrough and Howgill, and accused him implicitly of abandoning his prophetic vocation when it became clear that he would not do so. At this moment the Quaker movement was facing a crisis, very much to its own surprise; Nayler found himself at the center of it and had no choice but to respond in some way.

Exeter Jail and the Breach with Fox

In August 1656, after a little more than a year in London, Nayler set out for the west. Fox had been imprisoned since January at Launceton in Cornwall, a Royalist stronghold, and Nayler intended to visit him there, presumably with the intention of seeking some sort of reconciliation after the troubles in London. The authorities were on the lookout for traveling Quakers, however, with a view to preventing their gathering in support of Fox. Nayler and a number of companions were therefore arrested on the way, charged with being rogues and vagabonds, and imprisoned at Exeter.

To be in jail was not necessarily a disaster, since if you are determined to reject the world, incarceration can help to confirm that you have done so. Bunyan, who after 1660 was in jail more often than out, wrote in his *Prison Meditations*,

> This gaol to us is as a hill,
> From whence we plainly see
> Beyond this world, and take our fill
> Of things that lasting be.[55]

Nayler himself, in a letter written in Appleby jail, indicated that inner freedom was promoted by forcible exclusion from the things of the world:

> I see myself set here as a sign to a people wholly given over to fulfill the lusts of the flesh, in all things beyond measure. I was made after the Sessions to refuse their diet, and since [then] to live upon bread and water, which cannot be believed by them; not that it is any bondage to me within or without, for it is my liberty and freedom, whereby the Lord hath set me above all other created things. Oh dear Friends, rejoice with me, for I see that to be taken out of all created things is perfect freedom, but no freedom till then.[56]

In negative terms, imprisonment was a barrier against all created things; in positive terms, Nayler was thereby exalted, "set *above* all other created things." But of course in being so exalted he no longer acted as an independent self, but rather as a vehicle for divine communication: "I see myself set here as a sign." It was as a sign that he was about to have his unexpected moment upon the tragic stage.

A letter written by Howgill and Audland in August 1656 indicates that apprehension was felt in the movement as the Nayler group took to the road, and reveals also the disorganization and apparent randomness of their movements. The original punctuation conveys the writers' bafflement and anxiety:

> We write by the last post: of those people passing out of the town: as it appeared they would have gone unknown: but did not: some friends followed: and the other in hasting lost one another: so they were parted in three, the two men was together and the other each alone: and the two men was found next day and went to an inn: and so yesterday N. J. [James Nayler] went towards F. G. [George Fox] west and Jo: Bo: [John Bowron?] and Nic. Gan: [Nicholas Gannicliffe] with him: and Stringer [Stranger] said he would come for London. Han: [Hannah Stranger] came to us 5 day and had lost all the rest; and said she would go to G: [George] and she passed that way, but Martha [Simmonds] we have not heard on since: a mighty thing was in it that they should be so parted: even by nothing, as to the outward; and they were

disappointed, whatever they intended. We went with N. J. [Nayler] yesterday about 15 mile he said little to us but he did one whiles weep exceedingly so we returned, and they rode on. We were glad that they went.

The letter adds that Fox had written to warn, obscurely, that "the wrong in them was got above and N. J. had lost his dominion, but there was something in it."[57] Apparently the "something in it" was a continuing threat of "running out" implicit in the bumbling peregrinations of the group that couldn't keep together, and it seemed somehow to be "a mighty thing" that their mysterious purposes were balked. If they were parted "by nothing, as to the outward," perhaps it was the inward motion of the Spirit that was deflecting them from their goal, whatever that might be. At any rate Nayler's taciturnity and tears were disturbing, and his riding on came as a relief.

Since Nayler's mental state at this time is very much at issue, it is significant that immediately upon being imprisoned at Exeter he embarked on one of his frequent protracted fasts. Fox mentions that as early as 1652 when Nayler visited Swarthmoor "he was under a fast fourteen days."[58] In principle this practice was intended to demonstrate rejection of the body, asserting total control over its desires and needs.[59] Orthodox Puritans tended to be suspicious of heroic fasting, even though official fasts and Days of Humiliation were frequently mandated on a national scale at times of crisis. One Royalist of the time observed that a fast by the New Model Army could be counted on to presage some new act of mischief.[60] Quaker spokesmen, conversely, regularly denounced the practice of ritual public fasts—"hanging down the head for a day," as Fox contemptuously called it[61]—while the extravagant duration of their own private fasting attracted attention, as it was undoubtedly meant to do, and gave scandal by seeming to mimic the prophets of old. According to Higginson, Quaker fasts were not in the least humble exercises of prayer, "but undertaken as a foolish imitation of the miraculous forty days' fasts of Moses, Elias, Christ, and the long three weeks' abstinence of Daniel, and three days' fast of the apostle Paul, and as is conceived for the procuring of revelations and inspirations, as they think, of the Spirit." Higginson added that such protracted fasts tended to be obviously damaging in their effects: "Many of them have fasted themselves so weak, they could scarce go [i.e., walk], and till their faces have gathered blackness . . . But where are such ungodly murtherous fasts as these prescribed in the Word?"[62]

In light of this kind of criticism, Nayler's practice of sustained fasting was virtually a polemical statement, a challenge to Puritan ministers who preached self-denial but failed to practice it. Earlier in 1656 he had written bitterly,

> You seem to reproach the Quakers, saying, You know some of them who fasted 30 or 40 days. I say, if you had lived in the days of Moses, Elias, David, Daniel, and other the saints of God and the apostles, who made proof of their ministry in fastings and prayings; yea Christ himself should have had no better from you than scorn and reproach therein, fasting being a thing which your generation knows little of, nor are exercised in, whose care in the first place is for your bellies, and all must fast about you before you want [i.e., lack] your hire which you expect from them, which many times you do no work for, yet war is prepared if they put not into your mouths, [law] suits and prisons, yea many times where the children want bread, and whereof you stand in no need; so that there is little thoughts of your fasting.[63]

On this showing Nayler fasted in order to testify to spiritual purity and to achieve it, while Puritan ministers forced their parishioners to go hungry so that they themselves might feed heartily. In a marginal note Nayler added, "Let the adulterers cease seeking for a sign or a miracle in this generation, seeing this is witnessed with your own hands." His own "sign" at Bristol was therefore preceded by a protracted fast, which at once established his spiritual purity and exposed the impurity of his opponents; and, as Fogelklou notes, a connection may have been implied with Christ's fasting and temptation in the wilderness.[64]

In any case, Nayler's fast at Exeter could not fail to take its toll. According to one eyewitness, "For the most part he doth night and day take water in his mouth and put it out again after he has had it in some space . . . The life which I have once known to breathe forth, I find not."[65] Another reported, "James Nayler is here with me standing in the will of God, waiting in his own way, for he is precious and dear with God and is willing to bear reproach. He hath been in a fast, he ate no bread but one little bit for a whole month, and there was about a fortnight when I came to him he took no manner of food, but some days a pint of white wine, and some days a gill sprinkled with water."[66] As time passed Nayler grew weak and seriously depressed. His old friend Richard Hubberthorne, shocked at his passivity in Exeter prison while his female followers appeared to dominate him, wrote to Margaret Fell:

> The ball no question makes of ayes or noes
> But to and fro as strikes the player goes.

> J. N. his condition is pretty low and tender and dear, and tender love from my soul flowed forth to him. After a little time his heart was opened towards me and he let forth himself to me, but there came Martha Simmonds when I was there and when at any time we were together she would have called him away and he was so much subject to her.[67]

Nayler's companions also got the impression that he anticipated some potent occurrence, but they wrote about it with extreme circumspection, fearing no doubt that their letters might be intercepted. "James saw this thing long before it came, and thou knowest he wrote to thee of it that there must be a suffering. But he knew not how and when it came on him, but he stands innocent of things that are spoken and done and hath peace and comfort and inward joy."[68]

At this crucial juncture Martha Simmonds chose to travel to Launceton, where Fox was still imprisoned, and as he angrily wrote to Nayler in a letter that was transmitted from one jail to the other, she repudiated Fox's authority in the most vehement terms:

> James! Thou must bear thy own burden, and thy companies [i.e., companions] with thee whose iniquity doth increase and by thee is not cried against. Thou hast satisfied the world, yea their desires [which] they looked for, and thou and thy disciples and the world is joined [against the?] truth, it is manifest through your wilfulness and stubbornness, and this is the word of the Lord God to thee. Martha Symonds which is called your mother, she bid me bow down, and said I was lord and king, and that my heart was rotten, and she said she denied that which was head in me.[69]

Simmonds' accusation—"she said she denied that which was head in me"—is unclear, owing to Fox's characteristically elliptical style. Had

he permitted his carnal head to rule in place of the Spirit? More probably, the meaning is that he had exalted himself as head of the movement, when no human being should arrogate that kind of authority.
But even while rebuking Nayler for encouraging "disciples," Fox exhibited his usual confidence that he himself spoke directly for the
Almighty: "This is the word of the Lord God to thee." As for the
claim that Martha Simmonds was called Nayler's "mother," this later
came back to haunt Nayler during official interrogations, but he always explicitly denied it.

The pathos of individualism in its resistance to ingrained hierarchy
is deeply apparent here. The spirit should move alike in all men and
women, yet Fox must be the "head" and not be challenged. Nayler's
apparent defection was all the more painful because he had formerly
shown Fox great deference, perhaps even what Brailsford calls "intense love, amounting to worship." In 1652 Nayler wrote to Fox,
"My father, my father, the glory of Israel, my heart is ravished with
thy love above what can be declared. Let me live in thy bosom as a
seal set upon thy heart for ever."[70] Actually Fox was eight years
younger than Nayler, and if he was a "father" it must be in a spiritual
sense. In his classic study *Enthusiasm* Ronald Knox shrewdly sums up
Nayler's problem: "It was not that he was attempting to make himself equal with the Saviour of the world, but that he was attempting
to make himself equal with George Fox." This should not, however,
be taken to mean that Fox demanded homage as a settled policy. For
as Knox also says, Fox had been accustomed to "roam the countryside, cross-fertilizing hearts with the pollen of a doctrine which was
not so much his as everybody's," and it may well be that only in response to the Nayler challenge did he find himself turning irrevocably into an authority figure.[71] The revelation of disunity was deeply
threatening to a movement that had asserted a unity of the spirit in
which ordinary discipline was irrelevant, and their enemies were
quick to make this point. Thus Ralph Farmer introduced his account
of the Bristol affair: "Here thou shalt see James Nayler and George
Fox, their two chief leaders and their followers, at daggers drawing
one against another, which is a sufficient discovery of that cheat of
theirs, that they were all led by that one, true, and unerring, *infallible
spirit.*"[72]

Fox's own state of mind at this time was far from comfortable. After
he had been imprisoned at Launceton for two months the assizes were

held, and Sir John Glynne, Lord Chief Justice of England, found himself entangled in a characteristic exchange with Fox:

> Judge Glynne . . . said to the gaoler: "What be these you have brought here into court?"
> "Prisoners, my lord," said he.
> "Why do not you put off your hats?" said the judge.
> And we said nothing.
> "Put off your hats," said the judge again.
> But we said nothing.
> Then again the judge: "The court commands you to put off your hats."
> And then I replied and said, "Where did ever any magistrate, king, or judge from Moses to Daniel command any to put off their hats . . . Or show me where it is written or printed in any law of England where any such thing is commanded; show it me and I will put off my hat."[73]

After Fox finished this uncooperative speech he was dismissed to his cell, but eventually the court could no longer postpone hearing the case against him, which proved to rest on a claim by an army officer that Fox intended to raise an army and bring back King Charles II. This of course was preposterous, but Fox and his companions were nevertheless fined for refusing to take off their hats and were sent back to prison until they should pay.

The jailer, meanwhile, kept demanding hefty bribes for feeding and lodging the Quaker prisoners, and when they demurred,

> He grew very devilish and wicked, and carried us and put us into Doomsdale, a nasty stinking place where they said few people came out alive; where they used to put witches and murderers before their execution; where the prisoners' excrements had not been carried out for scores of years, as it was said. It was all like mire, and in some places at the top of the shoes in water and piss, and never a house of office in the place, nor chimney . . . The gaoler was in such a rage that he stamped with his foot and stick and took the pots of excrements of the prisoners and poured it down a hole a-top of our heads in Doomsdale, so that we were so bespattered with the excrements that we could not touch our-

selves nor one another, that our stink increased upon us. (pp. 252–253)

Accounts of this treatment reached Cromwell himself, who gave orders that it should be moderated, and after much delay the Quakers were finally released, having spent eight months in jail. Fox resumed his travels and a week later proceeded to Exeter to meet with Nayler. After what he had been through it is not surprising that he was in no mood for further trouble.

When Fox got to Exeter, where Nayler was still in jail, he demanded subservience in terms that Nayler flatly refused to comply with. In particular Nayler insulted Fox by keeping his hat on while Fox led prayers. This incident still infuriated Fox when he recalled it long afterward in his *Journal:* "But James Nayler and some of them could not stay the meeting but kept on their hats when I prayed. And they were the first that gave that bad example amongst Friends. So after I had been warring with the world, now there was a wicked spirit risen up amongst Friends to war against."[74] The problem was that although Quakers refused to doff their hats for other men, going willingly to jail rather than accord "hat honor," they did remove their hats when they prayed as an expression of humility before God. A fine point was involved here, but one with far-reaching implications, especially since the abominated Ranters were notorious for keeping hats on during prayer. (After Nayler's time the schismatic Quaker John Perrot, who inherited a number of his followers, likewise insisted on this practice.)[75] Nayler's refusal to remove his hat when praying was certainly an insult to Fox, but in Fox's view it was also an insult to God, or alternatively it tended to confirm that Nayler had indeed confused himself with Christ.

Hubberthorne sent Margaret Fell a long and highly interesting letter that described what happened next. On the whole it was presented from Fox's point of view, and of course it was written to the patron who was unwavering in her support of Fox against Nayler. Still, both sides in the dispute can be clearly made out, colleagues and rivals negotiating with each other in a strange code of symbolic gestures. Hubberthorne's letter deserves to be quoted at some length, since it gives us a rare glimpse of actual dialogue among the principals.[76]

When Fox made a second visit to the prison Nayler refused to speak to him and left the room, after which Fox went away. Hubberthorne, however, was anxious to make peace and waited until Nayler returned. "After a while I was moved to speak in tenderness to James, that he might see whom he now was subject unto and whom he rejected, and whether he did not know that those whom he now rejected and would not be subject unto nor answer, [such] as George [Fox] etc., had not as much of God in them to be obeyed as those whom he was subject unto, which if they bid him come or go either up or down he was subject." The burden of Hubberthorne's complaint was that Nayler was "subject" to his female disciples and did whatever they commanded. The alternative, however, was not that Nayler should be free of subjection to any person. On the contrary, it was Fox to whom he should be subject, and Fox certainly had "as much of God to be obeyed" as the women did.

At this point it was Fox who stood on his dignity. Nayler was clearly moved by Hubberthorne's plea. The jailers permitted him to leave the prison briefly to visit the inn where Fox was staying, "and he was broken and tender and wept and said to George that there was that which could never be separated from him; and much love and tenderness was from George to him. And he offered to give George an apple but he would not receive it." Just when one would appreciate some clarification, Hubberthorne is silent. Did Nayler intend the apple as a symbolic gesture that might reverse the primal discord of the Edenic fall? And why did Fox refuse it?

The next morning "George sent for James to come to him, he having something to speak privately to him which he would not have spoken in public, but he would not come." They then met in the street, evidently a neutral site where Nayler could avoid seeming to obey a summons, and a quarrel unexpectedly erupted.

> So then George spoke much to him in the street privately, but in the end something got up in him against George, and when George was turning away from him he openly uttered forth these words: "Take heed of lying and false accusings." And several in the street heard, both prisoners and others. But George passed away and would not reply openly. Then after we were passed away George sent me to him again and Edward Piate [Pyott] went with me to ask him wherein he could charge him with lying or false accusing, and I went to him and asked him: what was that lying and false accusing which he so publicly charged against

George in the street? He said that he did not charge him with lying nor false accusing. Then I told him that he spoke to none else but him in particular. Then he said that George knew what he meant: and that it was lies that he had received from others and so judged by them.

(Pyott, who had shared Fox's foul imprisonment at Launceton, was an army captain at Bristol who held meetings at his house and later went with Fox to London to plead with Cromwell for religious toleration.)[77]

The disgrace of this public confrontation was obviously upsetting to Hubberthorne, who misunderstood what he was hearing, as Nayler explained: he was accusing Fox not of lying but of giving credence to lies. In this atmosphere of mistrust and accusation Fox returned to the prison, where yet another symbolic scene was enacted.

Afterwards George passed to him again into the prison, where he and some others with him was sitting in a place where he lies which is lower than the rest of the chamber, and George spoke much to him. James wept and professed a great love and again offered George an apple and said, "If I have found favour in thy sight receive it." But he denied it and said, "If thou can say thou art moved of the Lord to give me it." James said, "Would thou have me to lie?" Then James having George by the hand, he asked him if he might kiss him. George standing above the low place would have drawn James out to him, but he would not come out; but George standing still could not bow down to him at his asking of him in that thing which if he had come out he could have suffered him to have done it. Then George gave him his hand to kiss but he would not, and then George said unto him, "It is my foot." So with some few more words we passed away.

Why did Fox demand that Nayler say he was "moved of the Lord" to offer the apple, and why did Nayler, who was clearly seeking reconciliation, refuse to say it? Fogelklou proposes one possible explanation: Nayler may have thought of the quarrel as ultimately trivial and Fox's demand as pretentious, so that it would have been a presumptuous "lie" to claim a divine mandate.[78] At any rate Fox was still willing to give Nayler a kiss of peace, but only on his own terms; apparently he felt that in attempting to draw him into the "low place" Nayler was trying to force him to "bow down." Martha Simmonds had demanded that Fox pay homage to Nayler, and now Nayler himself seemed to be staging this homage, perhaps even by a trick.

The tragicomedy of signification was concluded when Fox offered not his hand but his foot, a gesture that is somewhat obscure in Hubberthorne's account but was clarified twenty years later by Robert Rich in an open letter to Fox. Rich was a close ally of Nayler's and reported the story as Nayler remembered it, expressly drawing parallels with the temptation and crucifixion of Christ.

> It was the same spirit that acted in thee (and others of thy friends) against James Nayler in the day of his visitation and trial, when he was led by the Spirit into the wilderness to be tempted of the Devil; for did not G. F. (during J. N.'s imprisonment in the West) come thither to him, accusing, threatening and condemning him as one departed from the truth, and that had lost his authority; also tempting him with fair speeches and promises, if he would bow down and be obedient to him: To all which threats and promises J. N. being silent and regardless, and G. F. thereby thinking he was cast under his subjection, held forth thy hand for him to kiss as a testimony of thy favour to him, and of his obedience to thee; which he refusing to do, didst thou not immediately offer thy foot to him, saying, Thou wert mistaken, it should have been thy foot and not thy hand. I appeal to thine own conscience, whether this allegation be not true, for I assure thee I received it from J. N.'s own mouth, as I went with him from London to Bristol to receive his crucifixion there.[79]

This explanation would have come after Nayler's trial and punishment in London, when he was required to return to Bristol and ride backward on a horse to undo the damage caused by his scandalous performance there. But from Rich's point of view the entire story reenacted the passion of Christ, and Fox in refusing love had in effect played the role of the Devil. The slippage between second and third person is interesting: sometimes Fox is challenged as "thee"; at other times Fox is the "he" of a completed historical event.

Fox, for his part, appeared confident that he was acting as God's authorized representative, and that in demanding subjection of Nayler he was doing no more than God required. In his own retrospective account, "He would have come and kissed me, but I said, seeing he had turned against the power of God, 'It is my foot,' and so the Lord God moved me to slight him and to set the power of God over him."[80] In effect the two men were struggling over the *mana* of true prophecy. Nayler wanted Fox to accept the apple of reconciliation, give him his hand, and kiss him; Fox demanded that Nayler first acknowledge God's command to yield to Fox, which Nayler refused to do. Neither was willing to bow to the other, and Fox (moved by the power of God) ended by contemptuously proffering his foot instead of his hand.

In a letter to Nayler written immediately after the encounter Fox was more still more indignant:

> James! Thou hadst judged and written thy secret and false letters against him thou shouldst not, thou shouldst not deal so pre-sumptuously against the innocent and thereafter thou wouldst have kissed him when thou hadst done this. A innocency and justice is delivered from that and you all, and truth, innocency and justice is set atop of you all, and this thou must read and own.[81]

Again the third-person construction is interesting: Fox presents himself objectively, as if from outside, as "him" to whom respect and obedience are due. The crux of the dispute perhaps is Fox's recognition that Nayler was not acting alone, as the phrase "you all" groups him with his obstreperous followers.

What is most striking in all of this is the continual insistence on authority. Free spirits though the Quakers understood themselves to be, assumptions about hierarchy and obedience were deeply ingrained in the seventeenth century, and as the movement grew increasingly organized Fox emerged more and more clearly as the figure at the top—the very notion that Martha Simmonds and her group were attempting to dispute. Margaret Fell wrote angrily to Nayler,

> I have heard that thou would not be subject to him to whom all nations shall bow; it hath grieved my spirit. Thou hath confessed him to be thy father and thy life bound up in him and when he sent for thee and thou would not come to him, where was thy life then; was thou not then banished from the Father's house, as thou knows thou hath writ to me? . . . And when he [Fox] bended his knees to the most High God for the Seed's sake, and thou

would not bend nor bow nor join with him, how will thou answer this to Him who hath given him a name, better than every name to which every knee must bow? This is contrary to what thou wrote to me, where thou saith George is burying thy name that he may raise his own . . . Where the Seed suffers the Truth suffers; doth not the Seed and all the body suffer by that spirit that holds not the head, but rebels against him?

This was no merely personal quarrel. Nayler was in danger of taking the wrong side in the apocalyptic struggle: "Be tender of the Truth which thou hath [known?] before and suffered for, which draweth thine ear from unclean spirits which is like frogs which cometh out of the mouth of the dragon, the beast, and the false prophet. These was seen when the sixth Angel poured out his vial upon the great river Euphrates."[82]

Although Fox was furious at the report that Nayler had acknowledged Martha as his spiritual "mother," he evidently had no reservations about his own status as Nayler's "father." The fierceness of the dispute could not, of course, be acknowledged later on in the Quaker movement, when William Penn described the canonized Fox as "so meek, contented, modest, easy, steady, tender, it was a pleasure to be in his company. He exercised no authority but over evil, and that everywhere and in all, but with love, compassion, and long-suffering, a most merciful man, as ready to forgive as unapt to take or give an offence."[83] To this it is tempting to reply, "It is my foot." Fox himself later claimed that he had foreseen all along that Nayler would be at the center of some disaster. Leaving London for Cornwall, "I went out of the city and left James Nayler behind me in London. And as I parted from him I cast my eyes upon him, and a fear struck in me concerning him."[84]

The Entrance into Bristol

Martha Simmonds, who was clearly not the madwoman Quaker writers chose to depict her as being, just at this time took employment as a full-time nurse to the sick wife of Major General Desborough, who was no less a personage than the sister of Cromwell. The only payment she would accept was Nayler's release from the Exeter jail, and in due course Cromwell himself signed the order.[85] Martha Simmonds said afterward that she "was sent of the Lord, to watch with General Desbrow's wife, in whom there is a measure of God," and in Ralph Farmer's interpretation this was further evidence of her black arts: having turned up unannounced she managed somehow to ingratiate herself with the general and his wife, "and there (it seems) by her diligence and subtilty she so far insinuated, as that she procured the enlargement of Nayler and his company."[86] They were discharged on October 20, and on October 24 they entered Bristol.

Along the way Nayler and his companions may have attempted to attract recruits to their party, and it is possible that they had made specific plans concerning the sign they were about to enact.[87] There is also some evidence, little remarked at the time and unnoticed by later historians, that the Nayler group enacted the identical performance at Wells and Glastonbury before they repeated it at Bristol. This at least was Farmer's claim in *Satan Inthron'd in his Chair of Pestilence*, adding that during her interrogation Hannah Stranger acknowledged that she "spread [her] garments at Wells, &c. to honour him."[88] When Nayler himself was examined by Parliament he declared that the Lord had commanded "what has been done as I passed through these towns,"[89] the plural noun implying similarly that the incident at Bristol was not unique but culminated a series of symbolic actions.

Bristol was not chosen at random. The leading seaport and commercial center in the west, it had developed a strong Quaker community, which excited strong resistance since the local leaders were generally royalist in sympathy. When the activities of the Quakers began to alarm persons in authority, their main support against repression came from the Puritan army, from which many of their preachers, like Nayler, had emerged. In 1654 a correspondent wrote to Fox, "We have here in Bristol most commonly 3,000 to 4,000 at a meeting. The priests and magistrates of the city begin to rage, but the soldiers keep them down."[90] From the point of view of orthodox Calvinists, the Quaker presence was an embarrassing scandal; Farmer admitted, "Our city and government are (we doubt not) voted and noised abroad as much corrupted, inclined to and favouring much these blasphemous Quakers."[91] Nayler himself, along with Fox and several other leading Quakers, had been named as a suspicious person in a warrant of the previous year, and on at least one occasion a house had been searched by the constables on suspicion that he was conducting a meeting there.[92] In the autumn of 1656 the Quakers of Bristol were far from eager to associate themselves with peculiar behavior that might strengthen their enemies' hand. Fox, still fuming from the confrontation at Exeter, had written to warn them against Nayler's arrival, and no member of the large Quaker community was willing to take him in.

The fullest account of what happened was recorded not by Quakers, who tended to refer to it with uneasy allusiveness, but by John Deacon, one of the "priests" who had a record of stirring up mob action against them. Along with his fellow ministers Ralph Farmer and William Grigge, who also brought out accounts of what happened, Deacon took part with the Bristol magistrates in interrogating the Nayler group. Shortly afterward he published in London a fifty-page pamphlet entitled *The Grand Impostor EXAMINED: Or, The Life, Tryal, and Examination of JAMES NAYLER, The Seduced and Seducing QUAKER with The Manner of his Riding into BRISTOL.* The largest word on the title page is "Quaker." Also on the title page appears an extraordinarily equivocal epigraph: "We have a law, and by our law he ought to die; because he made himself the Son of God" (John 19: 7). The full context deserves to be recalled: Jesus has just been scourged by Pilate.

> Then came Jesus forth, wearing the crown of thorns, and the purple robe. And Pilate saith unto them, Behold the man! When the chief priests therefore and officers saw him, they cried out, saying, Crucify him, crucify him. Pilate saith unto them, Take ye him, and crucify him: for I find no fault in him. The Jews answered him, We have a law, and by our law he ought to die, because he made himself the Son of God. (5–7)

Ecce homo, indeed! Deacon's implication must be that the Jews were wrong to condemn Jesus to death only because he really *was* the Son of God. James Nayler, having blasphemously impersonated the Son of God, should die—indeed, should supplement his impious entrance into Bristol with a reenactment of its logical sequel, the crucifixion— because the text "we have a law" does indeed apply to his case.

In Deacon's narrative the actual act of alleged blasphemy is surprisingly brief and undramatic. Nayler approached Bristol with a small party of four men and three women, some on horseback and some on foot, trudging knee-deep in mire "through the dirty way in which the carts and horses and none else usually go." (Four of the group were often mentioned in later analyses of the affair: Martha Simmonds, Hannah and John Stranger, and Dorcas Erbery. The others were Samuel Cater, Robert Crab, and Timothy Wedlock.) One George Witherley, whose sworn testimony seems to have been the source for this account, "asked them to come in the better road, adding that God expected no such extremity; but they continued on their way, not answering in any other notes but what were musical, singing 'Holy, holy, holy, Lord God of Sabbath,' &c." Witherley added that "they sang sometimes with such a buzzing melodious noise that he could not understand what it was" (1–2). This lack of conventional intelligibility was in fact a deliberate feature of Quaker worship. Just as prayer was to be spontaneous, so also singing ought to be "making melody in your heart" as enjoined in the Epistle to the Ephesians (5: 19). As Fox later described it, "I was to bring them off from all the world's fellowships, and prayings, and singings, which stood in forms without power . . . that they might pray in the Holy Ghost, and sing in the spirit and with the grace that comes by Jesus, making melody in their hearts to the Lord."[93] Non-Quakers tended to perceive the melody differently: "I have heard them hum like a swarm of bees, as if Beelzebub, the God of Flies was there."[94]

What seems to have especially struck the few onlookers was the travelers' indifference to a pelting downpour in which they "received the rain at their necks and vented it at their hose and breeches" (19). Farmer adds that as one of the party, Timothy Wedlock, was coming along "the spouts on the bridge (which is a narrow place) poured on his bare head so that it ran out at his knees." As usual the presence or absence of the hat was symbolically charged, as the subsequent interrogation made clear: "You will not put off your hat to a magistrate, and yet you came bare in a hard rain through the town before him [i.e., Nayler]." To this Wedlock replied, "I must do it if God command me; I did it as I was moved by the Spirit."[95] This could certainly be taken as an indication that Nayler was perceived to be divine, since Quakers removed their hats only when praying to God; and indeed, when Howgill heard what Wedlock had done he was "almost struck dead."[96] As soon as the group entered the town they were arrested and detained in jail pending further examination. A Quaker writer long afterward admitted, "so extraordinary a procession and acclamation could not fail of attracting the notice of the police of any well-regulated city."[97] But the demonstration was certainly not as publicly spectacular as hostile reports later made it seem, as in the eighteenth-century German illustration that shows a dozen people exclaiming "Holy," Palm Sunday branches as well as garments being strewn, and a huge crowd of onlookers in the distance (see Figure 1).

This is really all that happened. As for what it meant, Nayler in his formal examination was superbly noncommittal.

> Being asked his name, or whether he was not called James Nayler, he replied: "The men of this world call me 'James Nayler.'"
>
> Q. Art not thou the man that rid on horseback into Bristol, a woman leading thy horse, and others singing before thee "Holy, holy, holy, Hosannah," &c.
>
> A. I did ride into a town, but what its name was I know not, and by the Spirit a woman was commanded to hold my horse's bridle; and some there were that cast down clothes, and sang praises to the Lord, such songs as the Lord put into their hearts; and it's like it might be the song of "Holy, holy, holy," &c.
>
> Q. Whether or no didst thou reprove those women?
>
> A. Nay, but I bade them take heed that they sang nothing but what they were moved to of the Lord.[98]

In Nayler's responses the factual particulars dwindle away as irrelevant, in an existential limbo that might almost suggest *Waiting for Godot*. There was a town, which might have been Bristol. Even his personal identity grows hazy: "The men of this world call me 'James Nayler.'" His questioners probably construed this as a covert statement that his real name was Christ, recalling perhaps that Ranter self-deification included adopting as one's new name "I am that I am."[99] Actually Nayler was invoking the Quaker belief that his name was merely a name, convenient in "this world" but of no importance in the world of the Spirit. And the authority of the Spirit dominated the event, commanding the women to hold the bridle and sing hosannas. Nayler's one injunction was that they be true to the Spirit and sing nothing unless moved by it.

At this point the examiners produced two letters from Hannah Stranger, which had been discovered when the party was searched. The letters were written in a high style of scriptural exaltation, and to anyone unfamiliar with the erotic spirituality of Quaker discourse they

Figure 1. Nayler's entry into Bristol, in Alte und neue Schwarm-Geister-Bruth, und Quäcker-Greuel, *part 6 of* Anabaptisticum et enthusiasticum Pantheon *(Köthen and Frankfurt a.M., 1702), facing title page. The picture is headed "The Quaker James Nayler's Entrance into Bristol"; the verses at the bottom may be translated, "The madhouse raves in raucous cries that this knight of Christ should be Christ the Lord; two women lead his horse, the others strew garments on the way and cry 'Holy, holy.'"*

would certainly imply that Hannah identified Nayler as Jesus and herself as the spiritual spouse of the Song of Songs:

> Oh thou fairest of ten thousand, thou only begotten Son of God, how my heart panteth after thee; O stay me with flagons and comfort me with wine. My well beloved, thou art like a roe or young hart upon the mountains of spices, where thy beloved spouse hath long been calling thee to come away, but hath been but lately heard of thee. (10)

Still more damaging than this rhapsody was a postscript by Hannah's husband John, a London combmaker: "Remember my dear love to thy Master. Thy name is no more to be called James but Jesus" (11). At the interrogation John Stranger acknowledged the postscript to be his. "He confesseth he called James Nayler Jesus, and saith he was thereto moved of the Lord" (30).

Deacon's account continues with sixteen pages of further questioning in which Nayler sometimes denies accusations, sometimes deflects them, and sometimes refuses to answer them. The examiners are never named, and the dialogue is thus propelled by a series of disembodied queries:

> Q. Art thou the only Son of God?
>
> A. I am the Son of God, but I have many brethren. (11)

He is "the" son of God, which sounds unique, yet he has many brethren, each of whom is similarly "the" Son of God. (Farmer's version of this speech is characteristically more tendentious: "I am the Son of God, and the Son of God is but one.")[100]

In what followed Nayler distinguished clearly between his corporeal self and the divine spirit within:

> Q. Have any called thee by the name of Jesus?
>
> A. Not as unto the visible, but as Jesus, the Christ that is in me.
>
> Q. Dost thou own the name of the King of Israel?
>
> A. Not as a creature, but if they give it Christ within I own it, and have a kingdom but not of this world; my kingdom is of another world, of which thou wots not. (11–12)

Again and again the questioners harped on the central point: did Nayler actually believe that he was Christ? As the interrogation proceeded he stopped answering this kind of question, and it is apparent that he was simply refusing to be bullied when he had already explained his position.

Q. Is thy name Jesus?

A. —Here he was silent . . .

Q. Is there no other Jesus besides thee?

A. These questions he forbore either to confirm or to contradict them. (14–15)

This tactic directly reflects Nayler's own account of Christ, given several years earlier in a defence of Quaker silence:

Is there not a time to speak, and a time to be silent? [Ecclesiastes 3: 7] And was not Christ asked many questions, and answered nothing? And doth not the Scripture say, "Answer not a fool according to his folly?" And when Christ did answer the tempters, it was either with silence, or contrary to what they would have had.[101]

The second citation here implies a quite subtle program of answering and not answering: "Answer not a fool according to his folly, lest thou also be like unto him. Answer a fool according to his folly, lest he be wise in his own conceit" (Proverbs 26: 4–5).

As for his status as (the) Lamb of God, Nayler acknowledged it in terms that once again resisted identification as the sole incarnation of Christ.

Q. Wert thou ever called the Lamb of God?

A. I look not back to things behind, but there might be some such thing in the letter [by Hannah Stranger]; I am a lamb, and have sought it long before I could witness it. (13)

"I am *a* lamb," then; and it was a condition that had to be "sought for" over a period of time, not one to which Nayler was born as a literal messiah. When the questioners returned to this theme he hit back for once with sarcastic asperity:

Q. Art thou the unspotted Lamb of God, that taketh away the sins of the world?

A. Were I not a lamb, wolves would not seek to devour me. (18)

Christ said to the original seventy, "I send you forth as lambs among wolves" (Luke 10: 3).

It is remarkable that even Farmer, the crudest reasoner among Nayler's adversaries, managed in his contemptuous summary of Quaker theology to corroborate the very point on which Nayler rested his defence:

[Quakers hold that] the pure image of Christ must be brought forth in us, we must be perfect and free from all sin, and then we are justified, and then we are righteous, and not till then . . . And if thus they bear the greatest burthen in the work of their own redemption and salvation, no marvel if they themselves have the greatest share of the honor of being their own Jesus. And if the *thing* belong to them, much more the *name;* and then these people [Nayler's group] have done well, and not blasphemed: all that they have said belongs not to James Nayler only, but to every justified person; every one is Jesus.[102]

This was indeed Nayler's position; that Farmer could reproduce it so accurately and still dismiss it as irrelevant shows how repugnant Quaker beliefs were to those held by most Puritans.

Surprisingly, the interrogators showed little interest in exploring the erotic infatuation, veiled though it was in scriptural language, that Nayler's female admirers might have been thought to exhibit. At one point, however, a question addressed that relationship, and Nayler lashed out with unexpected violence:

Q. Wherefore didst thou call Martha Simonds mother, as George Fox [in the confiscated letter] affirms?

A. George Fox is a liar, and a fire-brand of hell: for neither I, nor any with me, called her so. (19)

Farmer did record the testimony of one Thomas Perkins, who happened to be in jail for debt at Bristol when the Nayler party arrived there and overheard a curious conversation:

The informant saith that the same evening there came into the said room a woman of this city named Alice Brock, and as soon as she came near the said James, she fell on her knees before him, and the said James put his two hands on her head, and said to her, "Stand fast, there is that that is pure;" and then she arose and said it was given to her to come to him for a *covering*, and he told her, "Thou art covered;" and then she told him that she had *seed* by another man who had left her, but now she *loved another man* who had a wife, whose wife was envious against her, but she loved her as well as him; and then she asked the said James Nayler whether he had any *seed*, and he replied, "Yea, my seed is pure." (23–24)

The obscure comment about "a covering" is explained by the text quoted earlier in which Nayler says a husband should be "a covering of the eyes for ever" to his wife.[103] One must surely conclude, whatever Perkins imagined, that Nayler and Alice Brock were talking about the universal Seed rather than about "seed" in a sexual sense, and at any rate the interrogators did not pursue the point. What struck Farmer most in Perkins's testimony was that Nayler laid his hands on the heads of Martha and Hannah while "making a groaning noise within himself" and then "clapped his hands on cross [in the sign of the cross?] a little remote over their heads," after which they left him. "This practice," in Farmer's opinion, "is so grossly idolatrous and suspicious of witchcraft, that I shall not need to animadvert upon it" (25).

And what did Nayler's followers believe? They too gave answers that were notable for their subtlety. Martha Simmonds's testimony is introduced by the summary statement, "She confesseth she knew James Nayler formerly; for he is now no more James Nayler, but refined to a more excellent substance."[104] There was understood to be a divine element in this spiritualized substance, but Martha apparently envisioned a process of refining that was not yet the same thing as deification.

Q. Oughtest thou to worship James Nayler, as thou didst upon thy knees?

A. Yea, I ought so to do.

Q. Why oughtest thou so to do?

A. He is the Son of Righteousness; and the new Man within him is the everlasting Son of Righteousness; and James Nayler will be Jesus, when the new life is born in him. (26–27)

In another response Martha indicated clearly that this divine principle was the "Seed" in Nayler rather than a unique reincarnation of Christ:

Q. Tell me, doth that Spirit of Jesus, which thou sayest is in Nayler, make him a sufficient Jesus to others?

A. I tell thee, there is a seed born in him, which above all men I shall (and every one ought to) honour. (27)

The closest thing to an unequivocal statement of Nayler's divinity was made by Dorcas Erbery (or Erbury), misdescribed by Deacon as "the widow of William Erbury, once a minister, but a seducing Quaker" (actually she was his daughter). William Erbery was a former Puritan who had become a Seeker; we will consider his views presently. At the Nayler inquiry Dorcas, whom the informant Perkins had seen kneeling before Nayler and kissing his feet,[105] identified Nayler with Christ more explicitly than others did. Moreover, she had a spectacular testimonial to give, which the examiners seem not to have anticipated, judging by the way she sprang it on them.

Q. Dost thou own him for the Son of God?

A. He is the only begotten Son of God.

Q. Wherefore didst thou pull off his stockings, and lay thy clothes beneath his feet?

A. He is worthy of it; for he is the holy Lord of Israel . . .

Q. Jesus was crucified; but this man you call the Son of God is alive.

A. He hath shook off his carnal body.

Q. Why, what body hath he then?

A. Say not the Scriptures, "Thy natural body I will change, and it shall be spiritual?" [1 Corinthians 15: 44]

Q. Hath a spirit flesh and bones?

A. His flesh and bones are new.

Q. Christ raised those that had been dead: so did not he.

A. He raised me.

Q. In what manner?

A. He laid his hand on my head, after I had been dead two days, and said, "Dorcas arise;" and I arose, and live as thou seest.

Q. Where did he this?

A. At the gaol in Exeter.

Q. What witness hast thou for this?

A. My mother, who was present. (34)

The interrogators of course thought that Dorcas, whether through naiveté or honesty, was the only member of the group to admit what the others secretly believed. "Though Nayler himself and some of the others did juggle in their answers," Grigge concluded, "yet Dorcas Erbury speaks the sense of them all."[106]

When Nayler was questioned about this claim he suggested that God had been working through him as a sign, but he did not exactly deny that Dorcas had died and risen again.

Q. Was Dorcas Erbury dead two days in Exeter? and didst thou raise her?

A. I can do nothing of my self: the Scripture beareth witness to the power in me which is everlasting; it is the same power we read of in the Scripture. The Lord hath made me a sign of his coming: and that honour that belongeth to Christ Jesus, in whom I am revealed, may be given to him, as when on earth at Jerusalem, according to the measure.[107]

Did Deacon, or whoever else may have transcribed this dialogue, get it a bit scrambled? Did Nayler say instead "Christ Jesus, who is revealed in me?" Or did he actually say, more oddly and suggestively, "In whom I am revealed?" At any rate he acknowledged that a miracle had been enacted through him, though it is conceivable that he thought Dorcas had been restored from grave illness rather than from death.

Fox and other Quakers at the time certainly believed in miracles. In

opposition to the general tide of religious thinking away from faith
healing, the radical sects all emphasized it, and none more than the
Quakers, whose "miracles" had a good deal to do with the initial success of their movement.[108] In a *Book of Miracles* (later suppressed, and
now lost except for its topical index) Fox kept a list of more than 150
cures that he himself had accomplished, including cases of blindness,
paralysis, and a broken neck. Few of these were mentioned in the
printed versions of Fox's *Journal*, whose editors were not eager to
publicize the more "enthusiastic" aspects of their founder's early
years.[109] But there seem to have been no cases of claiming that the
dead had been raised. Deacon in another work promoted a much-
quoted anecdote: "There were (as I was informed for a certain truth)
some of this factious heresy [who] presumed so far on their delusions
that they slew a child, presuming to raise it from the dead; which when
they saw they could not accomplish, they were apprehended, and at
the Sizes condemned and executed for the said murder."[110] Deacon
gave no evidence for the "certain truth" of this tale, which in fact was a
badly distorted version of an actual incident in which a mentally distressed young Quaker in Worcester had drowned himself, after which
two women took the corpse from its grave and attempted to raise it.
When this failed they reburied the youth; Fox, in a letter to Margaret
Fell, dismissed the episode as a "mad whimsy."[111]

Rather than focusing on particular claims to have worked miracles,
one ought to recognize the far more comprehensive magical thinking
exhibited by the early Quakers. Fox remarked almost casually that
wherever he went he brought rain, and then generalized from this
fact:

When Oliver Protector gave forth a proclamation for a fast
throughout the nation for rain when there was such a mighty
drought; as far as Truth had spread in the north there was rain
enough and pleasant showers, when up in the south in places they
were almost spoiled for want of rain. And I was moved to give
forth an answer to Oliver Protector's proclamation that if he did
come to own God's truth he should have rain, and that drought
was a sign unto them of their barrenness of the water of life, as
you may see in that book given forth in answer to his proclamation. And the like observation and expectation they have beyond
the seas. When there is a drought they generally look for the

Quakers' General Meetings, for then they know they shall have rain; and as they receive the Truth and become fruitful unto God, they receive from him their fruitful seasons also.[112]

This is not a question of miracles that contravene the ordinary course of nature, but rather of being in harmony with the whole of creation so that inner fruitfulness coincides with outer. Conversely, a region that is barren of the water of life can expect the very real sign of a crippling drought. There is of course something charmingly naive in Fox's belief that it rained pleasantly wherever Quakers were to be found on the map and not elsewhere; but he was just as serious in his advice to Cromwell as Cromwell himself was in calling for a national fast.

In addition to these general suggestions of miraculous powers, the women around Nayler may have had a very specific typological parallel in mind, as can be deduced from a hint buried in Whitehead's highly unsympathetic narrative. He reports that when Nayler's female followers stepped up their attentions to him, "After some time they cried him up publicly in divers places, *bowing* and *kneeling* before him, magnifying him with high appellations: for which their bowing and falling down before him, the example of the Shunamite falling down at the feet of Elisha was pleaded; though that was in a different case and condition (2 Kings 4. 27, 37) and no just parallel."[113] As Whitehead's italics indicate, the actions of bowing and kneeling were particularly objectionable, and as usual the biblical reference is full of interest. The Shunamite woman "fell at his feet, and bowed herself to the ground" because Elisha had not only caused the Lord to give her a son when that seemed impossible, but had subsequently brought the son back to life in an a gesture of great physical immediacy: "He went up, and lay upon the child, and put his mouth upon his mouth, and his eyes upon his eyes, and his hands upon his hands: and he stretched himself upon the child; and the flesh of the child waxed warm" (2 Kings 4: 34). This allusion, though in Whitehead's opinion "no just parallel," points directly to the disputed event that took place not long afterward when Dorcas Erbery claimed that James Nayler did indeed raise her from the dead. It is as if that event had been proleptically envisioned when Martha Simmonds and her group invoked the Shunamite woman. From this it readily follows that the story of the Shunamite woman represented the kind of thing they believed Nayler to be capable of. Though not literally Christ he was Christlike, just as he also reincarnated in himself the mission the Old Testament prophets had embodied.

Deacon, having commented on his transcript, added some miscellaneous aspersions, including the familiar charge of sexual misconduct:

> In a letter I had in my possession, but now lent to a friend, subscribed by the pastor and other members of that congregation in the north, whereof Nayler once was a member, till for his apostasy he was excommunicated, it is offered to be proved, and by them testified to be true, that one Mrs. Roper, her husband being gone on some occasion from her a long voyage, this Nayler frequents her company, and was seen to dandle her upon his knee and kiss her lasciviously, and in that time of his society with her she was brought to bed with a child, when her husband had been absent seven and forty weeks to a day from her; and on a time he was seen to dance her in a private room; and having kissed her very often, she took occasion to say, "Now James, what would the world say if they should see us in this posture?" to which he said somewhat, but he was so low, that it could not be heard.[114]

Deacon follows this anticlimactic nonquote with an incoherent account of a shouting match between himself and Nayler, each calling the other a liar, and then gives a physical description of Nayler that is remarkable for its portrait of utter averageness:

> He is a man of a ruddy complexion, brown hair, and slank [thin, lank, *OED*], hanging a little below his jaw-bones; of an indifferent height; not very long visaged, nor very round; close shaven; a sad downlook, and melancholy countenance; a little band, close to his collar, with no bandstrings; his hat hanging over his brows; his nose neither high nor low, but rising a little in the middle. (44)

Not very thin, not very fat; a man memorable chiefly for his hair (longer than the Puritan norm) and for the Quaker hat that partly concealed his gloomy downward gaze. What is most notable in this rather dim portrait is what is missing: any suggestion that Nayler attempted to look like Christ. Surely if that had been the case, the furious Deacon would have made a point of it?

The claim that Nayler did cultivate a resemblance to Christ, which Hobbes later retailed and Hume used to satiric effect,[115] first appeared in an anonymous pamphlet called *The Quakers Quaking* (probably by Jeremiah Ives) published in 1656 before the Bristol episode:

> He is about four and thirty years of age—a man of good complexion, brown hair which he wears of an indifferent length, but his beard is short. He is of a melancholy aspect and he wears his hat hanging over his brows, his clothes very plain. He wears a little band close to his collar, without any bandstrings, as doth the other great Quaker, George Fox. He doth strive in his looks and posture to imitate the picture of our Saviour as it was sent up to Rome in the days of Tiberius Caesar, and he strives to wear his hair as it were with a seam on the crown of his head and so flowing down on each side of it. (p. 4)

Actually Nayler was thirty-eight in 1656, but this estimate puts him closer to the Christological age of thirty-three. Farmer added a couple of further details: "parting the hair of his head, cutting his beard forked."[116] Early Quakers did have a fondness for the spurious document known as the Epistle from Lentulus to the Roman Senate, which describes Christ as having a short, forked beard and shoulder-length hair parted in the middle, and when Nayler's companions were searched one of them had a copy of it on his person.[117] In 1661 an engraved portrait, supposedly of Nayler, appeared in an updated edition of Ephraim Pagitt's *Heresiography* (see Figure 2). I have chosen to reproduce not Pagitt's engraving, but rather a sketch in pen with which an early reader replaced it in a copy, now at the Houghton Library at Harvard, from which the original had been cut out. The sketch catches the likeness to Christ, and it endows Nayler with a tranquil mildness of expression that stands as an implicit reproach to the furious indignation of Pagitt. The verses beneath the picture, transcribed from the original in Pagitt, read as follows:

> Of all the Sects that Night & Errors own
> And with false Lights possess the world ther's none
> More strongly blind or who more madly place
> The light of Nature for the light of Grace.

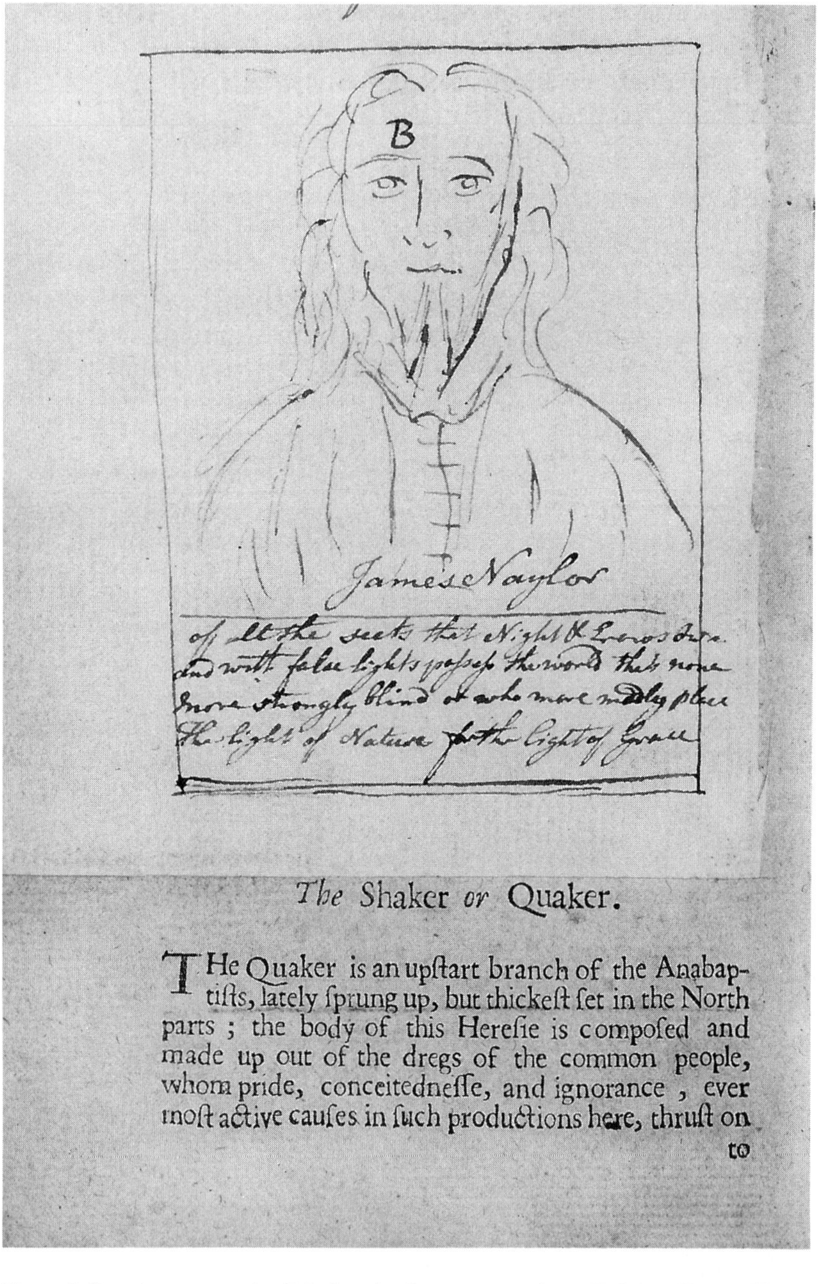

Figure 2. Imaginary portrait of Nayler: sketch in pen pasted into Ephraim Pagitt, Heresiography, 6th ed. (1661), p. 244, to replace the missing original engraving.

What Did It Mean?

As we have seen, Nayler was reluctant to exert authority even when the people around him demanded it. It is therefore extremely difficult to know to what extent he planned or anticipated the reenactment of Christ's entrance into Jerusalem. The event might have been manipulated by others, or it might conceivably have happened spontaneously. This much at least is clear: Nayler was involved in a performance that was intended to recall a crucial moment in the life of Christ; he did not discourage people from noticing a physical resemblance to Christ; he did not deny that he was in some sense the agent of a miracle in Exeter jail in which Dorcas Erbery believed she had been resurrected from death; and while he was in jail he did receive a number of letters that emphasized the messianic theme. Martha Simmonds's husband Thomas saluted him as "Thou King of Israel and Son of the Most High," and Richard Farman called him "son of Zion, whose Mother is a Virgin, and whose birth is immortal."[118]

Undoubtedly, then, Nayler enacted or impersonated Christ, but that was not at all the same thing as a delusive belief that he *was* Christ, except in the sense that Christ was present (in "measure") in all of the saints. Indeed, earlier in the same year Nayler had denounced John Toldervy, a renegade Quaker, for believing "that Christ Jesus which died at Jerusalem was a figure of him, and that he was the true Christ, . . . imitating the crucifying and burying of Christ, and much such like bewitched imaginations."[119] In one copy of Nayler's pamphlet (see Figure 3) an early Quaker reader sketched a hand in the margin pointing to Nayler's declaration that this behavior was "the devil's work." Whatever Nayler intended by his own enactment at Bristol, it was not to assert the literal second coming of the Messiah.

What, then, was the meaning of Nayler's sign, in an age that looked to "signs and wonders" (Acts 7: 36) as important signals of truth? William Simpson, one of a number of Quakers who were given to symbolic displays of public nakedness, wrote a statement entitled *Going Naked as a Sign* in which he said that "a necessity was laid upon me from the Lord God" even though at first he would have preferred to die.[120] At Oxford in 1654 a sixteen-year-old named Elizabeth Fletcher, "a very modest, grave young woman, yet contrary to her own will or inclination, in obedience to the Lord, went naked through the streets of that city, as a sign against that hypocritical profession they

(16)

going on to tell of his filthie practifes, being led with flies to crucifie himfelf, and to burn his Legs, and prick Needles in his Thumbs, and fuch filthie bewitched ftuff not worth the mentioning, being the devills work.

You blafphemers, did thofe truths of God beforementioned lead to thefe things? how are you filled with fubtil envie againft the truth? was there ever fuch a neft, to fet your hands to flander the truth? fhall not the Lord find you out, and bring your wickednefs upon your ownpate? fhal your ioyning hand in hand keep your wickednefs from being punifhed? what you have done in fecret the Lord wil reward you openlie, the daie of Revelation is at hand, and you can be no longer hid.

You go on to tell how he was moved not to pull off the hat to any man; to fpeak the word THEE and THOU; not to bow or worfhip any man, not to direct his mind in drinking to any; to pul off his Points at his knees, and his Buttons that were unneceffarie, and fuch like things which you vvould loath fee go dovvn, and therefore give it as though it vvas the Spirit of the devill that bare vvitnefs againft thefe things, and fo vvould condemn the fpirit of God and practife of the Saints, for the upholding of the Devills vvork, vvho is not divided againft himfelf, vvho hath too many amongft you to make covers for pride and excefs, to fet any on vvork to crie it dovvn, or your flattring titles either. Did ever the Spirit of God ufe any other language to a particular than *Thou* or *Thee?* Doth it not forbid bovving or vvorfhipping any man? Or did ever any vvho are guided by the Spirit of God put off their hats one to another in vvaie of Worfhip or Complement? Or did they ever ufe the practife of you Drunkards, drinking one to another, enticing one another to devour the creatures upon your lufts, by your heathenifh cuftomes? Or did they ever ufe Points at their knees in your manner of filthie pride? May not all fee what you are about to uphold? Are you

the

Figure 3. Nayler, Foot Yet in the Snare *(1656), p. 16, with marginal sketch of a hand pointing to Nayler's criticism of John Toldervy's impersonation of Christ.*

then made there, being then Presbyterians and Independents, which profession she told them the Lord would strip them of." The result was an officially mandated whipping.[121] It cannot have helped that the Ranters were widely understood to have seen clothes as symptoms of the loss of innocence, adopted by Adam and Eve after the fall. Returning to nakedness was for them symbolic of lifting the curse and abrogating the moral law; to go naked without shame would thus be to deny the existence of original sin, that most cherished of Puritan tenets.[122] The Quaker position, however, was a very different one: the enacting of the sign of nakedness expressed a renunciation of selfhood that made ordinary shame irrelevant.

If the spectators, however, felt shame, that was welcome evidence that the sign was having its desired effect. Richard Sale went through the streets of Derby "as a sign, barefoot and barelegged, dressed in sackcloth, with ashes on his head, sweet flowers in his right hand and stinking weeds in his left, the people struck into astonishment, though some set their dogs at him."[123] In a letter to Fox, Sale himself interpreted the consternation of the onlookers as proof of his prophetic authority: "My countenance was as fierce as a lion which was dreadful unto the wicked, and when the lion roared through the streets, the beasts of the field began to tremble and many faces gathered paleness before me . . . for my mouth was opened in much power."[124] In such cases the modern reader cannot help thinking of unconscious exhibitionism, and when an early Quaker reports "I went to the highway naked and great dread fell upon many hearts,"[125] one may suspect that there was more indignation (or even amusement) than dread. But in their own minds they were simply doing what the prophets did of old, in order to symbolize and foretell the fate of an unbelieving nation.

> And the Lord said, Like as my servant Isaiah hath walked naked and barefoot three years for a sign and wonder upon Egypt and upon Ethiopia, so shall the king of Assyria lead away the Egyptians prisoners, and the Ethiopians captives, young and old, naked and barefoot, even with their buttocks uncovered, to the shame of Egypt. (Isaiah 20: 3–4)

Shame indeed, by contrast with the Ranter idea, was a necessary component of the experience, intended to trigger spiritual awareness in the spectators lest they, like the Egyptians, experience a far greater shame.

The performance of the sign thus entailed a doubly negative aspect: in the person exhibiting it, a conviction of fulfilling a divine mandate in opposition to personal self-interest; and in those who witnessed it, an offense to ordinary social standards that actually served to authenticate it. Barbour observes that the believer would regard his or her own reluctance as proof that self-will was being overcome, the apparent rebuke to personal volition serving as a guarantee of divine origin. If the person was subsequently ridiculed for the sign, other Quakers would be all the more encouraged to emulate it. And since the Spirit was uninterested in speaking to unworthy persons, that is to say to the majority of persons, it was no objection to the sign that it might seem counterproductive in its effect.[126] The function of the sign was to bear prophetic witness rather than to get practical results; it fulfilled its purpose simply by being performed.

Fox made the point clearly: "Many ways were these professors [persons professing Puritan beliefs] warned, by word, by writing, and by signs"; he adds with satisfaction, "but they would believe none, so the Lord God brought his judgments upon all our old persecutors."[127] The intention of the warning was apocalyptic, not hortatory: the world would someday come to a very bad end, and those who had not experienced the interior apocalypse of the Quakers were already anticipatorily involved in that end. The duty of the prophet was to testify to this fact, not to argue with people who didn't choose to pay attention. Often—probably most of the time—the onlookers completely failed to understand what the Quaker signs were supposed to signify; displays of nakedness for example were regularly denounced as "shameless," "brutish," and so on.[128] This would have indicated failure if the purpose of the sign had been to communicate a message, but really its semiotic function was relevant only within the group of believers and potential recruits to their belief. Toward others it was meant to be a riddling challenge. In one of Blake's "Memorable Fancies" in *The Marriage of Heaven and Hell*, "I asked Ezekiel why he ate dung, and lay so long on his right and left side?" This was normally interpreted as a specific allusion to events in Jewish history, but in Blake's version Ezekiel "answered, 'the desire of raising other men into a perception of the infinite.'"[129]

Nayler's supporter Robert Rich demanded in one of his petitions to Parliament when Nayler was about to be punished, "Did not the prophets do many things that the wisdom of the flesh might count foolishness, and to be ridiculous?" Among other texts Rich cited Isaiah walking naked for three years "as a sign."[130] Not only were the early Quakers aware that they might look crazy, they were glad if they did. "O ye raging priests!" Nayler exclaimed in a 1654 tract entitled *The Stumbling-Block removed from weak Minds:* "The Lord . . . is manifesting his works, his strange works; his acts, his strange acts," by inspiring his servants to go in the streets "as signs of his wrath to come;" but the generation of priests has at all times "counted always what the prophets, Christ and the apostles did [as] madness, and called them mad fellows." Such behavior was particularly called for in a time of apocalyptic change. "The mighty God . . . hath always before his great judgments, which he has been about to bring on a people or nation, made some of his dearest servants to pass and act as signs to such nations of what was to follow."[131] At Bristol Nayler understood himself to be enacting such a sign, at a time when there was widespread speculation about the possibility of an imminent second coming of Christ, and some non-Quaker millenarians were specifically predicting that the world would end in 1656.[132]

Quaker signs were particularly disturbing to Puritans because they bore an unsettling affinity to the typological interpretation of life to which the Puritans themselves were committed. Many pro-Cromwell pamphleteers, for example, compared him elaborately with Moses,[133] in the mode of drawing parallels between Biblical "types" and modern history, which Dryden would later ridicule in *Absalom and Achitophel.* The Quaker way of using typology was very different, as Cotton Mather complained:

> This heavenly and spiritual body [i.e., according to Quaker teaching] . . . is the man Christ, a measure of which is in the Quakers; upon which accounts the Quakers made themselves to be Christs, as truly as ever was Jesus the Son of Mary. There is in every man a certain excusing and condemning principle; which indeed is nothing but some remainder of the divine image, left by the compassion of God upon the conscience of man after his fall; and this principle the Quakers called a *measure of the Man Christ,* the *light,* the *seed,* the *word.* The whole history of the Gospel they therefore beheld as acted over again every day as *literally* as ever it was in Palestine.[134]

The expression "condemning principle" belongs to Mather's Calvinism rather than to Quaker thinking. A Quaker would say that although the indwelling Spirit does indeed condemn sin and corruption, its goal is to bring freedom and delight to those who have been liberated from sin. But Mather's account of the literal reenactment of Christ's story certainly epitomizes what they taught and hoped to live.

Quaker understanding of typology thus inverted its usual Puritan sense, in which human lives were shadows or reflections of the one true story in the Bible. For the Quaker, not only were Old Testament events types and shadows of New Testament ones, but the New Testament too was but a shadowy anticipation of the present moment. Thus Isaac Penington, writing in 1666:

> This indeed is the main thing, . . . to witness the working out and the effecting of the salvation, as really in the substance, as Israel of old did in the shadow . . . Christ is as truly an healer of his people, in this ministration of life to them by his holy Spirit, as ever he was an healer of persons outwardly in the days of his flesh. That (with the other miracles which he wrought then) was but a shadow of what he would work and perform inwardly in the day of his Spirit and holy power.[135]

Typology operates, as it were, forward rather than backward: the point is not so much that our experience recapitulates events of the Bible as that reading the Bible helps to explain what the Spirit is enacting here and now.

In 1654 Fox, in a work coauthored with Nayler, gave a very interesting answer to critics who demanded "whether Christ in the flesh be a figure or not; and if a figure, how and in what?" Fox's response was to deny the distinction between the real (the historical Jesus) and the figurative (Jesus as a symbol):

> Christ is the substance of all figures; and his flesh is a figure; for every one passeth through the same way as he did, who comes to know Christ in the flesh: "there must be a suffering with him, before there be a rejoicing with him." Christ is an example for all to walk after; and if thou knew'st what an example is, thou wouldst know what a figure is, to come up to the same fullness.[136]

Symbols are real, and they only exist in real embodiment, so any distinction between "substance" and "figure" is meaningless. Christ is an example not only in the narrow sense that people may choose to imitate certain of his actions, but also in the wider sense that he dwells in them and they cannot help but retrace his steps in this world of sorrow. To know Christ "in the flesh" and not just theoretically, one must suffer with him before one can rejoice with him, as Fox indicates with a scriptural allusion: "Rejoice, inasmuch as ye are partakers of Christ's sufferings; that, when his glory shall be revealed, ye may be glad with exceeding joy" (1 Peter 4: 13).

When Fox himself was accused in 1652 of pretending to be Christ, he explained that Christ was in all people, not just himself, "and I said that if the power of God and the Seed spoke in man or woman it was Christ." According to Fox the crowd was impressed, but the accuser was not,

> And so I called him Judas, and all were satisfied except himself, and a professor [i.e., a Puritan], and his own false witnesses. So I told him again that he was Judas and that it was the word of the Lord and of Christ to him, and Judas's end should be his. And so the Lord's power came over all and all the people parted in peace, but this Judas went away and hanged himself shortly after, and a stake was driven into his grave.[137]

Although Fox was not personally *the* Christ, Christ spoke through him so effectively that a man who behaved like Judas got to reproduce the fate of Judas. One thing did irritate Fox, however: that ill-wishers could distort the plain meaning of this typological enactment. "And after, the wicked priest went and raised a slander upon us and said that a Quaker had hanged himself in Lincolnshire and had a stake driven through him. This they printed to the nation, adding sin unto sin, which the Truth was clear of; for he was no more a Quaker than the priest that printed it."

If, as the Quakers declared, all men and women have the Spirit within them, there is no need to wait for an individual, personal Messiah to appear. The end of history prophesied in the Book of Revelation will of course happen at some time, perhaps soon, but Christ's second coming is an internal and spiritual manifestation that is fully accomplished here and now. The Second Coming has always already occurred. Nayler and his companions were thus witnesses to an atemporal second coming, as he had indicated a year before the Bristol episode in an address to ye gazers, and mockers, and gluttonous ones, and drunkards, and evil beasts, whose God is your belly, who mind earthly things, and lives in the lusts of your own conceivings; who now lay [predict a date, *OED*] where is the time of his coming, and are observers of times, but sees him not where he is manifested, and makes a mock at his messengers which are his witnesses, and stone them in your streets, and casts them into holes and dungeons, corners and prisons and houses of correction, and whipping them, and beating them in your markets, stripping naked, setting your dogs upon them and tearing their clothes, beating them with cudgels and casting dirt upon them, who are made white through the blood of the Lamb.[138]

It is a grim catalogue but also a triumphant one: to be stoned and stripped and cudgeled and imprisoned is to be confirmed as the messenger of a Christ who has already come, who is present in the very people who suffer for testifying to his real existence in this world.

Nayler's sign at Bristol was symbolic, then, in a literal and not just an allegorical sense. A valuable clue is furnished by his antagonist Thomas Weld, who had earlier made a name for himself prosecuting antinomians in New England, in an attack on the alleged Quaker belief that "Christ in the flesh, with all he did and suffered therein, was but a figure, and nothing but an example." If that were true, Weld shrewdly remarked, then Christ's passion could no longer be seen as a decisive historical event but would need to be reenacted perpetually. This, I think, is precisely what Nayler did believe. Here is Weld's argument:

If but a figure, then he must type out another Christ yet to come, Col. 2. 17 ["which are a shadow of things to come; but the body is of Christ"]. But surely they do not mean the Jewish Messias; or do they intend a type of Christ in them yet to come, and to appear there in the time of their conversion, as their notion is? How absurd is such a doctrine, that all the acts of Christ, while here on earth, must be acted over again within them? . . . And all these not allegorized, but really, personally, and bodily acted in them, and as they were acted at Jerusalem, &c.[139]

In answer to this criticism Nayler acknowledged that Christ was a "figure" but rejected the implication that to say so was somehow to minimize Christ. "It is one thing to say Christ is a figure or example, and another thing to say, 'with all he did and suffered was but a figure, and nothing but an example.'"[140] In Nayler's interpretation a true figure must be more real, not less real, than a historical personage who lived and died long ago. One year after writing this he himself reenacted at Bristol Christ's entrance into Jerusalem, not allegorically but (to borrow Weld's words) "really, personally, and bodily."

A further comment of Weld's illuminates the deep conceptual gulf between Calvinist and Quaker notions of sin and election, not as abstract concepts but as aids or obstacles to spiritual tranquility.

> What comfort shall a guilty conscience ever find, but in the satisfaction of Jesus? and what peace shall he have, if Christ be only an example, unless he do fully come up in every tittle of his life and death also, to answer the pattern? which is it impossible for man to do, Heb. 4. 15 ["for we have not a high priest which cannot be touched with the feeling of our infirmities; but was in all points tempted like as we are, yet without sin"], he being without sin, and in that alone accepted, as to a likeness to us in all things: and the same impossibility is there of coming up to that pattern in the great matters of his nativity, death, and passion, and the like.[141]

In Calvinist doctrine all men are radically sinful but an inscrutable God elected a small minority of them, long before they were born, and though they continue to deserve damnation the elect are saved through the vicarious sacrifice and "imputed righteousness" of Christ. The Quaker position, as so often, inverts the Calvinist one. According to the Quakers, as we have seen, Calvinist doctrine imposes self-lacerating guilt even upon those who hope they are among the saved. The sacrifice of Jesus, however, can relieve the faithful from guilt, but only if they feel it to be comprehensively reenacted in their own lives. If it is merely an event that happened long ago in the Middle East, it will seem remote and unattainable. If it happens here and now in the interior self, then it becomes real; and in that case, Christ's sacrifice is neither a historical incident nor a mere "example," but a pattern of suffering that the believer literally and personally relives. Nayler's experience at Bristol not only *resembled* the passion of Christ, but in a real sense he must have believed that it *participated* in the passion of Christ.

The fundamental conflict between Puritans and Quakers over the significance of the Bible is replayed here, since this literalness of the Quaker imitation—recapitulation, really—of Christ is what needs to be understood. For the Puritans Christ died once and once only, and ever since then his sacrificial death and resurrection have protected certain humans from the consequences of their own iniquity. For the Quakers it was Christ's continual *presence* that mattered, not just the historical episode of his crucifixion. The point then was not, as their Puritan critics alleged, that Quakers minimized the crucifixion. On the contrary, they insisted on its absolute centrality and held that it was really the Puritans who minimized it by treating it as what someone else did and suffered, somewhere else, long ago.

Nayler wrote in prison in 1653, "The Cross is daily to be taken up, for the Cross is to the carnal, wild, heady, brutish nature in you, which lies above the Seed of God in you, and oppresseth the pure. Now giving this up to be crucified, makes way for that which is pure to arise."[142] What he did in Bristol three years later was to permit his followers to stage the passion of Christ, with himself as protagonist like an actor in a mystery play, enacting in a deliberately challenging form the daily taking up of the cross that was commonly invoked as a mere metaphor, but that needed to be internalized and lived as a potent sign. The tragic absurdity of the actual performance, the handful of bedraggled singers trudging knee-deep in mud, was actually essential to the enactment. To be despised and rejected, to be mocked by the world, was precisely to imitate Christ, as Nayler had said in the same work: a person who is born again in Christ "is willing to be a fool to the world and Serpent's wisdom, content to suffer wrongs, buffetings, persecutions, slanders, reviling, mocking, without seeking revenge, but bears all the venom the Serpent can cast upon him with patience . . . and is made perfect through suffering, and counts it joy, and rejoiceth in the Cross" (p. 77). But as Nayler elsewhere demanded of the Puritans, in words that are highly applicable to his own fate, "Are you like Christ, because you profess him, when you crucify every appearance of him to your selves afresh?"[143]

Richard Baxter, deeply though he despised the Quakers, accurately grasped the representational basis of their signs, as he indicated in his memoirs long afterward: "One while divers of them went naked through divers chief towns and cities of the land, as a prophetical act." Nayler at Bristol performed just such an act, as

Baxter acknowledged even while approving of the punishment he got for it: "Their chief leader James Nayler acted the part of Christ at Bristol, according to much of the history of the Gospel."[144] Nayler did not claim to be Christ, but he *acted the part* of Christ, reproducing the details of the entrance into Jerusalem as reported in the Bible.

As for the raising of Dorcas Erbery, this too gains intelligibility from the typological context, and what we know of her father's opinions suggests that she herself probably understood the experience in this way. She was no naive disciple. Her father, William, was a 1623 Oxford graduate and ordained minister of the Church of England, who had been ejected from his parish in 1638 for anti-episcopal preaching. During the civil wars he became an army chaplain and wrote energetically in favor of sweeping social reforms, more or less in the Leveller style, but he lost his position on account of his antinomian views and ended as a Seeker.[145] In Christopher Hill's account he is a moving figure of disappointment because "he seems to have abandoned hope of a political solution in his lifetime," in his own words "bewildernessed as a wayfaring man, seeing no way of man on earth or beaten path to lead him." "In this darkness," his friend and posthumous editor said, "he had rather sit down and wait in silence."[146] Erbery died in 1654, but not before he had outraged the orthodox ministers of Bristol; Farmer bitterly recalled that the magistrates refused to take action when he invaded Farmer's parish church, stood on a pew, and harangued the congregation.[147]

Some of Erbery's opinions are strikingly relevant to his daughter's involvement with Nayler, particularly the allegation by a Puritan opponent that he claimed "it is no such great matter to know that Christ suffered at Jerusalem; but to know that we suffer as the Son, that our sufferings are the sufferings of God, there is the mystery. I dare not say any more, for the time is not yet come to speak the truth."[148] Nayler's entrance into Bristol enacted just such a living renewal of the meaning of Christ's sacrifice. Erbery had also written, with reference to the Second Coming, "God comes reigning and riding on an ass, that is, revealing himself in majesty and glory in the basest of men." As Hill observes, this passage seems irresistibly prophetic of the Bristol episode.[149] Did Dorcas remember it?

Most striking of all in the "raising" of Dorcas Erbury is a scriptural reference that seems to have been entirely overlooked:

Now there was at Joppa a certain disciple named Tabitha, which by interpretation [i.e., in Greek] is called Dorcas: this woman was full of good works and almsdeeds which she did. And it came to pass in those days that she was sick, and died . . . But Peter put them all forth, and kneeled down, and prayed; and turning him to the body said, Tabitha, arise. And she opened her eyes: and when she saw Peter, she sat up. (Acts 9: 36–40)

In an atmosphere of extreme typological alertness, the parallel could hardly have been ignored when a modern Dorcas apparently died and rose again. If Nayler was instrumental in this miracle he would have been playing the role of the apostle Peter rather than of Christ. But he himself would have regarded this as an irrelevant distinction: it was the same Spirit that was at work when Christ raised Lazarus and when Peter raised Dorcas. What mattered in any case was the living urgency of typology, no mere system of hermeneutics but an opening to eternal life.

Finally, there survives a 1656 pamphlet, almost entirely ignored by those who have sought to understand what Simmonds and Nayler were up to, in which they themselves addressed the spiritual crisis of the age as they perceived it. In bibliographies this pamphlet is ascribed to Simmonds under the title *O England, thy time is come*, but in fact it has no title page and begins with a prophetic exhortation that is evidently signed by Nayler himself:

O England: thy time is come, God hath not taken thee until thou be full; yea, the fullness of thy time is come; with speed prepare to meet the Lord in judgment, lest thou be cut off; woe unto thee if he turn from thee before thou be refined. Remember, was not the Jews cut off that thou might be grafted in [Romans 11: 19]? Remember and take heed.

J. N.

The first and longest section of the pamphlet, signed by Martha Simmonds, prophesies a torrent of bloodshed that is clearly associated with the second coming of Christ:

O England, thy time is come that nothing will satisfy but blood; yea, yea the time is come that nothing will satisfy but blood.

Thou art making thyself drunken with the blood of the Innocent; he will be avenged of thee; till blood come up to the horse's bridle, thou art making thyself drunken with the blood of the Innocent, and now he will give thee blood to drink, for thou art worthy; for he will be avenged of thee till he is satisfied with thy blood . . . How cruelly have they beaten thy prophets, and now thy Son is come they conspire to kill him? (2–3)

The apocalyptic allusion is explicit: "And the winepress was trodden without the city, and blood came out of the winepress, even unto the horse bridles" (Revelation 14: 20). But nothing in this pamphlet suggests that Simmonds would have seen Nayler as the literal reincarnation of Christ, rather than as a prophet in whom Christlike suffering is recreated in the fallen world. Simmonds in fact goes on to make the standard Quaker point that since Christ is already within all people, there is no reason to be preoccupied with his return from the sky:

Why should it seem a strange thing to you to see Christ reign in his saints, and fit and prepare the vessels, and make our bodies fit for himself to dwell in, seeing our hearts are ready to bow to his will? And is it not more for his glory, though it be a greater cross to your wills, to purify these bodies and pour out the dregs thereof, than to bring down that body which was crucified at Jerusalem, seeing all are in his power and one Spirit rules in both? (5)

The bodies of all believers, then, are tabernacles of the divine spirit, and Nayler (or any other prophet, since no specific identification is made) testifies to an illumination that all can share: "Now I beseech you, is not this the manner of the reign of Christ to purify the bodies of his saints, to make them temples for himself and quicken them by his Spirit? And he that leads the way is the captain, king, or prophet, which in all ages the people loved and honoured" (5–6).

But if *O England, thy time is come* offers no evidence that Nayler's group mistook him for the sole Christ, it certainly does confirm that they anticipated a recapitulation in this world of Christlike suffering, in effect a repetition of the crucifixion in striking contrast to the descent in glory that was normally expected. Hannah Stranger, writing the next section of the pamphlet, makes this very clear:

So friends consider, that if it had pleased him [Jesus], he could have prayed to his Father, and he would have sent him legions of angels; but he chose rather to suffer, and thereby to cross his own will, and also all men's wills, for surely he is the same now as he was in former ages, who always appeared contrary to the expectations of all the world; but if he should appear in the way you have long looked for him, then man would have something to boast in; but now boasting is excluded, for . . . as he suffered at his going away, so doth he at his coming again, for so saith the Scripture, "he shall come in like manner as he went" [Acts 1: 11]. (7–8)

This was indeed the manner in which Nayler would soon reenact the sufferings of Christ, and in his own contribution to the pamphlet—for the most part a rhapsodic patchwork from the psalms—he declares significantly,

In thy will thou raised me, and sent me to the nations. A sign and a wonder thou hast made me, and a stranger to them who had well known me. Yea, how often hast thou changed me, so that I have not been known to my self? And thou hast hid me from such as have followed me. (12)

A strange sign and wonder Nayler indeed became, and he did seem radically changed to those who knew him—and very possibly to himself as well. The pamphlet ends with a poetic psalm, signed by Nayler:

Oh holy! holy! holy! still
Both night and day we cry,
Thy song most sweet, thy praises pure
Shall cause our foes to fly. (16)

At Bristol Martha and Hannah, cosigners of this pamphlet, sang "Holy, holy" before Nayler, and far from flying, their foes closed in upon them. And their foes were not just the Puritans in power. The Quakers, alarmed by antinomian literalism in their own group, had at first attempted to scapegoat their weakest members, concentrating on the "turbulent" women. Now the time had come to scapegoat one of their most admired leaders.

4

Trial and Crucifixion

The Politics of Toleration and Repression

Within a few weeks of the Bristol episode Nayler and his supporters were summoned to London to be examined by Parliament. This was not strictly a trial, since under the 1653 Instrument of Government Parliament did not have judicial powers, but in practical respects it turned out to be one. The Second Protectorate Parliament had been elected in the summer of 1656 and first met in September, just one month before Nayler's Bristol disaster. In his opening speech Cromwell stressed two issues—potentially contradictory ones—on which the Nayler case would soon hinge: one was liberty of conscience, the other was suppression of disorder and immorality. Underlying the debate on Nayler was a constitutional struggle between this Parliament and the Lord Protector, which greatly complicated the issues that were raised and helped to ensure that Nayler would be treated as a public scapegoat. The Bristol mayor, aldermen, and ministers who petitioned Parliament to take up Nayler's case stated plainly that their ability to suppress Quaker subversion was hampered by lack of "a law to punish and restrain," and they expressed the hope "that your honours would now take up the reins of government into your hands, which have too long lain loose in this particular, and curb the insolencies of all ungodly persons."[1]

Full transcripts of Nayler's preliminary interrogation were printed shortly afterward and were eventually collected by Cobbett in his multivolume *State Trials* (under a date that would have horrified the Puritan MPs, "8 Charles II"). But for the trial itself, which occupied nearly the whole of Parliament's time for a week and a half, no transcript at all was kept. By a fortunate chance, however, a very full and apparently accurate record does exist. Not published until 1828, it is the private diary of a member of Parliament named Thomas Burton, a justice of the peace from Westmoreland, which had been one of the first areas of Quaker proselytizing. Burton, about whom very little is known, gets into the *Dictionary of National Biography* only by virtue of having kept this diary. His sympathies were conservative, and on 16 October 1656 he had been required by the House to refute an accusation of disaffection towards Cromwell's government.[2] Not surprisingly, when the Nayler investigation began he was among those who favored the death penalty, but he nonetheless preserved an impressively unpolemical account of the debate, without which we would have only a sketchy notion of the complexity with which the Nayler case was argued out. The debate was tangled and extremely repetitive, so that a consecutive account of it would be exasperating in the extreme; for that reason I shall bring forward certain themes, while endeavoring (as other commentators have generally not done) to establish contexts for the quoted remarks and to say something about the speakers themselves.

On October 31, only seven days after the Bristol episode, a large committee of fifty-five members (later fifty-eight) was appointed to look into the case, "with power to send for the said Nayler and the said other parties, and such witnesses as they shall think fit." The committee was charged more largely with reviewing and if necessary rewriting the laws against blasphemy. Nayler and his most objectionable supporters—Martha Simmonds, Dorcas Erbery, and Hannah and John Stranger—were accordingly brought to London, as was reported in the *Mercurius Politicus* on November 5: "Divers strange and absurd pranks having been played lately by James Nayler, the Quaker, at Bristol, he is sent for by order of Parliament."[3] On November 15 a preliminary examination began, attended not only by the full committee but by many other members of Parliament as well; one of them later said that nearly 150 had been present.[4] The investigation eventuated in a report that was promptly reprinted in *A True Narrative of The Examination, Tryall and Sufferings of James Nayler*, edited by the Quakers Robert Rich and William Tomlinson. This pamphlet gives a sense of how fascinating the proceedings were by their very secrecy. The Quakers outside Parliament were intensely interested in the debate but could only speculate as to what was said, and their indignant marginal glosses surround a blank space. Today we are immensely remote from the passions and anxieties that people felt in 1656, yet thanks to Thomas Burton's diary we are also insiders in a way that contemporaries were unable to be.

Accounts of the trial have generally been by writers sympathetic to the Quakers and the cause of radical reform. It has been easy, therefore, to portray nearly all of the members of Parliament as villains, with those arguing for relatively mild punishment as less villainous than the others. Rather than assigning degrees of villainy, I want to try instead to understand why Nayler's alleged crime mattered so much to his contemporaries; whatever ulterior or "real" motives we may believe we recognize inside or underneath their arguments, they themselves took religious issues seriously and believed they were acting in (literally) good faith. The Nayler case becomes more interesting if we try to understand the feelings of all its participants. It is especially important to emphasize that the hard-line and "merciful" positions differed in degree rather than in kind. Every speaker claimed to be appalled by what Nayler had done and to want him punished. They disagreed only as to the severity of punishment that was appropriate, the legal standing of Parliament in ordering it, and the possible wisdom of lessening it for fear of making Nayler into a martyr.

The political situation in the 1650s was distressing to all concerned. After the heady excitement of the 1640s had waned it seemed increasingly evident, as one historian has put it, that "the hand of providence was no longer clearly visible in a history which was turning out to be one damn thing after another."[5] Distribution of power between Parliament, the army, and Cromwell had always been ambiguous, and attempts to resolve the ambiguity led to a jolting series of temporary expedients. In 1653, exasperated by the ineptness of the Rump Parliament, which had been sitting since the king's death and the abolition of the House of Lords four years earlier, Cromwell sent in troops to expel its members. As Blair Worden has pointed out in his study of the Rump, parliaments throughout the seventeenth century consistently opposed reform, which tended to be pushed through in spite of them. "Most MPs, whether Cavaliers or Roundheads, were apolitical in outlook, regarding political differences as of secondary importance to preservation of the ordered world they knew."[6] Likewise the theme of William Lamont's *Godly Rule* is that by the 1650s the preponderance of political and intellectual thought had given up on the idea of theocracy and was prepared to accept, in effect, godless rule. The mainstream also gave up on the idea of an imminent apocalypse, which as Lamont says "was increasingly becoming the property of the propertyless"; Calvinism was thereby "amputated" of what had formerly been an essential element, and "the Apocalypse was taken over by the political and social extremists."[7]

After the Rump was gone a stripped-down Nominated Assembly (later satirically nicknamed the "Barebones Parliament" by royalists) was appointed. Its members made serious efforts toward legal and financial reform, but collapsed into futile bickering and disbanded more or less of their own accord. At the end of 1653 a much more drastic innovation was tried. A written constitution known as the Instrument of Government, drawn up by Nayler's former commander John Lambert, installed Cromwell as Lord Protector to rule through an appointed Council of State—more than half of whose members were army officers—and somehow in tandem with an elected Parliament. For a long time the army had represented the last hope of radicalism. That doughty anti-Quaker Francis Higginson somewhat cautiously commented in 1653, "If I may without offence speak what I think and partly know, they presume to take this liberty to themselves [to 'show their teeth against ministers'] because they are apt to conceive that ministers are now almost friendless, that authority will not appear for them, and that they are the object of the wrath of divers soldiers in the army, whom they foolishly suppose to incline to their (as to them) unknown sect." Higginson allowed himself to hope, however, that in due course "the godly officers of the army," as contrasted with the soldiers, would "not only disown and detest, but also manifest themselves to be enemies of all their impieties, and enormous practices of this turbulent faction."[8] By the time of Nayler's trial in 1656 this had indeed taken place, and in fact the army leaders, like the members of Parliament with whom they overlapped, came largely from the gentry.[9]

Just how the powers of the Protector and his Council of State were to be coordinated with the parallel powers of Parliament was left unclear, as became glaringly obvious at the time of the Nayler debate. Cromwell himself might claim that his authority had been conferred by God, but many of his own supporters were not eager to rest the settlement on that kind of basis. An MP argued in 1654, "To say that my Lord Protector . . . hath it [his authority] by Providence: that argument is but like to a two-edged sword, and a thief may lay as good a title to every purse he takes upon the highway."[10]

When an elected Parliament duly convened in 1654 under the terms of the Instrument of Government, it too proved inconveniently bent on asserting its own supremacy. Cromwell began by excluding a hundred members who refused to sign an oath of loyalty to himself, and ended by dissolving the Parliament altogether after only five months. The 1656 elections, initially provoked by a desperate need to fund an ill-judged war with Spain, represented a second try at clarifying a fluid and unresolved constitutional situation.[11] For nearly two years Cromwell had governed with no Parliament at all, while attempting to install an unprecedented central administration on a national scale, the hated rule of the Major Generals in eleven districts across England and Wales. But this state of affairs could not continue indefinitely.

The 1656 Parliament was expected to be obedient to the Protector's wishes, since it included a large contingent of military officers and government officials, and since once again nearly a hundred elected members were considered unacceptable by the Council of State and were not allowed to take their seats.[12] Even so, a majority had served in the 1654 Parliament and soon showed an unwillingness to surrender their claim to ultimate authority. Throughout the country the election results had registered distrust of Cromwellian centralization and religious reform; in a number of areas the gentry organized successfully to reject the preferred candidates of the Major Generals, and many of the elected MPs had Presbyterian rather than Independent sympathies.[13] Even after Cromwell had purged the new Parliament of its least acceptable members it remained a potentially uncooperative body, and one that would welcome a test case on the issue of religious toleration.

As for Cromwell himself, on whose personality and impulses much depended, he combined fairly radical religious views with social conservatism, and throughout his career sought to conciliate the traditional governing classes and to keep them in place at the top of a hierarchical structure of society. His social attitudes were essentially those of the gentry class to which he belonged. In an attack on the Levellers in 1655 he declared that if the commonwealth were to perish, it would be some satisfaction "that it perish by men, and not by the hands of persons differing little from beasts; that if it must needs suffer, it should rather suffer from rich men than from poor men, who, as Solomon says, 'when they oppress, they leave nothing behind them, but are as a sweeping rain.'"[14]

The Quakers, like other radical groups, had no illusions as to the precariousness of their position. The conservative members of Parliament who sought to limit Cromwell's supremacy were no friends of theirs. In 1655 the Quaker William Dewsbury denounced not only the late king and his bishops, but "the late Parliament" too, "who all professed the name of Christ, but they would not obey his counsel, the light in their consciences, but walked after the counsel of their own hearts, and improved their power for their own ends, and would have dissembled with God and the country. But our righteous God hath overturned them, to their everlasting shame and contempt."[15] The 1656 Parliament was to prove even worse, and Quakers felt greater bitterness toward the Puritans than toward Anglican traditionalists: the Puritans controlled a government that condoned persecution if it did not actually encourage it, and they were particularly despicable as former allies who had turned into enemies. "Who hath changed their God like you?" Nayler demanded in 1659, after more than two years of imprisonment. "It's high time to cry aloud, not to spare the whore; for with an impudent face hath she backslided from her youth, and hath decked her self with the attire of a harlot."[16]

The problem of religious toleration was intractable and probably insoluble. On the one hand, Cromwell did believe in religious liberty and still hoped to reconcile it with the demands of property holders; on the other hand, his power depended on an uneasy alliance of conservative interests with the less conservative army, and Quakers in particular insisted on mounting an ostentatious challenge to that alliance.[17] In any case all groups at the time were opposed to toleration in the modern liberal sense, since untruth and wickedness should never be tolerated. Cromwell declared explicitly, "Civil liberty . . . ought to be subordinate to a more peculiar interest of God."[18] Even Milton's plea in *Areopagitica*, a decade earlier, that truth be permitted to grapple with falsehood "in a free and open encounter," was very different from the later liberal position that all ideas have an equal right to expression, simply *as* ideas. Rather, Milton's position reflected a pessimistic assessment of the fallen condition of mankind, in which "the knowledge of good is so involved and interwoven with the knowledge of evil, and in so many cunning resemblances hardly to be discerned, that those confused seeds which were imposed on Psyche as an incessant labour to cull out and sort asunder were not more intermixed."[19] By 1656, not many people in authority were willing to give falsehood a chance in free and open encounter.

It is true that Cromwell favored a greater degree of toleration than most members of Parliament did, but his position was an "authoritarian libertarianism" that had more to do with forestalling damaging dissension than it did with encouraging freedom of belief, and it always excluded people whose beliefs produced statements or actions that might be seen as disruptive.[20] As Worden observes in a magisterial essay, "The main reason for religious toleration in the Great Rebellion was the difficulty of stopping it." Each group wanted freedom for itself but not for everyone (anti-Catholic measures were favored by all) and such toleration as did emerge was a matter of uneasy compromises rather than of coherent principle.[21]

The Quakers themselves were not in principle tolerant, except in the specialized sense of demanding freedom from interference by magistrates in their own religious beliefs and practice. Francis Howgill and John Camm received a personal audience with Cromwell in 1654, but afterwards wrote sorrowfully to Margaret Fell, "Really, he is in great danger to be lost; for he hath got the form of Truth but fights against the power of Truth. For he holds that all the worships of this nation is the worship of God. But the blind cannot judge of Truth."[22] Ronald Knox says that the Quaker movement "had no sympathy with coercion, but it did not tolerate; agitation, of its very nature, is intolerant."[23] And the Quakers' own behavior made it inevitable that measures would be taken against them. Cromwell caused a proclamation to be issued in February 1655 against "divers men lately risen up under the names of Quakers, Ranters, and others, who do daily both reproach and disturb the assemblies and congregations of Christians in their public and private meetings and interrupt the preachers in dispensing the word and others in their worship contrary to just liberty and to the disturbance of the public peace." Such persons would henceforward be considered "disturbers of the civil peace" and be disciplined accordingly.[24]

The Quakers may have wanted to believe that they had withdrawn from the political arena altogether. "As for these things," Howgill wrote of protests against the exclusion of elected members, "they are nothing to us, we are redeemed from them. Praises to the Lord for evermore, who hath made us to reign above the world, and to trample on it."[25] But the authorities were not impressed by such claims, and even as the Quakers were attempting to trample on the world, the world took particular pains to trample on them. Moreover, it was generally taken for granted that anyone who claimed to teach religious truth would attempt to enforce it if he could. Hobbes said in *Leviathan* in 1651, in an attack on anti-establishment religious prophets, "He that pretends to teach men the way of so great felicity, pretends to govern them; that is to say, to rule and reign over them; which is a thing that all men naturally desire, and is therefore worthy to be suspected of ambition and imposture."[26] It was just this assumption of covert power-hunger that provoked the systematic suppression of the Quaker "prophets."

The Quakers, in turn, reproached the Puritans for having sold out the revolution. In a public letter to Cromwell in 1655, filled with reproaches for failing to promote freedom of conscience, Nayler said he was speaking "in love to you, with whom I have served for the good of these nations, between eight and nine years, counting nothing too dear to bring the government into your hands (for the liberty of freeborn men) as many can witness with me herein."[27] The betrayal was felt to be as much moral as political. In a pamphlet addressed to Parliament Nayler rather uncharacteristically evoked a specific place and occasion, complaining that even though the playhouses had been shut down, informal dramatic spectacles were still being tolerated:

> As I was passing down the borough of Southwark not many days ago, I saw the greatest abominations acted that ever mine eyes beheld: in several places in the open streets [there were] men upon scaffolds, by two, three, four or five upon a scaffold, transformed into several shapes, lifting wickedness up on high, and acting such abominable folly in words and actions, in the sight of the sun, as might make any tender heart, fearing God, to tremble at the sight of. And this was in many places of the streets openly, besides what was within the houses, where several trumpets were sounding to gather vain-minded people thereto; which wounded my heart to see, that ever such things should be tolerated under your government, for whom God hath so wrought that you might reform these evils.[28]

If these were really the greatest abominations Nayler ever beheld, it might seem that his nine years in army service were strangely sheltered from abominations; but his meaning must be that what was at stake was not merely individual transgressions, but rather an official willingness to look the other way when the hydra heads of the theater began to reappear. The point about these particular abominations is that they were flagrantly "acted," in public and in broad daylight, by men (not women, apparently) who denied their true nature by wantonly transforming themselves "into several shapes."

In the summer of 1656, while the Quakers were still protected in some areas by local authorities, they became targets of an organized drive to suppress them, with numerous arrests and increasing public resentment of a central government that seemed too lenient toward them.[29] There was a widespread feeling that the movement was dangerously anarchic, and repeated assertions that Quakers were no better than Levellers. That was certainly how they had struck their critics in the north from the very beginning:

> One Leonard Till, of their way in Lancashire, affirmed that one man ought not to have power over another. Another principal man of the sect in our country affirmed to a justice of peace, there would be Quakers in Westmoreland when there should be never a justice of peace in it; for which words he was indicted at the sessions January last . . . They hold that all things ought to be common, and teach the doctrine of levelling privately to their disciples . . . [One of them] affirmed that wheresoever Christ came, he came to destroy all property.[30]

But to translate the whole controversy into a fear of "levelling" would reduce its multilayered complexity. The Quaker challenge was couched in religious rather than political terms, and this placed a peculiar burden on a Puritan establishment that saw itself as divinely mandated. Its leaders were determined to assert political authority, but they also had to convince themselves that they did so in conformity with the noblest principles of Reformation Christianity.

Thus a need for religious legitimation ran closely parallel with the need for political legitimation. Parliament needed to punish Nayler as a warning to other dissidents and as a confirmation of its power; but the authority on which that power rested depended on a recognition that it was legitimate by virtue of being morally just (not the self-guaranteeing justification of power *by* power that was being urged by Hobbes). Many—I believe most—of the participants in the Nayler debate did not think of the occasion simply as a show trial. They cared about theological and ethical principles, and they wanted to convince themselves that Nayler's punishment was authorized by those principles. From a cynical point of view, one might say that the only point of a show trial is its result, and that the victim's "confession" is extorted merely as an extenuating cover for that result. But even then, one would have to add that many of the participants may be unwilling to admit to so cynical a view, and will be anxious to convince themselves that justice is being done. For this reason it was doubly important to establish Nayler's guilt and not just to find some legal excuse for condemning him. In the first place, the *facta*, the things he and his followers actually did, had to be proved to be morally and legally blasphemous—a claim that some members of Parliament were uneasy about, and that the Quaker community dismissed as grossly mistaken. And in the second place, Nayler had to be brought to declare in his own words the blasphemous beliefs on which the blasphemous actions had been based. If he refused to do that, he might still be punished for the *facta* themselves, but the result would look all too much like persecuting a deluded person for a delusion he could not help holding.

The Committee Report

The committee of fifty-five that examined Nayler was packed with supporters of Cromwell and might therefore have been expected to act according to his wishes.[31] When it immediately began to take a hard line it was evident that deep religious as well as political conflicts were coming to the surface. At Bristol, Nayler had been interrogated by a few local magistrates and ministers, accompanied by the loyal companions who had sung "Hosanna in the highest." Now, in a highly intimidating setting, he faced interrogation by a formidable body of the most distinguished men in the realm, including many of the powerful Major Generals through whom Cromwell ruled the entire country. Many of these inquisitors were already calling for a sentence of death. A marginal gloss in the Quaker *True Narrative*, in which the committee report was reprinted, bitterly demands, "Ought his accusers to

have been his judges? it was not likely that such could see his innocency" (27).

Nayler could, of course, have been tried in the normal way by a
local court at Bristol, as several members of Parliament pointed out;
that he was brought to London at all indicated a desire to make a public example of him for larger purposes. And indeed the extent of the
legal powers possessed by the newly unicameral parliament represented a disturbingly unresolved issue. The now-abolished House of
Lords formerly had the right to sentence certain malefactors, but it
was far from certain whether that right had passed to the Commons,
and even if it had, whether it was applicable in this case.[32] Moreover,
more than a few MPs were uneasy that legislation (called "ordinances") had proceeded from the Council without participation by
Parliament. From this point of view the Instrument of Government
was radically defective and the entire time of the Protectorate can be
seen, in Ivan Roots's words, as "the history of its deficiencies."[33] Political theory therefore merged with practical difficulties in a way that
made many members of parliament eager to see a restoration of the
"ancient constitution" with Lords, Commons, and Cromwell as
King.[34]

The report that the committee presented begins with a brief and
highly tendentious summary of Nayler's life, including the familiar accusation that he had been seen to kiss various women (these were just
"common salutations which then were not accounted evil," the
Quaker gloss retorts) and then gives a transcript of Nayler's testimony
as recorded by five members who had carefully compared notes.[35] At
the outset they declare what their conclusion will be:

The whole fact will fall under one of these two articles.

First, James Nayler did assume the gesture, words, honour, worship, and miracles of our blessed Saviour.

Secondly, the names and incommunicable attributes and titles of
our blessed Saviour. (3–4)

That is to say, not only did Nayler blasphemously impersonate the
historical Jesus, but still more blasphemously he arrogated to himself
the status of eternal godhead.

As to the first count, the committee report describes the women singing "Holy, holy" and strewing garments before Nayler, and also mentions the suspicion ("though much stress will not be lain on it") that he deliberately wore his hair and beard to mimic "the picture usually drawn for our Saviour" (6). The Quaker glosses here advance a double defense: that Nayler's companions had a perfect right to sing and strew garments in praise of the Lord, and that even if some of them did perhaps blaspheme, Nayler remained silent throughout and could hardly be held responsible. What the glosses evade is the obvious intention to enact a sign that would explicitly recall Christ's entry into Jerusalem. On the question of Nayler's alleged attempt to resemble Christ's appearance, however, a hint does come through. "To whom do you impute this fault, seeing there was no art used either to the head, beard, or feature, but was the work of the Creator? How do you here love your example, who count him the greatest offender that God hath made most like him?" (6). This writer (very likely Robert Rich, who contributed to the pamphlet, and who consistently emphasized Nayler's Christlike role) agrees that Nayler resembled Christ but claims that he couldn't help it. The implication is that it was God himself, not Nayler, who intended the resemblance and made it apparent. In any case it was hard to deny that his companions behaved toward him in ways that could only suggest worship: "And James Nayler being examined, whether any kneeled and kissed his feet, answered that there might be such things, though he did not mind it, being things that he did not glory in."[36] This was not a very satisfactory response. Christ himself might well have declared that he did not glory in being worshipped.

When the committee came to the alleged raising of Dorcas Erbery from the dead, they recorded testimony by Nayler suggesting that a miracle had occurred but that he, like the early apostles, had been only a conduit for divine power.

> To which Naylor being examined whether Dorcas Erbury was dead in Exon Gaol, as in her examination, answered, "If you speak of such a death as you may understand, she was dead." Being further asked how she was dead in his understanding, answered, "I shall say little of my self in that thing." And being further asked whether he raised her from the dead, answered, "I can do nothing of my self." Being asked whether any other did raise her by his hands, and if he laid his hands upon her, answered, "There is a

power in me from above." And being demanded whether he had such a power as to raise from the dead, answered, "I have said before, I cannot bear witness of my self in the thing." And being asked who bore witness of him, answered, "The Scriptures do bear witness to the power which is in me, which is everlasting."[37]

The interrogation kept going around in circles as the examiners tried to force Nayler to declare that he possessed supernatural authority, while he in turn maintained that a power "from above" used him as its instrument or vehicle.

In this confrontation a crucial dilemma of seventeenth-century Christianity stands exposed. On the one hand, an increasingly empiricist age had begun to demand "evidences" for Christian belief, and miracles were regarded as crucial evidence for the defense; yet—as Hume would later emphasize—the kinds of miracles that were supposed to be so authoritative in ancient times had somehow ceased to occur. Quakers, however, held that the Spirit was just as present in 1656 as in the first century A.D., and therefore as capable as ever of effecting miracles. For Nayler's interrogators, it was essential to believe in the primitive miracles but equally essential to be suspicious of modern ones. No wonder, then, that they so badly needed to define Nayler not as an inspired individual through whom spiritual power might really work, but rather as an impostor Messiah whose entire performance could only be an impious hoax.

Picking over the records of the Bristol testimony, the parliamentary committee was particularly disturbed by Nayler's answers when asked if he was the only begotten Son of God, in the sense in which "God sent his only begotten Son into the world, that we might live through him" (1 John 4: 9). Here the Quaker gloss seems embarrassed:

He that is a son of God, is he not the only begotten of God? Doth any help God to beget his children, save himself alone? Read James 1. 5. Were ye not wholly ignorant of the Scriptures and power of God, you would not stumble at these things. (17)

There is a *Through the Looking Glass* quality to the slippage of language here. The examiners, of course, wanted to know whether Nayler claimed to be the *only son* whom God had begotten, rather than a son whom *only* God had begotten. The text cited from James, incidentally, seems beside the point: "If any of you lack wisdom, let him ask of God, that giveth to all men liberally, and upbraideth not; and it shall be given him."

A later gloss is still more remarkable, invoking a biblical text in a hidden dialogue that lurks silently in the margin until one looks it up. The committee reports,

> And being examined again to the same question, whether he owned the title of the King of Israel, he answered, "As a creature, I deny any such thing further than as God manifested in the flesh. And if they give that title to Christ in me, then I do own it." (19)

On this the annotator exclaims, "Would you not have him to reign? Read Luke 19. 27." That text says alarmingly, "Those mine enemies, which would not that I should reign over them, bring hither, and slay them before me." Still more strikingly, in Luke's Gospel this text immediately precedes the triumphal entrance into Jerusalem that Nayler's Bristol episode imitated, with Christ's followers casting garments before him and singing hosannas. The biblical account continues, "Some of the Pharisees from among the multitude said unto him, Master, rebuke thy disciples. And he answered and said unto them, I tell you that if these should hold their peace, the stones would immediately cry out" (Luke 19: 39–40).

On the whole, however, Nayler's testimony, though guarded at times, should have convinced any fair-minded observer that he clearly distinguished between himself and Christ.

> "That you may clearly understand that [raising from the dead] wherein Dorcas Erbury, or any else do attribute unto me, as to a creature that hath beginning and ending, that I utterly deny; but that that any see of God in me, by the same Spirit that revealed any thing to them, that I do not deny. This may serve at one word; for there cannot be a more abominable thing than to take from the Creator, and give to the creature." . . . And being asked, if any prayed to Christ in him, whether he did disown it? answered, "As a creature I do disown it."[38]

As the committee's interrogation was ending the Quaker Anthony Pearson, hoping of course for the best, wrote to Margaret Fell that

"James Nayler answered all the questions with so much wisdom, meekness, and clearness, to the understanding of all indifferent persons, that the whole assembly (except some violent ones of the committee) were strangely astonished and satisfied with his answers."[39]

The "violent ones" had plenty of power, however, and at this juncture Burton gives a valuable piece of information: they felt they had already accumulated enough damaging evidence, and were reluctant to let Nayler reply.

> The Committee was ready to rise till Mr. Carey and Mr. Lister came in, and desired that Nayler might be asked something as to the substance of the whole charge against him. The sense of the Committee was against asking him any more questions, lest it should intricate the report; yet, for their satisfaction [i.e., Carey's and Lister's], that all might be clear, he was admitted to speak; and being asked if he had any more to say, he told us that he doubted [i.e., suspected] some had a design to entangle his innocency, and instanced in something that one said, the other day, at the Committee (it was Mr. Downing), "We have gotten enough out of him." Nayler said, this hath stuck upon his spirit ever since.[40]

George Downing was a prominent Presbyterian from Carlisle in the north, where the Quakers had made such notable progress. The *DNB* article on Downing, who was to remain active in public life under Charles II, says that he had obvious abilities "but his reputation was stained by servility, treachery, and avarice, and it is difficult to find a good word for him in any contemporary author."[41]

According to Burton, Nayler's final statement did him more good than anything he had said until then:

> I do abhor that any honour due to God should be given to me, as I am a creature. But it pleased the Lord to set me up as a sign of the coming of the Righteous One, and what has been done as I passed through these towns, I was commanded by the Lord to suffer such things to be done by me, as to the outward, as a sign, not as I am a creature. (11)

This would seem a clear enough statement of Nayler's position, and one that should have exonerated him from the charge of blasphemy, just as Fox had been exonerated at Lancaster. But that was not to be. Before we look more closely at the reasons why, we need to consider the complex way in which religious and political assumptions intertwined throughout the debate. And it should be noted that since Burton himself seems to have been less interested in theological disputation than many of his colleagues were, a full transcript of the debate might well have contained more of it than his summaries do.[42]

Parallel Languages: The Example of Catholic Penalties

The members of this Parliament had already showed in a related context that they found it normal to interchange worldly arguments with scriptural ones. Modern interpreters sometimes regard the worldly arguments as the "real" ones and the religious ones as a coded translation of them, but such a distinction would have made no sense to the speakers themselves. In their minds religious considerations *were* worldly ones. Earlier in the session the question of toleration—or rather, of limiting toleration—had come up in connection with a proposal to punish Catholic recusants by confiscating two-thirds of their estates. This met with general approval, but Denis Bond noted an alarming practical implication: "There is one desperate clause in it, as I understand it: if my wife turn Papist, I shall suffer sequestration of two-parts of my estate."[43] Other members thereupon retorted with scriptural texts. "Against the clause for marrying a Papist wife," Thomas Clarges said, "the believing husband shall convert the unbelieving wife" (p. 7). The solution to the problem was thus furnished not by British common law but by St. Paul:

> If any brother hath a wife that believeth not, and she be pleased to dwell with him, let him not put her away. And the woman which hath an husband that believeth not, and if he be pleased to dwell with her, let her not leave him. For the unbelieving husband is sanctified by the wife, and the unbelieving wife is sanctified by the husband: else were your children unclean; but now are they holy. (1 Corinthians 7: 12–14)

There is no reason to assume hypocrisy here. Clarges was perfectly willing to see Catholics' estates confiscated, but he was also willing to believe that marriage with a believer might convert an unbeliever, which would solve the problem supernaturally as well as naturally. If the wife refused to convert, so much the worse for the estate, two-thirds of which would be lost; but if she did convert, the Pope would lose another adherent, and so much the better for Protestantism and truth. Neither argument was disinterested. The language of social order and the language of scriptural truth ran in parallel, each reinforcing the other.

More usually the stern Presbyterians in this Parliament tended to summon texts from the Old Testament rather than the New, and even when these were not explicitly legalistic they could be counted on to abominate anyone whom the godly did not recognize as godly. Immediately after Clarges spoke, Downing commended the proposed bill: "That clause for marrying a Papist wife is the best part of it. It is against the Scripture. Solomon excepts against it" (pp. 7–8). The reference is not perfectly clear (Burton probably failed to record the entire speech) but as the nineteenth-century editor of his diary suggests, Downing must have had in mind a passage in the Book of Proverbs. The man of wisdom and understanding will be defended against evil persons,

> whose ways are crooked, and they froward in their paths; to deliver thee from the strange woman, even from the stranger which flattereth with her words; which forsaketh the guide of her youth, and forgetteth the covenant of her God. For her house inclineth unto death, and her paths unto the dead. None that go unto her return again, neither take they hold of the paths of life . . . But the wicked shall be cut off from the earth, and the transgressors shall be rooted out of it. (2: 15–22)

The lesson, then, is never to marry a "strange woman" in the first place.

Downing could not resist a further dig: "It was that which the late king lost not only two-thirds for, but all; by marrying of a Popish woman." This comment reflects the complex layering of contexts: righteous indignation out of Holy Scripture reinforces hardheaded realism about the estates and fortunes of disaffected persons, and is followed by a claim that Charles I lost his kingdom because he married a Catholic.[44] Charles's political crimes might then be seen as inseparable from his spiritual ones, and his downfall a condign punishment by the

Almighty for ignoring the express mandate of the Bible. Of course the Bible could speak with more than one voice, and the evident dissonance between Solomon and Paul indicates a chief reason why the Quakers—to the scandal of orthodox Calvinists—refused to grant unquestioned authority to it.

The extent to which Puritans were drawn to the Old Testament, and tended to identify with it, has often been remarked. The Quakers, with their emphasis on the immediate and full presence of Christ, preferred at all times to cite the New Testament; their writings do of course contain Old Testament citations, but usually in an attempt to refute arguments derived from them by Puritan opponents. When they came eventually to write formal theological treatises their own arguments were mainly buttressed by New Testament texts.[45] During the period of intense radical agitation in the late 1640s, voices had been heard demanding that the British legal system be replaced with the Law of Moses, the full system of prohibitions and penalties recorded in the Old Testament; but by 1656 there remained no significant political support for such a reform.[46] Appeals to the Law of Moses during the Nayler trial therefore tended to have an ad hoc and tactical quality as the members struggled to find plausible grounds for the punishment they knew they wanted to mete out. Among other points they argued solemnly as to whether particular Jewish laws were "ceremonial," in which case they might be no longer binding in the Christian era, or "moral," in which case they could still be invoked as relevant precedents. On this tendency of Puritans to endorse the more punitive aspects of Old Testament tradition, Quakers might well have agreed with Blake's comment: "The laws of the Jews were (both ceremonial and real) the basest and most oppressive of human codes, and being like all other codes given under pretence of divine command were what Christ pronounced them, the abomination that maketh desolate, i.e. state religion which is the source of all cruelty."[47]

Given the consistent overlap of political and religious languages, the ordinary rights of Englishmen might be suspended whenever the two languages coincided in identifying enemies of the people. On December 5, immediately before the report of the Nayler committee was presented to the full Parliament, a proposal to toughen laws against wandering rogues and vagabonds elicited a revealing reference to Quakers. Major Audley complained that unless wanderers were carefully defined, judges might abuse the law: "For aught I know I myself may be whipped, if I be found but ten miles from my own house." But this turns out to imply a less tolerant position than might at first appear:

> *Dr. Clarges.* Give liberty for five miles, that you may suppress the Quakers, who greatly increase, and pester and endanger the Commonwealth.
>
> *Major Audley.* Ascertain what this individuum vagum is, lest it be quidam homo, any man. I would have the persons ascertained. If they be Quakers, I could freely give my consent that they should be whipped.[48]

Clarges, incidentally, was brother-in-law of General Monck, who four years later would usher in the Restoration.

After the committee report on Nayler had been read, Major General Philip Skippon, who governed the London area and was a well-known enemy to the Quakers, launched the debate with an explicitly political rationale for punishing "blasphemy": the security of both ministers and magistrates was threatened by the Quakers.

> Every man is astonished to hear this report. I am glad it is come hither; I hope it will mind you to look about you now . . . It has been always my opinion that the growth of these things is more dangerous than the most intestine or foreign enemies. I have often been troubled in my thoughts to think of this toleration; I think I may call it so. Their [the Quakers'] great growth and increase is too notorious, both in England and Ireland; their principles strike both at ministry and magistracy. Many opinions are in this nation (all contrary to the government) which would join in one to destroy you, if it should please God to deliver the sword into their hands. Should not we be as jealous of God's honour as we are of our own? (24–25)

This establishes the profoundly ambiguous terms of the entire inquiry. Ostensibly it is a defence of God's honor against blasphemy, but the subtext is always the threat to established government if too much toleration were allowed. Opinions are not just opinions: they "would join in one to destroy you, if it should please God to deliver the sword into their hands." The role of the Parliament, accordingly, is to make sure that it does not please God to do any such thing. As always the religious arguments are felt to support the political ones; indeed, political arguments *are* religious ones. Skippon has been accurately described as "no mean religious fanatic."[49] A staunch Presbyterian, he had been an early and steadfast supporter of the Puritan revolution, and as Firth admiringly remarks, his principles were unquestioned: "In an age when soldiers were religious his faith was conspicuous as his courage, and it was not without right that he styled himself 'the Christian Centurion.'"[50]

Horrid Blasphemy

Nayler's crime, if crime it was, was blasphemy, or "horrid blasphemy" as many of the speakers called it (in the old sense of "exciting horror"). Nayler and Fox had both been accused of uttering "horrid blasphemies" as early as 1653 in a petition filed by a group of Westmoreland ministers.[51] The statute that seemed most applicable to Nayler's case was the Blasphemy Act of 1650, which had actually been intended to encourage toleration, replacing the hated Act of Uniformity with a much narrower definition of impermissible behavior. Years later, in 1659, Milton could still refer to it as "that prudent and well deliberated act." In Milton's opinion, accusations of heresy implied disputed beliefs that should not be subject to state interference, but blasphemy was a kind of libel, "evil speaking against God maliciously," and ought to be severely punished by the magistrate.[52]

The Blasphemy Act had never been more than sporadically enforced, and many magistrates virtually ignored it. Not more than twenty prosecutions are known (and only four under its astonishing companion act, which prescribed the death penalty for adultery).[53] Over the years there had been occasional instances of clearly demented persons who claimed to be the Messiah. In 1651 a Ranter named John Robins was imprisoned for declaring that he was God the Father and that his wife was pregnant with the new Christ; his fellow prisoners John Reeve and Lodowick Muggleton claimed to be the two witnesses prophesied in the Book of Revelation (and they eventually founded the splinter sect of Muggletonians).[54] But cases like these were always regarded as minor issues, dealt with promptly and firmly by local authorities.

The Blasphemy Act was principally aimed at Ranterish behavior, and as such had no relevance to Nayler. It prescribed punishment for anyone who

> shall presume to profess that . . . the acts of murther, adultery, incest, fornication, uncleanness, sodomy, drunkenness, filthy and lascivious speaking, are not things in themselves shameful, wicked, sinful, impious, abominable and detestable in any person, or to be practised or done by any person or persons; or shall as aforesaid profess that the acts of adultery, drunkenness, swearing and the like open wickedness are in their own nature as holy and righteous as the duties of prayer, preaching, or giving thanks to God . . . or that such acts are acted by the true God, or by the Majesty of God, or the Eternity that is in them.[55]

Neither Nayler nor the other Quakers were ever antinomian in this sense, and apart from a few perfunctory attempts to insinuate that he approved of adultery, no one ever claimed that Nayler could fall under these provisions of the act.

More promising was another part of the act, prescribing punishment for "every person and persons (not distempered with sickness, or distracted in brain) who shall presume avowedly in words to profess, or shall by writing proceed to affirm and maintain him or her self, or any other mere creature, to be very God, or to be infinite or almighty, or in honor, excellency, majesty and power to be equal and the same with the true God, or that the true God or the Eternal Majesty dwells in the creature and nowhere else, or whosoever shall deny the holiness and righteousness of God." If the members of Parliament in 1656, however, proposed to try Nayler on this basis they confronted a daunting double bind. On the one hand, they needed to maintain that he was sane, for if he was "distempered in his brain" he might seem a passive or even involuntary vehicle of sin and crime. But on the other hand, if he was indeed sane, then his own explanation of his beliefs had to be taken seriously. He never denied God's majesty and holiness, and he did deny that he thought himself equal to God, or that God dwelt in him in a different way from his simultaneous presence in all other creatures. Whatever the more hostile members of Parliament claimed to believe, Nayler's testimony, both at Bristol and in London, could not possibly be interpreted as blasphemous, except in the tendentious way that Nayler himself had predicted several years before in a critique of Puritan repression: "Others suffer for confessing the name of Christ, and witnessing him in them, in their measure, and they find him manifest in them to overcome sin, the world, and the devil, and reconcile them to God. And this is called *blasphemy*, and so proceeded against, though the saints have always witnessed the same, and it stands in Scripture for a witness against you."[56] To find Nayler guilty of blasphemy in a more narrowly legal sense, it was necessary to anticipate later theories of action as speech and to maintain that it was his actions that constituted blasphemy. For as Sewel commented long afterward, "Suppose there was blasphemy committed, yet his tongue seemed not properly guilty of it, since it was not proved that blasphemous words had been spoken by him."[57]

There was a further problem. The Blasphemy Act prescribed no greater punishment than six months in prison for a first offense and banishment for later ones. This must have seemed inconveniently lenient, and still more awkwardly, the 1653 Instrument of Government could be supposed to have superseded the Blasphemy Act with still milder penalties. "The Christian religion, as contained in the Scriptures" was officially proclaimed in Article 35 of the Instrument, and "able and painful teachers" were to be maintained to inculcate its principles and confute error. But toleration was explicitly called for. Article 36 made it clear that no one could be forced to conform in matters of belief: "That to the public profession held forth none shall be compelled by penalties or otherwise; but that endeavours be used to win them by sound doctrine and the example of a good conversation." Articles 37 and 38 were more ambiguous; they specified toleration for "such as profess faith in God by Jesus Christ," but failed to make clear how such faith was to be defined or tested.[58] Only under Article 37 were any grounds envisioned on which a case like Nayler's could be prosecuted:

That such as profess faith in God by Jesus Christ (though differing in judgment from the doctrine, worship or discipline publicly held forth) shall not be restrained from, but shall be protected in, the profession of the faith and exercise of their religion; so as they abuse not this liberty to the civil injury of others and to the actual disturbance of the public peace on their parts: provided this liberty be not extended to Popery or Prelacy, nor to such as, under the profession of Christ, hold forth and practice licentiousness.[59]

In practice neither Catholics nor high-church Episcopalian "prel-atists" were prosecuted as long as their religious beliefs did not extend to political action.[60] It was, then, for "civil injury and the actual distur-bance of the public peace" that Nayler would have to be punished, or else for the practice of "licentiousness." But was it so clear that he had caused injury, or disturbed the peace, or behaved licentiously?

Thus, neither the 1650 act nor the 1653 Instrument provided stern enough penalties to satisfy the majority of members, and Nayler's in-quisitors would be under severe constraints unless they treated the case as sui generis and made new law thereby. In view of these difficul-ties there was general agreement that Parliament would have to de-velop new rules as it went along, either by acting as a judicial body (though there was much doubt about the constitutionality of doing so) or by creating new legislation to meet the case (though many members disliked the expedient of post facto punishment under a law that had not yet existed when the offense was committed). To act as a legisla-tive body would require Cromwell's concurrence, which it was well known he would be reluctant to grant. The only alternative, and the one that was settled on in the end, was to regard this Parliament as a judicial body and to punish blasphemy according to criteria defined by itself.[61] As for the appropriate penalties if existing statutes were not to be invoked, these too would have to be determined.

Many MPs of course welcomed the chance to promote ad hoc con-stitutional innovation. The uncompromising Major Robert Beake de-clared, "You are no more bound to precedents than in Strafford's case. You may create a form when you please"; and again, "I conceive the judgment of Parliament is so sovereign, that it may declare that to be an offence which never was an offence before. The Roman senate did the like in cases of parricide."[62] Again political considerations joined with religious ones. Burton's nineteenth-century editor comments in a footnote: "The criminal was sewn up in a leathern sack, with a dog, a cock, a viper, and an ape, and so thrown into the Tiber. A new kind of expiation was also practiced, which consisted in loading a goat with the public execration, and then driving him out of Rome; . . . a cere-mony which seems to have been borrowed from the Jewish religion." The animal companions were omitted in Nayler's case, but he was un-questionably a scapegoat, loaded with the public execration.

There was an important precedent in the treatment of John Biddle, an accomplished biblical scholar who wrote against the Trinity from a highly intellectualist Socinian perspective (he was what would later be known as a Unitarian). Biddle escaped condemnation by the first Protectorate Parliament when it was dissolved in 1655, but his critics pursued him in the courts, and Cromwell removed him from the scene by committing him to prison in the Scilly Isles. The Biddle case shows just how deeply religious deviancy was feared, for as Worden observes, "Socinians, theologically the most subversive of the sects, were socially the least provocative of them; and Biddle was the most sober of sectaries."[63] All the same, the threat of Socinianism had long disturbed the leadership; in 1654 the Council of State commissioned John Owen of Oxford to produce a seven-hundred-page refutation of it.[64] The Quakers were much more threatening than the Socinians, whose beliefs they appeared to share; in Farmer's opinion, "One egg is not more like another, than the doctrines of the Quakers and Socinians."[65] Quaker behavior seemed to demonstrate that antinomian beliefs, far from being innocently theoretical, could easily inspire social transgression.

Nayler's Puritan judges faced a paradoxical dilemma. In the 1640s they had rebelled against the political and religious establishment, and were stigmatized as transgressive themselves. By now, however, they had constituted themselves as a new establishment and were compelled to make the same kinds of exclusions as the previous persecuters had. To define Nayler's crime as blasphemy was not simply to find an excuse for suppressing the Quaker movement; it was also to relegitimate the precarious new establishment's sense of itself as aligned with the true order of the universe, defining Nayler's behavior not just as crazy (a regrettable misperception of truth) but also as evil (a diabolical parody of truth).

At the beginning of the Nayler debate Major General Boteler reminded the house that "by the Mosaic law, blasphemers were to be stoned to death" and hoped that his colleagues would act accordingly (25–26). The political basis of this position was perfectly obvious: "They [the Quakers] are generally despisers of your government, contemn your magistracy and ministry, and trample it under their feet." But in Boteler's opinion Nayler's religious guilt was more dangerous than the guilt attached to ordinary crimes. It would be monstrous, he declared, "if we punish murder and witchcraft, and let greater offenses go, [such] as heresies and blasphemy . . . He that sets himself up in Christ's place certainly commits the highest offence that can be"

(26–27). Boteler was the most firmly anti-Quaker of the eleven Major Generals, and had had a rather nasty confrontation with Fox earlier the same year. As Fox remembered it long afterward,

> I was made to slight him for his speaking so lightly of the things of God; and one told me he was the Major General. "What," said I, "our old persecutor that has persecuted and sent so many of our friends to prison who is a shame to Christianity and religion: I am glad I have met with thee." And so I was moved to speak sharply to him of his unchristian carriages; but he fled away for he had been a cruel persecutor in Northamptonshire. And it was credibly reported in that country that his wife was with child as was thought but brought forth a monster which they knocked it in the head and conveyed it secretly away.[66]

When Boteler finished speaking, Downing picked up the religious theme and elaborated on it:

> Here is no liberty of conscience in this case, for he makes himself God himself. Our God is here supplanted. If he be God, then we must worship him. He is our God as well as the women's God . . . If ever there was a business for a Parliament, this is it. To supplant your God, oh, horrid! (27)

At this point Nayler's old commander Lambert testified movingly to his personal character, but like all of the other speakers he indicated that he took the threat of blasphemy very seriously indeed:

> It is a matter of sadness to many men's hearts, and sadness also to mine, especially in regard of his relation sometime to me. He was two years my quarter-master, and a very useful person. We parted with him with great regret. He was a man of a very unblameable life and conversation, a member of a very sweet society of an independent church. How he comes (by pride or otherwise) to be puffed up to this opinion I cannot determine. But this may be a warning to us all, to work out our salvation with fear and trembling. I shall be as ready to give my testimony against him as any body, if it appear to be blasphemy. (33)

Lambert was the hero of the Battle of Dunbar, where he had routed a much larger Scottish force in what Cromwell regarded as clear confirmation of divine mandate. Like many other young officers he had risen rapidly in influence during the civil war years; at the time of the trial he and Nayler were both in their late thirties. His motives for expressing sympathy with Nayler were no doubt complicated; Hobbes suggested that "Lambert, a great favourite of the army, endeavoured to save [Nayler], partly because he had been his soldier, and partly to curry favour with the sectaries of the army; for he was now no more in the Protector's favour, but meditating how he might succeed him in his power."[67] Still there is no reason to be suspicious of Lambert's testimonial on the one hand or of his expression of religious alarm on the other. He formerly knew Nayler to be an honest and pious man, but was shocked by what Nayler did at Bristol and was entirely willing to see him brought to judgment.

For many members scriptural precedents were decisive, or at least they talked as if they were. When debate resumed the next day the aptly named Mr. Church declared solemnly, "I desire . . . that you would set apart one of these three days to seek God in this business; for if we be not tender in God's honour, he will not honour us. We ought to be as zealous in this business as in Achan's case" (39). As so often, the scriptural reference turns out to be altogether chilling, justifying implacable retribution by the need—often invoked in the troubled England of the mid-seventeenth century—to placate an offended Almighty. Achan "took of the accursed thing," forbidden treasure from the destroyed city of Jericho, and the Lord commanded that the offender be found and punished. Achan thereupon confessed and was brought before Joshua with his sons and daughters.

> And Joshua said, Why hast thou troubled us? The Lord shall trouble thee this day. And all Israel stoned him with stones, and burned them with fire, after they had stoned them with stones. And they raised over him a great heap of stones unto this day. So the Lord turned from the fierceness of his anger. (Joshua 7: 25–26)

On this episode a modern biblical commentary says reassuringly, "The conception of God as a merciful father will later correct this primitive interpretation of his absolute dominion."[68] But it was precisely the license to read the Bible correctively that was in question in the 1650s, and for many members of Parliament Nayler unquestionably deserved the fate of Achan.

After much quarreling about precedents and procedures, it was finally agreed to bring Nayler before the bar in order to be "demanded several questions." The official narrative says only, "He was accordingly called in, and these questions demanded of him," to which the Quaker marginal gloss indignantly retorts, "But what these questions were is not yet certainly known, for there is no record kept of them."[69] Burton, however, did make an extensive record, though even he gave up in the face of "a great deal more . . . which I could not take [down]." Nayler again repudiated claims of sexual immorality, but again acknowledged the accuracy of the statements and events that had been reported from Bristol. The questioning then focused on what he understood the Bristol episode to mean, and in response he was even clearer on the concept of the sign than he had previously been.

Q. Why did you ride into Bristol in that manner?

A. There was never any thing since I was born so much against my will and mind as this thing, to be set up as a sign in my going into these towns; for I knew that I should lay down my life for it.

Q. Whose will was it, if not yours?

A. It was the Lord's will, to give it into me to suffer such things to be done in me; and I durst not resist it, though I was sure to lay down my life for it . . .

Q. Are there any more signs than yours?

A. I know no other sign. There may be other signs in some parts of the nation; but I am set up as a sign to this nation, to bear witness of his coming. You have been a long time under dark forms, neglecting the power of godliness, as bishops. It was the desire of my soul all along, and the longing expectation of many godly men engaged with you, that this nation should be redeemed from such forms. God hath done it for you, and hath put his sword in the hands of those from whom it cannot be wrested. That sword cannot be broken, unless you break it yourselves, by disobeying the voice, the call, and rejecting the sign set up amongst you to convince them that Christ is come. (47)

"He was not that Light, but was sent to bear witness of that Light" (John 1: 8). In this context at least, Nayler seems to have thought of himself not as Christ but as John the Baptist, whom he referred to in the same year as "the greatest of the Prophets,"[70] bearing witness against the "forms" of darkness. The civil wars were over, but the sword of the spirit remained unbroken. Nayler emphasized that he intended no civil disorder:

I am one that daily prays that magistracy may be established in this nation. I do not, nor dare affront authority. I do it not to set up idolatry, but to obey the will of my Father, which I dare not deny. I was set up as a sign to summon this nation and to convince them of Christ's coming. The fullness of Christ's coming is not yet, but he is come now. (48)

But of course a sign can be read in more ways than one, as Major General William Goffe contemptuously noted: "I am of opinion with Nayler in one thing, that he is set up as a sign. He has fulfilled a scripture, that false Christs should arise, 'to deceive, if it were possible, the very elect.' It ought to be a warning to us, to know how we stand. The Scripture is fulfilled saying, 'Lo! here, lo! there is Christ; but do not believe them.'"[71] Goffe was something of an illiberal fanatic and was known as "Praying Goffe" when he helped Cromwell defeat the radical wing of the army during the famous Putney Debates of 1647.[72] In 1655, when Quakers were proselytizing in the west of England, Goffe wrote that they were "doing much work for the Devil" and that he hoped for an opportunity to arrest them.[73]

As the proceedings went forward other members of Parliament occasionally gave some indication of grasping what Nayler's sign was supposed to have meant, Walter Waller for instance: "He hath not said that he is Christ, but only a sign. Now the sign is another thing than the thing signified. He says not that Christ dwells wholly, or personally, in him." Waller grasped better than most the distinctions Nayler repeatedly made: "That of assuming divine adoration: he does no such thing. He said not that Christ was in him more than he was in others." But understanding of this kind was very much in the minor-

ity, and while Waller was talking, Burton—our sole witness for the debate—got bored and tuned out: "He said a great deal more to extenu-
ate the crime, but I minded it not" (151–152).

When the debate resumed on Monday December 8 after a Sunday
recess, it centered on determining whether Nayler was guilty of "blasphemy" or of "horrid blasphemy," which some members saw as a
pointless distinction but others claimed to take very seriously indeed.
Walter Strickland, who represented Newcastle, where the Weld
group had tangled with Nayler, addressed the problem of belief in unusually thoughtful terms: "I believe [Nayler] is under the saddest
temptation of Satan that ever was, but I believe he does not believe
that he is the only Christ, that died at Jerusalem, or that the essence of
Christ is in him; but I fear he cannot distinguish of Christ's being in
him. I think his opinion is little else than as that of John Baptist, a
forerunner of Christ" (56). "I believe he does not believe": in addition
to the usual questions of fact that are attendant on any legal testimony,
this trial had to concern itself with the implications of belief, or in
Strickland's formulation with what Nayler did *not* believe.

From this, Strickland took up the whole problem of blasphemy,
horrid or otherwise. For Nayler to accept homage as the fairest of ten
thousand might smack of outrageous pride, but in what way was it
blasphemous? "He does not blaspheme God. He says he honours God
wherever he finds him. He nor curses nor reviles at God . . . He has no
evil spirit or malice in him against God; but he is under a sad delusion
of the devil . . . He believes that more of Christ is in him than in any
other creature; but he showed no malice to Christ, or envy." In short,
Strickland concluded, Nayler was a deluded person who deserved ostracism, not punishment for blasphemy, and ought merely to be sent
abroad as Biddle had been (56–57).

Judging from all the evidence, Strickland's interpretation seems theologically accurate, but at this point in the debate no concurring voice
was raised, and Major Beake was one of many who declared that blasphemy was indeed at stake: "It is a crime that deposes the majesty of
God himself, *crimen laesae maiestatis*, the ungodding of God" (59). The
too-penetrable barrier between mortal and divine is again at issue: the
quasi-Familist godding of Nayler is the ungodding of God. "He assumes Jesus instead of James," Beake added, recalling John Stranger's
letter to Nayler that was quoted in the Bristol transcript; and Downing remarked, "His being possessed of the devil is no extenuation of

the offence" (60). Moreover, "Christ never denied it to be blasphemy to make oneself equal with God, but he stood upon it that he was" (61). If Christ had not been God actually and in fact, then he too would have been a blasphemer. God's prestige is absolute and cannot be shared with any mortal being.

The root of Nayler's offense was clearly the antinomianism that bridged or even denied the gulf between creature and creator. Henry Lawrence, Lord President of the Council, who had published on the subject of baptism and been praised by Milton in the second *Defensio Populi Anglicani*, judiciously compared Nayler's errors to similar examples of extravagant belief:

> I wonder why any man should be so amazed at this. Is not God in every horse, in every stone, in every creature? Your Familists affirm that they are Christed in Christ, and Godded in God. This business lies heavy upon my heart. Imprudent persons run away with these notions, and not being able to distinguish, sad consequences arise . . . If you hang every man that says "Christ is in you the hope of glory" [Colossians 1: 27], you will hang a good many . . . I do not believe that James Nayler thinks himself to be the only Christ, but that Christ is in him in the highest measure. This, I confess, is sad. But if, from hence, you go about to adjudge it or call it blasphemy, I am not satisfied in it. (62)

As the debate rambled on, some continuing to urge the ruling of "horrid blasphemy" and others expressing doubts, all parties agreed upon the folly of Nayler's ill-judged sign. "His riding into Bristol," the Welshman Griffith Bodurda declared, "was a horrid piece of pageantry and impostery, but how to call that blasphemy in him I know not" (72). From this point of view, the group obsession with blasphemy reflects a pedantic legalism: they knew they wanted to suppress Nayler, but they needed to believe that they were suppressing him for a specifically religious lèse-majesté, such as might justify punishment with Old Testament rigor even if no English law had been clearly broken. "We know what Phineas did in such a case," William Briscoe urged, "and what was the consequence." The reference is ferocious in the extreme: after an angry Jehovah had killed 24,000 Israelites, a man of Israel named Zimri brought a Midianite woman into Moses' presence. Thereupon "Phineas . . . took a javelin in his hand,

and he went after the man of Israel into the tent, and thrust both of them through, the man of Israel, and the woman through her belly. So the plague was stayed from the children of Israel" (Numbers 25: 7–8). "Let us all stop our ears, and stone him," added Dr. Clarges (75).

The upshot was that two resolutions were moved for future vote:

Resolved, That James Nayler upon the whole matter in fact, is guilty of horrid blasphemy.

Resolved, That James Nayler is a grand impostor, and seducer of the people.[74]

The next day, Tuesday the 9th, the House finally turned its attention to other business of various kinds, but by the end of the morning it returned to Nayler and the problem of how to punish him, both because it was not clear that he had broken any existing law, and because even if he had the death penalty seemed excessive to many members. Colonel William Sydenham, a hero of the civil wars and a member of the Council of State, proposed an argument for moderation that was not likely to attract much support, since it implied a potentially devastating critique of the case for horrid blasphemy. "If Nayler be a blasphemer, all the generation of them [the Quakers] are so, and he and all the rest must undergo the same punishment. The opinions they hold do border so near a glorious truth, that I cannot pass my judgment that it is blasphemy" (86). To seriously contemplate the affinity between Nayler's views and orthodox accounts of the Spirit would have fatally jeopardized the trial, and no one was eager to follow up on Sydenham's hint (which may indeed have reflected Cromwell's wishes, since Sydenham, like his fellow moderates Strickland and Lawrence, was closely allied with Cromwell).

The next speaker, Judge George Smith, returned to the theme that it was God's honor and not Parliament's that was at stake.

I have as tender a conscience as any man to tender consciences, and I am also as tender of the honour of God . . . Our laws make it death for robbing a man, though he take but 12 pence from him. Burglary by night, though nothing be taken away, is death. Yet we make nothing of robbing God of his glory. My motion is that a bill of attainder may be brought in; and, if you have no other punishment, that you would fill up the blank with the old way of punishment, that he may be stoned to death. (86–87)

There is an eerie obsessiveness to these ferocious demands. Even if it was unclear what British law Nayler had broken, there was no obstacle to punishing him with a ritual murder based not on British law but on the Bible. Otherwise God would have been robbed of his glory.

Walter Strickland, who had argued earlier for moderation, repeated his suggestion that banishment would be punishment enough and added a striking reflection on the practical implications of heresy. "Heresies are like leaden pipes under ground. They run on still, though we do not see them, in a commonwealth where they are re-strained. Where liberty is, they will discover themselves, and come to punishment" (88). In this analogy heresy is a normal phenomenon that is bound to arise whenever free debate is permitted: "Where most power of the Gospel [is], most prodigies of heresies and opinions; which will happen always, unless you restrain the reading of the Scrip-tures" (88). Unrestricted interpretation of the Bible always produces conflicting interpretations; but since there can be only one truth, the mistaken interpretations, once enunciated, have to be punished. The alternative is to prohibit free expression, which will certainly drive heresy out of sight; but it will not then cease to exist, it will simply flow underground like water in pipes. This is as much as to say that heresy, like orthodoxy, has definition and purpose. It is better to keep it underground (modern metaphors of "repression" are irresistibly at-tractive here); but whether above ground or below heresy remains it-self, with its own coherence and reprehensible integrity.

Strickland himself evidently believed that truth was single, and was happy to see heresy repressed. But one need only twist the lens slightly to see heresy as a competing value-system whose status *as* heresy is a function of the power structure that keeps it below ground. When it surfaces, stimulated by a period of open debate, it manifests itself as heresy, or at least is so defined by those who reject it. When it stays below ground it is still itself, flowing through its regular conduits, but in its condition of invisibility its status as heresy becomes practically if not theoretically irrelevant. The subtitle of Thomas Edwards's polem-ical *Gangraena* was *A Catalogue and Discovery of many of the Errours, Heresies, Blasphemies and pernicious Practices of the Sectaries of this time, vented and acted in England these four last years.* The two verbs imply metaphors similar to Strickland's: when the lid was taken off in the 1640s all sorts of unwholesome doctrines were forcibly "vented," and still worse, having been vented they were "acted." By the mid-1650s the great majority of persons in authority, including many who had wholeheartedly supported revolution, were more than ready to see the lid put on again. Later on in the Nayler debate a different Strickland, Sir William, proposed a complementary metaphor: "It is sunshine makes these horrid things grow. I wish they were not tolerated" (220).

Just before Parliament adjourned—they had gone on debating until nine at night, far later than their usual time—Thomas Bampfield returned to Nayler's alleged impersonation of Christ and reiterated Beake's argument:

> The example of our Saviour's suffering is drawn thus. If he had not been really Christ, then had the Jews done justly in crucifying of him. For the Spirit of God holds this forth plainly, that the charge laid against him was that he, being a man, called himself God. And was this offence of Nayler's less than calling himself God, and assuming the name, title, and incommunicable attributes of our Lord and Saviour Jesus Christ, and the worship due to him? If this be not blasphemy, then there is no blasphemy in the world. (91)

Christ, then, was a potential blasphemer whose claims to divinity were not blasphemous only because they were true. A subliminal threat lurks just below the surface of Bampfield's statement: Christ *might* have been an imposter, and what then? This was no merely theoretical puzzle. One of Bunyan's deepest anxieties was "whether there were in truth a God or Christ, or no? and whether the holy Scriptures were not rather a fable and cunning story, than the holy and pure Word of God."[75]

Like all formulations in the Calvinist mode, Bampfield's depends on the utter incommensurability of God and man, the unbridgeable gulf between the real Christ and Nayler the fake Christ. The Quaker position, on the other hand, was that Christ's attributes, far from being "incommunicable," as Bampfield put it, were in fact communicated to all believers. Bampfield, insisting on the difference, felt no uneasiness about turning his scriptural texts upside down and proposing a punitive mirror image of the *imitatio Christi* that Nayler had enacted. What was done wickedly to Christ would be totally appropriate when done to Nayler:

> Then the Jews took up stones again to stone him. Jesus answered them, Many good works have I showed you from my Father; for which of those works do ye stone me? The Jews answered him, saying, For a good work we stone thee not; but for blasphemy; and because that thou, being a man, makest thyself God. (John 10: 31–33)

This is the ancient penalty specified in Leviticus, in the same context as "eye for eye, tooth for tooth" (24: 16, 20). Bampfield was no marginal figure in this debate: he was Recorder of Exeter, which had experienced Quaker evangelism similar to Bristol's. Together with Robert Aldworth of Bristol, Bampfield made sure the Nayler case was taken up by Parliament, chaired the committee that examined him, and coordinated the attack on him during the debate that followed. He was widely respected, and indeed became speaker of the next Parliament.[76] As it happens the speaker in 1656 was a much weaker figure, which may partly account for the disorganization of the Nayler proceedings.[77]

The question of punishment remained. Some speakers argued for leniency, but such things are relative: a typical moderate was Sir Charles Wolseley, a close confidant of Cromwell, who anticipated Nayler's eventual sentence by opposing the death penalty and proposing "a lesser punishment, as pillory, imprisonment, whipping, or the like" (90). Sir Richard Piggot—in his sole appearance in the four volumes of Burton's *Diary*—completed the thought by suggesting that "his tongue might be bored through" (91), as had been done in 1650 to the Ranter Jacob Bauthumley (or Bottomley), one of the first victims of the Blasphemy Act.[78] Colonel Robert Wilton[79] objected to any punishment less than death, stressing the social and political threat represented by the Quakers: "These vipers are crept into the bowels of your commonwealth, and the government too. They grow numerous, and swarm all the nation over; every county, every parish. I shall turn quaker too, but not in that sense." Nayler's "heinous crime" must not be passed over: "Remember Eli's case" (96). Eli failed to punish his sons for their licentious behavior as "sons of Belial"; as a result they were killed in battle, the ark of the covenant was stolen, and when Eli himself heard the news he fell off a gate and died of a broken neck

(1 Samuel 2–4). Lambert Godfrey elaborated a few days later on the relevance of the example: "That which is spoken against Eli, for honouring his sons more than God: he was a ruler, and yet spared his sons. That brought not only a judgment upon his family but upon the whole land. The ark departed. Let not, I beseech you, the tendering of your sons, the sons of Belial, though under your *pater patriae*" (142–143).

Colonel Thomas Cooper, who is not recorded as having spoken before, now delivered a speech of unusual subtlety, addressing the theological issue more carefully than most of the members had done. Nayler, he pointed out, had certainly not blasphemed in the usual sense by denying or cursing Christ. If in fact he had blasphemed at all, it was by implication, when he allowed his followers to worship him as Christ; and indeed his having done so was evidence of "darkness and a strong delusion." Moreover, Cooper foresaw that negative repercussions, moral as well as political, would flow from a death sentence. "I cannot say this person is innocent; yet if we take his life where God does not require it, that is a shedding of innocent blood." Even to speak in terms of God's commandments, as so many of the members had done, was in effect to concede that no human law had been violated. In addition there was the very real political danger of turning Nayler into a martyr: "I would have you use some endeavour to suppress the growth of them [the Quakers] in general. If you take this man's blood, you do certainly lay a foundation for them. Instead of taking away Quakerism, you establish it."

More clearly than most of the speakers, Cooper made it explicit that Nayler was on trial because he was no marginal figure, but on the contrary an intellectual leader and major theorist of the Quaker movement.

> For my part, I think, next to life [i.e., taking his life], you cannot pass a greater punishment than perpetual imprisonment, where he may not spread his leprosy. If you cut out his tongue, he may write, for he writes all their books. If you cut off his right hand, he may write with his left. The other punishments will certainly answer your ends more than if you take his life, and be a better expedient to suppress that generation of them. (96–98)

For Cooper the issue was not how best to vindicate God's glory, but rather how best to neutralize the growing Quaker movement and to silence its most eloquent writer. Speaking next, Denis Bond agreed: "Cut off this fellow, and you will destroy the sect." In Bond's opinion the death penalty was the only way to ensure it (98). And Skippon derided objections to invoking Jewish law: "It is against the tenor of the Gospel, they say. It is true we ought to love one another, but not so as to exclude our love to God . . . God has made a law to punish blasphemy, and what are we poor worms going about to repeal that law?" (103). As so often, Puritan expressions of humility were quite nakedly implicated in assertions of power: the poor worm was a Major General exhorting the most powerful body in the land to exercise its authority without remorse.

A similar irony is implied in a remark by Goffe the next day: "I am sorry to see this division amongst us, but I hope it will end in amity, love, and charity. For my part, I cannot be satisfied in myself to give my consent to less than the death of this man." Moreover, this company of regicides could still use the language of monarchy to justify ruthless action: "Christ is the King of this nation, and of all nations, and we ought to vindicate the honour of our King" (108–109). Boteler took the same line as Goffe did with respect to meekness and love: "We ought to be meek and lowly, it is true. But what says the same text, 'Bring my enemies and slay them before me.' Our zeal for God's glory is as well commanded under the Gospel as is meekness and lowliness" (114). This was no casual allusion. Boteler was citing Christ's seldom-quoted conclusion to the parable of the talents: "Those mine enemies, which would not that I should reign over them, bring hither, and slay them before me" (Luke 19: 27). Ivan Roots remarks that throughout the Nayler debate "Skippon and Boteler appear as ugly bigots, obsessed with sin, or at any rate anxious to give that impression."[80]

Major General William Packer, a Baptist who had commanded Cromwell's company of horse at Dunbar and was regarded by Fox as an enemy to the Quakers,[81] took a more moderate position, urging the inappropriateness of applying Jewish law to British cases and emphasizing the close affinity of Nayler's views with those of many unobjectionable believers. "This person tells you there is but one God, Father, Son, and Spirit. A strange notion that the Holy Spirit dwells personally and essentially in them [the Quakers], yet I know many godly men of this opinion" (99). From a somewhat different point of view Major General Thomas Kelsey, governor of the counties closest to London, summed up arguments for moderation with unusual clarity: there were legal pitfalls in condemning Nayler by a law that was only now being defined, and in any case claims to know God's will were surely presumptuous. "It may be any man's case here. He knows not how to walk securely, if a man shall be punished by a law *ex post facto*. To make a law in any case to this purpose is dangerous, much more in a matter of this nature, which is so dark and difficult to know what the mind of God is in this thing" (123). But ambiguities and doubts like these, whether legal or religious, were not what the majority wanted to hear about. On the contrary, most MPs gave every indication of relishing discussion of remote precedents, debating at some length whether the law of nature did or did not justify the ancient heathens when they put blasphemers to death, and why the Jews were forbidden to gather sticks on the sabbath, and whether this prohibition argued for or against applying Jewish law to Nayler. In the last instance Lambert Godfrey was fairly typical in urging that even if Moses showed hesitation, that was no argument for leniency toward Nayler: "They found a man that gathered sticks in that 16 Exodus [actually Numbers 15: 32–36]. Moses went to consult the manner of his death, which God directed. All the congregation should stone him. It is clear he knew the kind of punishment, but not the manner, and therefore, and for no other reason, he advised and consulted with God" (141).

Sentencing

The question was at last put whether Nayler should be condemned to death, and it failed by the not very large margin of 96 to 82; these 178 members represented about 60 percent of all who were eligible to vote.[82] "It seems you cannot have your will in this neither," comments the Quaker marginal gloss in the *True Narrative*, observing also that this was "the twelfth time the whole House assumed the debate about J. N." (pp. 32–33).

A lesser punishment now had to be determined, and a clamor of voices was raised, emphasizing the exemplary aspects and warning of unwanted consequences:

Colonel White proposed that his tongue might be bored through.

Colonel Barclay, that his hair might be cut off.

Major General Haines, that his tongue might be slit or bored through, and that he might be stigmatized with the letter B [for "blasphemy"].

Colonel Coker, that his hair might be cut off.

Sir Thomas Wroth. Slit his tongue, or bore it, and brand him with the letter B.

Major General Whalley. Do not cut off his hair; that will make the people believe that the Parliament of England are of opinion that our Saviour Christ wore his hair so, and this will make all people in love with the fashion. (153)

Implicit in this objection was the belief of many Puritans that Christ did not in fact wear his hair long (no cavalier he).[83] The penalty of boring through the tongue, which seems so appalling today, was treated by the debaters as unremarkable. "It is an ordinary punishment for swearing," said Major Lewis Audley; "I have known twenty bored through the tongue." If anything, this seemed the least that might be done. Downing exclaimed, "You ought to do something with that tongue that has bored through God," and Edward Whalley thought it would be a good idea if his lips were "slitted" as well. (154).

A word may be added about Whalley. According to Richard Baxter, who had been his army chaplain, Whalley had trouble with the radicals in his regiment because of his religious orthodoxy. As with many participants in this debate, however, what was conservative in one context became radical in another. Whalley was one of the regicides who signed the death warrant of King Charles I, and to escape execution in 1660 he had to flee to America, where he remained in hiding until his death many years later.[84] (This is why there is a Whalley Avenue in New Haven, Connecticut.)

Finally, at the end of the day on Tuesday, December 16, the full sentence was adopted:

Resolved, that James Nayler be set on the pillory, with his head in the pillory, in the New Palace Westminster, during the space of two hours, on Thursday next, and be whipped by the hangman through the streets of Westminster to the Old Exchange, London; and there, likewise, to be set upon the pillory, with his head in the pillory, for the space of two hours, between the hours of eleven and one, on Saturday next; in each of the said places, wearing a paper containing an inscription of his crimes: and that at the Old Exchange, his tongue shall be bored through with a hot iron, and that he be there also stigmatized in the forehead with the letter B; and that he be, afterwards, sent to Bristol and conveyed into and through the said city, on a horse bare ridged, with his face back [i.e., without saddle, and facing the rear], and there also publicly whipped, the next market-day after he comes thither: and that from thence he be committed to prison in Bridewell, London, and there restrained from the society of all people, and kept to hard labour till he be released by the Parliament: and, during that time, be debarred of the use of pen, ink, and paper, and have no relief but what he earns by his daily labour. (158)

The *True Narrative* reports that the clause "from the society of all people" was substituted for "the society of all men" (34), and Gilbert Pickering's comment makes clear why the change was thought necessary: "Either be strict in this, or you do nothing, for certainly this of *Quakerism* is as infectious as the plague. And that not only men, but women be kept from him. I have told you, it is a woman that has done all the mischief."[85] As for the provision that Nayler be imprisoned until Parliament decided otherwise, the unstated intention was to ensure that Cromwell, who still favored a policy of toleration, would not be able to release Nayler on his own initiative.[86]

An interesting glimpse of regional antagonism emerged when possible places of imprisonment were being proposed.

Mr. Highland [from Surrey]. Those that come out of the North are the greatest pests of the nation. The Diggers came thence.

Mr. Robinson [Yorkshire]. I hope that gentleman does not mean by his pests, all that come thence. He means not us, I hope. The origin of the Diggers was from London, a Blackwell-hallman thief.

Lord [Walter] Strickland [Northumberland]. I rather think these pests have come from Surrey, for there was the first rise of the Diggers.

Mr. Bampfield [Exeter]. I am glad every body apprehends this man to be such an one as that all are weary of him. He came from the North. It verifies the proverb *ab aquilone nil boni* [nothing good from the north wind]. I hope it will be a warning to them never to send us such cattle amongst us. (155–156)

Definitions of otherness were at stake: London and the southern counties were closing ranks. London was, and after the Restoration would remain, the stronghold of wealthy Nonconformist merchants, profoundly different in their values from the agrarian and artisan culture that produced the "First Publishers of Truth." Strickland's jibe about Surrey was well taken: Francis Drake, one of those who most fiercely denounced Nayler for "horrid blasphemy" (55), was lord of the manor of Cobham in Surrey and had been the chief persecutor of the Diggers in their short-lived attempt to establish claim to "common" land.[87]

There was now much discussion as to whether Nayler, after being informed of the judgment, should be permitted to speak again. An exchange between two of the Major Generals made the issue clear:

Major General Kelsey. This court, nor any court, but must mix mercy with judgment. It may be he may recant. None can tell what God in this time has wrought upon him. This is a new business. He has never been yet heard what he can say to it, why judgment should not be pronounced against him. You have no law for what you do.

Major General Boteler. If it had been the case of death, I confess I should have given him all the liberty that might be to speak for himself. But in the lesser punishment, you need not put an excuse in his mouth. (163–64)

Kelsey, as we have seen, was anxious to avoid precedents that could arbitrarily threaten the liberty of ordinary Englishmen, while Boteler, implacable hammer of the Quakers, wanted to avoid any risk that the chosen scapegoat might escape punishment. Nathaniel Bacon of Suffolk was even willing to assert that Nayler must not be *allowed* to recant: "You should consider how it stands with the honour of God, or of this House, to retract your judgment, though this man should say he repents. Have you not passed your judgment already?" (164).

Downing, whose hard-line position we have noted several times, was disgusted by this turn of affairs: "You have intricated yourselves into another debate" (165). But it is easy to see why this happened, since all along the issue of private understanding had been so crucial. If Nayler was simply being punished for what he had done, then his present state of mind would be irrelevant. But if what he had done was to be understood by ascertaining what he thought it meant, then his present state of mind was altogether relevant. Beyond that, if it should turn out that he had by now been converted to a "correct" state of mind, it would seem monstrous to punish him for a repudiated former state. All inquisitions have had to face this dilemma; Nayler's show trial would have concluded more promptly and convincingly if only he had been willing to grovel and acknowledge the justice of his punishment.

At length there was a vote, and by a margin of 107 to 85 it was resolved to bring Nayler back to hear the sentence but not to allow him to speak. While the sentence was being read he "offered two or three times to speak, and to say he desired to know what his crimes were; he knew none" (167). This was not permitted. As he was being taken away Nayler made a short statement that Burton had trouble hearing, but that is moving and generous even as he reports it (and Burton was one of those who had voted for the death sentence). "Nayler said, as he went out, 'God has given me a body; I shall willingly endure it;' or, 'I hope I shall endure it;' or, 'God will, I hope, give me a spirit to endure it.' I did not well hear. And said further, 'The Lord lay not these things to your charge. I shall pray heartily that he may not;' or, 'I shall pray for you.'" (167) The accuracy of Burton's record is confirmed by the similar wording reported in the Quaker *True Narrative:* "He that hath prepared the body, will enable me to suffer; and I pray that He may not lay it to your charge" (p. 57). It has not been noticed that Nayler was making a direct allusion here to the guilt of Saul before his conversion. When Stephen was being stoned to death "he kneeled down, and cried with a loud voice, Lord, lay not this sin to their charge . . . And Saul was consenting unto his death" (Acts 7: 60–8: 1). One remembers that the apologia published jointly by Fox and Nayler in 1654 was entitled *Saul's Errand to Damascus;* it was on the road to Damascus that Saul fell blinded to the ground, heard a voice crying "Why persecutest thou me?" and was converted as Paul.

According to Burton, "Sir John Reynolds and others said afterwards, it was hard he should not be heard out, and he doubted some were afraid he should recant. He doubted that was not so charitable" (167). Reynolds's sympathies were mixed, as was the case with not a few of his colleagues. Both lawyer and soldier, he had been given land in Ireland as a reward for his role in the campaign there and was a faithful supporter of Cromwell. During the civil wars he had been "popular with soldiers of advanced political views," but he helped to put down the Leveller mutiny at Burford, after which they "denounced him in their pamphlets as an apostate and a traitor."[88]

On December 18, the day after Nayler's sentence was handed down, an angry discussion erupted about the threat posed by the Quakers to law and order. William Strickland—like Nayler, from Yorkshire—summarized the arguments that many were raising: "They are a growing evil, and the greatest that ever was. Their way is a plausible way; all levellers against magistracy and propriety [i.e., property]. They say the Scriptures are but ink and paper. They are guided by a higher light. They deny all ordinances, as marriage, &c" (169). Calvinist rectitude is joined here with social conservatism: to claim to follow a "higher light" is to evade the institutional controls that are guaranteed by a right interpretation of the Bible, and the result must be a resurgence of the Levellers, defying magistrates, threatening property, and making light of officially sanctioned bonds. Bulstrode Whitelocke, a close associate of Cromwell's, drew the conclusion in lurid terms: "If there be any such people as deny magistracy and ministry, we may easily guess the consequence. Cutting of throats must necessarily follow" (170).

Yet Whitelocke was a moderate, and a particular kind of moderate who spoke for the future. In general it had been members of Cromwell's Council—Desborough (whose wife Martha Simmonds had nursed), Lambert, Pickering, Sydenham—who urged moderation toward Nayler, in part at least for prudential reasons.[89] But the strongest arguments for leniency were pressed by a small minority who stood outside the traditional categories to which the rest appealed, and who would help after the Restoration to bring about a new conception of toleration stressing liberty of conscience rather than theological soundness. Whitelocke, like Matthew Hale and Charles Wolseley, was a learned rationalist who sought to promote political peace under any regime, whether Puritan or royalist. It is interesting that he drew close to the Quakers in later years, when they too were putting theological controversy behind them; the publication of his posthumous writings was supervised by William Penn.[90] After the trial was over he was reported to have said that many people believed Nayler "was too furiously persecuted by some rigid men."[91] In the report of the debate in Cobbett's *State Trials*, the only extended speech by any MP is a learned discourse by Whitelocke, full of Hebrew and Greek, arguing against a death sentence for Nayler on both religious and judicial grounds.

Cromwell had remained officially aloof from the proceedings throughout the debate and sentencing, though apparently encouraging his surrogates in Parliament to work for relative leniency, but he now seized an opportunity to stress the constitutional issue. Parliament sat on Christmas Day, December 25, in contempt of that Popish festival. (In 1644 a parliamentary ordinance had called for the regular monthly fast on December 25 rather than any traditional celebration of the day "commonly called the Feast of the Nativity of Christ" on which "men took liberty to carnal and sensual delights, contrary to the life which Christ himself led on earth." A 1647 ordinance abolished the superstitious festivals of Christmas, Easter, and Whitsunday.)[92] On December 26 the Speaker read out a letter from the Lord Protector: "Having taken notice of a sentence by you, given against one James Nayler, albeit we do abhor such wicked opinions and practices, we, being interested [i.e., having an interest] in the Government, desire to know the grounds and reasons how you proceeded herein without our consent" (246).

Heated discussion ensued. Some members were panicky and feared Cromwell's wrath; others were confident that nothing needed to be justified. A few were stupid enough, or at least pretended to be, as to assume that their verdict of blasphemy was what needed to be explained. Most, however, were willing to discuss the real issue quite openly. Francis Rouse said, "We should return this short answer to his Highness's letter, 'We had power so to do'" (253). As Rouse and many others saw, they were participants in a historical process in which the constitution was being actively reinvented. Downing put it well: "The Instrument of Government is but new, and our jurisdiction is but new too. It is dangerous either for him [Cromwell] to question our power, or for us to question his, in matters that are for the public safety; we must both wink." (254) By now Nayler himself was no longer at issue. He had passed in effect into legend, subsumed into the Nayler case, from which precedents could be argued and consequences hoped or feared.

Lambert Godfrey, always keen-sighted on constitutional issues, urged the Parliament not to recede from the daring assertion of its own power that had just been taken: "If you revoke this, you must not only cry *peccavi* to James Nayler for what is passed, but to his Highness also, and also to the nation. Here is your power asserted on one hand; the supreme magistrate, on the other hand, desiring an account of your judgment. Where shall there be *tertius Arbiter?* It is a hard case. No judge upon earth" (249). Cromwell himself somewhat later, in a speech to army officers, suggested that the *tertius arbiter* should be a revived House of Lords, and accurately described the Nayler case as having exposed the weaknesses of the Instrument of Government. In Burton's summary of his remarks,

> It is time to come to a settlement, and lay aside arbitrary proceedings, so unacceptable to the nation. And by the proceedings of this Parliament, you see they stand in need of a check, or balancing power (meaning the House of Lords, or a House so constituted) for the case of James Nayler might happen to be your own case. By their judicial power they fall upon life and member, and doth the Instrument enable me to control it? (384)

If Nayler was being punished simply for horrid blasphemy, then God's honor was perhaps vindicated and future offenders warned. But if Nayler was the figurehead in a test case—and everyone knew he was—then the result served only to complicate matters. What exactly had been tested, and how conclusive were the results?

In the debate about how best to answer Cromwell's letter, Major General Lambert made a remarkable statement about the exclusion of some elected members when this Parliament first convened. "For that of keeping out the members, if such a course had not been taken, consider what a Parliament you might have had. If a Parliament should be chosen according to the general spirit and temper of the nation, and if there should not be a check upon such election, those may creep into this House who may come to sit as our judges for all we have done in this Parliament, or at any other time or place" (281). This was virtually to admit that the Puritans governed as a minority against the wishes of the majority of the population, sustained only by the power of the army. And it was also to anticipate, just beyond the horizon but rapidly approaching, the possibility of the Restoration. No doubt Lambert, who still hoped to be Cromwell's successor, felt that some of his colleagues were all too ready to position themselves for that eventuality. As Abbott says, "Men were already looking to the future, and many of them were already trimming their sails preparatory to setting a new course."[93]

In the event no answer at all was returned to Cromwell's letter, and he did not demand one. Although he clearly felt that Parliament had behaved illegally, he did nothing to reverse its action. Probably he did not dare to. Cromwell badly needed this Parliament to vote him funds, and in addition he believed that Nayler really had blasphemed, even if the punishment was excessive.[94] Meanwhile the constitutional point had been made, but how it was to be resolved remained unclear.

Equally unclear was the application of the Nayler judgment as a warning to the Quakers and other presumed subversives. Immediately after sentencing, Parliament received a large number of petitions from various parts of the country demanding that the Quaker menace be forcibly put down. The question then arose whether anyone could define what a Quaker was, much less show how Nayler's punishment should be understood as a blow to the Quakers in general. Colonel Sydenham put his finger on the problem: "I am as much against the Quakers as any man, but would not bring a law against Quakers by a general word." Walter Strickland concurred:

> You will not find in all your statute-books a definition of Quaker or Blasphemy. Other States [i.e., nations] never do it, further than as disturbers of the peace. We know how laws against Papists were turned upon the honestest men. We may all, in after ages, be called Quakers. It is a word nobody understands . . . We all know how the edge of former laws against Papists has been turned upon the best Protestants, the truest professors of religion, the honest Puritan, as they called him, a good profession, but hard to be understood, as this word Quaker will be in after ages. (172–173)

The remark about "after ages" was pointed, and had reference to the near future rather than the remote.

Crucifixion

Nayler's punishment was savage. He was to be whipped at each cross-street on the way to the pillory and did indeed receive "310 stripes as the hangman hath confessed, and should have had one more, for there are 311 kennels, but his [the hangman's] foot slipping it fell on his own hand and cut him much."[95] Rebecca Travers submitted a written protest that described the consequences of the whipping in vivid detail:

> To my best discerning there was not a space bigger than the breadth of a man's nail free from stripes and blood, from his shoulders [to] near his waist. And his right arm was sorely striped. His hands also were sorely hurt with the cords, that they bled, and were swelled. The blood and wounds of his back did very little appear at first sight, by reason of the abundance of dirt that covered them, till it was washed off . . . And others saw that he was much abused with horses treading on him, for the print of the nails were seen on his feet. (45)

This testimony had its effect on some members of Parliament, persuading them to postpone for a week the execution of the remainder of Nayler's sentence. When others suggested that the punishment had been merely symbolic, Colonel Richard Holland retorted, "A merchant's wife told me that there was no skin left between his shoulders and his hips. It was no mock punishment." But curiously, the extent of the punishment seemed doomed to remain hearsay, interpreted by each member as he thought best. Christopher Pack said the jailor had told him that "there were but three places where the skin was in any way hurt or broken, and it was no bigger than a pin's head," and Colonel Henry Markham agreed: "It is an abominable thing to hear such unjust things informed to this House, as that of his whipping so hard, or his being sick. I would have the merchant's wife that reported it sent for and whipped. I am informed it was quite otherwise."[96]

At least three accounts survive of Nayler's sufferings in the pillory. Burton, the self-effacing diarist to whom we owe our knowledge of the parliamentary debate, unexpectedly materializes in his own person as a witness of its outcome:

This day B—— and I were to see Nayler's tongue bored through, and him marked in the forehead. He put out his tongue very willingly, but shrinked a little when the iron came upon his forehead. He was pale when he came out of the pillory, but high-coloured after tongue-boring. He was bound with a cord by both arms to the pillory. Rich, the mad merchant, sat bare [i.e., bareheaded] at Nayler's feet all the time. Sometimes he sang and cried, and stroked his hair and face, and kissed his hand, and sucked the fire out of his forehead. Nayler embraced his executioner, and behaved himself very handsomely and patiently. A great crowd of people there. (266)

One writer suggests that "B" was Bampfield, with whom Burton had earlier dined at Richard Cromwell's.[97] Or perhaps it was Colonel Bethel, one of the party with whom Burton spent the rest of the day at the Sun Tavern. Did they celebrate there?

A fuller account was published by Nayler's old enemy John Deacon, who like Burton was a gratified eyewitness:

On Saturday December the 27th about 11 of the clock he was in a coach conveyed from the common gaol of Newgate to the Black Boy near to the Royal Exchange, London; in which house he continued till the clock had struck twelve at noon, when by divers on foot with holberts [halberds] he was guarded to the pillory, where when he came they presently put his head into the same, and having pinned it down, came up Martha Symonds, and with her two others, who was said to be Hannah Stranger and Dorcas Erbury; the first seated herself just behind him on the right side, the two latter before him, the one on the right hand, the other on the left, just at his feet, in imitation of Mary Magdalen and Mary the Mother of Jesus, and Mary the Mother of Cleophas, John 19. 25, thereby to witness their still blasphemous and presumptuous and heretical adoration of him, as Jesus the Christ, as is more evidently expressed by that act of Robert Rich, whom I saw stick up a paper over his head, in which it is said was writ, "This is the King of the Jews," word by word with that in Luke 23. 38 . . . When he had stood just one hour and three quarters, they took him forth of the pillory, and having bound him fast with his back to the same, the executioner pulled off his cap, and having hoodwinked his face and taken fast hold of his tongue, with a red hot iron he bored a hole quite thorough; which having done, and pulling the cloth off that covered his face, he put a handkerchief over his eyes, and so putting his left hand in his pole, he taking the red-hot iron-letter in his other hand, put it to his forehead, which gave a little flash of smoke; which being done, Rich licked the same, as did the dogs the wounds of Lazarus; and then sang, which he did often before, both stroking and kissing him, which he suffered with an admired impudence; so Naylor was first conveyed back to the Black-boy, and thence again to Newgate, where he rests till he sets forward to suffer deserved shame in like manner at Bristol. What I have said in this, I saw and therefore can witness.[98]

John 19: 25, incidentally, names the three Marys but says nothing about their positions at the cross; it must have been by allusion to traditional iconology that Nayler's followers presented their *tableau vivant*. Most striking in this account is Deacon's obvious approval of Nayler's suffering, his interpretation of Nayler's calm behavior as "impudence," and his irritation that the whole thing was stopped fifteen minutes before the prescribed two hours were up. One cannot help noticing, also, that no one objected to the presence of the women who had actually uttered blasphemy at Bristol, if blasphemy is what it was. A Quaker historian commented long afterward, "On the 18th December the house had referred to a committee the facts and crimes of the rest of the persons apprehended with him; and yet on the 27th, three at least of the women were so much at liberty as to come up on the pillory and seat themselves, two before and one behind him."[99]

Finally, there survives an anonymous Quaker account of the event, agreeing in all details but embedding them in an entirely different context of saintly endurance:

> The executioner took him out [of the pillory], and having bound his arms with cords to the pillory, and having put a cap over his eyes, he had him put forth his tongue, which he freely did; and the executioner with a red hot iron, about the bigness of a quill, bored the same, and by order from the sheriff held it in a small space, to the end the beholders might see and bear witness that the sentence was thoroughly executed; then having took it out,

and pulling the cap off that covered his face, he put a handkerchief over his eyes, and putting his left hand to the back part of his head, and taking the red hot iron letter in his other hand, put it to his forehead till it smoked, all which time James never so much as winced, but bore it with astonishing and heart-melting patience. Being unbound, he took the executioner in his arms, embracing and hugging him, after which Robert Rich through his ardent love licked the wound on his forehead.[100]

All that remained was for Nayler to return to Bristol and undo his crime by literally retracing his route backward. The *Mercurius Politicus* described with relish the highly circumstantial punishment decreed for him there:

Cause James Nayler to ride in at Lawfords-gate upon a horse bare ridged, with his face backward, from thence along Winestreet to the Tolzey, thence down High Street over the Bridge, and out of Rackly-gate; there let him alight, and bring him into St. Thomas Street, and cause him to be stripped and made fast to the cart-horse; and there in the Market first whipped, from thence to the foot of the Bridge there whipped, thence to the middle of High Street there whipped, thence to the Tolzey there whipped, thence to the middle of Broad Street there whipped; and then turn into Tailors-hall, thence release him from the cart-horse, and let him put on his clothes, and carry him from thence to Newgate by Tower Lane the back way.

The newspaper added that a number of Nayler's followers, notably Robert Rich, accompanied him bareheaded and singing on this grim journey.[101] Much to the indignation of William Grigge, who had been a prime mover in getting Nayler tried in the first place, influence was apparently exerted to lessen the severity and publicity of the punishment: "Now whereas customarily the bellman goes before and makes proclamation of the offence of the offender, yet this unparalleled blasphemer (though as vicious as erroneous) the keeper commands the bellman to the contrary, and suffers one Jones a coppersmith, and an ugly Quaker, to hold back the beadle's arm when striking, and in all the way the bell rang but six times."[102]

Most modern accounts treat all of this as a pathetic aftermath, with the real story already finished. But as Rich's actions and the glosses in *A True Narrative* show, for Nayler and his small group of supporters the story was still going on, and this was actually the most significant part of it. Bristol had been his Palm Sunday; now came his crucifixion. Persecution in this fallen world was an authentication of grace, and Nayler was now literalizing the metaphor that he and his colleagues so often invoked: "Being faithful to the Light . . . it will lead you to the death upon the cross, and crucify you unto the world and worldly things."[103] It was not just a case of welcoming martyrdom in psychological terms, though it may certainly have been that; it was also a case of confirming an apostolic mission by provoking the inevitable reaction of those who "have eyes and see not, ears and hear not," as Nayler had written in 1655.[104] This was to charge the Puritans not just with error, but with the total blindness and deafness to truth of which Christ had spoken: "Having eyes, see ye not? and having ears, hear ye not?" (Mark 8: 18). Not only were such false teachers cut off from Christ, but the parabolic message was cast in terms that would keep them that way: "Therefore speak I to them in parables: because they seeing see not; and hearing they hear not, neither do they understand" (Matthew 13: 13).

Nayler's text went on to describe Paul's sufferings in terms that directly anticipate his own treatment in the following year: "Paul was sent to open the blind eyes, yet was he sent to those who had eyes as you have, with which they could see to stone him and whip him, and ears to hear him, and call what he said *heresy* and *blasphemy*, as you do, and as ever the carnal judged of the spiritual, who have not an ear to hear what the spirit saith" (221). This kind of suffering was not sought as evidence of peculiar individual favor from God; the point was that Paul underwent what every true Christian ought to be willing to undergo. So Nayler demanded, "Can you receive him who is set as a sign everywhere to be spoken against? Will you bear his marks in your body? Will you take up his cross daily, and bear his reproach? Will you own him in whippings, stonings, mockings, and temptations, and to be counted the filth of the world and off-scouring of all things for his name's sake?" (244). To be "a sign to be spoken against," as Nayler himself became, was indeed to imitate Christ, for Simeon said when the child Jesus was brought to him in the temple, "Behold, this child is set for the fall and rising again of many in Israel, and for a sign which shall be spoken against" (Luke 2: 34).

Even before his punishment was completed Nayler played an apostolic role when five Puritan ministers were sent by Parliament to interview him in jail, just to make sure that he had not in fact repented of his dreadful crime. He refused to recant in terms they could accept and they left in a rage, burning their notes. They then informed Parliament of his intransigence, and on this one W. H. comments in the *True Narrative*,

> Query . . . whether any nation afford the like precedent, that four or five persons (a man's enemies) should be his examiners, and solely empowered to report his case to his judges, not admitting any to be present but themselves, as indifferent [i.e., impartial] witnesses betwixt them? If four or five of those silversmiths that made shrines for Diana, whose gain Paul's doctrine destroyed, if they had been sent to Paul to examine him and report his case to his judges, how unequal a thing would this be accounted? (60)

From the Quaker point of view professional clergy were no better than the pagans against whom Paul contended. At Cambridge in 1655, Fox recalled, the scholars "knew I was so against their trade, which they were there as apprentices to learn, the trade of preaching, that they raged as bad as ever Diana's craftsmen did against Paul."[105]

Of course for hard-line Puritans the biblical models were relevant in a totally different way: the Quakers were not persecuted apostles at all, but diabolical blasphemers. When it was suggested that petitions from the public should be heard, Downing responded furiously, "That text works much with me which is in Hebrews 10. 28 ['He that despised Moses's law, died without mercy']. We are God's executioners, and ought to be tender of his honour." Downing added that the report of the five ministers confirmed his sternness. "Had you anything from [Nayler] himself of recantation, it were something. But as the case is, if ten thousand should come to the door and petition, I would die upon the place before I would remit the sentence you have already passed."[106]

We have a number of indications that Nayler's supporters, and no doubt Nayler himself, were conscious of specific parallels with Christ's passion. The nail marks on his feet that Rebecca Travers described are surely reminiscent of the nails with which Christ was pierced. A later Quaker writer described him as having been "stigmatized,"[107] and the branding and tongue-piercing might indeed be regarded as a version of Christ's stigmata. In fact the marginal glosses in the *True Narrative* specify messianic typology for each component of Nayler's punishment. On the sentence of boring through the tongue they comment, "This was that the Scripture might be fulfilled, Rev. 1.7." The text in Revelation reads, "Behold, he cometh with clouds; and every eye shall see him, and they also which pierced him." As for the branding on the forehead, "this was also that the Scriptures might be fulfilled, Is. 52: 14" (p. 33). The Isaiah reference is to the prophecy of the Suffering Servant: "His visage was so marred more than any man, and his form more than the sons of men." Similarly the pillory, the whipping, and the inscription are directly connected in the *True Narrative* glosses to the punishment of Christ: "They clothed him with purple, and plaited a crown of thorns, and put it about his head, and began to salute him, Hail, King of the Jews!" (Mark 15: 17); "Then Pilate took Jesus, and scourged him" (John 19: 1); "They set up over his head his accusation written, THIS IS JESUS THE KING OF THE JEWS" (Matthew 27: 37). This last text was the one Rich invoked in what a modern Quaker writer regretfully refers to as "an allusive but ill-chosen inscription."[108]

Allusively but unmistakably, the point was being made that Nayler had reenacted Christlike signs in an overtly prophetic manner. "Though the Devil had power to cast some into prison," the *True Narrative* gloss adds after quoting Nayler's sentence, "yet the Lord's work will go on to the confounding of all his enemies, this assuredly will come to pass, and remember that a prophet hath been amongst you" (p. 35). And another biblical allusion confirms the typological statement that Rich had made, strangely enough with impunity, at the pillory:

> This was also very remarkable, that notwithstanding there might be many thousands of people, yet they were very quiet, few heard to revile him, or seen to throw any one thing at him; and when he was a-burning, all the people both before him and behind him, and on both sides of him, with one consent stood bareheaded. This was done that the Scripture might be fulfilled, Mark 15. 38. (p. 42)

Verse 38 seems not altogether apposite in itself, referring to the rending of the veil of the temple, but taken together verses 37–39 do tell a striking story:

And Jesus cried with a loud voice, and gave up the ghost. And the veil of the temple was rent in twain from the top to the bottom. And when the centurion, which stood over against him, saw that he so cried out and gave up the ghost, he said, Truly this man was the Son of God.

Nayler's supporters continued to invoke Christological parallels well after his punishment was over and he was consigned to solitary confinement. As Hubberthorne indignantly reported to Margaret Fell, Martha Simmonds and Mildred Crouch interrupted a large Quaker meeting and refused to let anyone else speak. They sang a psalm and Martha read a chapter from the Bible, both of which were Puritan practices that the Quakers repudiated. Still worse, "they broke bread and drunk drink and gave [it] to the rude multitude that would take any, and so fulfilled an imagination of their heart."[109] Imagination, as we have seen, was anathema in Quaker thought, and what it produced here, as Phyllis Mack observes, was a parodic holy communion.[110] It seems apparent that a direct comment on the Nayler episode was intended: now that he had been crucified, his followers must imitate Christ's disciples and consume the symbolic meal of body and blood. Rich years later referred explicitly to Nayler's return to Bristol as "his crucifixion there."[111]

Nayler himself was soon securely out of sight in Bridewell, rapidly receding into myth, where he has remained (more and more dimly) ever since. He still had four years to live, however, and during those years he wrote and even managed to smuggle out and publish a surprising amount. He also made several guarded and elliptical statements that later Quakers were eager to interpret as full-scale repentance. But it is far from clear that that was Nayler's intent. Certainly he regretted the damage he had caused the movement, and it goes without saying that he found ostracism by nearly all of his friends (and Friends) to be painful in the extreme. Still, he never repudiated the beliefs that had led to his notorious sign, and his disappearance from national memory is telling evidence of the double shift by which the Puritans first stamped out their antinomian rivals and then were themselves coopted and assimilated by a culture whose traditional attitudes proved more durable than anyone in the 1650s could have believed.

5

Aftermath

The Rise of Quakerism and the Reinvention of Nayler

Nayler's strange performance was something the Quaker movement definitely did not need. It came at a particularly inopportune moment in their struggle to win greater toleration, when they had just managed to secure an order of the Council of State to release a number of Quaker prisoners. Fox saw from the beginning that he had to repudiate Nayler unequivocally, as indeed he had already done before Nayler ever got to Bristol. As he complained in a letter he sent to Nayler in Exeter jail:

> Martha Simmonds, who is called your mother, she bade me bow down, and said I was Lord and King, and then my heart was rotten; and she said she denied that which was head in me. And one of them said she had stopped Francis Howgill's mouth and silenced him, and turned my words into a lie and into a temptation; and she came singing in my face, inventing words. And Hannah boasted and said, "If they were devils make them to tremble;" and she boasted what she would do and cry against.
>
> Many did not expect that thou wouldst have been an encourager of such as do cry against the life and power of Truth, but wouldst have been an encourager of Truth, and not have trained up a

company against it: and what is that which doth fulfill the world's prophecy and their desires? Therefore consider, and search thy self, if this be innocency. The light of God in you all I own, but this I judge.[1]

Against the sobriety and self-discipline of Quaker silence, the behavior of the women seemed ranterish and perhaps was meant to: "She came singing in my face, inventing words."

The Bristol authorities found this letter on Nayler, as Fox perhaps anticipated they would, and it served its purpose of exonerating Fox. But whether or not sending the letter was prudential, Fox's outrage was certainly sincere, as was that of the other Quaker leaders. When Francis Howgill, who had had to endure the abuse of Nayler's supporters in London, wrote to Margaret Fell about the episode in Bristol he could not bring himself to report the full details: "There is such filthy things acted there in such havoc and spoil and such madness among them as I cannot write, but there is about ten of them in all with him, and they call him 'I am' and the 'lamb.'"[2]

A few months later, when the debate in Parliament was in full cry, Fox addressed an epistle "To Oliver Cromwell and the Parliament" in which he pleaded for toleration—"it is not just that the mouth of the Seed should be stopped"—but added a postscript that unmistakably implied a repudiation of Nayler:

If the seed speak which is Christ he hath no other name, for the seed is Christ Jesus and it is not blasphemy but truth; but if the seed of the serpent speak and say he is Christ that is the liar and the blasphemy and the ground of all blasphemy and is not the seed which is Christ, but the seed of the serpent is to be bruised which is the cause of all enmity, strife, and debate with the seed of the woman which is Christ.[3]

Certainly the upshot was that the seed of the serpent was bruised. But still the damage had been done: petitions were pouring in to Parliament demanding anti-Quaker action, and in the months immediately following the Nayler case a series of measures cut down significantly on religious toleration. Cromwell, though more tolerant than many of the local authorities, endorsed new penalties proposed in the 1657 Humble Petition and Advice (which begged him to accept the crown);

laws against vagrancy and interrupting ministers were made more stringent; and local authorities stepped up prosecutions of Quakers.[4]

The Quakers in general were quick to dissociate themselves privately and publicly from Nayler's actions at Bristol. Ralph Farmer, one of the Bristol ministers who were present at Nayler's interrogation there, rushed into print with an account of the affair called *Satan Inthron'd in his Chair of Pestilence*. This drew an immediate reply from George Bishop, an army captain and Bristol Quaker, in a prolix treatise entitled *The Throne of Truth Exalted over the Powers of Darkness: From whence is judged the Mouth of Ralph Farmer (an Unclean and Bloodthirsty Priest of Bristol)*. Bishop deployed militant language to celebrate Nayler's former prowess when he still "walked in the light"—"How did he come upon the princes of all sorts as mortar, and as the potter treadeth clay?" (3)—but unequivocally condemned him for the Bristol performance. According to Bishop it was Nayler's seducing companions who deserved the principal blame, as Quakers at Bristol had already understood before the incident occurred:

> His hour of temptation being come, and darkness getting about him quick and sudden, his state was seen in the light by Friends at London, before he was brought thence to Bristol; and being at Bristol the latter end of the fifth month (the time of the fair) it was seen by Friends there how it had encompassed him; and that spirit which had darkened him was then denied by them, and also the woman from whom it had entered him, and the other two with her, and all their filth (whom not so much as one Friend owned of those thousands in that city and the country about it, as we have heard or have known). (4)

After leaving Bristol and being imprisoned at Exeter Nayler began to see the light once more, but "some came to him thither who tempted him again, and so he became again darkened." Against this erratic behavior, Bishop emphasized, the Quaker community responded at once with appropriate indignation. "Many papers were sent to him discovering that spirit, and that woman, her company, and their imaginations, and judging of both" (4). Yet what exactly *happened* is left obscure: the women were carriers of "filth" and they plunged Nayler into "darkness," but these vague metaphors do little to clarify the issues that were at stake.

At no time, then, according to Bishop's story, did any reputable Quakers show the slightest sympathy for Nayler, which means that they were not just defending themselves post facto after his disgrace (as Farmer had charged) but had already rejected him beforehand. In Bishop's account, Fox's letter played its role as a providentially inspired exoneration:

The wisdom of God foreseeing what hath come to pass, and how greedily this generation would catch at this opportunity to strike at the Truth and lambs . . . so ordered it that amongst the papers taken as aforesaid, some should be wherein expressly is discovered and judged that spirit, woman, company, and their practices, which should (and it doth) stand a full and undeniable record in the behalf of Truth and its Friends for ever. (5–6)

The obsessive textuality of this controversy is noteworthy: Quakers and anti-Quakers constantly reprinted and analyzed as many documents as they could find. The meaning of the event thus resolved itself, to a remarkable degree, into interpretation of the written and printed records that were generated by it. Bishop mentions that he had personally acted as amanuensis for Fox's denunciation of Nayler: "This letter was wrote by me out of George Fox his own handwriting (which handwriting of his I have by me) and sent as it was written by me from Reading to Bristol, to Dennis Hollister, with directions to him to send it thence to Exeter, which he sent by a messenger on purpose, and to J. N. it was delivered whilst he was at Exon a prisoner" (6). Bishop had associated closely with both Nayler and Fox and would have been well placed to supply an eyewitness's perspective; but from the point of view of his antagonists it was the documentary integrity of Fox's letter *before* the Bristol "sign" that mattered, and Bishop therefore focused on his own role only to confirm how the letter got written and sent. But Farmer had already noted this claim and dismissed it as irrelevant: the letter "was wholly written by the hands of George Bishop (that precious saint) but subscribed G. F.," and in Farmer's opinion it was a matter of indifference that Bishop was "the amanuensis, scribe, or pen-man (if not the inditer) of the letter of disclaimer."[5]

In this contest of interpretation, much could hinge on a single textual reading, as Bishop indignantly commented:

In the copy of the letter aforesaid [in Farmer's pamphlet] he hath thus put it, "The light of God in ye all I *am*, but this I judge;" whenas in the original letter it is, "The light of God in ye all I *own*, but this I judge": by which foul and dishonest dealing he holds him forth to the reader as saying that of himself which is only said of Christ Jesus, by whom the world was made, who is the Light of the World, and so (consequently) as a blasphemer under his own hand (which is what he would fain make him, and have him to be if he could, that in his blood he might wash his hands, and strike at the Truth which he witnesseth). What difference there is between "I own" and "I am," especially in this place; and what a devilish wickedness it is to forge in such a word, as for it, were it truly so, he would take away his life. (7–8)

"I own" (meaning "I acknowledge") is innocent; "I am," differing from it so minutely, is punishable by death.

These exchanges, at an early stage of modern print culture, embody a disquieting recognition of the spurious authority that print confers. Farmer had quoted from Weld's *Perfect Pharisee* the charge that Nayler denied the Christ who died at Jerusalem. To this Bishop responded that that charge had already been decisively refuted, but somehow the refutation remained maddeningly impotent: "So thou bringest *The Perfect Pharisee*, one of thy generation, and others bring thee; and because it's found in print under some of your hands, how false soever, therefore it must be truth, and if it be but so charged, it must be so made use of, though never so fully answered" (76). Laboring through Bishop's rambling treatise, a reader comes to feel that actual doctrinal positions have become all but irrelevant, as one struggles to winnow truth from error with the weary anxiety of Milton's Psyche.

Farmer replied two years later with an equally prolix book, deploying an extended ad hominem attack on Bishop's political and financial dealings "to let the world see how deeply and closely wickedness may lie lurking in our natures, and what a desperate evil hypocrisy is, that a man may continue in such wickedness unrepented of, and yet think himself a saint, and to have attained to perfection."[6] Farmer also commented shrewdly on the vagueness of Bishop's explanation of what went wrong in Nayler's case, using expressive italics to highlight its weakest points:

How comes it to pass that this *glorious son of the morning* is like *Lucifer* so cast down and darkened by that *woman* and her company, with all their filthiness and deceit, as he phrases it? What *spirit* was that, and what *darkness* was that which he speaks of, that *clouded* him? When *began* it? And is it not *still* upon him? And how came it to pass, that being *delivered*, he became dark *again?* These things would be known, that so we might say when James is in the *dark*, or when he is in the *light*, that so we might not be mistaken in him. (21–22)

As to the accusation that he had willfully substituted "I am" for Fox's "I own," Farmer protested that he had faithfully followed the court clerk's transcript, believing it to be correct, but that the original letter (now in Parliament's hands in London) had been hard to decipher and might indeed have been misquoted, or there might have been "a mistake of the printer, and the priest's [i.e., Farmer's own] oversight in correcting" (22). Was it a foul forgery, or an honest error, or a mere lapse in proofreading? Farmer was no doubt anxious to explain away his own misrepresentation, but he was expressing a very reasonable skepticism about textual evidence, which Bishop, who combined a radical distrust of textuality with a stubborn reliance on it, was less willing to entertain.

Textual cruxes had long been debated, sometimes with impressive pedantry, in the angry and badly printed pamphlets hurled between Quakers and their critics. Responding three years earlier to the Quaker charge that the "priests" were the chief organizers of mob action, Francis Higginson had noticed an interesting point buried among the "errata" printed at the end of the Fox-Nayler *Saul's Errand to Damascus:*

And where they say the raging priests continued shouting, crying, and throwing stones at him [Nayler] a quarter mile out of the town, their souls may blush for shame to print such a palpable execrable falsehood . . . At the close of the book I find the word Priests in this place among the *Errata's*, and that you should read not the raging Priests, but the raging People. A willing *Erratum* doubtless, and an excellent back door here is to avoid a lie. But how shall these *Errata's* which one of 100 reads not, and few in comparison know the use of, take off this base aspersion?[7]

Perhaps misprinting "raging priests" for "raging people" was a Freudian parapraxis; or perhaps Fox and Nayler thought there was really little difference, since the angry mob was inspired by the priests even if they pretended to stay aloof. Higginson himself, however, got entangled in his own indignant syntax: he meant to write "one of 100 reads," not "one of 100 reads not." In the pamphlet controversies of the 1650s words were blunt instruments that often missed their targets.

However energetically the Quakers rallied to defend the integrity of their movement, such a defense could only succeed if they utterly rejected Nayler, and this they willingly did. Samuel Butler observed in a satiric review of self-proclaimed Messiahs:

> [And] 'tis a miracle we have no more,
> But Nayler, to set up upon that score:
> Enough to settle infamy and shame
> Upon the Christian interest and name,
> But that fanatics have been found t' atone,
> And blot out all, with what themselves have done.[8]

When Nayler was first imprisoned Bishop wrote with satisfaction to Margaret Fell, "The Lord went forth with his power . . . to break the powers of darkness, and to chain them down so that Friends are all kept and preserved; none are hurt, none go to visit them (as I can hear of) and whatever is of God [is] raised and stirred up against this work of darkness."[9] Normally Quakers made great efforts to visit their fellows in jail, but Nayler's ostracism was complete, his action having been defined as a work of darkness. Earlier in 1656, as we have seen, Nayler himself had defined the behavior of the ranterish John Toldervy as Satanic and had participated in his ostracism by the group. Now it was his own turn.

Nayler's only visible allies in the months immediately following the trial were the handful of companions who had shared his notoriety and disgrace. After his humiliating return visit to Bristol and commitment to Bridewell, Fox addressed him in a letter that seems to have been intended for general circulation: "As Martha cried against the truth, and Hannah, so now do thy disciples come, and such as have had relation to the Ranters, which are got up, and come, and cry against the truth, with impudency and boldness." Fox went on to accuse Nayler of "railing speeches," which is what Ranters were notorious for, and suggested that the "liberty" his followers continued to assert was nothing more than ranterish license: "Such as had been loose, and at liberty formerly, who were come under the judgment of the truth, now are come to liberty, and thou art a tree to shelter them."[10] It was time for the movement to police its boundaries and to learn habits of discipline; Nayler the double scapegoat now stood for everything the leading Quakers did not want to be. And even the most intransigent found it hard to bear isolation from the group and were eventually reconciled with it. This was true of all of the women who had participated in the Nayler catastrophe, including Martha Simmonds and Hannah Stranger. But we know only that they ended up as members in good standing; as to the nature and significance of their reconciliation, no evidence survives.[11]

Nayler was deeply hurt by Fox's implacable refusal to see him, and wrote to Margaret Fell, "Truly for the hardness and unreconcileableness which is in some I am astonished and shaken lest the spirit of Christ Jesus should be grieved and depart. For, if I know anything of it, or ever have done, that is it which naturally inclines to mercy and forgiveness and not to bind one another under a trespass till the uttermost farthing [Matthew 5: 26], though this may be just and I do not condemn it."[12] But the entire movement, and not just Fox, had set itself against Nayler. By 1658 the anonymous author of *Rabshakeh's Outrage Reproved*, an extended reply to Grigge's *The Quaker's Jesus*, concentrated on a general defense of the Quakers and treated the Nayler case as essentially irrelevant, on the grounds that no person in Bristol had ever shown the slightest sympathy with him. Grigge's position could then be dismissed as utterly illogical. As this writer sarcastically summarized it: "If James Naylor came into Bristol with his disciples being *seven* in number, and there be in and about the same city more than *seven hundred* people called Quakers, of whom not *one* was of that number of *seven*, and by whom those *seven* were publicly disowned, then J. N. is the *Quakers Jesus*."[13]

Since the early Quakers rejected any kind of authority structure, it was all the more important to discipline behavior by mutual surveillance, and to head off cases of "running out" (as Fox always calls them in his *Journal*) that would give the movement a bad name. Nayler wrote in an early tract, "Dear friends, watch over one another, exhort, reprove, admonish in pure love and meekness of spirit, lest you also be tempted; and all know, that you are set as a city on a hill, as signs to this generation: therefore lift up your light to all the world, that all mouths may be stopped, and hearts convinced; so that all that see you, may see you to be children of light."[14] A city on a hill (Matthew 5:14) is all too conspicuous if it goes wrong, and the signs exhibited by the Quakers were capable of being very controversial indeed, as Nayler learned to his cost.

The fullest interpretation of Nayler's story was given long afterward, in 1716, when the eighty-year-old George Whitehead reprinted some of the writings of his former companion. Born in Westmoreland in 1636, Whitehead became interested in the Quakers at the age of fourteen and first heard Nayler preach in 1653. By 1654 he had begun his own career as an itinerant preacher, and endured repeated imprisonments and public whippings. He was a prolific author from 1655 onward, and his publications include an anti-tithe pamphlet coauthored with Nayler in 1659. After Fox's death in 1691, Whitehead was the leading survivor of the original "First Publishers of Truth" and became the de facto leader of the Quaker movement, providing it, as their historian says, with "cautious and pedestrian guidance; . . . he was the embodiment of drab respectability, devoid of genius, and of little humour, but industrious and politic."[15] Such a man was perhaps uniquely placed to rehabilitate part at least of Nayler's memory. Certainly that had not been possible during Fox's long lifetime; Fox's most recent biographer shows that in 1677 he blocked a project of reprinting Nayler's writings, and it seems clear that he or his associates destroyed correspondence in the Quaker archives that tended to put Nayler in a favorable light.[16] On at least one occasion a manuscript epistle by Nayler was printed—with emendations that toned down its theological radicalism—with the signature of George Fox.[17]

Whitehead's review of the crisis in which he had personally taken part gives an unusually clear picture of the changes, intellectual as well as organizational, that developed in the Quaker movement after 1660. The most remarkable feature of Whitehead's biographical introduction is its complete silence about the Bristol episode. It jumps from a description of Martha Simmonds to the "cruel and barbarous usage which the said J. N. met withal" when he was punished by Parliament.

For a man to be sentenced to stand two hours in the pillory at Westminster, and from thence to be whipped by the common hangman over every kennel as far as the Old Exchange with three hundred and ten stripes, and there again to stand two hours in the pillory, and bored through the tongue with an hot iron, under pretence of blasphemy, when no real proof could be made thereof against him. Which treatment and usage the said J. N. met withal. This might seem intolerable barbarity exceeding Jews or Turks. Many sober men and persons of quality were ashamed thereof, and greatly pitied him . . ."[18]

But why is there no mention of Bristol? In effect, Whitehead must be conceding the accuracy of the accounts of what Nayler did, while refusing to talk about why he did it. At the very center of the story is a blank.

From Whitehead's point of view, the accusation of blasphemy was in any case simply a cover for persecution of "the people called Quakers" and was essentially political rather than doctrinal. At the end of 1656 "Presbytery and Independency swimmed and floated in profession, and with their long lectures against us cried out, 'These are the Antichrists come in the last times, &c.'" While the best-organized sects or parties managed to swim or float, those that were more individualist tended to sink, and not by accident either: "Note, it was observable how busy the proud, covetous and envious priests were in those days to incense the magistrates against us, to make them their servants and drudges in persecution, supposing *that* a fit opportunity given them to brand us with blasphemy, and under that pretence to suppress us by force of persecution" (xii). The adjectives for the "priests" were not idly chosen: they were proud, because inspired by personal ambition rather than vocation; covetous, because determined to get an income by their preaching; and envious, because unpaid and unauthorized preachers like Nayler were more inspiring than they.

At this point Whitehead reenters the story in person. Having been released from prison in Suffolk, "I came to London, and went to see the said J. N. then prisoner in the gatehouse at Westminster, but could not get into the room where he was, but saw him and spake to him through the grate of the door, to know how he did." This moment of near-contact only produced a further opacity: "He looked on me, but said little: he seemed to be in a suffering condition of spirit, as well as body" (xiii–xiv). Much to his indignation, Whitehead found himself instead in the company of "the said Martha Simmonds, with some other women that had cried him up," and they told him angrily, "All that I had done must come to the fire." After a fruitless attempt to expostulate Whitehead left, "for I was sensible a great darkness was then over them" (xiv).

To Whitehead's disgust, Nayler's "fall" gave license for mockery of the embarrassed Quaker leadership. "Some other persons of a loose ranting spirit got up, and frequently disturbed our Friends' meetings in London by their ranting, singing, bawling and reproaching us, crying out against divers of our faithful ministers and their testimonies, in this manner, viz. 'You have lost the power; you have lost the power,' &c." (xvi). Whitehead recalled in particular "one Mildred, an impudent woman, and two or three rude boisterous fellows, who were Ranters; and this kind of their disturbance continued for some weeks, until the Lord by his power stopped and confounded them, so as they came to naught." How exactly the Lord accomplished this is lost to memory, but not the exasperating image of impudent Mildred Crouch and her boisterous accomplices. In the opinion of these jeerers the original *mana* had departed. "The power" was a term regularly used by Quaker writers to contrast with conventional "forms," as when Nayler condemned those "who know not Christ nor his power, but runs after men into notions and forms, but denies the power."[19] Rebecca Travers, one of Nayler's non-ranting supporters, wrote in 1659, "This is not ink and paper, or words, which the worst of men, or the devil may read or talk of; but it is spirit, life, and power, killing and making alive; as a fire in the bosom."[20]

Given Whitehead's righteous indignation against these indecorous spirits, what follows in his account is rather surprising, and long as it is, it deserves to be read in full. The merchant Robert Rich, who licked Nayler's wounds at the pillory and was probably responsible for the Christological allusions in *A True Narrative*, was both hottempered and peculiar, and held strong views about the presence of the divine in human beings. Whitehead clearly believed that his recollections of Rich contain clues to the meaning of the Nayler episode, but equally clearly he was unwilling to be explicit.

One Robert Rich, a merchant in London, who had been convinced of Truth, he was a great admirer of J. N. and did much appear and solicit for him while he was under prosecution and examination before the Parliament, and also stood by him on the pillory, when he suffered under the cruel sentence of boring through the tongue and stigmatizing with an hot iron, and then publicly licked his wounds, thereby showing his great affection to him.

After some time the said Robert Rich went into Barbados, where (as we had account) he was turbulent in our Friends' meetings with noisy singing, &c. to the offence of sober Friends there. After some years he returned to London and came into some of our meetings, and walked up and down therein in a stately manner (having a very long white beard) in his black velvet coat, with a loose hanging cloth one over it [i.e., an un-Quakerlike opulence of dress]. When he heard something declared that pleased him, he would cry "Amen, Amen, Amen."

After a meeting in White-Hart-Court in Gracious Street he came up into Gerard Roberts' room to some of us, and declared unto me these words, viz. "I am one of the dogs that licked Lazarus his sores."

I had some discourse with the said R. R. another time about the Seed of God (the Eternal Word) in man and the soul of man; and he could not distinguish them, putting no difference between the soul or spirit of man, and that which saves it; to wit, the ingrafted immortal Word, which is able to save the soul. So that he seemed to leave no room for the immortality of the soul of man, but only of the immortal Seed or Word of God; but discoursing him a little closely upon the point, he put me off with an evasive slight, saying, "Thou art wise in the letter, but I am in that which is above thy wisdom; to wit, in the mystery, &c." (xvi–xviii)

As so often, Whitehead's "&c." ends the sentence just when one would have liked it to go on, but the general drift is clear. Rich believed that the divine Seed or Word was so fully "ingrafted" into the human soul that there was no effectual difference between them, and dismissed Whitehead's objections as derived from the letter rather than the spirit of "the mystery, &c."

The equation of Seed and Word is particularly telling. As Word, Christ is the primal *logos* of ontology, as proclaimed in the most Platonic of the Gospels: "In the beginning was the Word, and the Word was with God, and the Word was God" (John 1: 1). But as Seed, Christ is the physical person who participates in a natural process of human reproduction: "Jesus Christ our Lord, which was made of the seed of David according to the flesh" (Romans 1: 3). The whole paradox of the Incarnation is implied in these two metaphors, and if they are merged together in a single imaginative whole, a sort of deification of mankind is at least conceivable. In various places in the New Testament this merging of the metaphors actually occurs, for example in the parable of the seed that fell on good ground and bore a hundredfold; and it is precisely here that Christ speaks of "mysteries" that are hidden from the unenlightened multitude:

> And his disciples asked him, saying, What might this parable be? And he said, Unto you it is given to know the mysteries of the kingdom of God: but to others in parables; that seeing they might not see, and hearing they might not understand. Now the parable is this: The seed is the word of God. (Luke 8: 9–11)

Surely the identity of Seed and Word, pronounced by the incarnate Word himself, is the "mystery, &c." of which Robert Rich spoke. This is "the engrafted word, which is able to save your souls" (James 1: 21) in Rich's other scriptural allusion that Whitehead recalls. And it follows logically, in Rich's opinion, that the incarnation of Christ as the Word-Seed renders sinless all in whom he dwells. For this, too, there is a plausible (if disturbingly Gnostic) text: "Whosoever is born of God doth not commit sin; for his seed remaineth in him: and he cannot sin, because he is born of God" (1 John 3: 9). But it was precisely this aspect of Quaker belief in the 1650s that later Quakers wanted to forget.

Rich's distinction between two modes of wisdom also reflects Quaker thinking in the 1650s. "Wisdom" in itself was not necessarily a good thing. The "carnal wisdom" of the world was a favorite target of Puritans generally; Bunyan's Mr. Worldly-Wiseman is its most famous avatar. In its carnal form wisdom served as a tool to oppress and humiliate the dispossessed and the simple. Nayler made the distinction clearly in a formal treatise, *A Discovery of the Wisdom which is from Beneath, and the Wisdom which is from Above* (1653):

> By your wisdom you can overreach your brethren, oppress the poor to get riches, to make your selves great in the earth, and

thereby *Lord it* over your brethren; by it you can go to law, and beggar your brethren for trifles, to fulfil your own wills; by it you can deceive the simple and harmless man, and make him your laughing-stock when you have done; by it you can contrive mischief on your bed [Micah 2: 1], and when the morning is come you put it in practice against those whom you envy.[21]

This is a very rich, indeed virtually a Blakean, critique of social practices. Carnal wisdom makes laws, laws make rich people richer, and—as Nayler's italics on *"Lord it"* suggest—laws and riches cooperate to undergird a hierarchical society with lords at the top. Not only is the harmless man oppressed, but he is also mocked, and those who mock him are consumed by a twisted form of envy that masks itself as natural superiority.

In the years following the Nayler debacle, the antinomian challenge refused to go quietly. In particular, Quakers in the 1660s had to deal with alarming aftershocks in the "hat controversy" associated with John Perrot.[22] Perrot, "convinced" by Burrough in Ireland in 1656, had been welcomed among the London Quakers and had left for the Mediterranean in 1658 with the intention of converting the Pope and the Sultan of Turkey. In Rome he was arrested by the Inquisition and imprisoned in a madhouse for three years, after which he returned to England and immediately got embroiled in a controversy that was taken extremely seriously by everyone involved. Perrot claimed to have received a revelation that men should not remove their hats when praying to God, and Fox retorted, with characteristic vehemence and indistinctness, in an epistle that raised this issue to a position of central importance:

Friends, the power of the Lord God is over all them that keep on their hats in prayer, and they [Perrot's group] do not keep on their hats in prayer neither by the motion, nor the power of God, nor by the spirit of God, but (by an earthly, dark spirit) against it, and them that are in the power of God. This was the first ground of it, both in John Perrot and his company, when he run out, and J[ames] N[ayler] when he run out; and this first was done in opposition to them, that were in the truth and in the power of God; but the power of God will crush to pieces that feigned, dark, earthly spirit, and to the earth and pit it must go.

This was to place a particular kind of ritual action in the largest possible context, as an expression of the duel to the death between heaven and earth. More pragmatically, Fox recognized that the controversy was furnishing ammunition to anti-Quakers: "Ye with your earthly spirit and earthly form, have given occasion to the world to say that the people of God called Quakers are divided, some with their hats on, and some with them off, and so they are opposite one to another." Perrot's challenge was really a last-ditch plea for the freedom of the free spirit. Fox's reply was an assertion of institutional unity that no longer had room for freedom of this kind: "The people of God called Quakers are one (and not divided) in the power of God and his truth; and in God's power and spirit they are in unity in the truth and power of an endless life."[23]

Even more sinister than the refusal to doff the hat was the beard that appeared on Perrot's face, which looked like a deliberate allusion to Nayler, and indeed some of Nayler's old followers gathered around Perrot as a counterweight to the growing authority of Fox. Predictably, Robert Rich was one of them, and he too grew a beard. Another supporter left a defiant manuscript declaration, "It is well known that J[ames] N[ayler] and J[ohn] P[errot] in their day was as amiable and beautiful in the eye of the chaste virgins in Israel as David was when he conquered Goliath and deserved as much honor for they had many combats with Israel's enemies and came off victorious conquerors."[24] More accurately Nayler was a failed David who had been demolished by the parliamentary Goliath. As for Perrot, the movement closed ranks and was soon rid of him, since he was imprisoned in 1662 (along with Burrough) and got his freedom by agreeing to emigrate to the colonies. He died in Jamaica in 1665, exchanging broadsides with Fox right up to the end.

Quakers who "ran out" could expect to vanish from the collective memory of the movement. For example, one Christopher Atkinson, though initially an admired martyr imprisoned with other Quakers in Norwich, fell into sexual misconduct and was disowned as a "filthy spirit." Even worse, Atkinson went on to publicly renounce the Quakers and to express regret for having interrupted sermons in church. The result was that his name completely disappeared from Quaker records (it has been recovered from the Norwich court Sessions Book); he vanished into the general category that Norwich Quakers obliquely described, long afterward, as "in early days stumbling blocks and stones of offence."[25] Nayler had been too prominent a preacher and writer, and his case was too notorious, for total erasure of this kind, but something like it was nevertheless attempted. He generally appears as an unnamed "other person" in memoirs of the early Quaker movement, and from most early accounts of activity in London, in which every one of Fox's occasional visits is recorded, one would not guess that such a person as James Nayler had ever existed.[26] Whitehead's retelling of the story, critical of Nayler and his supporters though it was, has to be seen therefore as an attempt at rehabilitation, recovering those of his writings that might still have some edifying value.

A few years after the publication of Whitehead's *Collection of Sundry Books*, the retrospective rewriting of the movement's early history was completed in a massive work by the Dutchman William (or Willem) Sewel, *The History of the Rise, Increase, and Progress of the Christian People called Quakers* (1722). This account was heavily indebted to Fox's *Journal*, alternating systematically between brief descriptions of other people and lengthy excerpts from Fox. The effect was to confirm Fox as the fountainhead of the movement. Nayler's quarrel with Fox has remained ever since an embarrassment for Quaker historians, who have been anxious to believe, in the words of one of them, that "the power of the Spirit to bring men into unity was one of the happy discoveries of the early Friends, and served as a final test of the guiding of the Light."[27]

In actuality Fox did exert a decisive influence on the movement, but not exactly in the way its later chroniclers asserted. Far from inculcating a new faith or system of belief, as his followers increasingly claimed, it was his organizational skills that mattered most in a movement that had originally rejected the very idea of organization. From the outset he was highly effective in bringing together like-minded groups of Seekers and other antinomians, and as has been well said, "Fox did not teach his followers a new set of concepts for talking about a universal experience; he introduced them to a new institution."[28] Whatever the theoretical primacy of the individual inner Light was supposed to have been, it was the authority of the Quaker meeting that prevailed, and survivors from the Nayler period like Perrot and Rich were sternly disciplined and, if they resisted discipline, decisively ejected.

We have seen how deeply Nayler was drawn to a wandering life, regarding it as a direct command from God and shunning the temptation to assume headship over a settled flock. In the aftermath of Nayler's "fall" Fox, consolidating his position of supremacy as the movement stabilized, urged that it was better to pursue one's vocation at home than to live on the road:

> Now there is a great danger too in traveling abroad in the world, except a man be moved of the Lord, by the power of the Lord, for then he keeping in the power is kept in his journey and in his work, and it will preserve him to answer the transgressed and keep above the transgressor . . . For now though one may have openings when they are abroad to minister to others, but as for their own particular growth, [it] is to dwell in the life which doth open. So if any one have a moving to any place and have spoken what they were moved of the Lord, return to their habitation again, and live in the pure life of God and fear of the Lord. And so will ye in the life and the sober and seasoned Spirit be kept.[29]

It is easy to imagine that the recent catastrophe of Nayler, who had certainly failed to "keep above the transgressor," was in Fox's mind when he composed this discourse, but its message confirms the larger tendency of Quaker practice at the time. Of course, "to dwell in the life which doth open" is a characteristically vague Foxian phrase. Well might he dispute with Nayler whether the power really came from the Lord and whether the life that was opened was a life of perpetual prophecy. A "sober and seasoned spirit," in particular, implied a style of preaching as well as of life that Nayler's charismatic style must inevitably violate.

The erasure, and eventual partial rehabilitation, of Nayler's memory were inevitable consequences of the evolution of the Quakers from a charismatic movement to an organized sect that might indeed be called Quakerism.[30] Above all it was the intense pressure of persecution that compelled the movement to organize itself more systematically. Whatever the tensions had been between Quakers and the authorities in the 1650s, they grew much more severe after the Restoration. Between 1660 and 1680 more than ten thousand Quakers were imprisoned (Fox included), many for long periods of time, and nearly two hundred and fifty died in prison. One result was that the first generation of leaders was largely wiped out. Nayler's two London rivals were both gone by the end of the decade: Edward Burrough died in prison in 1663 at the age of thirty, and Francis Howgill in 1669 after a harsh imprisonment of nearly four years to which he was sentenced for refusing to take the Oath of Allegiance, though like all Quakers he had assured the court that he meant no disloyalty by his refusal to swear oaths. William Dewsbury, who had labored hard to bring about Fox's eventual reconciliation with Nayler (which will be considered presently), lived until 1688 but spent the last nineteen years of his life in prison.[31]

As the movement settled down, some of its members complained that "Foxonian-unity" was threatening "to deprive us of the law of the Spirit and to bring in a tyrannical government: it would lead us from the rule within to subject us to a rule without."[32] William Penn, looking back in 1694 at early dissensions in the movement, was clearly uneasy about the fine line between "good order" and excessive control: "Some weakly mistook good order in the government of church affairs for discipline in worship . . . And they were ready to reflect the same things that dissenters had very reasonably objected upon the national churches that have coercively pressed conformity to their respective creeds and worships." Fox's detractors, then, were in error because they mistook discipline in conduct for discipline in belief; but Nayler and his group would have retorted that Quakers more than anyone else should understand that belief and conduct were inseparable, since conduct ought to be simply the living enactment of belief. Penn added that although Fox "never abused" his power, he did possess it by right, since "God had visibly clothed him with a divine preference and authority, and indeed his very presence expressed a religious majesty."[33]

In many ways, indeed, the movement converged with the Puritan sects it had originally struggled against, as antinomianism was swallowed up in domesticated Nonconformity. It was increasingly assumed that even though Quakers were in principle free they would tend to express similar doctrines in similar language; the Bible was regularly invoked as ultimate authority; and a few experienced and distinguished members began to exercise discipline formally as "weighty Friends."[34] Not least of the consequences was a return by many Quakers, reluctant perhaps but unmistakable, to the old hard-line Calvinist conception of sin; and this reaffirmation of sin was essential to the eventual recognition of Quakerism as an acceptable sect among other sects, as it relinquished its antinomian challenge to the very assumptions that made sectarianism possible.

Nayler's "Repentance" and His Afterlife

The James Nayler whom institutional Quakerism remembered, when it remembered him at all, was an unfortunate figure who "ran out," repented, and was subsequently reconciled with the movement in a way that confirmed its institutional mandate and integrity. "This is certain," Sewel solemnly declared in 1722, "that James Nayler came to very great sorrow, and deep humiliation of mind; and therefore because God forgives the transgressions of the penitent, and blotteth them out, and remembereth them no more, so could James Nayler's friends do no other than forgive his crime, and thus take back the lost sheep into their society."[35] The story of his repentance was of course essential to any rehabilitation of his memory. "That he fell is not denied," Bevan wrote in 1800, "but that he rose from his fall is equally true; and it shows that either he possessed principles which, in the hours of his retreat, were sufficient to discover to him his errors, or that he acquired them in his humiliation."[36] In any case, what happened at Bristol had to be fully repudiated by Nayler himself, so that sympathetic historians could move beyond the embarrassment of his "fall" and see the story as heartwarming and exemplary. "In the end," Geoffrey Nuttall writes, "Nayler proved able to use not only his sufferings but his errors, terrible though these had been, for the expression of a gospel far truer, because saner as well as sweeter, than the gospel of many of his contemporaries." (To the piety of this summation, however, should be added Nuttall's dry comment, "Practically never in my researches have I come across a Friend who acknowledges a mistake. Nayler does so: which at once puts him in a class by himself.")[37]

But the real story is more interesting. To understand it fully we need to go back to the years immediately following the trial and listen to Nayler's own voice. During imprisonment he continued to write with his usual energy and clarity, and even managed to get some of these writings smuggled out and printed, but surprisingly none of his biographers—let alone historians who glance at him in passing—have made adequate use of this material. Brief passages are sometimes quoted with a misleading reference to *Works*, but without recognition of their post-1656 date or reflection on what they might tell us about Nayler's own understanding of what had happened to him, especially if one ponders the submerged personal implications in discussions that were deliberately couched in universal terms. Only a few texts have been quoted in this context, and they are ones in which Nayler is understood to have "repented" or even "recanted." But matters are far less simple than that.

In a number of testimonies written in Bridewell Nayler did express grief at the trouble he had caused the Quaker movement "in this time of great trial and temptation," and he invoked the Psalms both for consolation and for assurance that his example might prove helpful to others. "The Almighty God of Love, who hath numbered every sigh and put every tear in his bottle, reward it a thousand-fold into your bosoms in the day of your need, when you shall come to be tried and tempted."[38] The allusion is to Psalm 56, "Thou tellest my wanderings: put thou my tears into thy bottle: are they not in thy book?" Insofar as he had wounded the movement Nayler was certainly filled with regret, for as he wrote from Bridewell "To all the Dearly Beloved People of God," "There is nothing dear and precious to me in this world but God's Truth, and his life of righteousness, for which I have forsaken all the world; and whatever was dear to me therein, I have hated and counted it as an enemy."[39] He seems indeed to have developed in prison a strong sense of tranquility and relief, as he wrote to Rich at the end of his first year there:

> I know there is that amongst them [the other Quakers] which must be purged, and I have learned it; yet are they the people of God . . . Truly my table is spread, and my cup over-runs with love, and peace, and joy in the Spirit, wherein I am covered from the delights of the flesh, and not seen to the world; but truly my peace flows as a river, as my Father did me promise when I was in the fire, . . . and truly my soul hath fullness, indeed, of the best since I was stripped of all.[40]

Perhaps the suffering Nayler had undergone now seemed a purgative fire that had burned away the last vestiges of the despised selfhood; certainly prison afforded a welcome exclusion from the world and "the delights of the flesh."

Yet it is far from clear that Nayler "repented" in any fundamental way, or that he ever disavowed the antinomian beliefs that had infuriated the Calvinist Puritans and would become increasingly unpalatable to Quakers too. In prison, just as before, he wrote copiously and intel-

ligently on the usual topics, referring occasionally to a now-past period of imbalance and instructive suffering but not to a real "fall" into
sin. In a short pamphlet in 1659 he deplored "those ranting wild spirits" who had surrounded him at Bristol, and claimed that even at the
time he knew Stranger's letter to be incriminating:

> And also that letter sent to me to Exeter by John Stanger [sic]
> when I was in prison, with these words, "Thy name shall be no
> more James Nayler, but Jesus;" this I judge to be written from the
> imaginations, and a fear struck me when I first saw it, and so I put
> it in my pocket (close) not intending any should see it, which they
> finding on me spread it abroad, which the simplicity of my heart
> never owned; so this I deny also that the name of Christ Jesus is
> received instead of James Nayler or after the flesh, for the name is
> to the Seed in all generations, and he that hath the Son hath the
> name which is life and power, the salvation and the unction, into
> which name all the children of Light are baptized.[41]

Nayler's denial of any specific assertion of Christhood is explicit, but
so is his assertion of a general identification with Christ on the part of
all true believers. This had always been his position, and the Bristol
episode did nothing to change it. Some years earlier he had stated it
clearly in answer to an opponent who charged that Fox had said "I am
the way, the truth and the life." Nayler's response was that Fox might
indeed have said that, in the sense in which any one of the saints could
say it: "Where Christ speaks in male or female, he is what he testifies
himself to be; if thou canst receive it thou may."[42]

Nayler's fullest attempt to interpret his own story was a short pamphlet entitled *To the Life of God in All* (1659), which Whitehead long
afterward reprinted at the beginning of *A Collection of Sundry Books*.
(I follow the first edition here; Whitehead's text faithfully reproduces
the original, but adds punctuation and paragraphing that tend to regu-
larize the onrolling urgency of Nayler's prose.) This account is highly
abstract and heavily allegorical, but if read with care it gives a clear
sense of what Nayler thought had happened to him. When he began
to preach in London, he says, he was inspired by the "presence and
power" of the Spirit, but unexpectedly he was led astray. At this point
an extremely long sentence, which all but refuses to end, traces the full
trajectory of Nayler's interior journey, in language so allusive that it

will be best to interrupt it from time to time to comment on what is implied.

> But not minding in all things to stand single and low to the motions of that endless life, by it to be led in all things within and without, but giving way to the reasoning part, as to some things which in themselves had no seeming evil, by little and little drew out my mind after trifles, vanities, and persons which took the affectionate part, by which my mind was drawn out from the constant watch and pure fear into which I was once begotten, and spiritual adultery was committed against that precious pure life which had purchased me unto himself alone, and is grieved with the least departure from him in body, spirit or mind . . . (p. 2)

By "the reasoning part" Nayler means, I think, his former willingness to dispute and theorize; by "the affectionate part" he means the love of "creatures," of any and all created things, which as we have seen the Quakers reprehended even more sternly than Puritans did.

By "spiritual adultery" Nayler certainly does not imply literal sexual involvement with his female disciples; this he continued to deny at all times, and the vehemence of his denials deserves notice: "As that accusation, as if I had committed adultery with some of those women who came with us from Exeter prison; and also those who were with me at Bristol the night before I suffered there: of both which accusations I am clear before God, who kept me at that day both in thought and deed, as to all women, as a little child, God is my record."[43] In 1660, just before his death, he was still at pains to defend his reputation from accusations "as that I had a woman in bed with me the night before I suffered at Bristol, when there was six or seven persons in the room that night, and a man (to wit) Robert Rich in bed with me."[44] (If anyone at the time, incidentally, suspected Nayler of homoerotic feelings toward Rich or anyone else, no trace of it has survived.)

But if Nayler always denied improper relations with women, the account in *To the Life of God in All* does concede that his indulgence in "reasoning" led him into a too-emotional relationship with them. When this happened he was committing spiritual adultery against Christ the spouse ("which had purchased me unto himself alone") and thereby placed himself in opposition to the divine Spirit that had previously entered his life:

. . . even that eternal pure and zealous Spirit from above had drawn me near into himself, and that pure Word was become my life, who said, "He that doth but look upon a woman to lust, commits adultery, and in whose sight the least coveting or letting any visible object into the affections, is idolatry," into that life I was comprehended . . .

That is to say, Nayler had at one time been "comprehended" in the life of a Word so pure that sexual thoughts were just as repugnant to it as sexual acts, for as Christ said in the Sermon on the Mount, "Whosoever looketh on a woman to lust after her hath committed adultery with her already in his heart" (Matthew 5: 28). In this pure state, at one with the holy Word, Nayler was immune from every kind of idolatrous love of visible objects,

. . . and the apple of that pure eye was opened in me, which admits not of an evil thought, but is wounded and bruised with the least appearance of evil, even this birth was born, which reigns through righteousness, and suffers till all righteousness be fulfilled in every particular, and this is the Son of God for ever, and into this Life and Kingdom I was translated, and I was in him that is true, in whom there is no sin, and He alone lived and ruled in this his temple, which to himself he had purchased with his precious blood, and his delight was in me, and his presence was glorious, and not the least evil could appear, but I could feel him in spirit lifting up his witness against it . . .

Having been "translated" into the life of the Son of God, Nayler's individual selfhood was abolished, and he became for a time the living temple in which Christ alone lived and ruled.

Something, however, went dreadfully wrong:

. . . but when I reasoned against his tender reproof, and consulted with another, and so let the creatures into my affections, then his temple was defiled through lust, and his pure Spirit was grieved, and he ceased to reprove, and he gave me up, and his light he withdrew, and his judgement took away; and so the body of death and sin revived again, and I possessed afresh the iniquities of my youth, and that which had of old been buried arose and stood against me, and so the temple was filled with darkness and the power of death, and my heart with sorrow, and Satan daily at my right hand to tempt me farther to provoke the Lord, and to take away my life.

The God who could enter Nayler could also withdraw, precipitating his fall into the merely carnal condition that Paul, that great theorist of dualism, lamented so passionately: "For we know that the law is spiritual: but I am carnal, sold under sin . . . For I delight in the law of God after the inward man: but I see another law in my members, warring against the law of my mind . . . O wretched man that I am! who shall deliver me from the body of this death?" (Romans 7: 14, 22–24). God and Satan: the universe is a battleground contested by two rival powers, and Nayler had fallen prey to the mighty enemy of Truth and Life. Or to translate his experience into modern terms, his charismatic power had always been energized by the erotics of faith, and its inherent tensions—evident at the time to critics inside the movement as well as outside it—now burst into the open.

As Nayler understood it in retrospect, his brooding silence shortly before the Bristol episode, which so many people had noticed, had been the outward symptom of a desperate effort to regain his balance. "Thus having in a great measure lost my own guide, and darkness being come upon me, I sought a place where I might have been alone to weep and cry before the Lord, that his face I might find, and my condition recover." The expression "lost my own guide" poignantly recalls Nayler's account, years earlier, of a deranged young man who was tempted to throw himself into the fire and to perform other self-destructive acts: "About midnight he [heard] a voice which said, 'Up, get thee hence'; and he did arise, and went forth; but the mind not waiting to be guided, but running before, he lost his guide, and so returned home again."[45] What made recovery impossible was the interference of others, and Nayler now endorsed the view that he had become a passive victim. "I gave myself up wholly to be led by others, whose work was then wholly to divide me from the Children of Light [the original name of the Quakers], which was done" (3). Far from embodying Christ fully in himself, he had separated from Christ and had become *merely* himself: "I give all glory to the Life for ever more, and to him it is due, and all the evil hath been from self" (4). In a single elliptical sentence Nayler recalled the adulation he once received, and now he firmly disavowed it: "Whatever of that worship or honour hath any way by any creature been given or received to my person which belongs to that Eternal Spirit, for ever by me it is denied and condemned as idolatry" (5). At the end of the pamphlet appears the striking line "Printed for Thomas Simmons at the Sign of the Bull and Mouth near Aldersgate, 1659." The Bull and Mouth was the former tavern that had become the Quakers' headquarters in London, and the place where opponents like John Deacon came to dispute with them. Thomas Simmonds was the husband of Martha, the ringleader of those whom Nayler now rebuked for having falsely seduced his spiritual affections, and perhaps his carnal ones as well. But Simmonds remained his publisher.

Thus Nayler's moment of apparent exaltation in Bristol had actually been a capitulation to the "flesh," just as Adam capitulated when Satan tempted him in Eden. In a posthumously published pamphlet, *How the Ground of Temptation is in the Heart of the Creature*, Nayler further developed this interpretation in a generalized discussion that had an obvious basis in his own experience:

> As to this ground and part in the creature, it is flesh, and hath the fleshly motions and actions (arising in and proceeding from it) through a tickling delight of fancy, that works therein; for that delight was first fancied in the flesh (when Adam began to look out at the glory of the state he was first placed in, and was thereby struck into a deep sleep, in the dream of which was fancied the delight of the flesh, and she took from him that which promoted that work in secret, and loves the secrecy of pleasure she takes therein); and were there real satisfaction in what answers that part (in which the creature hath a sense and knowledge of good and evil) he should never more hunger therein; but the contrary being experienced, I need not go far for a testimony hereof, in that many do know that the Tempter overpowering the desire of him that wants opportunity (always to put in practice what the mind lusteth into and longeth after) being ready to attend with evil, as opportunity serves him therein, doth as enviously accuse, as subtily tempt.[46]

Seeking to escape from self and reenact the passion of Christ, Nayler had instead tasted the forbidden fruit of good and evil and had been cut off from the tree of life.

In a letter written in Bridewell in 1658 Nayler explicitly placed his relationship with his erstwhile disciples in a similar perspective. He had been seduced, he now acknowledged, by wicked spirits who pretended to humility and holiness in the service of Satan "the Murtherer and Devourer." In this disguise they "steal into simple minds; but being got in, exalt themselves above the Seed of God, and trample the meek spirit under foot, and so darken the vessels, and being exalted in the imaginations, lead the creature (as God) above that of God, and so against that of God he [i.e., Satan] wars in others, where God is above."[47] As usual, the expression is highly abstract, but full of meaning. Nayler's own mind could hardly have been called "simple," so he was evidently referring to his enthusiastic disciples who exalted themselves above the Seed of God; but just because Nayler was not simple, he tried especially hard to be meek, and this meekness they trampled underfoot.

In all of this it was deluded "imaginations" that ran out of control, a constant threat for inner-light sects and a constant target of criticism for their conservative enemies. The highly positive valuation of imagination from the Romantic poets onward has made it difficult to appreciate with what suspicion many people once regarded it. Imagination was the faculty of forming images, and if the only true images were those existing beyond the individual self—in God's creation, according to traditional theology, or in natural phenomena, according to the emerging empiricist philosophy—then any mental images formed entirely by and within the self were bound to be erroneous. A Romantic poet would see imagination as the power that creates form and brings light into darkness; in Nayler's usage imagination is a direct product of the darkness that has obscured the divine light of John's Gospel, and any forms it may generate are corrupt reshapings of that darkness. He wrote in 1656, shortly before his own disaster, "And self having got the form, into the imagination, above the life, cannot receive the light that's hid and condemns it. So all the world lies in darkness, yea, *thick darkness* is upon all the seas, and the great depth is covered with gross darkness; and from thence is the imagination spread over all."[48]

When Nayler said in the Bridewell letter that Satan stole in against "that of God" and exalted "the creature," he was tacitly acknowledging that his followers had treated him—a creature—as if he were God. That is certainly how Whitehead interpreted what happened, with a similar reference to imagination:

Some of those followers and admirers of J. N. (when in his clouded condition) were puffed up in their imaginations concerning him, as vainly conceiting his growth and attainments in Christ amounted to more equality with Him (when on earth) than is attainable by any particular member; probably mistaking that scripture, Ephes. 4. 13. "Till we all meet together (or come) into the unity of the faith, and of the knowledge of the Son of God, and to a perfect Man, unto the measure of the stature (or of the age) of the fullness of Christ." Which is not predicated of any particular member, but of the whole Body or Church, as united to Christ the head or principal thereof; which therefore is said to be the "fullness of him that filleth all in all," Ephes. 1. 23.[49]

Whitehead's parenthesis, "or of the age," seems intended to block any suggestion that an individual believer might actually share in Christ's "stature." Rather, it is a question of waiting until the not-yet-accomplished period when full union of the church-body with its Christ-head will take place.

Nayler himself consistently denied that he believed himself to be literally Christ, but he now apparently conceded that others had asserted it and that if he permitted them to do so he was implicated in their error. "This mystery of deep iniquity," he continued, "hath the Lord God in the Spirit of the Lamb revealed unto me, whose powerful working I have found, working in me against the pure measure and unspotted life of God;" and he added that he now perceived it to be "the old spirit of the Ranters" (xxxii). In another Bridewell letter he again referred to "those ranting wild spirits, which then gathered about me in the time of darkness," and explicitly denounced their actions at Bristol: "all their casting off their clothes in the way, their bowings and singings, and all the rest of those wild actions which did any way tend to dishonour the Lord."[50]

The most striking thing in all of Nayler's reflections is his renewed commitment to passive waiting in preference to ostentatious prophetic impulses.

The body of Christ is felt in the Light . . . If there appear to thee voices, visions, and revelations, feed not thereon, but abide in the Light and feel the body of Christ, and there wilt thou receive faith and power to judge of every appearance and spirits, the good to hold fast and obey, and the false to resist. Art thou in darkness? Mind it not; for if thou dost, it will fill thee more; but stand still and act not, and wait in patience till light arise out of darkness to lead thee . . . And this I have learned in the deeps, and in secret when I was alone, and now declare openly in the day of my mercy, glory to the Highest for evermore. (lv–lvi)

No more voices and revelations now, no more intoxication with appearances; just patient waiting for the light to dispel the darkness, and the body of Christ to be not seen but "felt."

Nayler's beliefs thus remained exactly what they were before 1656, including the essential conviction that each person has Christ fully present within. What he did acknowledge and regret was a tendency to relish reasoning too much, which led in turn to a deluded imagination that attached itself too deeply to "the creatures." Surely this does not constitute "repentance" as the term is ordinarily understood. He seems, indeed, to have been deeply concerned that he not be misrepresented as repudiating everything he had done, either at Bristol or in his subsequent testimony about it. The Bristol sign had certainly been coopted by turbulent spirits for their own purposes, but to acknowledge this was not at all to recant. In 1659 Thomas Simmonds published a little four-page pamphlet by Nayler with the title *Having heard that some have wronged my words which I spoke before the Committee of Parliament, concerning Jesus Christ, and concerning the Old and New Testament, some have printed Words which I spoke not; Also some have printed a Paper, and called it James Naylor's Recantation, unknown to me. To all which things, I shall speak a few words, which may satisfy such as loves the truth.* In this document Nayler acknowledged that "after I was put into the hole at Bridewell," Quaker meetings were violently interrupted by "a sort of people, who pretend that they owned me," but he maintained that he never wavered in his belief in Christ and never intended that his own actions should occlude the faith of others. The difference between himself and Christ was reaffirmed in an urgent rush of language:

And whereinsoever this earthen vessel or any thing therein hath been set up in the minds of any, to diminish the glory of that invisible power, or to draw any one from the measure of the same spirit in themselves, or to offend the least measure of that pure and tender spirit in any of his people, all that I condemn and deny as a thing never intended by me; but is the work of the Adversary, who seeks all occasion against the truth of God to devour, in whom it is begotten, who took his advantage in the time of my trial and sufferings to stir up enmity and despite against the spirit of truth, and with all his power sought to dishonour the name of the Lord Jesus Christ, for which I have denied all that I loved in this world, which name stands in the power and nature of that eternal spirit, and to the power the name is given, and not to James Nayler, as himself hath said, John 14. 26, and in the eternal Seed is the Sonship, and the Lamb is he that bears all things.

To say that Satan made use of Nayler's plight is not in the least to concede that Nayler's behavior was satanic; in this document he does not even say that it was sinful at all. The significance of his nonrecantation was certainly not lost on other Quakers at the time, such as Samuel Fisher, who indignantly denounced Baxter and others for claiming that "J. N. had forever renounced the Quakers as unclean spirits and Ranters and such like; whenas it's most evident to any but the blind that as J. N. still justifies the Truth and Light, and all the Quakers that abide in it, and to which by the grace of God he now stands a true and faithful servant, so that his recantation and renunciation is of no other than of that old spirit of the Ranters, which makes head against the light of Christ, condemning filthiness in every conscience, and the life of the Cross."[51]

However much he had come to admit that he had fallen into some kind of error at Bristol, Nayler never repudiated the symbolism by which the crucifixion was to be witnessed and internalized by the individual believer. In 1659 he wrote that Puritan preaching was committed to "vain words" that cannot give "the knowledge of God in the face of Jesus," but that "the living faith worketh and conforms to Christ, within and without, to live his life and manifest his life to the world in their mortal bodies, and to bear his name and nature, his marks and sufferings in their conversation before his enemies, showing him to be the same today, blessed for evermore; and such are baptized into his likeness in death and resurrection in a true measure."[52] In his own *imitatio Christi* Nayler had borne those marks and sufferings both in "conversation before his enemies" and, very literally, in his "mortal body."

One senses in Nayler's later writings a determination not to be autobiographical, to express general truths that confirm the successful extinction of the selfish individual personality. Still, moments of strong feeling sometimes surface:

> The power of holiness and truth in the inward parts is not known but in the depth, when the fire of wrath comes upon all vain hopes and hypocritical confidence, when all that is without a man is removed far away; when all relations, friends and acquaintance are become farther off than strangers, and whatever thing the creature seeks to for comfort turns against him and adds to his grief; then is known the power of holiness and truth in heart with God . . . He that hath proved it [i.e., experienced it] commends it to you, who have been stripped of all, that ye might learn and know the treasure of life, and holiness with God.[53]

Nayler had indeed been stripped of all. Those who ought to have been his comforters had turned against him, and his friends had become farther off than strangers.

Nayler again sought to explain his position in a 1660 pamphlet, co-authored with Richard Hubberthorne, responding to *The Fanatick History* by Richard Blome. Here he pondered his own case in terms of unusual complexity:

> As for thy charge thou hast [made] against J. Nayler, through the everlasting mercy of my God, I have yet a being amongst the living and breath to answer for my self, though against the intents of many bloody cruel spirits who pursued my soul unto death (as much as in them lay) in that day of my calamity, when my Adversary was above, and wherein I was made a sign to a backsliding generation, who then would not see nor hear what now is coming upon them, but rejoiced against this piece of dust, and had little pity towards him that was fallen into their hands; wherein God was just in giving me up for my disobedience, for a little moment, as a Father to correct; yet should not they have sought to aggravate things against me, as thou [i.e., Blome] dost, for it was a day of deep distress, and lay sore upon my soul, and the pitiful God saw it, who though he was a little displeased, yet his thoughts

were not to cast off for ever, as it is at this day, glory be to his name from my delivered soul eternally.[54]

This slowly evolving sentence traces a circuitous path through the obscurities of Nayler's sad passion. He was "made a sign to a backsliding generation," but he now understands that this happened under the aegis of the diabolical accuser ("when my Adversary was above"). Nayler's behavior was therefore disobedient to God and he had to suffer "for a little moment" under paternal correction; yet the sign had been a true sign, the backsliders did need to be warned, and the events of 1660 subsequently confirmed "what now is coming upon them."

As with the Miltonic *felix culpa*, Nayler's action was wrong but God used it for his own ends, and God certainly did not want Nayler's worldly enemies to pursue him "unto death" (Nayler must have remembered how narrowly he escaped a death sentence in 1656). As for his former companions, Nayler was as elliptical as ever, though he seemed now to claim that he never really surrendered to them in his heart: "And in that day there was many spirits flocked about me, and some whom while my candle shone upon my head I ever judged and kept out from me, who then got up and acted and spoke several things not in the light and truth of God, by which they who sought occasion against me then was strengthened to afflict this body" (2–3). But perhaps this is to concede that the candle did not always shine upon Nayler's head, and that when it temporarily flickered out he was no longer competent to judge those who gave convenient "occasion" to his persecutors.

In any case Nayler did not specify which words and actions were "not in the light and truth of God," much less how he would now revise or replace them. And in more than one of these late writings he stressed not his own errors but rather the criminal folly of the Puritan regime, which had lost its divine mandate, a prime instance of which was its treatment of the Quaker martyrs. "Then did the Lord raise up signs and wonders among you," wrote Nayler, who had served as a sign and wonder himself, "but these you used worse than formerly, and your rage increased in stocking [putting in the stocks], beating, whipping and imprisoning, until the cry of oppression was so great that there was no remedy; and then the Lord arose and shaked you in pieces, as a mighty one in his anger, and broke you with such a breach so as you could not be healed, nor be a power any longer."[55]

In 1661 a posthumous work by Nayler was published, *Milk for Babes, and Meat for Strong Men*, with a preface by Mary Booth that allusively developed an explanation of what had happened to him. In Booth's preface, Nayler's prophetic mission was unequivocally affirmed—"He had the mind of God, and the secrets of the Almighty did abide upon his tabernacle"—and his Christlike role was clearly hinted at: "a follower of the Lamb in many tribulations . . . made like unto him through sufferings." Nayler's sufferings and tribulations turn out to have been an instrumentality by which God exposed the sins not so much of Nayler himself as of those who persecuted him:

> The Lord did never leave him or forsake him, although Satan had power to winnow him as wheat; yet his precious life was hid with God, and the evil one could not touch it; and the trial came not upon him for his own sins only, nor the sins of others, but it was to try some, that all flesh may be silent, and that none should glory in his presence, who setteth up and casteth down, who kills and makes alive, according to the good pleasure of his own will . . . Mark this: he was set as a sign for the rise and fall of many, that the secrets of many hearts might be made manifest, and for to prove that generation that then had power in their hands, but improved it not, but went on in the counsel of their own corrupt hearts to persecute the innocents . . . The Lord God hath pleaded with that generation of men which now are passed away, and their very memorial is become an evil savour, for they showed no mercy; therefore in the day of their distress they could find no mercy.[56]

Mary Booth does not deny that Nayler sinned in some way, and his companions likewise, but she emphasizes that "the trial came not upon him for his own sins only, nor the sins of others." It was Nayler's role "as a sign" that was important, just as he himself had continued to assert. Even if it was indeed Satan who was "winnowing" Nayler when he entered Bristol in the manner of Christ entering Jerusalem, God nonetheless intended the Christological sign to be instructive for a "generation of men" who persecuted Christlike behavior just as their forebears in Israel persecuted the Lamb of God himself. These men were therefore the true subjects of the Nayler episode. They held power for good but used it for evil, and having been found wanting it was they and not Nayler who found no mercy from God.

The pamphlet itself represents Nayler's own final attempt to generalize from his own experience for the use of others. The full title, *Milk for Babes, and Meat for Strong Men: A Feast of Fat Things; Wine well refined on the Lees*, employs biblical allusions to indicate that it is addressed above all to those who are just beginning to heed the call,[57] and whose addiction to controversy reveals how far they still are from spiritual maturity.

> And I, brethren, could not speak unto you as unto spiritual, but as unto carnal, even as unto babes in Christ. I have fed you with milk, and not with meat: for hitherto ye were not able to bear it, neither yet now are ye able. For ye are yet carnal: for whereas there is among you envying, and strife, and divisions, are ye not carnal, and walk as men? For while one saith, I am of Paul, and another, I am of Apollos; are ye not carnal? (1 Corinthians 3: 1–4)

One recalls how Quakers in London complained that Nayler attracted a personal following that proclaimed "I am of James." Emerging now from his sufferings—the title page promises "the breathings of the Spirit through his servant James Nayler, written by him in the time of the confinement of his outward man in prison, but not published till now"—Nayler firmly repudiates that kind of competitiveness. But his appeal is not to novices only; he is also addressing those who have grown in the spirit, as a further allusion to Paul indicates: "Strong meat belongeth to them that are of full age, even those who by reason of use have their senses exercised to discern both good and evil" (Hebrews 5: 14). And the title embodies a historical reference as well: the mighty city of the Puritan regime had to be shattered so that God's humble servants might flourish at last. "For thou hast made of a city a heap; of a defensed city a ruin: a palace of strangers to be no city . . . And in this mountain shall the Lord of hosts make unto all people a feast of fat things; a feast of wines on the lees, of fat things full of marrow, of wine on the lees well refined" (Isaiah 25: 2, 6).

Milk for Babes begins with an appeal to all "tender hearted ones" to be patient and "wait low" for the wellspring of living water to flow, and then offers reassurances that are certainly based on personal experience:

But dear children who seek this to attain, think it not strange when for the attaining hereof, you come to be *rejected of all, denied, condemned, contradicted,* and *tempted* with all manner of spirits and evils, *assaults within* and *without,* with *fears* and *dread,* in *weakness, watchings* and *fastings,* with *tears* of *sorrow* night and day; to be led into the *wilderness,* and there *tempted, tried* in the night with *great temptations,* and see no way out, led on a way you know not, a way of wrath and terror, and passing by the gates of Hell, and none to pity you, nor take your part; chastened alone, that you may be proved to the uttermost.[58]

If Nayler had indeed enacted a Christlike role, it was in enduring the temptation in the wilderness, and he now admits to a dreadful isolation. Seeking to abolish his individual selfhood in the perfection of sinlessness, it may seem that Nayler is anticipating the uncharted "way" of Bunyan's pilgrim, benighted and desperate in the Valley of the Shadow of Death. Far from affirming complacency about the continuous presence of the radiant inner Light, he now acknowledges its opposite: "Though at some times the clouds may be so thick, and the powers of darkness so strong in your eye that you see him not, *yet love him,* and *believe,* and you have him present" (3). What is this but the far-off *deus absconditus* of Luther and Calvin, hidden from human beings who must believe him present though they see him not?

The answer now must be that it is precisely in isolation and rejection that the *imitatio Christi* consists. "Come to him that seeks not himself, who hath not his rest in things on earth, who is rejected of men, denied of his own kindred, and forsaken of all; and as you come to him, you will come to be proved whether you can forgo all these [worldly things] for him alone, and that he may make his appearance in you, and cover you with himself" (11). This is perhaps a more external Christ than the one Nayler had formerly celebrated, one who is no longer internalized within the believer but rather "covers the believer with himself." But faith in him will lead eventually out of the darkness, so long as the "wayfaring man here on earth" (15) persists in his wearisome pilgrimage, and so long as he represses every temptation to pay attention to the world he ought to be leaving behind.

Remember Lot's wife; and the wrath of God will ever be upon that mind which looks back into old things . . . Wrath will arise, and confusion will be to that mind which is double, where the eye is not single, kept forward in the belief of the Spirit only, but looks back into the loss, and to that which is dying and condemned; there is the *smoke*, and *darkness*, and *torment*, and *temptations*, being enticed back into the old; but if the eye be single, the whole body is full of light, and the faith ariseth to endure to the end of the world, and to look to the beginning and finishing of the new work of regeneration. (31–32)

To preserve that resolutely monocular vision, intensely difficult though it is to do so, becomes the chief concern of the pilgrim in this dark journey. Nayler may still reject Calvinist theology, but in his allegorical understanding of a world of sin and probation he has rejoined the Puritans at whose hands he suffered so bitterly.

The image of the "covering" deity is now that of the psalms: "He shall cover thee with his feathers, and under his wings shalt thou trust" (91: 4). And Mary Booth concludes the pamphlet with a meditation of Nayler's (omitted in the *Sundry Books* reprint) that she describes as "A Psalm of James, the servant of Jesus, or a song of praise which he sung in the day of his deliverance," telling how the Lord had sustained him in "the day of the deep trial of his innocent lamb" and at last "brought him to know himself, and then exalted him over death, and delivered him out of the pit in the sight of his enemies" (24). Always in these late writings Nayler stressed the example of Christ as suffering servant rather than of Christ as apocalyptic judge. The true believer can be recognized by his *imitatio* in this kind: "his righteousness, his meekness, his patient sufferings, his lowly-mindedness, his faith and obedience to the Father, his love and tender compassion towards all men, being richly furnished with all manner of godliness, shall declare him whose image he bears, and whose son he is, and from whence he comes."[59]

During the years of Nayler's imprisonment, the world of politics continued on its uncertain way. The constitutional crisis stumbled onward with ever-increasing complexity and ever-decreasing optimism. Cromwell, probably fearing army resistance, turned down the proposal that he become king; he dismissed his erstwhile right-hand man Lambert, who had expected to be his successor but came to a disappointing end, and named his son Richard instead.[60] From the very beginning the Parliament that condemned Nayler had shown itself to be undisciplined and petty, bogging down in a myriad of local bills rather than undertaking the broad program of legal reform that Cromwell had called for. (Many of its members were themselves lawyers, and not inclined to share the Army's exasperation with the legal profession; it is entirely possible that the emphasis on trivial matters was a deliberate delaying tactic.) By 1658, when he finally dissolved this Second Protectorate Parliament, Cromwell grimly told its members what he thought of his own embattled role as Lord Protector: "I cannot [but] say it in the presence of God, in comparison of which all we that are here are [like] poor creeping ants upon the earth, that I would have been glad, as to my own conscience and spirit, to have been living under a wood-side, to have kept a flock of sheep, rather than to have undertaken such a place as this was."[61] He had seven months left to live. After Cromwell's death a time of intense political confusion ensued, with alliances that shifted almost daily among various military and civilian figures. His son Richard governed for a few months as head of a new Council of State. After Richard Cromwell's abdication in May 1659, a handful of survivors of the Rump Parliament constituted themselves a Parliament and sat until October, when military rule was once again imposed. It was this body, responding to a short-lived mood of religious tolerance, that set free Nayler and more than a hundred other Quaker prisoners. The date of his release was September 8, 1659, nearly three years after he was first imprisoned.

At long last Nayler met Fox again and the old scene of refusing to kneel was played out, in a strange parallel to the parliamentary sentence that had compelled Nayler to retrace his Bristol ride. William Dewsbury traveled all the way from Yorkshire to promote the (rather grudging) reconciliation, at which Fox once again demanded that Nayler kneel before him. This time Nayler complied.[62] A few months later he set out on a journey to his home to Yorkshire; this seems to have been exacted by Fox as a further token of obedience, in part at least to get Nayler out of London, where his preaching was once again drawing a large following.[63] But he never reached home. A quite full account (though not an eyewitness one) was left by John Whiting, who invested it with all the solemnity and edification of a saint's life, which for him it was:

> At last departing from the city of London, about the latter end of the 8th month, 1660, towards the North, intending to go home

to his wife and children at Wakefield in Yorkshire, he was seen by a Friend of Hertford (sitting by the wayside in a very awful weighty frame of mind), who invited him to his house, but he refused, signifying his mind to pass forward, and so went on foot as far as Huntingdonshire, and was observed by a Friend as he passed through the town, in such an awful frame, as if he had been redeemed from the earth, and a stranger on it, seeking a better country and inheritance. But going some miles beyond Huntingdon, he was taken ill, being (as 'tis said) robbed by the way, and left bound; whether he received any personal injury is not certainly known, but being found in a field by a countryman toward evening, was had, or went, to a Friend's house at Holm, not far from King's Rippon, where Thomas Parnel a doctor of physic dwelt, who came to visit him; and being asked, if any friends at London should be sent for to come and see him: he said, "Nay," expressing his care and love to them. Being shifted [his clothes having been changed], he said: "You have refreshed my body, the Lord refresh your souls;" and not long after departed this life in peace with the Lord, about the 9th month, 1660, and the 44th year of his age.[64]

As so often, Nayler's inner feelings remain concealed. The "very awful weighty frame of mind" that two witnesses noticed may imply readiness for death, but Nayler (or Whiting) did not explain. And the nature of the mugging remains frustratingly unclear. Could it conceivably have been the act of someone who recognized Nayler and wanted to get rid of this troublemaker, who had been so inconveniently released from prison and was gathering admirers once again? But ill health had forced Nayler to leave the army a decade before, fasting and imprisonment had doubtless taken their toll since then, and he may well have died of entirely natural causes.

Directly following *Milk for Babes* in the 1716 collection, Whitehead printed a text that has been regularly cited by Quaker writers (without any commentary or analysis) as evidence of Nayler's final beatitude. Whether or not he actually spoke these words as he lay dying can never be known. They were first published in 1660, immediately after his death, and it is certainly conceivable that he dictated them and perhaps even initialed them after hearing them read back to him.[65] The text deserves to be quoted in full:

His Last Testimony, said to be delivered by him about two Hours before his Departure out of this Life; several Friends being present.

There is a spirit which I feel that delights to do no evil, nor to revenge any wrong, but delights to endure all things, in hope to enjoy its own in the end. Its hope is to outlive all wrath and contention, and to weary out all exaltation and cruelty, or whatever is of a nature contrary to itself. It sees to the end of all temptations; as it bears no evil in itself, so it conceives none in thoughts to any other; if it be betrayed it bears it; for its ground and spring is the mercies and forgiveness of God. Its crown is meekness, its life is everlasting love unfeigned, and takes its kingdom with entreaty and not with contention, and keeps it by lowliness of mind. In God alone it can rejoice, though none else regard it or can own its life. It's conceived in sorrow, and brought forth without any to pity it; nor doth it murmur at grief and oppression. It never rejoiceth but through sufferings, for with the world's joy it is murthered. I found it alone, being forsaken; I have fellowship therein with them who lived in dens and desolate places in the earth, who through death obtained this resurrection and eternal holy life.

J. N.

This statement is certainly consistent with the views Nayler had been expressing in his final writings, though the cadences do not sound much like his and seem too artfully rhetorical for a dying man; if he did indeed express some version of these remarks, somebody else must have edited them afterward. Suffering has now become a decisive form of authentication for a spirit that "delights to endure all things," and militant opposition, which he had once practiced and which friends like Robert Rich continued to practice, is now repudiated. The spirit aspires to "weary out" persecution by simple endurance, and "if it be betrayed it bears it." Nayler the individual still speaks—"I found it alone, being forsaken"—but his isolation is gathered into the communal solitude of all those who have dwelt in desolate places and have achieved eternal life. He speaks not for himself but for "a spirit which I feel" that is generalizable in a way that enlarges his personal experience into an exemplary universality. Whether or not this text accurately reproduces Nayler's last words, it certainly crystallizes what the Quaker movement needed to make of him, if it was not to erase him entirely from collective memory.

Perhaps it is Robert Rich, among Nayler's contemporaries, who should get the last word. In 1678 he published a pamphlet with the indignant title *Hidden Things Brought to Light: Or the Discord of the Grand Quakers among Themselves, Discovered in some Letters, Papers, and Passages written to and from George Fox, James Nayler, and John Perrott.* In his preface the wealthy merchant remarks pointedly on Fox's rise from obscurity: "Fox . . . is become of an inconsiderable shoemaker or mean servant, a general teacher and leader of a numerous company of men and women, who all profess to be guided by the Light within them, which they say errs not." But in faithfully following Fox and accepting his discipline, Rich urges, they have in fact "betrayed their great principle of the Light in every man his unerring guide, and even the principle of Protestantism and all the Reformation, which requires every man to judge for himself, and follow his own judgment against any number whatsoever."[66] After reprinting Nayler's last words, Rich comments bitterly that both Nayler and Perrot "declared that they had received greater wounds from the house of their Friends, than from the house of their enemies" (22). As usual Rich has Christological symbolism in mind: "And one shall say unto him, What are these wounds in thine hands? Then he shall answer, Those with which I was wounded in the house of my friends" (Zechariah 13: 6).

In effect the Quaker leaders had developed exactly the same kind of authoritarian ministry they had originally opposed. And perhaps their final act in reappropriating Nayler was to abridge his own solemn last words; for after the text of "His Last Testimony" as Whitehead would later reprint it, Rich adds the following:

Thou wast with me when I fled from the face of mine enemies, then didst thou warn me in the night; thou carriedst me in thy power into the hiding place thou hadst prepared for me; there thou coveredst me with thy hand, that in time thou mightest bring me forth a rock before all the world. When I was weak thou stayedst me with thy hand, that in thy time thou mightest present me to the world in thy strength; in which I stand and cannot be moved. Praise the Lord, O my soul. Let this be written for those that come after, Praise the Lord. (21–22)

Those that came after silently deleted it. Nayler the penitent could still be useful for their purposes; Nayler the rock, in all the complexity and ambiguity of his story, had to disappear. Rich himself was firmly rejected by the Quaker movement, continuing until his death in 1679 to speak out on religious issues and to attempt to sustain a universalist "Church of the First-Born" in what he understood to be the tradition of James Nayler.[67]

Looking back on the confused and unhappy history of the 1650s, modern hindsight inevitably uses lenses that did not then exist; but it is clear that even then people were conscious of living through immense changes that traditional categories were ill-equipped to explain. Nayler and Fox saw themselves as persecuted prophets like those memorialized in the Acts of the Apostles, but in their rejection of bibliolatry and their insistence on an indwelling spirit that resisted definition they seem to have been groping toward something new as much as confirming something old, "Being by Calvary's turbulence unsatisfied, / The uncontrollable mystery on the bestial floor."[68] The early Quakers proclaimed Christ, but their enemies kept forcing them to admit that they were more interested in an indwelling spirit than in the person who was born in Bethlehem and died in Jerusalem long ago. In one sense Nayler's imitation of Christ—including the turbulence of Calvary—was an affirmation of the continuing relevance of the Gospel story, but in another sense it pointed to the need to remake that story as part of a general campaign against established beliefs and practices. Milton's *Paradise Lost* was an intellectualized and aestheticized version of the same effort: to recover confidence in the integrity of the old symbolic story by replaying it in a new way for a new age, asserting continuity and sameness but haunted always by discontinuity and difference.

During the Restoration, however, the old values and their literary and intellectual conventions changed beyond recognition, and the controversies of the 1650s were foreshortened into parodic travesties by people who wanted no part of them. The claim of the radicals to be living a biblical mission was now dismissed as self-serving propaganda, whose only parallels with Scripture were with the rebellions recounted there:

> The Jews, a headstrong, moody, murmuring race,
> As ever tried the extent and stretch of grace;

God's pampered people, whom, debauched with ease,
No king could govern, nor no God could please
(Gods they had tried of every shape and size
That god-smiths could produce, or priests devise) . . .[69]

Inspiration by the Spirit was dismissed as delusionary "enthusiasm" not just by empiricist psychologists, but also by a Platonist like Henry More. "Enthusiasm is nothing else but a misconceit of being inspired," and its origin is physiological: "The spirit then that wings the enthusiast in such a wonderful manner is nothing else but that flatulency which is in the melancholy complexion, and rises out of the hypochondriacal humour upon some occasional heat."[70] From this it was but a short step to the debunking sarcasms of Swift's *Mechanical Operation of the Spirit,* and if Nayler was remembered at all he was reduced to the saturnine portrait typified by "the great liar and false Messiah James Nayler, King of the Quakers" in the *Anabaptisticum et Enthusiasticum Pantheon* (see Figure 4).

In this book I have attempted to breathe some life into that long-ago controversy with its compelling central figure, and to give James Nayler a chance to speak. But as I have sat reading the faded records of those distant passions in the well-appointed comfort of a modern university library, I have had to reflect on the immense gulf that separates Nayler and his contemporaries from any modern interpreter. The copy I have been using of the 1716 *Collection of Sundry Books* has a history that deserves reflection. On the flyleaf an early purchaser inscribed his name: "Jn. Pemberton, London 6th mo., 20th. 1750" (he paid the considerable price of five shillings and sixpence for what must by then have been a used book). Pemberton was twenty-two years old at the time. The ninth of ten children of a Philadelphia merchant, he had sailed to Europe in search of improved health, had come under the influence of a Quaker minister with the allegorical name of John Churchman, and was now beginning what would turn into a three years' preaching tour in Churchman's company. Pemberton died in 1795 after a lifetime of proselytizing, interrupted only by a distressing period of imprisonment in 1777–78 when his principles prevented him from cooperating with armed colonial resistance against England.[71] This was a reader who would have wanted to know what Nayler had to say about Truth, and for whom most of the questions modern interpreters ask would have seemed impertinent if not incomprehensible.

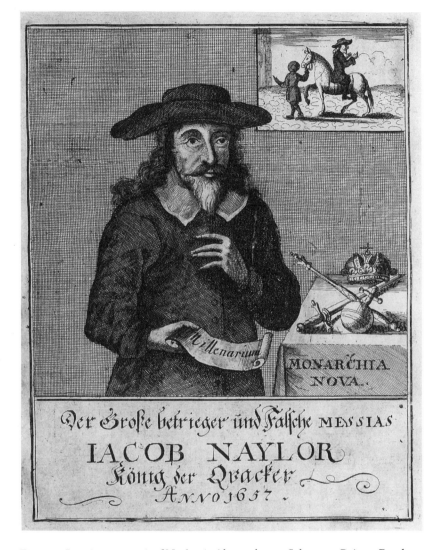

Figure 4. Imaginary portrait of Nayler, in Alte und neue Schwarm-Geister-Bruth, *facing p. 112.*

Inside the front cover a printed label is pasted, belonging to the Friends' Library of Philadelphia, with the annotation "The Gift of John Pemberton." There the book must have remained for many years, but also pasted in the cover is the bookplate of the Earlham College Library, with a picture of a man and woman in Quaker dress gazing at a forest above which an institutional building rises upon a cloud-capped hill. In 1929 this copy of Nayler's *Sundry Books* had fallen at last into the hands of professional academics, albeit ones who were sympathetic to the movement; Hugh Barbour, one of the most distinguished of Quaker historians, later taught at Earlham. A few years later the book came to the Houghton Library at Harvard as part of an exchange of duplicate materials, and there it has remained.[72] Now, another sixty years later (and two and a half centuries after its purchase by young John Pemberton) it is being asked to yield up answers its author and first readers never thought of. But it has also, I hope, helped to illuminate what they did think and believe, and thereby to contribute to the understanding of a cause célèbre that can still reveal much about the experience of the seventeenth century.

Notes

Index

❖ *Notes*

Abbreviations of Frequently Cited Works

Barbour and Roberts   Hugh Barbour and Arthur O. Roberts, eds., *Early Quaker Writings, 1650–1700* (Grand Rapids, Mich.: Eerdmans, 1973)

Bittle   William G. Bittle, *James Nayler, 1618–1660: The Quaker Indicted by Parliament* (York, England: William Sessions, 1986)

Brailsford   Mabel Richmond Brailsford, *A Quaker from Cromwell's Army: James Nayler* (New York: Macmillan, 1927)

Braithwaite   William C. Braithwaite, *The Beginnings of Quakerism* (1912), 2nd ed., revised by Henry J. Cadbury (Cambridge: Cambridge University Press, 1955)

Burton, *Diary*   *Diary of Thomas Burton, Esq., Member in the Parliaments of Oliver and Richard Cromwell from 1656 to 1659*, ed. John Towill Rutt (4 vols., 1828), repr. with an introduction by Ivan Roots (New York: Johnson Reprint Corporation, 1974)

DNB   *Dictionary of National Biography*, ed. Leslie Stephen and Sidney Lee, 22 vols. (Oxford: Oxford University Press, 1917–22)

Fogelklou   Emilia Fogelklou, *James Nayler: The Rebel Saint*, tr. from the Swedish by Lajla Yapp (London: Benn, 1931)

Fox, 1911 *Journal*   *The Journal of George Fox*, ed. Norman Penney, 2 vols. (Cambridge: Cambridge University Press, 1911)

275

Fox, 1952 *Journal*   *The Journal of George Fox*, ed. and revised by
                             John L. Nickalls (Cambridge: Cambridge
                             University Press, 1952)

Higginson, *Brief Relation* [Francis Higginson], *A Brief Relation of the
                             Irreligion of the Northern Quakers* (1653)

Nayler, *Sundry Books*   *A Collection of Sundry Books, Epistles and Pa-
                             pers, Written by James Nayler, Some of which
                             were never before Printed. With an Impartial
                             Relation of the Most Remarkable Transactions
                             Relating to His Life* [ed. George Whitehead]
                             (London, 1716)

OED   *The Oxford English Dictionary*, 20 vols., ed. J.
                             A. Simpson and E. S. C. Weiner (Oxford:
                             Clarendon Press, 1989)

Introduction

1. My own title is borrowed from *The Quaker's Jesus* by William Grigge, an account of the affair that appeared in 1658.

2. David Hume, *The History of England*, 6 vols. (Indianapolis: Liberty Classics, 1983, following the edition of 1778), 6: 145–146.

3. Thomas Hobbes, *Behemoth, or, The Long Parliament*, ed. Ferdinand Tönnies, 2nd ed. with intro. by M. M. Goldsmith (London: Frank Cass, 1969), p. 187. This work was finished in 1668, when Hobbes was eighty. The king refused publication and it did not appear until just before Hobbes's death in 1679, and then only in a pirated edition; the first accurate edition was in 1682.

4. My own attempt to explore these issues was *God's Plot and Man's Stories: Studies in the Fictional Imagination from Milton to Fielding* (Chicago: University of Chicago Press, 1985).

5. Thomas Babington Macaulay, "Milton," in *The Works of Lord Macaulay* (New York: Longmans, Green, 1897), 5: 23.

6. Thus in Van A. Harvey's entry for "antinomianism" in *A Handbook of Theological Terms* (New York: Macmillan, 1964): "On the grounds that the Christian is saved by grace and not by works or moral effort, some Christians have claimed that the saved man is free from all moral obligations or principles" (p. 23).

7. *A True Discoverie of Faith, and A Brief Manifestation of the Ground upon which we stand, to those who desire to know it; With a Declaration why we cannot repair the Idolls Temples, Nor pay wages to a Clerk* (1655), p. 11.

8. Brailsford, p. 170.

9. As noted by Barbour and Roberts, p. 83.

10. See Ormerod Greenwood, "James Nayler's 'Last Words,'" *Journal of the Friends' Historical Society* 48 (1958): 200–201.

11. As Joseph Gurney Bevan remarked in his 1800 *Life of James Nayler*, included in *A Refutation of Some of the More Modern Misrepresentations of the Society of Friends* (London: William Phillips, 1800), p. 91. Bevan specialized in biographies of religious personages, including Isaac Penington and St. Paul.

12. *Studies in Christian Enthusiasm, Illustrated from Early Quakerism* (Wallingford, Pa.: Pendle Hill, 1948), p. 69. Nuttall's little book concludes, "We are to use all God's gifts to the full . . . Better far to make mistakes, in the freedom of the children of God, than to dismiss the way of Christian enthusiasm as altogether too dangerous" (p. 90).

13. Braithwaite, p. 61.

14. William M. Lamont, *Godly Rule: Politics and Religion, 1603–1660* (London: Macmillan, 1969), p. 167.

15. *Religion and the Decline of Magic* (New York: Scribner's, 1971), p. 136. Thomas's footnote cites a passage in Nuttall's *The Holy Spirit in Puritan Faith and Experience* (Oxford: Blackwell, 1946, p. 182) that refers to Quaker failures to distinguish between the spirit and the earthly vessel, but expressly *rejects* the idea of messianic delusion.

16. Ivan Roots, *The Great Rebellion, 1642–1660* (London: Batsford, 1966), p. 205.

17. Theodore A. Wilson and Frank J. Merli, "Naylor's Case and the Dilemma of the Protectorate," *University of Birmingham Historical Journal* 10 (1965): 45–46.

18. *The World Turned Upside Down: Radical Ideas during the English Revolution* (London: Penguin Books, 1975), pp. 249, 250–251, 256.

19. *The Experience of Defeat: Milton and Some Contemporaries* (New York: Viking Penguin, 1984).

20. In *Symbol and Truth in Blake's Myth* (Princeton: Princeton University Press, 1980) I have put forward evidence for this interpretation.

21. *The World Turned Upside Down*, p. 341.

22. *The Causes of the English Civil War* (Oxford: Clarendon Press, 1990), pp. 8, 7.

23. See M. G. F. Bitterman, "The Early Quaker Literature of Defense," *Church History* 42 (1973): 206.

24. Account of a hearing in Boston in September 1656, printed in the government-controlled *Mercurius Politicus*, no. 341, 18–24 December 1656 (clearly timed to coincide with reactions to Nayler's sentence for blasphemy the previous week).

25. *Clio, A Muse, and Other Essays* (London: Longmans Green, 1930), p. 150.

1. The Quaker Menace

1. A transcript of the interrogation was reprinted in *Saul's Errand to Damascus* (1654), p. 30. Nayler and George Fox signed the two most extensive sections of this pamphlet, but other writers were probably involved as well.

2. On one occasion in 1659 a William Nayler was reported to have interrupted a church service in London, but James Nayler denied that any brother of his had ever been in London. See H. Larry Ingle, *First among Friends: George Fox and the Creation of Quakerism* (Oxford: Oxford University Press, 1994), p. 322.

3. Andrew Marvell, *An Horatian Ode upon Cromwell's Return from Ireland* (1650).

4. "On the New Forcers of Conscience under the Long Parliament" (not published until 1673).

5. There is a concise account in G. E. Aylmer, *Rebellion or Revolution? England, 1640–1660* (Oxford: Oxford University Press, 1986), pp. 136–137.

6. Quoted from Lilburne's *The Hunting of the Foxes* (the foxes were Cromwell and his henchman Henry Ireton) by Derek Hirst, *Authority and Conflict: England, 1603–1658* (Cambridge, Mass.: Harvard University Press, 1986), p. 293.

7. Manuscript record of Christopher Copley's troop, at Worcester College, Oxford; see David Underdown, *Revel, Riot, and Rebellion: Popular Politics and Culture in England, 1603–1660* (Oxford: Clarendon Press, 1985), p. 190.

8. See Fogelklou, pp. 40–41. Emilia Fogelklou, whose biography of Nayler is still valuable over sixty years after it was published, was a pioneer Swedish feminist, holder of a degree in theology, and teacher. Her book grew from an interest in the Quaker movement and dissatisfaction with its increasing institutionalization; her rather critical treatment of George Fox drew indignant retorts from numerous Quaker writers. See the biographical introduction in *Reality and Radiance: Selected Autobiographical Works of Emilia Fogelklou*, intr. and tr. by Howard T. Lutz (Richmond, Ind.: Friends United Press, 1985), esp. pp. 48–49.

9. Burton, *Diary*, 1: 33. Lambert's view of Nayler will be considered more fully in ch. 4.

10. See Mark Kishlansky's comprehensive study, *The Rise of the New Model Army* (Cambridge: Cambridge University Press, 1980), and also Aylmer, *Rebellion or Revolution?*, pp. 96–97.

11. Declaration of the army in Scotland, 1 August 1650, in *Puritanism and Liberty*, ed. A. S. P. Woodhouse (London: Dent, 1950), pp. 474–477.

12. See, e.g., Nigel Smith, *Perfection Proclaimed: Language and Literature in English Radical Religion, 1640–1660* (Oxford: Clarendon Press, 1989), pp. 10–12.

13. *Sundry Books*, p. 697 (among works described there as "never before printed"). The "grounds" were the usual ones, which will be discussed in the next chapter: preaching from set texts in church buildings, "sprinkling infants" in baptism, and so on.

14. 1952 *Journal*, p. 73.

15. Ingle (*First among Friends*, pp. 13–15) traces the "faint trail" left by Anthony Nutter, who was ejected from Drayton-in-the-Clay in 1605 (long before Fox's birth in 1624, but leaving a legacy of independence and seriousness that influenced Fox's highly religious family) and who then moved to West Ardsley and remained there until his death in 1634, at which time Nayler was sixteen.

16. *Saul's Errand to Damascus*, p. 30.

17. In 1653, shortly after Nayler's first judicial interrogation, there were rumors of sexual misconduct, which would continue to plague him thereafter, and his wife made a journey to offer him support. That he may have had doubts about her intentions is suggested by his comment in a letter, "I see she was sent of my Father and fitted by him not to be a hinderer, but a furtherer of his works" (quoted from the Swarthmore manuscripts in the Friends' House Library, London, by Bittle, p. 20). The second occasion was a visit when Nayler was imprisoned in Bridewell in 1657; she successfully petitioned Parliament to ameliorate his treatment.

18. *The Experience of Defeat*, p. 138.

19. Thomas Weld et al., *The Perfect Pharisee . . . in the Generation of Men called Quakers* (1653), p. 2.

20. *Saul's Errand to Damascus*, pp. 30–31.

21. *A Brief Relation of the Irreligion of the Northern Quakers* (1653), p. 70.

22. Matthew 4: 18–20. My biblical quotations throughout are taken from the King James Bible, which was the one regularly used by Quaker writers during the 1650s, as is confirmed by a scholar who has studied Fox's works intensively and has identified many scriptural allusions for which Fox makes no explicit reference; see Douglas Gwyn, *Apocalypse of the Word: The Life and Message of George Fox* (Richmond, Ind.: Friends United Press, 1986), p. vii.

23. See Fogelklou, p. 78, and Bittle, pp. 7–9.

24. *The World Turned Upside Down*, p. 378.

25. *The Resurrection of John Lilburne, Now a Prisoner in Dover-Castle* (1656), p. 5. Hill (*The Experience of Defeat*, p. 138) claims misleadingly that Lilburne here makes only a passing and derogatory reference to Fox. Lilburne's point was not at all to denigrate Fox, whom he genuinely esteemed, but rather to insist on the spiritual independence of every believer. Lilburne's wife had urged him to send a statement of principle to Cromwell as Fox had done in order to counter misunderstandings about his conversion, but Lilburne refused: "George Fox though even then a precious man in my eyes, his particu-

lar actions being no rules for me to walk by, unless I lived in the very same life and power of spiritual enjoyments that he did, and had the very self-same motions in spirit from God, that led him to a freedom and ability to do such and the like particular actions" (p. 9).

26. *Saul's Errand to Damascus*, p. 30. The charge reappeared during Nayler's parliamentary trial in 1656.

27. As Geoffrey Nuttall shows in "Overcoming the World: The Early Quaker Programme," *Studies in Church History* 10 (1973): 145–164.

28. *The Nature of the English Revolution* (London: Longman, 1993), p. 25.

29. *Love to the Lost* (1656), in *Sundry Books*, p. 315.

30. On these developments see Morrill, *The Nature of the English Revolution*, ch. 7, and Morrill and J. D. Walter, "Order and Disorder in the English Revolution," in *Order and Disorder in Early Modern England*, ed. Anthony Fletcher and John Stevenson (Cambridge: Cambridge University Press, 1985), pp. 137–165.

31. Quoted by Geoffrey Nuttall, *The Holy Spirit in Puritan Faith and Experience*, p. 11n.

32. Morrill, *The Nature of the English Revolution*, p. 149–150.

33. See Michael G. Finlayson, *Historians, Puritanism, and the English Revolution: The Religious Factor in English Politics before and after the Interregnum* (Toronto: University of Toronto Press, 1983), p. 62. I cannot, however, accept Finlayson's nominalist conclusion that there were no such people as "Puritans" (or "Anglicans" either). Still less persuasive is the often-cited claim of C. H. George that there was never any such thing as a Puritan and that we owe this misconception entirely to the malign influence of Max Weber ("Puritanism as History and Historiography," *Past and Present* 41 [1968]: 77–104). The term "Puritan" was very widely used in contemporary polemics, and there is even a seventeenth-century precedent, in Latin, for the term *Puritanismus* (Richard Baxter's *Church History*, quoted by Nuttall, *The Holy Spirit in Puritan Faith and Experience*, p. 10n).

34. On these last see Claire Cross, "The Church in England, 1646–1660," in *The Interregnum: The Quest for Settlement, 1646–1660*, ed. G. E. Aylmer (London: Macmillan, 1974), p. 107.

35. *The Causes of the English Civil War*, p. 84.

36. See Russell, ch. 4, and also Peter Lake, *Anglicans and Puritans? Presbyterians and English Conformist Thought from Whitgift to Hooker* (London: Unwin Hyman, 1988).

37. The five doctrines endorsed by the Synod of Dort were total depravity, unconditional election, limited atonement (Christ died only for the elect, not for all men), irresistibility of grace, and perseverance of the saints (the elect, even though continuing to be sinners, could not lose their election).

38. Worden, "Providence and Politics in Cromwellian England," *Past and Present* 109 (1985): 55–99.

39. *The Rise of Puritanism, Or, The Way to the New Jerusalem as Set Forth in Pulpit and Press from Thomas Cartwright to John Lilburne and John Milton, 1570–1643* (New York: Columbia University Press, 1938), p. 193.

40. "Religion and the Struggle for Freedom in the English Revolution," *The Historical Journal* 35 (1992): 508. As Nuttall summarizes the Puritan-Quaker relationship, "The Quakers in the exclusive sense are not Puritans but the Puritans' fiercest foes, but yet repeat, extend, and fuse so much of what is held by the radical, Separatist party within Puritanism that they cannot be denied the name" (*The Holy Spirit in Puritan Faith and Experience*, p. 13).

41. *Authority and Conflict*, p. 323.

42. *Fear, Myth and History: The Ranters and the Historians* (Cambridge: Cambridge University Press, 1986), p. 104.

43. *Behemoth*, p. 136.

44. Joshuah Miller, *Antichrist in Man the Quakers Idol* (1655), p. 2.

45. *The Quakers Catechism, or, The Quakers Questioned, their Questions Answered*, unpaginated prefatory material.

46. See Barry Reay's Introduction in J. F. McGregor and Reay, eds., *Radical Religion in the English Revolution* (London: Oxford University Press, 1984), pp. 25–27.

47. *Brief Relation*, p. 12.

48. See Nigel Smith, *Perfection Proclaimed*, pp. 7–8.

49. *Reliquiae Baxterianae: Or, Mr. Richard Baxter's Narrative of the Most Memorable Passages of his Life and Times*, ed. Matthew Sylvester (1696), p. 76.

50. Quoted by William Haller, *Liberty and Reformation in the Puritan Revolution* (New York: Columbia University Press, 1955), pp. 165–166.

51. See J. F. McGregor, "Seekers and Ranters," in McGregor and Reay, *Radical Religion in the English Revolution*, pp. 121–139.

52. See George Arthur Johnson, "From Seeker to Finder: A Study in Seventeenth-Century English Spiritualism before the Quakers," *Church History* 17 (1948): 299–315.

53. Winthrop S. Hudson carefully reviewed the evidence many years ago (and offered plausible conjectures about missing evidence) in "A Suppressed Chapter in Quaker History," *Journal of Religion* 24 (1944): 108–118. Henry J. Cadbury responded immediately and with asperity in "An Obscure Chapter of Quaker History" (same volume, 201–213), attempting to exonerate later Quaker writers from the charge of distortion, but did not really address Hudson's argument, as Hudson pointed out in "Quaker History: Dr. Hudson Replies" (279–281).

54. Letter to his daughter Bridget Ireton, 25 October 1646, in *The Writings and Speeches of Oliver Cromwell, with an Introduction, Notes, and an Account of His Life*, ed. Wilbur Cortez Abbott, 4 vols. (Cambridge: Harvard University Press, 1947), 1: 416.

55. *The Social Development of English Quakerism, 1655–1755* (Cambridge, Mass.: Harvard University Press, 1969), p. 29, quoting Dewsbury's *Faithful Testimony*.

56. John Bunyan, *Grace Abounding to the Chief of Sinners* (1666), ed. Roger Sharrock (Oxford: Clarendon Press, 1962), p. 6.

57. See Gwyn, *Apocalypse of the Word*, pp. 153–154.

58. *A Word to the Seed of the Serpent, or Ministers of Antichrist, or Man of Sin, wherever found* (1653), in *Sundry Books*, pp. 62–63.

59. *The Power and Glory of the Lord, Shining out of the North* (1653), in *Sundry Books*, pp. 35–36.

60. *The Railer Rebuked, in reply to a paper subscribed Ellis Bradshaw* (1655), pp. 1, 7.

61. *A Few Words, Occasioned by . . . A Discourse concerning the Quakers* (1653), in *Sundry Books*, pp. 113–114.

62. *Weakness above Wickedness, and Truth above Subtilty . . . Clearly seen in an Answer to a Book called Quakers Quaking, Devised by Jeremy Ives* (1656).

63. Braithwaite, p. 570.

64. *Visionary Women: Ecstatic Prophecy in Seventeenth-Century England* (Berkeley: University of California Press, 1992), p. 8.

65. See Barry Reay, *The Quakers and the English Revolution* (London: Temple Smith, 1985), pp. 26–31, which contains interesting maps of Quaker distribution in three representative counties.

66. Quoted by R. C. Richardson, *The Debate on the English Revolution Revisited*, 2nd ed. (London: Routledge, 1988), p. 111.

67. See Reay's introduction in McGregor and Reay, *Radical Religion in the English Revolution*, p. 7.

68. See Underdown, *Revel, Riot, and Rebellion*, ch. 2, and Hugh Barbour, *The Quakers in Puritan England* (New Haven: Yale University Press, 1964), ch. 3. In contrast to studies that have stressed an artisan base for the Quaker movement, recent work suggests that there were rather more farmers among the early Quakers than used to be supposed (Reay, *The Quakers and the English Revolution*, pp. 24–25).

69. See Vann, *The Social Development of English Quakerism*, ch. 1–2. Vann's findings are confirmed in detail for a local region by Alan Anderson in "The Social Origins of the Early Quakers": "There is little evidence to support the view that the first Friends were drawn from the 'economically pressed' sectors of Lancashire society;" rather, they seem to have possessed "solid, though middling, wealth" (*Quaker History* 68 [1979]: 39).

70. Braithwaite, p. 94.

71. *The Experience of Defeat*, p. 118.

72. Reay, *The Quakers and the English Revolution*, pp. 67–68.

73. "Her class and wealth enabled her to become a powerful leader and

pierce through traditional gender constraints of her era, and thus awe people in a way that Fox could not" (Bonnelyn Young Kunze, *Margaret Fell and the Rise of Quakerism* [Stanford: Stanford University Press, 1994], p. 231). See also Mack, *Visionary Women*, esp. pp. 222, 239–240.

74. Braithwaite, p. 508.

75. *A True Discoverie of Faith* (1655), p. 13.

76. Richard Baxter, *One Sheet against the Quakers* (1657), p. 11.

77. This topic will be considered more fully in Chapter 3, in connection with the group of women who surrounded Nayler.

78. "Quakerism and the Social Structure in the Interregnum," *Past and Present* 43 (1969): 90. The son remained "hostile to her and Fox for their Quakerism" (William C. Braithwaite, *The Second Period of Quakerism* [London: Macmillan, 1919], p. 263), especially when, a decade after Judge Fell's death, Margaret Fell married George Fox.

79. *Thomas Camm's Testimony concerning John Camm and John Audland*, the unpaginated first item in Camm and Charles Marshall, *The Memory of the Righteous Revived* (1689).

80. Nayler and Fox, *Several Petitions Answered, That were put up by the Priests of Westmoreland* (1653), p. 18. This passage is signed by Nayler.

81. See Reay, *The Quakers and the English Revolution*, p. 40.

82. Max Weber, *The Protestant Ethic and the Spirit of Capitalism*, tr. Talcott Parsons (New York: Scribner, 1958), p. 44.

83. *Brief Relation*, p. 39.

84. Quoted from the Swarthmore manuscripts by Braithwaite, p. 73. At the time of Aldam's conversion "the power and spirit of God caused his bones to shake and his limbs to tremble" (p. 60).

85. *Charles Marshall's Testimony*, in Camm and Marshall, *The Memory of the Righteous Revived*, sig. E6. The symbolism of the "Seed" will be discussed in the next chapter.

86. *A Few Words, Occasioned by . . . A Discourse concerning the Quakers* (1653), in *Sundry Books*, p. 130.

87. *The Way how all Flesh come to Know the Lord and Fear Him, by his Terrible Shaking the Earthly Part in Man, witnessed by the Holy Men of GOD in Scripture* (1653), in *Sundry Books*, pp. 53–57.

88. *Brief Relation*, p. 16.

89. *The History of the Life of Thomas Ellwood* (2nd ed., 1714), p. 15.

90. Quoted by Braithwaite, p. 508.

91. Burton, *Diary*, 1: 128. The speaker was Bernard Church of Norwich.

92. See the very full survey in J. F. Maclear, "Popular Anticlericalism in the Puritan Revolution," *Journal of the History of Ideas* 17 (1956): 443–470.

93. A number of established ministers, including Baxter, attempted to prove that the Quakers were secret Papists or at least Papist dupes, arguing

even that overtly anti-Catholic writings by Quakers were red herrings designed to deflect suspicion. See Stephen A. Kent, "The 'Papist' Charges against the Interregnum Quakers," *Journal of Religious History* 12 (1982): 180–190; and Reay, *The Quakers and the English Revolution*, ch. 4.

94. Quoted by Claire Cross, "The Church in England, 1646–1660," in Aylmer, *The Interregnum*, p. 117.

95. *Brief Relation*, p. 1. Little is known of John Spoden (or Snowden?). Samuel Thornton remained active in the Quaker movement for decades, enduring imprisonment in 1662 and 1683.

96. *Several Petitions Answered, That were put up by the Priests of Westmoreland* (1653), pp. 1–5.

97. Quoted from the Swarthmore manuscripts by Mack, *Visionary Women*, p. 224.

98. *An Account from the Children of Light* (1660), in *Sundry Books*, pp. 629–630.

99. *Satan Inthron'd in his Chair of Pestilence, or, Quakerism in its Exaltation: Being a true Narrative and Relation of the manner of James Nailer (that eminent Quaker's) entrance into the City of Bristol the 24 day of October, 1656* (1657), unpaginated preface that begins, "Reader, take this preliminary Epistle as manductive and giving some light to the ensuing Narrative." After this metaphysical introduction Farmer, a prominent Bristol minister who had been involved for some time in anti-Quaker activity, descends to a detailed review of the actions and statements of the Nayler group.

100. Shakespeare, *Othello*, 1. 1. 133–134.

101. *Religion and the Decline of Magic*, p. 59.

102. See Gwyn, *Apocalypse of the Word*, pp. 127–128.

103. 1952 *Journal*, p. 449.

104. Hill, *The World Turned Upside Down*, p. 106; Reay, *The Quakers and the English Revolution*, p. 43.

105. *Saul's Errand to Damascus*, pp. 21–22.

106. *An Account from the Children of Light* (1660), in *Sundry Books*, p. 608.

107. *The Power and Glory of the Lord, Shining out of the North* (1653), in *Sundry Books*, p. 43.

108. *The History of the Life of Thomas Ellwood*, p. 19.

109. *The Old Serpent's Voice; or, Antichrist discovered, opposing Christ in his Kingdom* (1655), in *Sundry Books*, pp. 200–201.

110. *One Sheet against the Quakers* (1657), pp. 5–6.

111. Letter to Sir Wilfrid Lawson, printed in the 1911 *Journal*, 1: 116. Lawson, a Cromwell supporter, was sheriff of Cumberland when Fox was imprisoned at Carlisle in 1653.

112. *Love to the Lost* (1656), in *Sundry Books*, p. 288, quoting phrases from Matthew 23 and Acts 13.

113. "Providence and Politics in Cromwellian England," p. 97.

114. *The Power and Glory of the Lord, Shining out of the North* (1653), in *Sundry Books*, p. 41.

115. Weld et al., *The Perfect Pharisee*, p. 44; Nayler, *A Discovery of The Man of Sin . . . Or, An Answer to a Book set forth . . . by way of Reply to an Answer of James Nayler's to their former Book, called The Perfect Pharisee* (1655), p. 46.

116. *Brief Relation*, p. 22.

117. Quoted in the notes to the 1911 edition of Fox's *Journal*, 1: 439; the paper is annotated in a contemporary hand, "When she was 8 years old 1655." William Lampitt, an Independent, was rector of Ulverston near Swarthmoor; Judge Fell had given him the living in place of an ejected Episcopalian. Isabel Ross reports that Mary Fell was a sensitive child (*Margaret Fell: Mother of Quakerism* [London: Longmans, Green, 1949], p. 27; on Lampitt, see pp. 4, 10).

118. *A Dispute between James Nayler and the Parish Teachers of Chesterfield* (1655), p. 1.

119. *DNB* 2: 496–497 (quoting Calamy).

120. Underdown, *Revel, Riot, and Rebellion*, p. 236; see also pp. 240 and 252.

121. From the *Lancaster Quarterly Meeting Minutebook*, in Barbour and Roberts, pp. 62–63.

122. *Saul's Errand to Damascus*, pp. 24–25.

123. *Brief Relation*, p. 66.

124. 1952 *Journal*, p. 223.

125. As Richard Bauman observes in *Let Your Words Be Few: Symbolism of Speaking and Silence among Seventeenth-Century Quakers* (Cambridge: Cambridge University Press, 1983), p. 72.

126. *Brief Relation*, p. 25.

127. *A Fool Answered according to his Folly . . . in an answer to George Emmot of Durham* (1655), p. 9.

128. See Alan Cole, "The Quakers and the English Revolution," in *Crisis in Europe, 1560–1660: Essays from "Past and Present"*, ed. Trevor Aston (London: Routledge, 1965), pp. 341–358.

129. *Some Considerations needful to be taken into mind by such as are in Place*, in *Sundry Books*, pp. 752–753 (among undated works described on p. 697 as "never before printed").

130. See Derek Hirst, "The Lord Protector," in *Oliver Cromwell and the English Revolution*, ed. John Morrill (London: Longmans, 1990), p. 137; and also Morrill, *The Nature of the English Revolution*, p. 122.

131. *Middlemarch*, ed. David Carroll (Oxford: Oxford University Press, 1988), I, vi, p. 43.

132. *Satan's Design Discovered . . . Clearly laid open in an answer to Thomas Moor* (1655), p. 13.

133. *From the Spirit of the Lord, written by one whose name in the flesh is William Dewsbury* (1655), in Barbour and Roberts, p. 96.

134. *Good Work for a Good Magistrate*, quoted by Hill, *The World Turned Upside Down*, p. 98.

135. *The Quakers Catechism* (1655), pp. 6–7.

136. *One Sheet against the Quakers* (1657), p. 7.

137. *To Oliver Cromwell* (1654), in *Sundry Books*, pp. 185–186.

138. *The Old Serpent's Voice; or, Antichrist discovered, opposing Christ in his Kingdom* (1655), in *Sundry Books*, p. 203. Nayler supported the absolute rejection of covetousness by New Testament citations from Ephesians, Colossians, and Hebrews.

139. *To the Gathered Churches* (1659), in *Sundry Books*, p. 578.

140. *An Account from the Children of Light* (1660), in *Sundry Books*, p. 628.

141. Nayler, *A Salutation to the Seed of God* (1655), in *Sundry Books*, p. 231. I follow the first edition (p. 20) in reading "days to conform to the world." *Sundry Books* has "a day to conform to the world," thereby losing the sense of the six weekdays as opposed to the Puritan sabbath.

142. *Natural Symbols: Explorations in Cosmology* (New York: Random House Vintage Books, 1973), p. 28. Douglas observes that "a violent source of antiritualism is opened up when persons are perceived to be behind the principles, or benefiting from them" (p. 181).

143. *An answer to that common objection against the Quakers, that they condemn all but themselves*, quoted by Vann, *The Social Development of English Quakerism*, p. 27.

144. The quotation that follows is taken from Higginson's *Brief Relation*, p. 11.

145. The connection between Puritan discipline and political activism is traced by Michael Walzer in *The Revolution of the Saints: A Study in the Origins of Radical Politics* (New York: Atheneum, 1973).

146. See J. C. Davis, "Against Formality: One Aspect of the English Revolution," *Transactions of the Royal Historical Society*, 6th series, 3 (1993), 265–288.

147. *Brief Relation*, pp. 40, 56–57, alluding to 1 Thessalonians 4: 11.

148. A petition in 1658, asking for the release of more than a hundred Quakers then in jail, resulted in statements from their judges that identified their offenses as follows: sixty in connection with tithes, forty-two for interrupting ministers, five for refusing hat-honor, three as "vagabonds" (i.e., unwelcome itinerant preachers), two for refusing to swear oaths, two for illegal meetings, and three for other charges (Barbour, *The Quakers in Puritan England*, p. 199).

149. Bauman's term in *Let Your Words Be Few*, p. 45. Bauman's Chapter 4

("Christ Respects No Man's Person: The Plain Language and the Rhetoric of Impoliteness") is a valuable examination of these issues from a sociolinguistic point of view.

150. 1952 *Journal*, p. 250.

151. *The Perfect Pharisee*, p. 32.

152. *A Discovery of the Man of Sin* (1655), p. 39.

153. John Deacon, *The Grand Impostor EXAMINED: Or, The Life, Tryal, and Examination of JAMES NAYLER, The Seduced and Seducing QUAKER with The Manner of his Riding into BRISTOL* (1656), p. 18.

154. *The History of the Life of Thomas Ellwood*, p. 26.

155. *Deceit brought to Day-Light* (1656), p. 15. On these points of usage see Barbour, *The Quakers in Puritan England*, pp. 164–165.

156. *Brief Relation*, p. 10.

157. 1952 *Journal*, p. 36, italics mine.

158. As J. S. Morrill and J. D. Walter observe in "Order and Disorder in the English Revolution," p. 147n.

159. *An Account from the Children of Light* (1660), in *Sundry Books*, p. 612.

160. *Brief Relation*, p. 28.

161. See Barbour and Roberts, p. 127n.

162. *Several Petitions Answered, That were put up by the Priests of Westmoreland* (1653), p. 60.

163. *A Discovery of the Man of Sin* (1655), pp. 3–4.

164. Quoted from *An Instruction to Judges and Lawyers* by Hill, *The Experience of Defeat*, p. 154.

165. *Saul's Errand to Damascus*, p. 29 (reporting Nayler's examination for blasphemy at the sessions at Appleby).

166. 1952 *Journal*, pp. 36–37.

167. *A Record of Sufferings for Tythes in England* (1658), quoted by Bitterman, "The Early Quaker Literature of Defense," p. 214. A Puritan opponent, incidentally, called Hubberthorne "the most rational calm-spirited man of his judgment that I was ever publicly engaged against" (Adam Martindale, quoted by Ann Hughes in "The Pulpit Guarded: Confrontations between Orthodox and Radicals in Revolutionary England," in *John Bunyan and His England, 1628–88*, ed. Anne Laurence, W. R. Owens, and Stuart Sim [London: Hambledon Press, 1990], p. 44).

168. Fox, *Newes coming up out of the North*; Howgill, *To the Camp of the Lord in England*; Audland, *The School-Master Disciplined*; all quoted by Hill, *The Experience of Defeat*, pp. 158, 149.

169. "Overcoming the World: The Early Quaker Programme," p. 163.

170. *Several Petitions Answered, That were put up by the Priests of Westmoreland* (1653), pp. 2, 11–12.

171. *Saul's Errand to Damascus*, pp. 1–2.

172. *The Power and Glory of the Lord, Shining out of the North* (1653), in *Sundry Books*, p. 48.

173. *A Discovery of the Wisdom which is from Beneath, and the Wisdom which is from Above*, in *Sundry Books*, pp. 67–68.

174. "Popular Anticlericalism in the Puritan Revolution," p. 460.

175. Blair Worden, "The Politics of Marvell's Horatian Ode," *The Historical Journal* 27 (1984): 528.

176. Letter to Margaret Fell, 1653, quoted from the Swarthmore manuscripts by Mack, *Visionary Women*, p. 143.

177. See Cole, "The Quakers and the English Revolution," p. 342.

178. Quoted by Mack, *Visionary Women*, p. 242.

179. *A Few Words in Answer to the Resolve of Some who are called Independent-Teachers* (1659), in *Sundry Books*, p. 564.

180. *To All Present Rulers, Whether Parliament, or Whomsoever of England* (1659), quoted by Mack, *Visionary Women*, p. 187.

181. Reay, *The Quakers and the English Revolution*, pp. 43, 40.

182. This is not to deny that some Quakers served as aldermen or as local officials of other kinds, or that Quakers sometimes took an interest in broad-based proposals for reform, such as the ones that surfaced when the Commonwealth was breaking down in 1659. A useful review of such concerns is provided by David Boulton, "Public Policy and Politics in Fox's Thought: The Un-militant Tendency in Early Quakerism," in *New Light on George Fox*, ed. Michael Mullett (York: William Sessions, 1993).

183. *To the Parliament, the Army, and all the Wel-affected in the Nation*, quoted by Cole, "The Quakers and the English Revolution," p. 345.

184. *Father and Son* (New York: Norton, 1963), p. 19.

185. "Esthétique du Mal," in *The Collected Poems of Wallace Stevens* (New York: Knopf, 1961), p. 325.

2. God in Man

1. *Literature and Revolution in England, 1640–1660* (New Haven: Yale University Press, 1994), p. 118.

2. *Babylon the Great Described*, quoted by Hill, *The Experience of Defeat*, p. 123.

3. Epistle IX, "To some that were backslidden," in *Sundry Books*, p. 722 (among undated works described on p. 697 as "never before printed").

4. *Brief Relation*, p. 38.

5. *A Discovery of the Beast, Got into the Seat of the False Prophet . . . Or, An Answer to a Paper set out by T[homas] Winterton* (1655), p. 2.

6. As I have argued in "Hobbes as Reformation Theologian: Implica-

tions of the Free-Will Controversy," *Journal of the History of Ideas* 40 (1979): 339–352.

7. 1952 *Journal*, p. 123.

8. Nuttall, *The Holy Spirit in Puritan Faith and Experience*, ch. 5, "The Spirit and Prophesying."

9. *A Lamentation . . . over the Ruins of this Oppressed Nation* (1653), in *Sundry Books*, p. 99.

10. Epistle no. 10, in Barbour and Roberts, p. 487.

11. *Paradise Lost* 2: 557–561.

12. John Donne, *Satire 3*, lines 79–82.

13. *Satan's Design Discovered* (1655), p. 24.

14. *Antichrist in Man, Christ's Enemy* (1656), p. 1. Nayler was responding to Joshua Miller's attack entitled *Antichrist in Man the Quakers' Idol*.

15. *Paradise Lost* 11: 351, 354.

16. *Foot Yet in the Snare* (1656), p. 32.

17. *The Holy Ghost on the Bench* (1656), quoted by Nuttall, *The Holy Spirit in Puritan Faith and Experience*, p. 49.

18. *Paradise Lost* 4: 423–427.

19. See Nigel Smith, *Perfection Proclaimed*, pp. 237–240.

20. *A Dispute between James Nayler and the Parish Teachers of Chesterfield* (1655), pp. 13–14.

21. *Areopagitica*, in *The Prose of John Milton*, ed. J. Max Patrick (New York: Doubleday Anchor Books, 1967), p. 287.

22. 1952 *Journal*, p. 27.

23. John Whiting, *Persecution Expos'd, in some memoirs relating to the sufferings of John Whiting, and many others of the people called Quakers, for conscience sake* (1715), p. 177.

24. *One Sheet against the Quakers* (1657), p. 3. The first formal "sum or body" of Quaker belief was Robert Barclay's *Apology for the True Christian Divinity*, published in Latin in 1676 and in English in 1678.

25. *A Second Sheet for the Ministry, Justifying our Calling, Against Quakers, Seekers, and Papists, and all that deny us to be the Ministers of Christ* (1657), p. 16.

26. *An Answer to a young unsettled Friend, who before* [i.e., previously] *inclining strongly to Anabaptistry, at last fell in with the Quakers,* part of the unpaginated prefatory material in *The Quakers Catechism* (1655), sig. B4.

27. Quoted by Hirst, *Authority and Conflict*, p. 325 (Hirst calls Baxter "a pastoral genius").

28. See Thomas, *Religion and the Decline of Magic*, pp. 76–77, 151–166.

29. In the 1688 twelfth edition of *The Saints' Everlasting Rest*, p. 520 (Part 3, ch. 14, sec. 10). This passage does not appear in the first edition (1650).

30. *Love to the Lost* (1656), in *Sundry Books*, p. 309.

31. *A Discovery of the Wisdom which is from Beneath, and the Wisdom which is from Above*, in *Sundry Books*, pp. 88–89.

32. *1952 Journal*, p. 79.

33. Samuel Butler, *Hudibras* (1662), 1: 81–82.

34. *George Fox's Address to Friends in the Ministry* (1657), in Barbour and Roberts, pp. 490–491.

35. *To the Gathered Churches* (1659), in *Sundry Books*, p. 579.

36. Report of the Kelk Monthly Meeting, in Barbour and Roberts, p. 58.

37. Hill, *The Experience of Defeat*, p. 128 ("a great falling off from the taut prose of Overton, Walwyn, Winstanley, Coppe").

38. "Seventeenth-Century Quaker Style," *PMLA: Publications of the Modern Language Association* 71 (1956): 725–754.

39. *Let Your Words Be Few*, p. 78. "Collaborative expectancy" is a phrase of Kenneth Burke's, from *A Rhetoric of Motives*.

40. Ronald Knox, in his comprehensive study *Enthusiasm: A Chapter in the History of Religion* (New York: Oxford University Press, 1950), traces the word's popularity to a 1680 anti-Quaker sermon by George Hickes, *The Spirit of Enthusiasm Exorcised* (pp. 6, 368–369).

41. Rufus Jones, *Studies in Mystical Religion* (London: Macmillan, 1909), p. xv. Jones quotes the philosopher Josiah Royce as saying that "the mystic is a thorough-going empiricist"—not, it need hardly be added, in the sense that Locke or Hume understood empiricism.

42. See William P. Alston, "Ineffability," *Philosophical Review* 65 (1956): 506–522.

43. *Brief Relation*, p. 12. "Rope of sand" was a cliché in controversial writing; the Quaker George Bishop applied it to anti-Quaker polemics in *The Throne of Truth Exalted* (1656), p. 76.

44. *Let Your Words Be Few*, p. 11.

45. Both quoted by Bittle, pp. 78, 79.

46. *An Exact History of the Life of James Naylor* (1657), p. 4.

47. E.g., Brailsford, p. 33 ("Suddenly the curtain lifts between one century and another," p. 31).

48. *A Discovery of the Man of Sin* (1655), p. 51, answering *The Perfect Pharisee* by Thomas Weld and his minister colleagues.

49. *Brief Relation*, unpaginated introductory address "To the Seduced Followers of George Fox, James Nayler, etc."

50. *The Quakers Catechism* (1655), unpaginated introduction.

51. Whiting, *Persecution Expos'd* (1715), p. 176. Braithwaite (p. 242) notes that Whiting misdates this event in 1654; it should be 1656.

52. *The World Turned Upside Down*, p. 95.

53. *Behemoth*, p. 21.

54. *Saul's Errand to Damascus*, pp. 14, 18.

55. *A Publike Discovery of the Open Blindness of Babel's Builders* (1656), p. 17.

56. *A Relation of the Imprisonment of Mr. John Bunyan*, in *Grace Abounding*, p. 111.

57. *The Perfect Pharisee*, p. 27.

58. *Brief Relation*, p. 4.

59. Braithwaite, p. 89.

60. *A Discovery of the Man of Sin* (1655), pp. 36, 37.

61. See the reminiscence by Charles Marshall quoted in Chapter 1 above.

62. See the very full account, "Thomas Weld of Gateshead: The Return of a New England Puritan," in Roger Howell, *Puritans and Radicals in North England: Essays on the English Revolution* (Lanham, Md.: University Press of America, 1984), pp. 83–111. Weld began his career as a vicar in Essex, was disciplined for Puritan tendencies, and emigrated to New England in 1632. He returned to England in 1641 as a financial and political agent for the Massachusetts colony, and eventually took up the parish of Gateshead, just outside Newcastle, in 1650. The formal complaint came in 1657, but Weld had cultivated powerful patrons in the Newcastle establishment and it turned out to be his critics who were disciplined.

63. *Christian Directory* (1673), quoted by John R. Knott, *The Sword of the Spirit: Puritan Responses to the Bible* (Chicago: University of Chicago Press, 1980), p. 71.

64. "A paper of G. F.'s what was spoken to Friends in the ministry at John Crookes 1658," in 1911 *Journal*, 1: 321.

65. *The Protestant Ethic and the Spirit of Capitalism*, pp. 148–149.

66. *Grace Abounding*, pp. 29, 43, 53, 66, 77.

67. 1952 *Journal*, p. 109.

68. See Christopher Hill, *The English Bible and the Seventeenth-Century Revolution* (London: Allen Lane/Penguin Press, 1993), p. 18. The army in Scotland, where Nayler was stationed, placed a bulk order at 1s. 8d. per copy.

69. *Deceit brought to Day-Light* (1656), p. 8.

70. *An Exact History of the Life of James Naylor*, p. 21.

71. 1952 *Journal*, p. 159.

72. *Saul's Errand to Damascus*, p. 33.

73. *A Few Words, Occasioned by . . . A Discourse concerning the Quakers* (1653), in *Sundry Books*, p. 119.

74. *Satan's Design Discovered* (1655), p. 7. The dispute was held in Lincolnshire in May of 1655 with the Manifestarians, "a rather obscure sect which had been gathered by Thomas Moore, an equally obscure individual" (Bittle, p. 73). Wray was a justice in Gainsborough who had offered his house for the occasion.

75. *The Railer Rebuked* (1655), pp. 5–6.

76. *A Disputation on Holy Scripture* (1588), quoted by Knott, *The Sword of the Spirit*, p. 34.

77. *Love to the Lost* (1656), p. 271.

78. John Donne, *Devotions upon Emergent Occasions* (Ann Arbor: University of Michigan Press, 1965), Expostulation 19, p. 125.

79. *To them of the Independent Society*, in *Sundry Books*, pp. 698–699 (among undated works described on p. 697 as "never before printed").

80. *Several Petitions Answered, That were put up by the Priests of Westmoreland* (1653), pp. 15, 26.

81. *The Royal Law, and Covenant of God* (1655), p. 3.

82. See A. L. Morton, *The Everlasting Gospel: A Study in the Sources of William Blake* (London: Lawrence & Wishart, 1958), pp. 37–39. It is hard to prove, however, that there was a coherent tradition, and as Nuttall observes, Fox and other Quakers' use of the phrase "the everlasting gospel" proves that they had read Revelation 14: 6 but not that they had read Joachim (*The Holy Spirit in Puritan Faith and Experience*, p. 104n).

83. *A Discovery of the Man of Sin* (1655), p. 7.

84. Joseph Wright, *A Testimony for the Son of Man* (1660), p. 78. On this subject see T. L. Underwood's judicious survey, "Early Quaker Eschatology," in *Puritans, The Millennium and the Future of Israel: Puritan Eschatology 1600 to 1660*, ed. Peter Toon (Cambridge: James Clarke, 1970), pp. 91–103.

85. *Brief Relation*, unpaginated preface "To my Christian Readers."

86. *What the Possession of the Living Faith Is* (1659), in *Sundry Books*, p. 459.

87. Quoted by Barbour, *The Quakers in Puritan England*, p. 145.

88. *Magnalia Christi Americana: Or, the Ecclesiastical History of New-England*, 7 vols. bound in one (London, 1702), 7: 22.

89. *Saul's Errand to Damascus*, p. 8.

90. See Gwyn, *Apocalypse of the Word*, ch. 6.

91. *A Salutation to the Seed of God* (1655), in *Sundry Books*, pp. 216–217.

92. *Some Gospel-Truths Opened*, in *The Miscellaneous Works of John Bunyan*, ed. Roger Sharrock et al. (Oxford: Oxford University Press, 1976—), 1: 44, 86.

93. Fox, 1952 *Journal*, p. 63. Fox is recalling here his arguments with Rice [Rhys] Jones, a former Baptist and Quaker apostate who did deny the historical Jesus.

94. *Satan's Design Discovered* (1655), p. 11; *Love to the Lost* (1656), in *Sundry Books*, pp. 261, 265.

95. Geoffrey Nuttall, *James Nayler: A Fresh Approach* (London: Friends' Historical Society, 1954), p. 5. Nuttall makes a good case for the affinity of Nayler's beliefs with Familist ones, although his attempt to prove direct Familist connections may be unconvincing (see Bittle, p. 79). Pordage, incidentally, was an admirer of Jakob Boehme, whose writings were later a major influence on William Blake.

96. Quoted from Niclaes's *Exhortatio I* (1574) by Jean Dietz Moss, "'God-ded with God': Hendrik Niclaes and His Family of Love," *Transactions of the American Philosophical Society* 71, pt. 8 (1981): 41. Moss notes (5) that the Familists practiced outward conformity and concealed their secret obser-vances, which made them hard to detect at the time and even harder for later historians to trace.

97. Quoted from Coppin's *Divine Teachings* (1653) by Hill, *The World Turned Upside Down*, p. 220. Coppin was jailed for his beliefs in 1655.

98. *Love to the Lost* (1656), in *Sundry Books*, p. 256.

99. Fox, 1911 *Journal*, pp. 66–67. Nayler's questioner was William Mar-shall, referred to by Fox as "priest Marshall" (p. 62).

100. Nayler, *Love to the Lost*, in *Sundry Books*, p. 348 (emended from the first edition of 1656, as indicated below).

101. Quoted from the Swarthmore manuscripts by Braithwaite, p. 179. (Fox's account is headed "Sufferings at Leicester, 1653," but Braithwaite shows that it must actually be 1655.)

102. *The Short Journal and Itinerary Journals of George Fox*, ed. Norman Penney (Cambridge: Cambridge University Press, 1925), p. 279, n. 2 to p. 17.

103. Epistle XII, "Exhorting to Mercy and Forgiveness," in *Sundry Books*, p. 731 (among works described on p. 697 as "never before printed").

104. *A Vision of the Last Judgment*, in *Complete Poetry and Prose of William Blake*, ed. David V. Erdman (Berkeley: University of California Press, 1982), pp. 556–557. In Blake's vision of the united Zoas of humanity "they walked / To and fro in eternity as one man" (*Jerusalem* 98: 38–39, p. 258).

105. Henry Crabb Robinson, in *Blake Records*, ed. G. E. Bentley, Jr. (Ox-ford: Clarendon Press, 1969), p. 310.

106. 1952 *Journal*, p. 47. This happened in Coventry in 1649.

107. *A Discovery of the Man of Sin* (1655), pp. 12–13.

108. Higginson, *Brief Relation*, p. 71.

109. *Satan's Design Discovered* (1655), p. 51.

110. 1952 *Journal*, p. 27.

111. *The Lamb's War against the Man of Sin* (1658), in *Sundry Books*, p. 394.

112. On specific differences between Calvinist and Quaker thought see William J. Frost, "The Dry Bones of Quaker Theology," *Church History* 39 (1970): 503–523, based on the 1676 codification by Robert Barclay.

113. *A Door Opened to the Imprisoned Seed* (1659), in *Sundry Books*, pp. 506, 519 (the 1716 text gives "born of the spirit" in place of the first edition's "born of the freedom").

114. For example, in 1643 Jeremiah Burroughs published *Jacob's Seed: Or the Generation of Seekers*; in 1647 the Leveller John Saltmarsh wrote, "Christ is already in all his [i.e., all his people] in spirit and truth, and as the eternal seed, and his fullness is already in the saints, or all true Christians": *Sparkles of*

Glory: Some Beams of the Morning Star Wherein are many discoveries as to Truth, and Peace, quoted by A. L. Morton, *The World of the Ranters: Religious Radicalism in the English Revolution* (London: Lawrence & Wishart, 1970), pp. 61–62.

115. *A Salutation to the Seed of God* (1655), in *Sundry Books*, p. 236.

116. *The Light of Christ, and the Word of Life: Cleared from the Deceipts of the Deceiver, and his litterall Weapons turned upon his owne head* (1656).

117. 1952 *Journal,* p. 21.

118. See Frost, "The Dry Bones of Quaker Theology," p. 511.

119. *A Door Opened to the Imprisoned Seed* (1659), in *Sundry Books*, p. 545.

120. *Sundry Books,* p. 58.

121. "A paper to papists and all professors and others," in the 1911 *Journal,* 1: 333.

122. *Love to the Lost* (1656), in *Sundry Books,* p. 260.

123. *A Discovery of the Man of Sin* (1655), p. 6.

124. *A Door Opened to the Imprisoned Seed,* in *Sundry Books,* p. 547.

125. Preface to *Sundry Books* (1716), p. vii.

126. "To all dear brethren and friends in Holderness, and in the east parts of Yorkshire" (1653), in *Sundry Books,* p. 33.

127. *A Salutation to the Seed of God,* in *Sundry Books,* pp. 210–211.

128. *A Few Words, Occasioned by . . . A Discourse concerning the Quakers* (1653), in *Sundry Books,* pp. 117–118.

129. *An Answer to a young unsettled Friend, who before* [i.e., previously] *inclining strongly to Anabaptistry, at last fell in with the Quakers,* part of the unpaginated prefatory material in *The Quakers Catechism* (1655), sig. C1.

130. 1952 *Journal,* pp. 51–52.

131. *Brief Relation,* p. 21.

132. *A True Discoverie of Faith* (1655), p. 13. The dog returning to his vomit appears in Proverbs 26: 11 and in 2 Peter 2: 22.

133. *The Diary of Cotton Mather,* ed. Worthington C. Ford, 2 vols. (New York, 1957), 1: 237 (entry for 16 October 1697).

134. *Heaven on Earth* (1654), in *The Complete Works of Thomas Brooks,* ed. Alexander Grosart, 6 vols. (Edinburgh: Nichol, 1866), 2: 347.

135. *Weakness above Wickedness, and Truth above Subtilty* (1656), p. 15.

136. *Love to the Lost* (1656), in *Sundry Books,* p. 285.

137. *Sundry Books,* pp. 58–59.

138. *Sundry Books,* pp. 427, 436. This tract was first published in 1659.

139. *What the Possession of the Living Faith Is,* in *Sundry Books,* p. 452, citing Hebrews 10: 26–27.

140. Eugène Portalié, *A Guide to the Thought of St. Augustine,* tr. Ralph J. Bastian (Chicago: Regnery, 1960), p. 108.

141. *The Lamb's War against the Man of Sin* (1658), in *Sundry Books,* p. 382.

142. *Love to the Lost,* in *Sundry Books,* pp. 341–342.

143. *What the Possession of the Living Faith Is*, in *Sundry Books*, pp. 432, 434 (with an emendation from the first edition, p. 9).

144. In *Fear, Myth and History* J. C. Davis has argued that there was never such a thing as a movement that could be identified as Ranterism, and only a few writers who can properly be called Ranters; he concludes that the myth of a menacing Ranter underground was generated for polemical purposes in the early 1650s. See also J. F. McGregor's essay "Ranterism and the Development of Early Quakerism," *Journal of Religious History* 9 (1977): 349–363. Davis's argument has a polemical purpose of its own, to show that in the mid-twentieth century the Ranters were resurrected by Marxist historians, who needed to believe that a potent radical movement was generated by the Revolution, was savagely "repressed," and then went "underground" (see Davis's reply to angry reviews of his book in "Fear, Myth and Furore: Reappraising the 'Ranters,'" *Past & Present* 129 [1990]: 79–83, and the ensuing "Debate" in the same volume, in which four historians reply to his reply). In any case there were certainly more than a few people whose attitudes struck the authorities as blatantly Ranterish, and as been well said, "If the Ranters were a fiction, they were one of their own as well as of others' making" (Nigel Smith, *Perfection Proclaimed*, p. 9n).

145. *A Looking-Glasse for the Quakers*, p. 7.

146. *Reliquiae Baxterianae* (1696), p. 77. Coleridge's copy is held by the Houghton Library at Harvard—or, more accurately, it holds the copy of George Frere, who noted on the inside front cover that he lent it to Coleridge at Hampstead and got it back again, heavily annotated, only after Coleridge's death.

147. *A Vindication of The Book called Some Gospel-Truths Opened*, in *Miscellaneous Works*, 1: 139.

148. *Grace Abounding*, p. 17.

149. *A Few Words, Occasioned by . . . A Discourse concerning the Quakers* (1653), in *Sundry Books*, p. 115.

150. *Love to the Lost* (1656), in *Sundry Books*, p. 336.

151. *One Sheet against the Quakers* (1657), pp. 9–10.

152. *Behold you Rulers, and hearken proud Men and Women, who have let the Spirit of the World into your hearts* (1658), p. 3.

153. *A Salutation to the Seed of God* (1655), in *Sundry Books*, p. 218.

154. Testimony from the Selby Meeting, Yorkshire, 1704, in Barbour and Roberts, p. 59.

155. Letter in the Swarthmore manuscripts, in Barbour and Roberts, pp. 157–158.

156. *The Four Zoas*, Night the Ninth, in *Complete Poetry and Prose of William Blake*, ed. Erdman, p. 404.

157. Douglas, *Natural Symbols*, p. 17.

158. Epistle XI, *Not to strive, but overcome by suffering,* in *Sundry Books,* p. 730 (among works described on p. 697 as "never before printed").

159. *Love to the Lost* (1656), in *Sundry Books,* pp. 328–329 (restoring a reading from the first edition).

160. *To them of the Independent Society,* in *Sundry Books,* p. 699 (among works described on p. 697 as "never before printed").

161. Letter in 1653, quoted from the Swarthmore manuscripts by Nuttall, *Studies in Christian Enthusiasm,* p. 45.

162. *A Salutation to the Seed of God* (1655), in *Sundry Books,* pp. 229–230.

163. *A Discovery of the Wisdom which is from Beneath, and the Wisdom which is from Above* (1653), in *Sundry Books,* p. 67.

164. *A paper of G. F.'s to all professors* (1654), in the 1911 *Journal,* 1: 172.

165. *The Lamb's War against the Man of Sin* (1658), in *Sundry Books,* p. 390.

166. *The Forbidden Fruit* (1642), translation of Sebastian Franck's *Von dem Baum des Wissens guts und boses* (1538), p. 4; quoted by Nigel Smith, *Perfection Proclaimed,* p. 125.

167. *A Vision of the Last Judgment,* in *Complete Poetry and Prose of William Blake,* ed. Erdman, p. 565.

168. See Gwyn, *Apocalypse of the Word,* pp. 84–86.

169. *Jerusalem and Albion: The Hebraic Factor in Seventeenth-Century Literature* (New York: Schocken, 1964), p. 101. The quoted phrase is from Calvin's *Institutes,* II. xii.

170. 1952 *Journal,* pp. 9–10.

3. Nayler's Sign and Its Meanings

1. Quoted by Elisabeth Brockbank, *Edward Burrough: A Wrestler for Truth, 1634–1662* (London: Bannisdale Press, 1949), pp. 57–58.

2. See Barbour, *The Quakers in Puritan England,* p. 193.

3. *Brief Relation* (1653), p. 29.

4. Quoted by Nuttall, *The Holy Spirit in Puritan Faith and Experience,* p. 184. Fogelklou (p. 189) cites numerous pamphlets that apparently took Nayler's "headship" for granted. Long afterward Richard Baxter, an implacable enemy of the Quakers, still referred to "their chief leader James Nayler" (*Reliquiae Baxterianae,* p. 77), though he may have done this for polemical reasons, since the context was Nayler's deserved punishment for blasphemy.

5. Ingle reviews evidence that Fox's associates recognized "that something in his style did not go over as well in London as elsewhere" (*First among Friends,* p. 128).

6. John Spooner, quoted from the London Friends House collection by Bittle, p. 59.

7. *An Exact History of the Life of James Nayler* (1657), pp. 18–19.

8. Richard Roper, 20 October 1656, quoted by Isabel Ross, *Margaret Fell,* pp. 101–102.

9. Quoted from the Barclay manuscripts by Bittle, p. 22.

10. Braithwaite, pp. 105–106. Margaret Fell married Fox in 1669, more than a decade after the death of her first husband.

11. See Richard Bailey, *New Light on George Fox and Early Quakerism: The Making and Unmaking of a God* (San Francisco: Mellen Research University Press, 1992), pp. 128–129, quoting these salutations (by Burrough and Howgill, Thomas Curtis, and Richard Sale) and many others like them. Unfortunately Bailey rests his entire book on an unproved and extreme claim that Fox developed (and later suppressed) a highly specific concept of "inhabitation" by the flesh and bone of Christ.

12. Quoted by Barbour, *The Quakers in Puritan England,* p. 38; I have not attempted to punctuate this somewhat ambiguous exclamation.

13. Both quoted from the Swarthmore manuscripts by Nuttall, *Studies in Christian Enthusiasm,* pp. 43, 72.

14. Richard Nelson, letter of May 1655, quoted from the London Friends' House collection by Bittle, p. 76.

15. 1952 *Journal,* p. xxxiii; see also Reay, *The Quakers and the English Revolution,* p. 70. Higginson (*Brief Relation,* p. 19) gave the fullest account of Fox's disturbing gaze: "It has been his custom in these parts to fix his eyes earnestly on such strangers as came into his company a good while together, as though he would look them through. If anyone please to look on him steadfastly again, it is his manner impudently to outstare them. His followers say he can out-look any man, and that he doth it to know what is in them, but if there be such a thing as fascination by an evil eye, I should rather suspect him guilty of that, than of any ability to discern the complexions of men's souls in their faces."

16. See Mack, *Visionary Women;* also Keith Thomas, "Women and the Civil War Sects," in *Crisis in Europe, 1560–1660: Essays from "Past and Present,"* ed. Trevor Aston (London: Routledge, 1965), pp. 317–340; and Richard L. Greaves, "Foundation Builders: The Role of Women in Early English Nonconformity," in *Triumph over Silence: Women in Protestant History,* ed. Greaves (Westport, Conn.: Greenwood Press, 1985), pp. 75–92; and see Greaves's introduction to the volume, esp. pp. 7, 12.

17. Alfred Cohen, "Prophecy and Madness: Women Visionaries during the Puritan Revolution," *Journal of Psychohistory* 11 (1984): 411–430.

18. Dorothy P. Ludlow, "Shaking Patriarchy's Foundations: Sectarian Women in England, 1641–1700," in *Triumph over Silence: Women in Protestant History,* ed. Richard L. Greaves (Westport, Conn.: Greenwood Press, 1985), p. 95; on acceptance of women as harmless visionaries rather than preachers, see p. 103.

19. See Mack, *Visionary Women,* pp. 133, 174.

20. *Brief Relation*, pp. 3–4. Higginson's anecdote was reprinted on a page by itself by Deacon, under the heading "A most Remarkable Story yet very true, of that mad, blind and presumptuous spirit in them" (*An Exact History of the Life of James Naylor*, p. 43).

21. *Exact History*, p. 55.

22. See Underdown, *Revel, Riot, and Rebellion*, pp. 39 and 253, and Barbour, *The Quakers in Puritan England*, pp. 166–167.

23. See Mack, *Visionary Women*, esp. pp. 222 and 239–340.

24. Mack, *Visionary Women*, pp. 162–164.

25. *To all the World's Professors and People, that you may see where you are, and repent* (1654), in *Sundry Books*, pp. 176–177.

26. Ann Audland, letter of 8 February 1655, John Audland 3 January 1656, both quoted from the Caton and Swarthmore manuscripts by Mack, *Visionary Women*, pp. 153–154.

27. Quoted from the Swarthmore manuscripts by Nuttall, *Studies in Christian Enthusiasm*, p. 50.

28. Thomas Camm and Charles Marshall, *The Memory of the Righteous Revived* (1689): the unpaginated first item, *Thomas Camm's Testimony concerning John Camm and John Audland*. These passages are quoted in part (with elisions that obscure the difference between John Camm and Thomas Camm) by Mack, *Visionary Women*, pp. 224–225.

29. Letter from Dublin to Margaret Fell, 3 September 1655, quoted by Barbour, *The Quakers in Puritan England*, p. 122.

30. *Purity and Danger: An Analysis of the Concepts of Pollution and Taboo* (London: Routledge & Kegan Paul, 1969), p. 158.

31. See the texts from Fox and others quoted by Mack, *Visionary Women*, pp. 227–228.

32. *An Answer to a young unsettled Friend*, in *The Quakers Catechism* (1655), sig. C3.

33. *Behemoth*, p. 26.

34. Burton, *Diary*, 1: 24.

35. From the account of Nayler's testimony at his 1656 trial in Burton, *Diary*, 1: 48. Nayler was responding to the report that "one Sarah Blackbury came to him and took him by the hand, and said, 'Rise up, my love, my dove, my fair one, and come away; why sittest thou among the pots?' And presently put her mouth upon his hand, and sunk down upon the ground before him." William Cobbett, ed., *Cobbett's Complete Collection of State Trials and Proceedings for High Treason and other Crimes and Misdemeanors from the Earliest Times to the Present Day*, 33 vols. (London: R. Bagshaw, 1810), 5: 817.

36. *The History of the Rise, Increase, and Progress of the Christian People called Quakers, written originally in Low Dutch, and also Translated into English* (1722), pp. 159n, 139.

37. The wife of Myles Halhead, quoted by Ross, *Margaret Fell*, p. 60. Ross adds, "She lived however to change her mind, and become a true supporter, like the others."

38. Christine Trevett, "The Women around James Nayler: A Matter of Emphasis," *Religion* 20 (1990): 249–273. Kenneth L. Carroll's "Martha Simmonds, a Quaker Enigma," *Journal of the Friends' Historical Society* 53 (1972): 31–52, though limited in its effort at interpretation, is a useful review of the surviving evidence.

39. Between them, Calvert and Simmonds published the majority of tracts by the Levellers, the Diggers, Jakob Boehme, and the Family of Love, as well as by the Quakers (see Barbour, *The Quakers in Puritan England*, p. 193).

40. *A Lamentation for the Lost Sheep of the House of Israel, With an Invitation to have them turn in their minds to the true Shepheard of their souls* (1655), p. 6.

41. Letter from James Parnell to William Dewsbury, quoted by Carroll, "Martha Simmonds, a Quaker Enigma," p. 34.

42. Letter of 26 July 1656, quoted by Carroll, "Martha Simmonds, a Quaker Enigma," p. 40.

43. See Ingle, *First among Friends*, p. 130.

44. Quoted from the Markey manuscripts by Carroll, "Martha Simmonds, a Quaker Enigma," pp. 40–41. The remark about "goats, rough and hairy" may allude to Esau, or perhaps to the apocalyptic dream in Daniel 8.

45. Richard Hubberthorne to Margaret Fell, 26 August 1656, quoted from the Caton manuscripts by Patricia Crawford, *Women and Religion in England 1500–1720* (London: Routledge, 1993), p. 175. In her rather uncritical review of the case Crawford takes it for granted that it would be welcome evidence of female empowerment if "Martha Simmonds was, for a brief period, one of the leaders of the Quaker movement" (p. 176).

46. Letter to Margaret Fell, quoted by Carroll, "Martha Simmonds, a Quaker Enigma," pp. 39–40.

47. As Bailey argues in *New Light on George Fox and Early Quakerism*, pp. 143–144.

48. Quoted from the Markey manuscripts by Carroll, "Martha Simmonds, a Quaker Engima," p. 41.

49. Quoted by Fogelklou, p. 142.

50. No. 340 (11–18 December 1656), reprinted in *Making the News: An Anthology of the Newsbooks of Revolutionary England, 1641–1660*, ed. Joad Raymond (Moreton-in-Marsh, Gloucestershire: The Windrush Press, 1993), p. 412. In October 1655 Cromwell had ordered strict application of licensing laws, and thereafter the *Mercurius Politicus*, edited by the compliant Marchamont Nedham, enjoyed a monopoly in disseminating what passed for the news (p. 336).

51. From the interrogation at Bristol, as quoted by Farmer in *Satan Inthron'd in his Chair of Pestilence* (1657), pp. 10–11.

52. *History of the . . . Quakers*, p. 138.

53. As Phyllis Mack points out; she examines the Simmonds-Nayler relationship in interesting detail in *Visionary Women*, pp. 197–208.

54. Martha Simmonds, Hannah Stranger, and "J. N.," *O England, thy time is come* (1656), pp. 9–10. This passage is signed by Simmonds.

55. *Miscellaneous Works*, 6: 47.

56. Quoted from the Swarthmore manuscripts by Nuttall, *Studies in Christian Enthusiasm*, p. 73.

57. Francis Howgill and John Audland to Edward Burrough, August 1656, reprinted in the *Journal of the Friends' Historical Society* 48 (1956): 90–91.

58. 1952 *Journal*, p. 119.

59. Nigel Smith observes that Anna Trapnel's much-remarked feats of self-denial might today be diagnosed as anorexia, "a rejection of food for the sake of personal control over the body, as if she were trying to make herself pure" (*Perfection Proclaimed*, p. 50).

60. See Thomas, *Religion and the Decline of Magic*, pp. 114–115, 147.

61. *A Warning from the Lord to all Such as hang down the head for a day*, quoted by Hill, *The English Bible and the Seventeenth-Century Revolution*, p. 100.

62. *Brief Relation*, p. 20.

63. *Foot Yet in the Snare* (1656), p. 14.

64. Fogelklou, p. 163.

65. John Bolton to Margaret Fell, quoted from the Swarthmore manuscripts by Bittle, p. 88.

66. Thomas Rawlinson to Margaret Fell, quoted from the Swarthmore manuscripts by Brailsford, p. 104.

67. Quoted from the Swarthmore manuscripts by Brailsford, p. 108.

68. Rawlinson to Margaret Fell, quoted by Bittle, p. 89.

69. Quoted from the Swarthmore manuscripts by Fogelklou, p. 162.

70. Brailsford, quoting Nayler's letter from the Swarthmore manuscripts, p. 57.

71. *Enthusiasm*, pp. 161, 144.

72. *Satan Inthron'd in his Chair of Pestilence* (1657), unpaginated introductory Epistle.

73. 1952 *Journal*, p. 243.

74. 1952 *Journal*, p. 268.

75. See Bauman, *Let Your Words Be Few*, pp. 128, 140. We will return to Perrot in Chapter 5.

76. The letter, from the Gibson manuscripts, is printed in full by Fogelklou, pp. 164–167.

77. See Braithwaite, pp. 171, 364, 385, 437.

78. Fogelklou, p. 167.

79. Rich, *Hidden Things brought to Light: Or the Discord of the Grand Quakers among Themselves, Discovered in some Letters, Papers, and Passages written to and from George Fox, James Nayler, and John Perrott* (1678), p. 37. Rich also reprinted (p. 42) a 1757 letter that he had written to Nayler, reviewing the same points: "Thou may call to mind (what thou told me in our journey to Bristol) how he came to thee when imprisoned in the West, tempting thee with fair words, and what he would give thee if thou would bow down to him; and supposing he had prevailed, held out his hand for thee to kiss; which thou refusing, did not he then lift up his foot, saying, he was mistaken, it should have been his foot, and not his hand?"

80. 1952 *Journal*, p. 269.

81. Quoted from the Swarthmore manuscripts by Fogelklou, p. 169.

82. The full letter (15 October 1656) is printed as an appendix in Isabel Ross, *Margaret Fell*, pp. 396–397.

83. Penn's Preface to Fox's *Journal*, p. xliv in the 1952 edition.

84. 1952 *Journal*, p. 230.

85. See Fogelklou, p. 159.

86. *Satan Inthron'd in his Chair of Pestilence*, p. 12.

87. See Bailey, *New Light on George Fox and Early Quakerism*, p. 161.

88. *Satan Inthron'd in his Chair of Pestilence*, pp. 3–4, 16.

89. Burton, *Diary*, 1: 11 (repeated in a similar context on p. 47).

90. Quoted by Bittle, p. 66.

91. *Satan Inthron'd in his Chair of Pestilence*, p. 45.

92. See Maryann Feola-Castelucci, "'Warringe with ye worlde': Fox's Relationship with Nayler," *Quaker History* 81 (1992): 65–66.

93. 1952 *Journal*, p. 35; see Gwyn, *Apocalypse of the Word*, pp. 172–173.

94. Joshuah Miller, *Antichrist in Man The Quakers Idol* (1655), p. 29.

95. Farmer, *Satan Inthron'd in his Chair of Pestilence*, p. 17.

96. Quoted by Ingle, *First among Friends*, p. 142.

97. Bevan, *The Life of James Nayler* (1800), pp. 76–77. Bevan saw the subsequent treatment of Nayler, however, as motivated mainly by "a desire to crush the rising society of Friends."

98. Transcript in Deacon, *The Grand Impostor Examined*, pp. 5–6. Deacon's transcript and commentary were later reprinted in the *Harleian Miscellany* and in Cobbett's *State Trials*, 5: 830–838.

99. See Nigel Smith, *Perfection Proclaimed*, p. 61.

100. *Satan Inthron'd in his Chair of Pestilence*, p. 14.

101. *A Few Words, Occasioned by . . . A Discourse concerning the Quakers* (1653), in *Sundry Books*, pp. 125–126.

102. *Satan Inthron'd in his Chair of Pestilence*, pp. 28–29.

103. *To all the World's Professors and People, that you may see where you are, and repent* (1654), in *Sundry Books*, pp. 176–177.

104. Deacon, *The Grand Impostor Examined*, p. 43.

105. Farmer, *Satan Inthron'd in his Chair of Pestilence*, p. 23.

106. *The Quaker's Jesus* (1658), p. 23.

107. Deacon, *The Grand Impostor Examined*, p. 18.

108. See Thomas, *Religion and the Decline of Magic*, pp. 125–127.

109. See the very full introduction by Henry J. Cadbury to *George Fox's "Book of Miracles"* (Cambridge: Cambridge University Press, 1948).

110. *An Exact History of the Life of James Naylor*, p. 49.

111. See Braithwaite, p. 391.

112. 1952 *Journal*, p. 293. The work Fox refers to is *A Warning from the Lord to all such as hang down the head for a day* (1654).

113. *Sundry Books*, p. x.

114. *The Grand Impostor Examined*, pp. 41–42.

115. Hume's account is quoted above in the Introduction.

116. *Satan Inthron'd in his Chair of Pestilence*, p. 27.

117. See Braithwaite, p. 243. Henry J. Cadbury, the reviser of Braithwaite's book, says that Quakers often carried this document in their Bibles (pp. 564–565).

118. Quoted by Brailsford, pp. 109–110.

119. *Foot Yet in the Snare* (1656), pp. 19–20. Fox too joined in the attack on Toldervy, whom the movement regarded as a Ranter who had never really been a Quaker at all; see Barbour, *The Quakers in Puritan England*, p. 128.

120. Quoted by Carroll, "Early Quakers and 'Going Naked as a Sign,'" *Quaker History* 67 (1978): 79.

121. Thomas Camm's report, as quoted by Braithwaite, p. 158.

122. See A. L. Morton, *The Everlasting Gospel*, p. 53.

123. Braithwaite, p. 126.

124. Letter of 28 October 1655, quoted from the Swarthmore manuscripts by Mack, *Visionary Women*, p. 183.

125. Thomas Holme in 1655, quoted from the Swarthmore manuscripts by Carroll, p. 79.

126. See Barbour, *The Quakers in Puritan England*, pp. 116, 133.

127. 1952 *Journal*, p. 84.

128. See Bauman, *Let Your Words Be Few*, pp. 86–92.

129. *Complete Poetry and Prose of William Blake*, ed. Erdman, p. 39.

130. Robert Rich and William Tomlinson, *A True Narrative of The Examination, Tryall and Sufferings of James Nayler* (1657), p. 35 (in a sequence of misnumbered pages: this is Query 5 in the first of Rich's petitions).

131. *Sundry Books*, pp. 143–144.

132. See Hill, *The World Turned Upside Down*, pp. 96–97. The year 1656 was chosen because it was calculated that there were 1,656 years between the creation of the world and Noah's flood (see Thomas, *Religion and the Decline of*

Magic, pp. 141–142, and Nuttall, *The Holy Spirit in Puritan Faith and Experience,* p. 109n, quoting an apocalyptic prophecy by the Welshman Morgan Llwyd).

133. See John Morrill, "Cromwell and his Contemporaries," in *Oliver Cromwell and the English Revolution,* ed. Morrill (London: Longman, 1990), pp. 271–272.

134. *Magnalia Christi Americana,* 7: 22. Mather conceded that William Penn and others had redirected the Quaker movement away from the "blasphemies and confusions" of "the old Foxian Quakerism."

135. *Concerning the Sum or Substance of Our Religion Who Are Called Quakers,* pp. 12–13.

136. *Saul's Errand to Damascus,* p. 14.

137. 1952 *Journal,* p. 96. This happened at Gainsborough.

138. *The Royal Law, and Covenant of God* (1655), p. 4.

139. *The Perfect Pharisee* (1653), pp. 8–9.

140. *A Discovery of The Man of Sin . . . Or, An Answer to a Book set forth . . . by way of Reply to an Answer of James Nayler's to their former Book, called The Perfect Pharisee* (1655), p. 19.

141. *The Perfect Pharisee,* p. 9.

142. *A Discovery of the Wisdom which is from Beneath, and the Wisdom which is from Above,* in *Sundry Books,* p. 68.

143. Epistle IX, "To some that were backslidden," in *Sundry Books,* p. 722 (among works described on p. 697 as "never before printed"). Since this text is undated, it is not possible to know if it was written before or after the episode at Bristol.

144. *Reliquiae Baxterianae* (1696), p. 77.

145. The sketch of Erbery in the *DNB* (6: 802) is loftily contemptuous of his beliefs: in a disputation with some ministers in 1653 "Erbery declared that the wisest ministers and the purest churches were then 'befooled and confounded by reason of learning,' that 'Babylon is the church in her ministers and the Great Whore the church in her worshippers,' and made a number of other equally absurd statements, which caused the meeting to end in a riot."

146. Hill, *The World Turned Upside Down,* p. 196; *The Experience of Defeat,* p. 92 (quoting the posthumous *Testimony of William Erbery,* 1658) and p. 95 (quoting John Webster's preface to the *Testimony*).

147. *Satan Inthron'd in his Chair of Pestilence,* pp. 48–49.

148. Francis Cheynell, *An Account given to the Parliament by the Ministers sent by them to Oxford* (1647), quoted by Hill, *The Experience of Defeat,* p. 91. The soldiers stationed at Oxford had appreciated Erbery's opposition to the official Presbyterianism of the university (p. 85).

149. Hill, *The Experience of Defeat,* p. 89, quoting from Erbery's *Testimony,* pp. 23–24.

4. Trial and Crucifixion

1. The petition appears in Farmer, *Satan Inthron'd in his Chair of Pestilence*, pp. 34–36.

2. *DNB* 3: 469.

3. Quoted in the editorial notes to Burton, *Diary*, 1: 10. (Since the entire Nayler debate is contained in the first volume, subsequent references will be by page numbers only.) Timothy Wedlock, Robert Crab, and Samuel Cater, whose testimony at Bristol seemed insufficiently incriminating of Nayler, were not summoned.

4. Major Robert Beake, in Burton, *Diary*, p. 43.

5. Derek Hirst, *Authority and Conflict*, p. 335.

6. *The Rump Parliament, 1648–1653* (Cambridge: Cambridge University Press, 1974), p. 58.

7. *Godly Rule*, pp. 144, 181.

8. *Brief Relation*, pp. 23–24.

9. G. E. Aylmer, Introduction to *The Interregnum: The Quest for Settlement, 1646–1660* (London: Macmillan, 1974), p. 23.

10. Burton, *Diary*, p. lxix (entry for 11 November 1654; the speaker is not identified). As is explained in the editor's preface, the first part of the volume, paginated in Roman numerals, is not by Burton but is the much briefer diary of Guibon Godard (or Goddard).

11. The issues are summarized by Aylmer, *Rebellion or Revolution? England, 1640–1660*, ch. 7.

12. In all 460 MPs were elected, of whom more than a hundred were excluded as unfit (Aylmer, *Rebellion or Revolution?*, p. 175).

13. See Underdown, *Revel, Riot, and Rebellion*, pp. 237–238, and Hirst, *Authority and Conflict*, p. 341. "The regimes of the 1650s were radical only in the circumstances that brought them into existence. In most other respects, there was a rush to restoration: a return to familiar forms of central and local government; . . . the silencing of radical demands for land reform or greater commercial freedom; a renewed social paternalism" (Morrill, *The Nature of the English Revolution*, p. 24).

14. Speech on the dissolution of Parliament, January 22, in *The Writings and Speeches of Oliver Cromwell*, ed. Abbott, 3: 584. The reference is to Proverbs 28: 3.

15. *From the Spirit of the Lord, written by one whose name in the flesh is William Dewsbury* (1655), in Barbour and Roberts, p. 96.

16. *Give ear you gathered Churches, so called* (1659), pp. 4, 7.

17. See Alan Cole, "The Quakers and the English Revolution," p. 349.

18. Speech to Lord Whitelocke and a committee urging Cromwell to accept the kingship, 3 April 1657, in *The Writings and Speeches of Oliver Cromwell*, ed. Abbott, 4: 445.

19. *Areopagitica* (1644), in *The Prose of John Milton*, ed. Patrick, pp. 327, 287.

20. The phrase "authoritarian libertarianism" is John Morrill's in his introduction to *Oliver Cromwell and the English Revolution* (London: Longman, 1990); see also J. C. Davis's essay "Cromwell's Religion" in that volume, esp. pp. 191–196.

21. Blair Worden, "Toleration and the Cromwellian Protectorate," in *Persecution and Toleration: Studies in Church History* 21, ed. W. J. Sheils (Oxford: Blackwell, 1984): 199–233; the quotation is from 205.

22. Letter of 27 March 1654, in Barbour and Roberts, p. 385. It is possible that Cromwell's willingness to meet with Fox and other Quakers was due not to sympathy with their views, as Quaker historians have naturally wished to believe, but rather to a desire to please the remaining radicals in the army on which his power depended (see Hirst, "The Lord Protector," pp. 129–130).

23. *Enthusiasm*, p. 146.

24. Proclamation of 15 February 1655, quoted by Samuel Rawson Gardiner, *A History of the Commonwealth and Protectorate, 1649–56*, 4 vols. (London: Longmans, Green, 1903), 3: 261.

25. Letter quoted by Brockbank, *Edward Burrough*, p. 80.

26. Thomas Hobbes, *Leviathan: Or the Matter, Form and Power of a Commonwealth Ecclesiastical and Civil*, ed. Michael Oakeshott (Oxford: Blackwell, 1946), ch. 36, p. 283. On the consensus that all governments ought to enforce religion, see Conrad Russell, *The Causes of the English Civil War*, pp. 64–66, 214–215.

27. *To Oliver Cromwell*, in *Sundry Books*, p. 187.

28. *To the Parliament of the Commonwealth of England* (undated), in *Sundry Books*, p. 748 (among works described on p. 697 as "never before printed").

29. See Reay, *The Quakers and the English Revolution*, pp. 52–53.

30. Higginson, *Brief Relation*, pp. 9–10.

31. See Theodore Wilson and Frank Merli, "Naylor's Case and the Dilemma of the Protectorate," p. 48.

32. The Lords had criminal jurisdiction only over their own members, except for cases involving violation of the privileges of the House and impeachment for political crimes. Their appellate jurisdiction was limited to civil cases, which would not have been relevant here.

33. "Cromwell's Ordinances: The Early Legislation of the Protectorate," in *The Interregnum: The Quest for Settlement, 1646–1660*, ed. G. E. Aylmer (London: Macmillan, 1974), p. 144; on members of Parliament who were critical of legislation by "ordinance," see p. 161.

34. See Johann Sommerville, "Oliver Cromwell and English Political Thought," in *Oliver Cromwell and the English Revolution*, ed. John Morrill (London: Longman, 1990), pp. 257–258.

35. Rich and Tomlinson, *A True Narrative of the Examination, Tryall and Sufferings of James Nayler* (1657), p. 3. The accuracy of this transcript is confirmed by the version in Cobbett's *State Trials*, vol. 5, where a few parts of the examination are reported at greater length.

36. I follow here the somewhat fuller text in Cobbett, *State Trials*, 5: 807.

37. *A True Narrative*, p. 15.

38. Cobbett, *State Trials*, 5: 808.

39. Quoted from the Swarthmore manuscripts by Bittle, p. 116.

40. Burton, *Diary*, p. 11.

41. *DNB*, 5: 1306. Vol. 4 of the 1974 reprint of Burton's *Diary* has an invaluable appendix identifying the full names of the speakers in the debate.

42. As Worden remarks: "Toleration and the Cromwellian Protectorate," p. 224.

43. Burton, *Diary*, p. 6.

44. Conceivably this was intended as a joke, but Henrietta Maria was a constant target for anti-Catholic anxieties, and Charles Harding Firth assumes that Downing meant what he said; see Firth, *The Last Years of the Protectorate, 1656–1658*, 2 vols. (London: Longmans, Green, 1909), 1: 76.

45. In Barclay's *Apology for the True Christian Divinity* there are 656 New Testament citations and 165 Old Testament ones, a ratio of five to one; Barclay's catechism has 559 references to the New Testament and only 40 to the Old (Frost, "The Dry Bones of Quaker Theology," p. 520n).

46. See Aylmer, *Rebellion or Revolution?*, p. 126.

47. Annotations to *An Apology for the Bible* (1797) by Bishop Richard Watson, in *Complete Poetry and Prose of William Blake*, ed. Erdman, p. 610 (citing Matthew 24: 15).

48. Burton, *Diary*, pp. 22–23.

49. Maurice Ashley, *The Greatness of Oliver Cromwell* (London: Hodder and Stoughton, 1957), p. 332.

50. *The Last Years of the Protectorate*, 1: 86.

51. Nayler and Fox, *Several Petitions Answered, That were put up by the Priests of Westmoreland* (1653), p. 2 (a Quaker reply, reprinting the original petition).

52. *A Treatise of Civil Power in Ecclesiastic Causes: Shewing that it is not lawful for any power on earth to compell in matters of religion*, in *The Prose of John Milton*, ed. Patrick, p. 453.

53. Hirst, *Authority and Conflict*, p. 296.

54. See J. F. McGregor, "Seekers and Ranters," in *Radical Religion in the English Revolution*, ed. McGregor and B. Reay (London: Oxford University Press, 1984), p. 133.

55. In *Acts and Ordinances of the Interregnum, 1642–60*, ed. Charles Harding Firth and R. S. Rait, 3 vols. (London: H.M. Stationery Office, 1911), 2: 410.

56. *A Lamentation . . . over the Ruins of this Oppressed Nation* (1653), in *Sundry Books*, p. 102.

57. *History of the . . . Quakers* (1722), p. 140.

58. See Worden, "Toleration and the Cromwellian Protectorate," pp. 215–218.

59. In *The Constitutional Documents of the Puritan Revolution, 1625–1660*, ed. Samuel Rawson Gardiner, 3rd ed. (Oxford: Clarendon Press, 1906), p. 416.

60. See Claire Cross, "The Church in England, 1646–1660," pp. 114–115.

61. There is a concise review of the subject in Firth, *The Last Years of the Protectorate*, 1: 79–82, 90–91.

62. Burton, *Diary*, pp. 44, 58.

63. "Toleration and the Cromwellian Protectorate," p. 204; Worden gives the clearest and fullest account available of the Biddle case (see esp. pp. 203–205, 220–222).

64. See Hill, *The English Bible and the Seventeenth-Century Revolution*, p. 101.

65. Ralph Farmer, *Satan Inthron'd in his Chair of Pestilence* (1657), p. 28.

66. 1911 *Journal*, 1: 260; in Nickalls' 1952 edition the remark about the monstrous child is quietly relegated to summary in a footnote.

67. *Behemoth*, p. 187.

68. *New Jerusalem Bible* (New York: Doubleday, 1985), p. 291.

69. *A True Narrative*, p. 30.

70. *The Light of Christ, and the Word of Life* (1656), p. 3.

71. Burton, *Diary*, p. 52, quoting Matthew 24: 23–24.

72. See Roots, *The Great Rebellion*, p. 119.

73. See Braithwaite, pp. 202–203.

74. *A True Narrative*, p. 30 (reported in nearly identical language in Burton, *Diary*, p. 79).

75. *Grace Abounding*, p. 31.

76. On Bampfield see Firth, *The Last Years of the Protectorate*, 1: 85–86, and Worden, "Toleration and the Cromwellian Protectorate," p. 225.

77. Cromwell's failure to influence the Nayler debate actively has often been noted, and it did not help that for his leader in the House he chose "a fatally weak Speaker in the time-serving lawyer Sir Thomas Widdrington" (Hirst, *Authority and Conflict*, p. 342). Certainly in Burton's record of the debates there is never any sense of direction being given, by Widdrington or by anyone else.

78. Bauthumley (also spelled Bottomley) was punished for his book *The Light and Dark Sides of God* (see Hill's account of Bauthumley in *The World Turned Upside Down*, pp. 219–220). J. C. Davis notes, however, that no other Ranter or alleged Ranter was punished so brutally, so that Bauthumley's treatment does not really support the notion of a "savage repression" of "Ranterism" (*Fear, Myth and History*, pp. 44–48). In 1655 Bauthumley turned up to ir-

ritate Fox: "The next day Jacob Bottomley came from Leicester, a great Ranter, but the Lord's power stopped him and came over them all" (1952 *Journal*, pp. 182–183).

79. Burton's text mistakenly gives Wilton as "Milton"; his modern editors correct the error (p. 29 of the "Index of Speakers" appended to vol. 4).

80. "Swordsmen and Decimators: Cromwell's Major Generals," in *The English Civil War and After, 1642–1658*, ed. R. H. Parry (Berkeley: University of California Press), p. 83.

81. 1952 *Journal*, pp. 195–196.

82. After 460 members had been elected, the Council of State excluded 100, and another 50 withdrew in protest. Of the approximately 300 who remained, many were so lax in attendance that they had to be threatened with fines and other sanctions. On December 13 Burton recorded a vote to adjourn as 108 yea, 175 no, but these figures (later reproduced by some historians) are in error. The original manuscript of the diary, corroborated by the Journal of the House of Commons, gives the vote as 108 to 75, for a total of 183 voting members on that occasion. William G. Bittle, in "The Trial of James Nayler and Religious Toleration in England" (*Quaker History* 73 [1984]: 29–33), shows that the misprint in Burton's *Diary* has encouraged a mistaken notion that a hundred more members of parliament were present than took part in the death-penalty vote.

83. As Bittle observes, *James Nayler*, p. 131.

84. *DNB*, 20: 1305–1307.

85. Burton, *Diary*, p. 155.

86. As Hill notes, *The World Turned Upside Down*, p. 365n.

87. Hill, *The World Turned Upside Down*, p. 365.

88. *DNB*, 16: 933–934.

89. As Ashley notes, *The Greatness of Oliver Cromwell*, p. 332.

90. On the careers of these three *politiques* see Worden, "Toleration and the Cromwellian Protectorate," pp. 228–233. Burton records Wolseley as speaking only a couple of times during the Nayler debate, and then only to warn against establishing dangerous precedents. Hale was not a member of the 1656 Parliament (he was elected in 1658).

91. Cobbett, *State Trials*, 5: 802.

92. Quoted by Morrill, *The Nature of the English Revolution*, p. 153.

93. *The Writings and Speeches of Oliver Cromwell*, ed. Abbott, 4: 367.

94. See Hirst, *Authority and Conflict*, p. 344.

95. *A True Narrative*, p. 38.

96. Burton, *Diary*, pp. 247, 264.

97. Bittle, p. 142.

98. *An Exact History of the Life of James Naylor*, pp. 35–37 (misnumbered in the original as 35, 44, 45).

99. Bevan, *The Life of James Nayler* (1800), p. 84.

100. "A Further Account of the Burning of James Nayler, by a different Person," in an anonymous collection of documents entitled *Memoirs of the Life, Ministry, Tryal and Sufferings of that Very Eminent Person James Nayler* (1719), p. 69.

101. No. 345 (15–22 January 1657) in Raymond, *Making the News*, p. 418.

102. *The Quaker's Jesus*, pp. 20–21.

103. John Camm and John Audland, *The Memory of the Righteous Revived* (1689), p. 258.

104. *A Salutation to the Seed of God*, in *Sundry Books*, p. 221.

105. 1952 *Journal*, p. 219, alluding to Acts 19.

106. Burton, *Diary*, pp. 217–218.

107. Bevan, *The Life of James Nayler*, p. 83.

108. Brailsford, p. 154.

109. Letter of 26 August 1656, quoted from the Caton manuscripts by Mack, *Visionary Women*, p. 198.

110. *Visionary Women*, p. 199.

111. *Hidden Things Brought to Light* (1678), p. 37.

5. Aftermath

1. Quoted by George Bishop, *The Throne of Truth Exalted* (1656), p. 6. Bishop claimed (p. 9) that other transcriptions had been published in which some words were omitted and others maliciously mistranscribed. See also Feola-Castelucci, "'Warringe with ye worlde': Fox's Relationship with Nayler," 70.

2. Quoted from the Etting manuscripts by Bittle, p. 103.

3. Printed in the 1911 *Journal*, 1: 266.

4. See Reay, *The Quakers and the English Revolution*, pp. 56–57.

5. *Satan Inthron'd in his Chair of Pestilence* (1657), pp. 9, 35.

6. *The Impostor Dethroned* (1658), unpaginated "Epistle to the Reader."

7. *Brief Relation*, p. 58.

8. Undated manuscript poem, "Religion," in *Satires and Miscellaneous Poetry and Prose*, ed. René Lamar (Cambridge: Cambridge University Press, 1928), p. 280. Excerpts from Butler's manuscripts were first published in 1759; this poem was not printed in full until the edition of 1928.

9. Letter of 27 October 1656, in Barbour and Roberts, p. 484.

10. Quoted from the Markey manuscripts by Fogelklou, p. 234–236.

11. See Mack, *Visionary Women*, pp. 208–210.

12. Quoted from the Swarthmore manuscripts by Braithwaite, p. 273.

13. *Rabshakeh's Outrage Reproved; or, A Whip for William Grigge of Bristoll, Tanner, To Scourge him, For his many notorious lies . . . in a late fiery Pamphlet, (pub-*

lished under his name) *entituled, The Quakers Jesus* (1658), p. 15. Rabshakeh was sent by the King of Assyria to threaten the Jews, and was reproved by Isaiah (2 Kings 18–19, repeated in Isaiah 36–37). This writer also dismisses as irrelevant (pp. 13–14) Grigge's assertion that Nayler "rode to the White Hart in Broad Street, being the house of Dennis Hollister and Henry Roe, both eminent Quakers," citing legal evidence that the White Hart was in fact leased to a non-Quaker named Nicholas Fox, who paid rent to four sisters (two of whom were the wives of Hollister and Roe) who had inherited it from their brother in 1649.

14. "To all dear brethren and friends in Holderness, and in the east parts of Yorkshire" (1653), in *Sundry Books*, p. 34.

15. Braithwaite, *The Second Period of Quakerism*, pp. 177–178. Braithwaite quotes the opinion of a Quaker who was present when Whitehead read a discourse to King George I: "Though not very long, yet considering it was not lively, was too long in the occasions" (p. 200).

16. Ingle, *First among Friends*, pp. 271, 323.

17. An undated epistle by Nayler beginning "All Friends everywhere, who with the light that never changeth are convinced and turned from darkness" was reprinted (with emendations) in 1698 in the *Epistles* of Fox, with the signature "James Nayler" altered to read "G. F." See Geoffrey F. Nuttall, "A Letter by James Nayler Appropriated to George Fox," *The Friends' Quarterly* 55 (1988): 178–179.

18. Introduction to *Sundry Books*, p. xi.

19. *A True Discoverie of Faith* (1655), p. 2.

20. *For Those That Meet to Worship at the Steeplehouse called John Evangelist in London* (unpublished manuscript tract, 1659), quoted by Phyllis Mack as epigraph to *Visionary Women* (full reference given at p. 7n).

21. *Sundry Books*, p. 95.

22. Braithwaite gives a concise account of Perrot's career (*The Beginnings of Quakerism*, pp. 420–426, and *The Second Period of Quakerism*, pp. 228–241). The original sources are carefully studied by Kenneth L. Carroll in *John Perrot: Early Quaker Schismatic* (London: Friends' Historical Society, 1971).

23. Quoted by Carroll, *John Perrot*, pp. 57–59. Carroll dates the epistle at 1662 or possibly even later (p. 59).

24. John Harwood, *The life of innocency vindicated that was manifested in two famous ministers in their day* (1667), quoted by Carroll, *John Perrot*, p. 83.

25. See Vann, *The Social Development of English Quakerism*, pp. 18–19, citing the Norwich Quarter Sessions Book for 1 August 1655 and the "Epistle of Norfolk Quarterly Meeting to London Yearly Meeting" for 1725.

26. See Fogelklou, pp. 283–285.

27. Barbour, *The Quakers in Puritan England*, p. 122.

28. Claire Disbrey, "George Fox and Some Theories of Innovation in Religion," *Religious Studies* 25 (1989): 71.

29. *George Fox's Address to Friends in the Ministry* (March 1657), in Barbour and Roberts, p. 490.

30. Richard Bauman uses this distinction effectively, drawing on Max Weber's classic formulation, in *Let Your Words Be Few*, ch. 9.

31. Braithwaite, *The Second Period of Quakerism*, pp. 98n, 26–27, 37, 449.

32. An anonymous *Spirit of the Hat* (1673), quoted by Braithwaite, *The Second Period of Quakerism*, p. 292 (plausibly substituting "Foxonian" for the otherwise mysterious "Foxoman" of the original). Nuttall attributes this pamphlet to William Mucklow (*The Holy Spirit in Puritan Faith and Experience*, p. 46).

33. Penn's preface to Fox's *Journal:* in the 1952 *Journal*, pp. xlvi, xlvii.

34. See Barbour and Roberts, p. 514, introducing selections from Robert Barclay's 1674 treatise *The Anarchy of the Ranters, and Other Libertines*.

35. *History of the . . . Quakers*, p. 153.

36. *The Life of James Nayler*, p. 66.

37. *James Nayler: A Fresh Approach*, pp. 1, 16.

38. "To all the Dearly Beloved People of God," in *Sundry Books*, p. xxx. Nayler adds at the end, "By a way unexpected did the Lord open a way to declare these words, all other means of writing being taken from me" (xxxi). The manuscript had to be smuggled out of Bridewell.

39. *Sundry Books*, p. xxvii.

40. Reprinted by Rich, *Hidden Things Brought to Light* (1678), p. 43. Rich dates this letter "about the latter end of Anno 1657 [or] in the beginning of 1658."

41. *Glory to God Almighty who Ruleth in the Heavens* (opening words of an apparently untitled four-page pamphlet, printed by Thomas Simmonds in 1659), p. 2.

42. *Weakness above Wickedness, and Truth above Subtilty* (1656), p. 12. Nayler was answering *The Quaker's Quaking* by Jeremiah Ives.

43. *Sundry Books*, p. liv.

44. Nayler and Richard Hubberthorne, *A Short Answer to a Book called The Fanatick History*, p. 4.

45. Letter to Margaret Fell, April 1654, quoted from the Swarthmore manuscripts by Nuttall, *Studies in Christian Enthusiasm*, p. 76, who notes the echo in the late autobiographical account.

46. *How the Ground of Temptation is in the Heart of the Creature* (1662?), p. 3.

47. "To all the People of the Lord, every where, Gathered or Scattered," in *Sundry Books*, p. xxxii.

48. *Love to the Lost*, in *Sundry Books*, pp. 262–263.

49. *Sundry Books*, p. xviii.

50. *Sundry Books*, p. 11.

51. *The Testimony of Truth Exalted* (1662), p. 621.

52. *To the Gathered Churches* (1659), in *Sundry Books*, p. 583.

53. *A Door Opened to the Imprisoned Seed* (1659), in *Sundry Books*, p. 541.

54. *A Short Answer to a Book called The Fanatick History*, p. 2. Nayler's apologia was reprinted in the 1716 *Collection of Sundry Books* with a few minor changes (e.g., "merciful God" in place of "pitiful God," p. 651).

55. *To Those who were in Authority, whom the Lord is now Judging*, in *Sundry Books*, p. 593.

56. Preface by "M. B." to Nayler, *Milk for Babes* (1661), first two unnumbered pages. *Milk for Babes* was included in the 1716 *Collection of Sundry Books*, but without Mary Booth's preface.

57. In 1646 the American Puritan John Cotton had published a popular catechism called *Spiritual Milk for Babes*.

58. *Milk for Babes*, p. 2; also in *Sundry Books*, pp. 665–666; italics in the original.

59. *A Message from the Spirit of Truth, unto the Holy Seed* (1658), in *Sundry Books*, p. 414.

60. When a new constitution was adopted in 1657 under the terms of the Humble Petition and Advice, Lambert refused to swear allegiance and was stripped of his office. In exile, he continued to hope to come to power eventually, and in 1659 attempted to lead an army against the forces of General Monck, which were about to bring about the restoration of Charles II. This effort collapsed and he ended his days in the Tower of London. (See Aylmer, *Rebellion or Revolution? England, 1640–1660*, pp. 181, 195, 198.)

61. Speech of February 4, in *The Writings and Speeches of Oliver Cromwell*, ed. Abbott, 4: 729.

62. See Bittle, p. 173.

63. See Fogelklou, p. 280.

64. Quoted by Sewel, *History of the . . . Quakers*, p. 155. Whiting, who was born in 1656, developed this account long after Nayler's death. Nayler was actually forty-three when he died.

65. The documentary evidence is carefully reviewed by Ormerod Greenwood in "James Nayler's 'Last Words,'" *Journal of the Friends' Historical Society* 48 (1958): 199–203.

66. Unpaginated preface to *Hidden Things Brought to Light*.

67. See Geoffrey F. Nuttall, "The Last of James Nayler: Robert Rich and the 'Church of the First-Born,'" *The Friends' Quarterly* 23 (1985): 527–534.

68. "The Magi," in *The Collected Poems of W. B. Yeats* (New York: Macmillan, 1956), p. 124.

69. John Dryden, *Absalom and Achitophel* (1681), lines 45–50.

70. More, *Enthusiasmus Triumphatus* (1662), pp. 2, 12.

71. *Dictionary of American Biography*, ed. Dumas Malone, 20 vols. (New York: Scribner's, 1928–36), 14: 413–414.

72. I am grateful to Professor Thomas D. Hamm of Earlham College for informing me that when the Friends' Library in Philadelphia was broken up in 1929 its contents were distributed among several Quaker colleges. Earlham already had a copy of the Nayler volume, and gave this one to Harvard as part of the exchange in 1935.

❖ Index

Abbott, Wilbur Cortez, 221, 281n54
Achan, 202
Act of Uniformity, 196
Acts of the Apostles, 22, 34, 103, 163, 174, 176, 217, 269, 284n112, 309n105
Adam, 74, 97, 163, 254
Aldam, Thomas, 33
Aldworth, Robert, 210
Alston, William P., 290n42
Amos, 41, 64, 65, 121
Anabaptists. *See* Baptists
Anderson, Alan, 282n69
Anglicans, 23–24, 38, 51, 79, 99, 199
Antichrist, 41–42, 52
antinomians, 5, 25, 42, 90–91, 197, 206, 243
apocalypse, 28, 34, 62–68, 90–91, 99, 108–110, 166–167, 175, 180
Appleby, 18, 64, 96, 118, 135
Arminians, 23, 72
army, 2, 16–18, 65, 77, 147, 180, 202, 218
Ashley, Maurice, 306n49, 308n89
Atkinson, Christopher, 244
Audland, Ann, 123
Audland, John, 30, 62, 86, 124, 300n57, 309n103
Audley, Lewis, 194–195, 214
Augustine, 105
Aylmer, G. E., 304, 278n5, 304nn9,11,12, 306n46, 312n60

Bacon, Nathaniel, 216
Bailey, Richard, 297n11, 299n47, 301n87
Bampfield, Thomas, 209–210, 216, 223, 307n76
baptism, 76
Baptists, 21, 23–26, 32, 84–85, 91, 99, 106, 121, 212
Barbados, 241

Barbour, Hugh, 166, 272, 275, 277n9, 282n68, 285n121, 286nn133,148, 287nn155,161, 290nn34,36, 292n87, 295nn154,155, 296n2, 297n12, 298nn22,29, 299n39, 302nn119,126, 304n15, 305n22, 309n9, 310n27, 311nn29,34
Barclay, David, 213
Barclay, Robert, 289n24, 293n112, 306n45
Barebones Parliament, 180
Barwick, Grace, 66
Bauman, Richard, 81, 82, 285n125, 286n149, 300n75, 302n128, 311n30
Bauthumley, Jacob, 210, 307n78
Baxter, Richard, 26, 27, 31–32, 42–43, 51, 75–77, 84, 87, 101, 107–108, 125, 172–173, 214, 258, 280n33, 283n93, 296n4
Beake, Robert, 199, 205, 304n4
Beckett, Samuel, 150
Beelzebub, 149
Benson, Col., 61
Bethel, Slingsby, 223
Bevan, Joseph Gurney, 248, 277n11, 301n97, 309nn99,107
Bible, as authority, 24, 27, 34–35, 39, 55, 58, 84–91, 193–194, 218, 247. *See also individual books*
Biddle, John, 199–200
Billingsley, John, 45–47
Bishop, George, 232–234, 236, 290n43, 309n1
Bitterman, M. G. F., 277n23, 287n167
Bittle, William G., 275, 279n23, 290n45, 292n95, 296n6, 297nn9,14, 300nn65,68, 301n90, 306n39, 308nn82,83,97, 309n2, 312n62
Blackbury, Sarah, 298n35

315